MMOs FROM THE OUTSIDE IN

THE MASSIVELY-MULTIPLAYER ONLINE ROLE-PLAYING GAMES OF PSYCHOLOGY, LAW, GOVERNMENT, AND REAL LIFE

Richard A. Bartle

Apress®

ISBN-13 (pbk): 978-1-4842-1780-1

ISBN-13 (electronic): 978-1-4842-1781-8

Managing Director: Welmoed Spahr
Lead Editor: Ben Renow-Clarke
Editorial Board: Steve Anglin, Pramila Balen, Louise Corrigan, Jim DeWolf, Jonathan Gennick,
    Robert Hutchinson, Celestin Suresh John, Michelle Lowman, James Markham,
    Susan McDermott, Matthew Moodie, Jeffrey Pepper, Douglas Pundick,
    Ben Renow-Clarke, Gwenan Spearing
Coordinating Editor: Melissa Maldonado
Copy Editors: James Compton, Kim Wimpsett
Compositor: SPi Global
Indexer: SPi Global
Artist: SPi Global

Distributed to the book trade worldwide by Springer Science+Business Media New York, 233 Spring Street, 6th Floor, New York, NY 10013. Phone 1-800-SPRINGER, fax (201) 348-4505, e-mail orders-ny@springer-sbm.com, or visit www.springeronline.com. Apress Media, LLC is a California LLC and the sole member (owner) is Springer Science + Business Media Finance Inc (SSBM Finance Inc). SSBM Finance Inc is a Delaware corporation.

For information on translations, please e-mail rights@apress.com, or visit www.apress.com.

Apress and friends of ED books may be purchased in bulk for academic, corporate, or promotional use. eBook versions and licenses are also available for most titles. For more information, reference our Special Bulk Sales–eBook Licensing web page at www.apress.com/bulk-sales.

To those whom worlds would make

Contents

About the Author

Dr. Richard A. Bartle has been playing and designing MMOs longer than anybody, having in 1978 co-written *MUD*—the progenitor of the entire genre. His famous Player Types model has seen widespread adoption by the MMO industry and beyond, and the online test bearing his name has been taken more than 800,000 times. His first book, *Designing Virtual Worlds*, is the classic text on the subject, and he is an influential writer on all aspects of online game design. In 2010, he was the first recipient of the prestigious Game Developers Choice award of Online Game Legend. He is Honorary Professor of Computer Game Design at the University of Essex, England, where it all began. He's also innumerable characters in MMOs.

Acknowledgments

Because this book was prepared at the same time as *MMOs from the Inside Out*, its acknowledgments ought to be the same as those of its older sibling.

They are.

Taking my cue from Universal movies of the 1920s, which insisted "a good cast is worth repeating," here you go!

This book would not have been written were it not for:

Ben Renow Clarke at Apress, who decided to take on a project so unlike other Apress projects that I can only guess at what blackmail material he holds on key members of Apress management.

The army of editors who swarmed over my text to convert it from British English to American English in time to meet the publication deadline. The Z key on your Macs must be worn thin by now.

My wife, Gail Bartle, who isn't a gamer but understands. She'll probably read this once the final volume of *A Song of Ice and Fire* has come out.

I'd also like to thank the hundreds of students, blog readers, e-mail correspondents, game designers, journalists (whether clueless or clueful), academics (likewise), and players who have given me cause to think about MMOs over the years. If only you'd realized at the time what it would lead to…

Introduction

This is the companion volume to *MMOs from the Inside Out: The History, Design, Fun and Art of Massively-Multiplayer Online Role-Playing Games*. You should probably read that one before this one, unless you don't mind coming across articles with titles such as "Games You Should Have Played #8" without having read "Games You Should Have Played #1–#7".

I wrote both books at the same time and originally planned to publish them as a single unit. Unfortunately, the physical practicalities of book manufacturing put to rest that idea, but the connection between both volumes still holds. It's not like a comma-relationship, in which *MMOs from the Outside In* flows seamlessly from *MMOs from the Inside Out* and I could have broken up the narrative at any theme boundary; neither, however, is it like a period-relationship, with both books as stand-alone discourses on unrelated topics. It's more of a semicolon-relationship, in which the second says something that should be considered in the light of the first but that does make sense all on its own.

The difference between the books is one of perspective. *MMOs from the Inside Out* spends its time arguing that MMO design is an exalted profession, asserting that players can gain from MMOs in ways that can't be even attempted elsewhere and concluding that this gives us untold power that would liberate humanity if only we recognized it. Yes, there may be a modicum of hubris involved.

MMOs from the Outside In, as its title suggests, comes from the other direction. Rather than preaching to the converted, it examines what the yet-to-be-converted preach about MMOs. *Reality* always wins, so what wider society thinks *is* actually important.

It's also important that MMO players and designers understand this. I've presented the case that they have the power to change the world, but of course if they do have power, then they must also have responsibility. They can't simply do what they want to do and tell the real world to suck it up. They must accept and appreciate the implications of their actions beyond the magic circle of the virtual world, so as not to make the real world worse instead of better.

That said, in many areas the real world misunderstands MMOs to such a degree that, frankly, it deserves all that MMOs can throw at it. It genuinely has it coming. However, in other cases it's the real world that has it right and MMOs that are going to cause damage.

The format of *MMOs from the Outside In* is, unsurprisingly, much the same as *MMOs from the Inside Out*. It contains several hundred articles arranged in an intertwingled fashion that advances an overall line of reasoning but gives the reader a chance to think along the way. There are five main themes, plus two interludes that are more tangential (but no less ranting).

It would be nice if, 50 years from now, people were to read this book with a growing sense of disbelief that what it describes could ever have been so. Did scientists really used to think that about games? Was the government really considering implementing such a law? Did designers really not address the implications of their work? Are those newspaper extracts real or made up (and what's a newspaper anyway)? Of course, as time moves on, old problems are resolved and new problems arise that we don't currently even recognize as distant possibilities. So, yes, it would indeed be nice if all the issues raised here about the relationship of MMOs and the wider world were wrapped up or irrelevant in 2066, but there'll be a whole new raft of questions to take their place.

That's if we still have MMOs in 2066, of course.

I wrote this book in the hope that in some small way it would raise the probability that we might.

Have fun!

Richard A. Bartle

December 2015

CHAPTER 1

On Psychology

Real-Life API: AddWorry

CPopulation::AddWorry

int AddWorry(int *nWorry*, **CComplex** *cInitWt***)**

- *nWorry*: Specifies the worry.
- *cInitWt*: Specifies the initial weight of the worry.

Remarks

nWorry is one of:

- *W_ANTISOCIAL*: Destroys social lives.
- *W_ADDICTION*: Play every day or get withdrawal symptoms.
- *W_CHILD_ABUSE*: Think of the children!
- *W_MURDER_DEATH_KILL*: Makes players violent.

Return

0 on success, otherwise:

- *E_WAE*: Population already has this worry.
- *E_EDU*: Population is too educated to worry about this.

How It Works: Research Funding

This is how government funding for research into games (or indeed anything policy-related) works:

1. Government really, really wants proof that X is true even though it isn't.

2. Government instructs funding agencies to divert funds toward proving X.

3. While attempts by scientists to prove X fail, government encourages funding agencies to allocate more resources to be thrown at proving X.

4. Once X has been proven, research funds for people trying to prove X are cut to zero.

This means that scientists will find themselves stuck in the while loop at step 3, which would be dispiriting were it not for the possibility of being able to milk funding agencies until the point that either someone breaks ranks for the glory of it or there's a statistical anomaly that produces the "right" result.

Interestingly, were scientists to organize as a cartel, this script would also work if the government wanted to prove something that was, in fact, true.

Can People Become Addicted?

One of the three things that journalists in search of an anti-MMO story habitually write about is MMO addiction (the other two are how MMOs turn people violent and how they and their players prey on children).

A headline reading "MMOs Are Addictive" is an easy sell for a journalist (although journalists will tend to use another term rather than MMO—"MMOGs" or "online games" or similar). To get this headline from an interview (as opposed to reading the often-scrappy research papers written in this area), the journalist will usually ask either "Are MMOs addictive?" or (for more experienced journalists) "Can players become addicted to MMOs?" Note that these are different questions, although they both lead to the same headline.

The reason for phrasing the question the second way is that some people genuinely *can* become addicted to MMOs. This happens in two main ways beyond the usual "there's bound to be someone in the world addicted to riding a unicycle" outliers.

First, they could be getting the wrong message from their play, reinforcing a negative self-image that causes them want to play more (to dispel it) but that succeeds only in feeding back and making matters worse. People who behave like this are generally fairly easy to spot because they're pains in the backside to be with. There aren't many of them, especially in modern MMOs where it's hard to do anything that makes you feel bad about yourself, but there are still some.

Second, people can become addicted to MMOs is if they have a gambling predisposition. The way that rewards are produced in return for effort in a virtual world resembles the kind of operant conditioning exploited by slot machines. However, because the time between feedback events is much longer than for slot machines, very few people are going to be affected by it. Some will be, though.

So yes, people *can* become addicted to MMOs, but almost none of them *are* addicted to them. They play because the world is *compelling*, not because it's *addictive*.

As for *why* it's compelling...

Correlation and Causality

Social scientists are studious about the difference between *correlation* and *causality*.

Suppose you make observations about two different things, X and Y, at the same time. You make many of these paired observations under different conditions. Let's say you notice it's never the case that one of them changes and the other doesn't. To keep it simple, suppose they both go up or go down together by proportionately the same amount.

As an example, consider X="wind speed" and Y="windmill rotation speed." If the wind is faster, then windmills rotate faster; if windmills rotate faster, then the wind is faster. There's a clear relationship between the two—a *correlation*. However, merely from looking at the set of recorded speeds, we can't tell whether higher wind speed *causes* higher windmill rotation or whether it's the other way round. If we'd studied fans instead of windmills, it would indeed have been the other way round.

Correlation can arise because there is an underlying relationship between two variables, but (importantly) it can also come from simple coincidence. For example, since 1825 the leaders of Russia have alternated between being bald and being not bald—but it would be hard to argue that having a full head of hair *caused* the next leader of Russia to be bald (and *vice versa*).

There's also the possibility that two variables are linked together not because one causes the other but because both are caused by something else. The number of deaths by drowning correlates with ice cream sales because both are caused by warm weather. The hotter it is, the more people go swimming and the more ice creams people buy.

This is why social scientists always talk in terms of correlation rather than causality. Correlation can be used to identify *possible* causation, but you'd need to find the underlying mechanism to be sure it *was* causation.

There are various degrees of correlation. For example, fuel consumption in a car correlates with distance traveled, but not always by the same amount. Driving on a flat, straight, open road uses less fuel than crawling from traffic light to traffic light in rush (ha!) hour.

This is still pretty good compared to other correlations, though. There is an obvious correlation between a country's surface area and the number of people living there, but it's not the case that a rise in one is automatically accompanied by a rise in the other.

The strength of a correlation is measured by the *Pearson product-moment correlation coefficient*, developed in the 1880s by Karl Pearson to calculate linear dependency. A value of 0 means there's no correlation, and a value of 1 means there's complete correlation (or -1 for negative correlations—when the variables do the opposite to each other). If you see something such as "correlation 0.95," then that means there's a very strong correlation; 0.05 would be a very weak one.

Correlations concern *populations* of things that have the properties you're analyzing. Sometimes you'll have full information (for example, number of prisoners per county), but sometimes you won't (for example, number of cigarette smokers per county). To correlate without access to a full population, your best option is to survey a representative sample and use that as a proxy.

In academic papers, the Greek letter rho (ρ) is used to refer to the correlation between members of a full population; r is used for correlation between members of a sample of a population. Social science surveys will therefore use r rather than ρ, because you can rarely survey an entire population. As for how to interpret something like "r=.3" (irritatingly, the 0 before the . is always dropped), well, the answer is that you square the figure for r (0.09) and multiply by 100 (9) to get the percentage of the variation in one variable that is related to the variation in the other. So, r=.3 means that 9 percent of the variation is related; r=.75 means that 56.25 percent of it is.

A related statistical concept used by social scientists is p (which, annoyingly, looks rather like ρ). A p-value is essentially the probability that a set of observations could have arisen at random. For example, the chance of tossing a coin and getting 10 heads in a row is 1 in 1,024. Therefore, if you toss a suspect coin 10 times and it comes up heads on each occasion, there's a 0.0009765625 probability the coin isn't double-headed. This 0.0009765625 is the p-value.

Social scientists calculate p-values for their correlation results to see whether they could be the result of chance. A p-value of 0.05 or less is deemed to be "significant," meaning that there's only at most a 5 percent chance that the results obtained could have arisen if there were no correlation.

Note that this is not what the public thinks the word *significant* means.

Uses and Gratifications

Game genres aren't defined by their dressing but by their gameplay.

People play games that tend to give them what they want from playing them. This isn't just true for games; it's true across the board for leisure activities (and even many nonleisure activities). People are attracted to them based on how well they expect them to satisfy their needs.

The area of Psychology that addresses this relationship between what people want and what they do to get it is called Uses and Gratifications theory. It originated in the 1940s for studying why people listened to particular radio shows, so it tends to be applied mainly to media in Communications Studies, but it does have more general applications (Maslow's famous Hierarchy of Needs[1] came out of it). The key insight introduced by Uses and Gratifications theory was to regard media as something that audiences *use*, rather than something that *influences* audience behavior; it puts the audience in the driving seat, not the media- producer.

Uses and Gratifications theory has been applied to a wide range of media (including online games). It has two main problems:

- The identifying of gratifications is primarily determined by the researcher rather than the people being studied, so it's not entirely objective.

- Few gratifications can be studied directly, so studies often rely on subjects' (unreliable) self-reporting rather than hard data.

Another issue, to do with the fact that different people using the same media may gain radically different gratifications from it, has been addressed by constructing dynamic models rather than simple categorizations.

This is particularly interesting for us because different people play MMOs to gain radically different gratifications.

---

[1]Abraham Maslow: *A Theory of Human Motivation. Psychological Review* v50 (4) pp 370–396, 1943. http://psychclassics.yorku.ca/Maslow/motivation.htm

Significance

Social scientists discussing the relationship between two possibly correlated variables will talk about the *significance* of the relationship. This is a technical term from Statistics; it means that the probability your findings show a relationship when there isn't one is less than some threshold (typically 5 percent in Psychology).

For example, suppose you are investigating sexism in employment. You look at the board of directors of a company and discover that all six members are of the same gender. Assuming a 50/50 male/female split in the general population, the probability of having six people all the same gender is 1 in 32 (that is, 1 in 64 that they would be all male plus 1 in 64 that they would be all female); 1 in 32 is 3.125 percent. Because 3.125 percent is less than your significance threshold of 5 percent, you can say that your findings are statistically significant: there's a less than 5 percent chance that you would have obtained this result if sexism wasn't a factor.

The natural sciences have much tighter criteria for significance. In Physics, for example, the threshold is five standard deviations from the norm, or about 1 in 3,500,000 (rather than the 1 in 20 used by psychology). When CERN announced it had discovered the Higgs boson, it was because researchers could say that only one experiment in 3.5 million would have exhibited the signal they observed if there were no Higgs boson (note that this is *not* the same as saying that there's a 1 in 3.5 million chance the Higgs boson doesn't exist).

Now there's absolutely nothing wrong with this use of statistical significance. If everyone in your particular field accepts the threshold of significance to be $p < 0.05$, then that's perfectly okay The problems come when people *outside* the field look at what you say. They'll use your technical words nontechnically in their ordinary, everyday meanings.

Suppose a newspaper article states, "There is a significant relationship between playing violent video games and aggression." Would the reader think that this means there is less than a 5 percent chance a relationship was found when there isn't one? Well, no. They would think that the relationship between playing violent video games and aggression is worryingly *important*.

Outliers

Some correlations are very strong except for a few exceptions known as *outliers*. For example, you could take a list of common baby names and ask people to say whether they're for boys or girls. Almost everyone will agree, but you might find someone who believes that baby names shouldn't be gendered and that a boy could be called Mary and a girl Mohammed if that's what the parents want.

Outliers are often rejected by studies because they have disproportionate influence. However, sometimes they're the key to understanding what's going on. Study after study found that heterosexual men admitted to having more sexual partners than did heterosexual women; as this makes no sense, the conclusion was that either the men were boasting or the women were ashamed. It turned out that both groups were being honest, a fact that became clear only when one survey happened to trawl a prostitute who'd had 3,000 sexual partners.

On EvE

Officially, it's *EVE Online*, but you just know that the EvE reference (as opposed to PvE or PvP) can't be accidental.

EVE is one of my favorite MMOs in terms of its design. Yes, it has its flaws (its mercilessly harsh learning curve being the most obvious one), but nothing is perfect.

What I like about *EVE* is the "no concessions" attitude of its designers. They remain 100 percent true to their original vision: they have no knee-jerk reactions to apparently alarming goings-on, they don't rush things out, and they make every decision in the context of the MMO as a whole. As a result, *EVE* remains as coherent and consistent today as it was when it launched in 2003.

If only more developers had sufficient faith in their designers to allow this degree of integrity.

One Size Fits All

Psychologists have an alarming tendency to view all computer games (or *video games*, as they prefer to call them) as being the same. They'll ask in surveys how *often* you play games, or for how *long* you play games, but not ask *which* games. It doesn't matter to them whether it's *Candy Crush Saga* or *Dragon Age: Inquisition*. You rarely see a research paper that restricts itself to one particular game or genre of games.

That said, they do make a distinction between video games and all other games. Playing *Mahjong* on a computer is, it would seem, different in Important Ways to playing it on a table. Video games based on contact sports seem to merit more study than the contact sports upon which they are based.

Fortunately, there is a newer generation of psychologists who are more game-savvy than their predecessors. They look at the reasons *why* a particular behavior is observed and construct experiments to try to explain what they've observed.

Therefore, when you read in a news report what "researchers have found" about video games, you need to be objective. It may be garbage, but it may actually be true!

Looking at the Past

With *MUD*, we had no precedents. Therefore, a designer looking at *MUD* can do so in the knowledge that everything we put there, we put there for a reason; they can then hypothesize what that reason might be (or, if they realize we're not dead yet, ask me or Roy).

A designer looking back at *MUD* won't learn anything new to put in their MMO, but, through *reflecting* on its design, they might learn more about themselves as a designer.

Operant Conditioning

Earlier, I mentioned operant conditioning.

Operant conditioning is a psychological technique that has been used for millennia. It's basically a system of rewards and punishments: you *reward* behaviors that you want to encourage and *punish* ones you want to discourage. So, fairly innocuous, then?

Well, that depends on how you use it.

The area of psychology that owns rewards is Behavior Therapy. The key difference between operant conditioning and general observational learning is that the individual is able to associate the reward or punishment with a particular action. This association may be wrong, of course. The ancient Egyptians left offerings for the gods because they wanted the Nile to flood, but the Nile would have flooded anyway. Also, it's not always obvious who's conditioning whom. From an Egyptian perspective, did the gods train the ancients to give them offerings by flooding the Nile, or did the ancients train the gods to flood the Nile by giving them offerings?

Rewards and punishments are subdivided into *positive* and *negative* types:

- A positive reward is when you receive something good ("Here's a box of chocs").

- A negative reward is when something bad is removed ("I've switched off that annoying buzzing").

- A positive punishment is when you receive something bad ("Take this, varlet! And this!").

- A negative punishment is when something good is removed ("You're grounded!").

A reinforcement *schedule* says how often you receive a reward or punishment. A *fixed ratio* schedule gives its reinforcement after a set number of intervals (pull this lever 20 times and you get $1); a *variable ratio schedule* gives its reinforcement after an undetermined number of intervals (pull this lever and there's a 5 percent chance of your getting $1).

Variable ratio reinforcement schedules for positive rewards are common in gambling and are very moreish. Moreish does not mean fun, though. Putting these schedules into games *will* keep people playing, but not for fun.

The Zeigarnik Effect

It's the 1920s, and you're sitting in a restaurant watching waiters take orders. You notice that they remember what they've been asked to bring until they've brought it but that shortly afterward they have completely forgotten.

This phenomenon was noted by an eminent Gestalt psychologist, Kurt Lewin, who asked one of his students to look into it. This student, Bluma Zeigarnik, conducted a series of experiments that demonstrated the effect that now bears her name: people are nagged by tasks they have started but not yet finished.

In MMOs, quests are like this. If you need to kill X mobs or collect X objects, you won't want to stop at X-1. When you finally get X of them, it is enjoyable—but perhaps only in the same way that stopping hitting your head with a hammer is enjoyable. Of course, the moment you hand the quest in, you are immediately offered another quest that you feel you have to complete before you log off. It's like the "just one more turn" phenomenon experienced in turn-based strategy games, but rather less unavoidable.

Related to the Zeigarnik effect is the Ovsiankina effect, identified in 1928 (a year after Zeigarnik's study) by another of Lewin's students, Maria Ovsiankina. What she found was that when you're doing something and are interrupted before you've finished, you will tend to want to finish it even if you don't really have to do so. Again, this is something that happens a lot in MMOs. For example, you may start a quest to pass the time before your Tuesday raid starts, and then after the raid you go back to finish it (rather than logging off) even though it was just a filler. It's rather harder to design for than the Zeigarnik effect, though.

So, should designers design MMOs deliberately to exploit the Zeigarnik effect? Should they be OK with it if it happens "naturally" but not go out of their way to put it in? Or should they studiously avoid it?

Operant Conditioning, Sure…

Let's suppose that MMOs really are addictive and that this addiction really is caused by their ample use of the psychological technique of variable ratio reinforcement scheduling, leading to operant conditioning. This is an argument I've heard at several conferences, particularly from lay attendees (as opposed to academics).

Well, if that *were* what caused addiction, why would MMOs have to be online? Blizzard could bring out a single-player version of *World of Warcraft* and people would get addicted to it just like they do the online version.

Except, of course, they wouldn't. Ask any player of *WoW* whether they would play a solo version of it for 2 to 4 hours most evenings for 18 straight months, and the prospect would probably be met with horror.

Therefore, whatever it is that keeps people playing MMOs, it's *not* operant conditioning. As a result, we can confidently state that players' playing habits are not reflective of a form of addiction caused by operant conditioning.

This doesn't stop people making those statements, of course, but it does mean you can legitimately laugh in their faces when they do so.

Possibilities

In a textual world, I can stand in my own mouth, seeing my surroundings get light and dark as I open and close it. I can be part of a painting I am carrying under my arm. I can appear as a frog to one person and a handsome prince to another. I can photograph an opinion. I can share control of my body with someone else. I can juggle Penrose triangles. I can be of no gender. I can be plural. I can unerupt a volcano, store the world in a box, hold a soul in the palm of my hand, and dance with the color cyan.

Do *that* in your graphical world.

Do it in your real world, come to that.

Cheap Psychological Tricks

Operant conditioning, and to a lesser extent flow and the Zeigarnik effect, are examples of what designers call *cheap psychological tricks* (CPTs). Yes, that's the actual technical term we use.

Most established designers want people to play their games for fun, not because of mind control. They're trying to communicate through their design; limiting their vocabulary to a few magic words does not allow them to say much. Also, designers tend to care for their players, so regard deliberate attempts to make people continue to play after they should have stopped as being immoral.

The counterargument is that variable rate reinforcement schedules for positive rewards are hard to avoid in game design whatever, so if you're going to have them anyway, then you may as well do it properly. I personally don't buy this. There's a difference between having such mechanisms occur "naturally" and purposefully designing games around them. Games aren't generally supposed to have periods of boredom in them either, but no one uses that as an excuse to design boring games (they use "it's edutainment" as an excuse instead).

The fact is, any game designer worth a jot knows full well what the effects of cheap psychological tricks are. If they choose to design so as to exploit them, they're doing so knowing what the results will be. Unfortunately, one of those results is that you can make an awful lot of money by applying CPTs in combination with micropayments, so CPT use is not something that is going to go away until players wise up to it. Indeed, it might not go away even then. New designers, who have grown up playing games that employ these techniques, might come to believe they're the norm. That in turn will make them the norm.

Developers develop games so as to make money; they're businesses after all. However, players play games so as to have fun. If they're not having fun, they simply won't play—and then games as a whole will be diminished.

Cheap psychological tricks work, but only for as long as people can be tricked.

Ask Dr. Psycho

From this week's *Practical Serial Killer*:

> *Dear Dr. Psycho,*
>
> I have heard that most serial killers exhibit obsessive-compulsive behavior but learned recently that I don't. Can you suggest an "MMORPG" I can get addicted to in order to cultivate such a habit? I was originally hoping to try heroin, but it's very expensive and, I understand, against the law.
>
> —Chuck

> *Dear Chuck,*
>
> Sorry to be the bearer of bad news, but to become addicted to an MMO you need to have the very obsessive-compulsive behavior that you seek—it's a catch-22 situation. This is because MMOs are compelling and engrossing, but they're not actually addictive. You won't feel empowered to go out and kill someone if you can't play for a few days. Believe me, I've tried it.
>
> You are correct in your understanding of the legal situation regarding heroin: possession of this class A drug can lead to a stiff fine. However, all is not lost! Because of a quirk in the law, another powerful drug with the street name "cigarettes" is readily available at a reasonable price in most supermarkets. Although it's not quite as potent as heroin, failure to use it for a few hours will soon have you clawing at the walls in anguish.
>
> Just what the doctor ordered!
>
> —Dr. Psycho

Integration

Ultimately, MMOs will be integrated into everyday life. That's fine, but I'd like to reserve the option to prevent everyday life from becoming integrated into every MMO.

Games You Should Have Played #8

A game you wrote yourself that no one else has played.

Game design is actually hard to do well, but you're not going to know quite *how* hard unless you try it yourself. In the attempt, you'll come to understand more about games and what makes them tick—but only if you actually play the resulting game. If it needs more than one player, play it against yourself—professional designers do this every time.

If you actually *are* a game designer, playing a game of your own that no one else has played is something you will have done on many, many occasions already, of course; just make sure you keep doing it. All game designers have a corpus of games in various stages of completion that they have never shared with anyone else simply because doing the design itself was the fun part; putting it out there for people to play takes unfun effort.

I'm a bit low on computer games in this list, so as my own example I'll go for one I did called *Mombasa* about the exploration of Africa. It's not all that good, but the point is that I wouldn't have known that if I hadn't played it.

After Next

So we have gesture recognition and stereoscopic 3D. What comes next?

So we have reading facial expressions. What comes next?

Do you want it to come next? What's the end point of "next"?

What's the point of "next"?

"It's Just a Game"

There is always something that, if it were in a game, would be sufficient to shock you out of the magic circle. Some of the players of *WoW* who did The Art of Persuasion quest said there was *nothing* that the game could throw at them that would faze them enough to stop doing something that got them XP. They'd do anything within the game that they were asked to do if the rewards were decent enough.

Oh, so they'd do <their most abhorrent idea of sexual assault> to a representation of <the deity they worship>, would they? Or they'd have their character rape a child NPC for XP? Why not, if it's "just a game"?

An action doesn't even have to be immoral to shock people out of their immersion. If you were playing a fantasy game and were told, in-game, that you could get XP for clicking a wall and watching a car ad projected onto it, I'd guess that would probably be sufficient. If your cat walked over your keyboard, that would do it too. Major competitive sports will immediately stop play when someone is injured, and if it's serious, then an entire match could be abandoned. As Wednesday Addams once said, "It's all fun and games until someone loses an eye; then, it's just fun."

Everyone has *something* that would introduce enough of real life into their MMO experience to shock them out of it. What players mean when they say they would do "anything" for XP is that they would do anything within their concept of what constitutes the magic circle.

People have different ideas of where the boundaries lie, but all should intersect with a minimum set inside which the designer covenants play will take place. If the designer doesn't constrain play to this area, the game is being offered on a false prospectus; in my view, this would be immoral. Sometimes things happen beyond the designer's control that can shock players out of a game—injury, for example—and clearly those are not the designer's responsibility. It's when the designer breaks their *own* boundaries without the explanation of a subframe that we get problems.

Psychology and Games

Psychologists don't look at games; they look at *players* of games. This is easy to forget when you read about the "psychology of games," but it's an important point. Games may use psychological techniques, but the psychology is that of the players (and, to a certain extent, the designers), not of the games themselves (which can't think).

I've talked a little about how designers can apply psychology to game design, but what do psychologists themselves think about it? Psychology is a subject with a very large and active research base, and game-oriented work makes up less than 5 percent of the total research output. That's still a lot, though.

So, what are the main areas related to games that psychologists consider hot topics?

This is only a *very* approximate breakdown, which I obtained anecdotally by asking the opinions of people who work in the field to give estimates, but it seems that academic papers about players of games appear in roughly the following proportions:

- 70 percent games and aggression
- 20 percent games and addiction
- 5 percent games and children
- 5 percent everything else

Hmm. That appears rather, well, unbalanced.

Therapy

MMOs have been used successfully as a rehabilitation tool for psychotherapy since the early 1990s. Unfortunately, they don't get a lot of publicity because of the nature of what goes on in them.[2] This means few psychiatrists know about the potential benefits of virtual worlds for rehabilitation or other therapy, and practically none of their patients do.

---

[2]Elizabeth Reid: *Cultural Formations in Text-Based Virtual Realities*. University of Melbourne, 1994. www.aluluei.com/cult-form.htm

Postscript

When I raised my concerns about the design of The Art of Persuasion, I wasn't expecting to get close to a thousand emails on the subject and spark similar numbers of forum postings. As far as I was concerned, I was making a point about good form in design. That's not how it was received.

Here are some of the more general themes I saw, with a couple of outliers thrown in for fun:

- **WoW is not real life**: I know; real life is more expensive.

- **The Geneva Conventions don't apply there**: I never said they did, I said the Alliance operated *as if* they did.

- **It has killing, which is worse than torture**: True, but that doesn't mean that if you kill, then torture is OK. See the aforementioned Geneva Conventions.

- **Death Knights torture**: Yes, but that's flagged. It's fine. It's the Art of Persuasion I was complaining about.

- **It's just a game**: Come back and say that when you yourself have been tortured in real life.

- **You didn't complain about other immoral WoW quests**: No, but if I get pilloried for highlighting something as apparently trivial as torture, how is "killing innocent animals for their body parts" going to go down?

- **You don't *have* to torture him if you don't want.** No, but I don't want even to be asked to do so in the first place.

- **You have to torture him or the world will be destroyed**: This contradicts "You don't *have* to torture him if you don't want."

- **You don't like *Manhunt***: I'm fine with it. Analogy: if I watch *South Park*, I expect a stream of profanities; if I watch *The Simpsons*, I don't. Being alarmed at profanities in *The Simpsons* doesn't mean I dislike *South Park*. *WoW* content doesn't affect *Manhunt* content.

- **You're growing a vagina**: No, I'm not (I've just checked).

- **You're anti-*WoW***: As a designer, I like *WoW*—it's one of my favorite MMOs. That's why this one slip-up stood out.

- **You're the new Jack Thompson**: Don't you think they'd give the job to someone who wasn't a pro-games advocate?

- **You get credit for inventing an early MUD you didn't invent**: It's not my fault I get sole credit for inventing *MUD*; I myself always make a point of saying I only co-wrote it.

- **You're negative**: Oddly, "Richard Bartle likes *WoW's* vehicle quests" didn't make the headlines.

- **You're confusing stories with moralizing**: So, stories don't have morals?

- **Sewing would be more your speed**: This would be a fine rebuttal of my argument if it were, indeed, my argument it was rebutting.

- **Some people will do anything for experience and reputation**: That explains the boom in the number of MMO prostitutes, or "gold farmers" as they are sometimes known.

Obviously, there were other themes that were rather less friendly (I don't think I got great numbers of death threats on this occasion, though). There were also some brave souls agreeing with my point. These people tended to be the ones who had also been surprised by the quest in question, although not all (some had missed its message but now were re-evaluating it without resorting to "it's just a game").

If you say anything negative about a popular MMO, don't expect many of the responses you get to be much to do with what you said. People write about what they think you said, what someone else said you said, what they think you must think, and what stereotype they wish you to conform to. They'll also make *ad hominem* attacks with free abandon and make irrelevant points as if they were relevant.

Fortunately, some will also take the point seriously and add a cogent contribution that advances the discussion or even settles it one way or the other. Those are the people you thought would be reading what you wrote at the time you wrote it.

Keep heart, they do exist!

What Is Required to Be a Successful Game Designer?

Luck.

Note that I didn't say "good" designer. I said "successful."

Gamification

Gamification is a term several decades old. It used to mean "turning something not a game into a game" but now means "turning a game into something not a game." Formally, it's putting game design patterns to nongame use. It's typically utilized for marketing purposes but can be profitably employed to encourage people to do things. When you got a star for your schoolwork as a child, that was an example of what we'd now call gamification.

Gamification differs from Serious Games in that the latter wants a game at the end whereas gamification doesn't. This is just as well, because games are play you can lose at whereas gamified activities are not play and you can't lose at them. Interestingly, Serious Games started out using simplified gamification techniques but abandoned them because they didn't deliver.

There are several ways to gamify an activity, but most of what goes on is what is termed (rather disparagingly) *pointsification*; I suspect the reason this approach has traction is that gamification tends to be undertaken by people who aren't game designers.

A key aspect of gamification concerns rewards. *Intrinsic rewards* are inherent to an activity itself. Play is ultimately an intrinsic reward: people play because it's fun. *Extrinsic rewards* are acquired for completing an activity, for example phat lewt. Gamification exclusively uses extrinsic rewards.

Games tend to offer extrinsic rewards for activities that the player already finds intrinsically rewarding. Gamification makes receipt of the reward itself be the reward. This means that the rewards do have to *be* rewarding. They can be so either intrinsically (such as a fun, jaunty victory tune) or extrinsically (such as points you can spend on stuff).

What gamification comes down to, then, is bribery. You want someone to do something, so you pay them to do it. Sometimes, this is something they want to do anyway—promising yourself a Mars Bar if you manage to lose a certain amount of weight this week, for example. Other times, it's to help you make up your mind—say, buying one kind of fizzy drink in preference to another because you could win a year's supply of the stuff.

Now the thing is, if you want to bribe someone to do something, then the reward you offer has to be valuable to them; if it isn't, it's not a reward. Points, leaderboard positions, badges, and achievements can't be turned in for goods and services so will be regarded as valuable only for so long. You didn't still get stars on your work at the end of your school career because by then every-one had realized that they didn't actually mean a great deal.

Intrinsic rewards are almost always universally good (unless an individual gets so rewarded by them that it leads to an addiction). Extrinsic rewards can be used to supplement intrinsic rewards, but there are dangers if recipients take them for granted. External incentives then serve to *reduce* intrinsic motivation, and when the extrinsic rewards stop, then the intrinsic motivation doesn't return. This disassociation of (in our case) player from content is called the *overjustification effect,* and it could explain why so many people did the *Wrath of the Lich King* torture quest without a second thought: they regarded it as simple work for pay.

Gamification is currently in vogue. Whether it will still be in vogue a few years' hence is another matter. If too much of it goes on, people will realize that worthless extrinsic rewards are indeed worthless. MMO players accept that raiding-game rewards will be worthless come the next expansion, but at least they find participating in raids fun; gamified activities don't have that intrinsic reward to support them. The more that activities are gamified, the more often people will spot what's going on and the less effective the method will become.

It may sound from this that I don't think a great deal about gamification. Actually, I believe it has a lot of potential when it's being used to encourage people to do things they want to do anyway or to boost an intrinsic reward or as a way of easing people into an activity until they do find it intrinsically rewarding (reading novels, say). I have deep concerns about generic pointsification, however, even though (or perhaps because) it uses Player Type theory to underpin it.

I also have concerns about some of the particular game design techniques that gamification adopts. In particular, it sometimes takes a dark path. . .

Games and Addiction

People used to describe computer games (and MUDs in particular) as being "addictive" in order to sell them.

The word was used figuratively, of course, but following the "computer addiction" and "Internet addiction" media panics of the 1980s and 1990s, respectively, the perception grew among nonplayers that games were addictive *literally*.

So, is this perception correct?

Well, there are two things we need to know if we are to answer:

- What games are we talking about?

- What's the definition of addiction?

Unfortunately, as I mentioned earlier, psychologists have tended to regard video games as much of a muchness. When it comes to addiction, MMOs are the same as casual games and AAA console titles.

As for the definition of *addiction*, well, there's no universally accepted one because particular indicators that may be available for (say) substance abuse may not be available for (say) risk-taking or cosmetic surgery. That said, there is one definition that has wide acceptance and is often used in reference to computer games: Griffiths' Component Model.[3]

Griffiths asserts that addictions of all kinds have six similar biopsychosocial (!) components:

- **Salience**: The activity is the most important thing in your life and dominates your thinking.

- **Mood modification**: The activity gives you a buzz/high or escape/numbing.

- **Tolerance**: You need more to get the same effect that a little used to give you.

- **Withdrawal symptoms**: Unpleasant feelings or physical changes come from stopping the activity.

- **Conflict**: The activity compromises your relationships with those around you.

- **Relapse**: You haven't been doing an activity for ages but then start up again.

---

[3]Mark M. Griffiths: A 'Components' Model of Addiction within a Biopsychosocial Framework. *Journal of Substance Use* v10 (4) pp 191–197, 2005.

Conflict is the weak point of this model because it relies on the attitudes of other people, not of the subject individual. Nevertheless, on the whole, Griffiths' criteria do look eminently reasonable.

So, using this and other models, psychologists routinely find that computer games addict 5 percent to 10 percent of their users—pretty well regardless of which games are studied. To put that into context, the equivalent capture rates for various drugs are as follows: cannabis, 9.1 percent; alcohol, 15.4 percent; cocaine, 16.7 percent; heroin, 23.1 percent; tobacco, 31.9 percent.[4] Yes, almost a third of the people who have tried tobacco have become addicted to it.

Of course, how serious being addicted to something is does rather depend on what it is to which you are addicted. An addiction to heroin is going to screw you up much more than is an addiction to texting or exercising, say. Unfortunately, studies on game addiction don't tend to talk about the consequences of addiction, focusing mainly on the incidence of it.

You have to wonder how transient these addictions are, too. For example, let's assume a capture rate of 5 percent. Do 5 percent of the players of the 1985 RPG *Ultima IV* still play it? Well, no. Do they play RPGs? Very likely, yes, but the same could be said of nonaddicted *Ultima IV* players. Do they play computer games of any kind? Well, almost certainly—as does well over half the population. So, what exactly *were* those who were addicted to *Ultima IV* in 1985 addicted to, and for how long did their addiction last?

Most games don't make addicts of people. They're *compelling* but not addicting. Some, however, genuinely *are* psychologically addictive; anything that includes a variable ratio reinforcement schedule for rewards in its core loop risks addicting some players to some degree. Thus, although it may be tempting to dismiss "video game addiction" research as a misreading of what's actually going on, you can't; some of it is frighteningly valid.

Incidentally, frontline health professionals who treat addiction never call it that. They talk instead about *dependence*. Psychology and Psychiatry are different things.

---

[4]James C. Anthony, Lynn A. Warner and Ronald C. Kessler: *Comparative Epidemiology of Dependence on Tobacco, Alcohol, Controlled Substances, and Inhalants: Basic Findings From the National Comorbidity Survey. Experimental and Clinical Psychopharmacology* v2 (3) pp 244–268, 1994. www.umbrellasociety.ca/web/files/u1/Comp_epidemiology_addiction.pdf

But Is It Art?

In April 2005, I attended a talk in Milwaukee that concerned digital and public art. The talk was given by Christiane Paul, the adjunct curator of New Media Arts at the Whitney Museum of American Art.

What she was saying was edgy stuff for the art establishment because it pushed at boundaries as to what is high concept and what isn't. To those of us immersed in digital culture, some of what she described was mundane, but other stuff was too Real Art to be accessible. Some of it was, however, interesting to game designers. Given that she had a broad audience to talk to, I think this was probably a good hit rate.

Let me summarize the Q&A session that followed her talk:

- Ted Castranova said that a lot of what she described was boring.

- She said it was challenging.

- Ted said that some of what she described completely misunderstood and patronized the medium of computer games, for example, the pitiful *agoraXchange*.

- She said that computer game design wasn't art.

- I laid into her with some ferocity.

I had no problem with her describing what she discussed in her talk as being art. I even had no problem with her saying that *agoraXchange* was art, although it would have been nice if she'd understood why it was bad art. Where I did have a problem was in her denial that what I myself do is art. Telling an artist that what they do isn't art is almost guaranteed to annoy them, and it did me.

She never did acknowledge that computer game design is art. She didn't see any art in violent first-person shooters, so by extension there was no art in any computer game. It's a shame, but there you have it.

I agree that you do have to play these games a lot to be able to pick up on the art as a player, but if I can accept that art exists that it would take a course in art appreciation to make sense of, then surely she could accept the mere possibility that there might be art in games she hasn't played? Or, come to that, in games she has played but not enough to internalize them?

All I wanted was an acknowledgment that it was possible, but it never came.

I suspect it'll be a while before Sid Meier gets an exhibition at the Whitney.

There were 18 BAFTAs awarded for computer games that year.

Games You Should Have Played #9

An MMO.

This is because I co-wrote the first one, and therefore the more people who play these, the higher my kudos rises. I assume, given the nature of this book, that you probably have this one covered. Still, you might be an academic who's fiercely proud of never having had your objectivity corrupted by actually playing the games you study, in which case go for it.

I'll list as my example the last MMO I'd played through up to the level cap at the time the question that led to this thread was asked: *Rift*. I came away not so much impressed by the game itself but by its developer, Trion Worlds, which is more understanding of its players than is any other developer I've encountered except perhaps CCP. If you've never played an MMO, you won't have the foggiest idea why that would be at all important.

Extrinsic Rewards in Games

Games mainly use intrinsic rewards. When you concoct your master plan in *Chess*, the intellectual stimulation you get from the exercise is an intrinsic reward. Winning a trophy because you won a *Chess* tournament would be an extrinsic reward.

In game design, extrinsic rewards can be used with good effect for a number of things, such as:

- To make implicit progress explicit. Experience points make your character improve as you, the player, improve.

- To breadcrumb players through directionless content. Yes, you were supposed to kill those guys—look, here are some points to prove it.

- To open new content or shortcut played-through content. With this stone you can teleport to the City of Gold.

- To indicate the end of a narrative cycle. That guy you killed was the boss of this dungeon wing, so here's some armor that might be useful for the next stage.

- To heighten the response from an intrinsic reward. Not only was that fun, but you get this!

Extrinsic rewards are used a lot in games, particularly MMOs, but intrinsic rewards dominate. What self-respecting game designer would be happy to release a game they thought was so bad that they had to bribe people to play it?

Games You Should Have Played #10

Mornington Crescent.

The last game on my list of games you should have played is different from the others in that it's an actual game, rather than a way to identify a game. Well, I suppose naming it *is* a way to identify it, but it's the only game I do name this way in the list.

Earlier, I explained the rules to *Mornington Crescent*—but not the fact that it's actually called *Finchley Central*, which is how I first encountered it in the monthly magazine *Games and Puzzles* that my dad bought when I was in my teens in the 1970s.

Either way, this is a game that everyone should play, because it gets to the heart of what a game *is*: you can see exactly what happens when you freely and knowingly bound your behavior according to a set of rules in the hope of gaining some benefit. You play it for just so long as it's fun, with people who also play it for just so long as it's fun, which is how all games should be.

So, at last we reach the end of my top 10 list of games that people should have played (which is to say, should play if they haven't already). If you'd already played them, I apologize for having wasted your time. If you haven't played them, I envy you the treasure trove of discovery that lies ahead.

Declining Standards

Players of MMOs are doing what they've always done—they're trying to "win." So as to gain customers, designers are therefore changing the gameplay to allow them to win; all too often, however, this is being done in such a way that it makes winning a worthless concept.

If this carries on, MMOs are going to lose all vestiges of whatever made them special. People are going to wonder, 10 or 15 years from now, what all the fuss was about. There'll be some resonance through the cultural changes that persist, but it will dampen down over time. All we'll see will be ripples of what once was. We'll have millions of people playing, sure, but what they'll be playing will lack the essence that makes MMOs so importantly different from ordinary computer games.

Now if people really want to turn MMOs into ordinary computer games, well, that's up to them. I just don't want for them to be able to turn *every* MMO into an ordinary computer game.

If they do, we'll have lost something special, precious, and unique in human history, and it will be *decades* before it re-emerges.

Mope

So many MMO designers have lost touch with what they can do, they don't even know what it is they're undermining anymore. It's not just designers, either. Researchers talk of MMOs in terms of property and contract law and social capital and government, all the while missing what's on offer. Players think of the future only in terms of *WoW* or *GW2* or *WildStar* or *SW:TOR* or *Dungeon Fighter Online* or whatever else their current world of choice is; they refuse to contemplate the mere possibility that there may be other ways of doing things, let alone that these ways could be better.

In the drive to make virtual worlds mass market, they've been gradually losing what it is that makes them special. It's both sad and frustrating to watch.

In the very, very early days of *MUD*, players had freedom but didn't realize it. They played as themselves, with no role-playing—much as they might play *Monopoly* or *Tennis*. It was only when I showed them by example that they finally got what was possible (although it would surely have happened eventually without my intervention).

From that time onward, they had the freedom to do and to be whatever they wanted. They took it, too. Their ability to interact with other players was immense: you could attack and kill (permadeath) other player characters, you could steal things from them, you could lock them in rooms from which they couldn't escape—there were many ways to be absolutely awful to them. However, there were many more ways to be nice to them. Being awful was rapidly assessed to be a losing strategy (as it was designed to be). People built up trust, friendships, expertise, and knowledge; in so doing, the game world asked them questions that they answered through deeds, learning more about themselves in the process.

This potentially unfettered interaction (which is no worse than what is available in real life) is nevertheless not viable in modern MMOs. You can't do anything much at all to other player characters. This makes the world more palatable at one level, if those things you might want to do were grief-related, but it makes it less embracing at another, in that sometimes you want to be able to help others in ways that are no longer possible.

Over time, players have become accustomed to being wrapped in cotton wool. They've grown used to having decisions made for them. You want to be a mage, so you select class mage—it's just too confusing if you have to, you know, *act* like a mage. More and more constraints are being added to protect players from the twin demons of other players and of having to think; eventually we're going to end up with a useless mush that's suitable only for 10-year-olds.

I do see a little light ahead, though. Some players and designers do sense the possibilities. If production costs were to come down, they could experiment with new designs, in new directions, recapturing some of what was lost and, it's to be hoped, breaking out to bring us more than we ever had before.

If we end up in a situation where MMOs are so bland that people think they're just another social network, we're in trouble. Unfortunately, we're actually getting close to that.

Now I'm starting to mope.

Child Psychology and Games

There's little controversy about the potential effect of games on children. Society has long kept children away from anything it deems to be inappropriate and has also encouraged children to engage in a broad range of activities rather than just a few (which is just as well, given that they have shorter attention spans than adults).

Children feature strongly in research on games and violence, but such research is less "about" the children than it is "about" the violence. Children don't feature anywhere near as much in research on games and addiction, except perhaps for adolescents.

Work on the child-specific psychological effect of games tends to be of the games-and-learning kind. This feeds into the more general research on pedagogy undertaken by educationalists, so although it's informed by other research on Psychology and Games, it tends to have a more practical agenda.

Of course, if you're going to make games specifically for the use of children, you do have to consider the important issue of child protection.

This is especially the case for MMOs.

Player Type Misuses #3

Some designers apply Player Types in a superficial, bullet-point kind of way. For them, it's a bandwagon that they're jumping on for no reason other than everyone else is jumping on it.

We saw this with gamification —the use of game techniques for nongame purposes (normally selling people stuff, but it could also be for educational, instructional, creative, health, or other reasons). Originally, Player Types were picked up by gamification in an analogy-style mapping, as in, "Hmm, people play MMOs for different reasons, so perhaps people respond to gamification for different reasons?" However, once a bandwagon developed, all sense of the analogy was lost. People started creating off-the-shelf solutions for gamifying web sites (or whatever), that assumed there *were* four types that you *would* get and that *would* respond to the typed content in predictable ways. It was cookie-cutter stuff.

When I said "superficial" back there, by the way, I meant it: some of these attempts didn't look deep enough to realize that achiever rewards (points, badges, leaderboards, "achievements") work only for achievers. They would reward socializers and explorers for socializing and exploring by giving them achiever rewards and then wonder why it didn't work.

It seems incredible that people will spend time and money implementing a sophisticated system that's based on a theory they didn't bother to read. Nevertheless, that doesn't seem to stop them doing so.

Awful Happenings

"What happens now that all the awful things we've been predicting would happen to MMOs for years are finally happening and they are indeed awful?"

I wrote that in 2010.

The answer is, they get worse.

Games and Aggression

If you thought "video games and addiction" sold newspapers and made research careers, you haven't met "video games and aggression."

Early research found no link between video games and aggression. This was not, however, what society at the time wanted to hear.

Whenever a new entertainment medium appears, the older generation doesn't understand it and so doesn't trust it. Sometimes, the older generation is right: narcotics really do mess you up. Most of the time, though, it over-reacts. In the past, society has been concerned about the effects of books, the waltz, music halls, penny dreadfuls, film, jazz, radio, comic books, TV, rock and roll, videos, rap, and the Internet. Such over-reaction leads to media panics and therefore, in today's world, government research funding.

As the older generation dies off, video games will lose their place as the latest threat to civilization. Indeed, it already looks as if social media (such as Facebook and Twitter) are being lined up to star as the next social evils that will rend the fabric of society. However, until that happens, the relentless narrative that video games cause players to be aggressive in real life will continue to play out, damaging the game industry in the process.

It's interesting to note that this research is almost entirely about *video games* and aggression, rather than nonvideo games (such as perhaps *Ice Hockey*) and aggression. Such research will usually compare the effects on aggression of violent video games only against those of nonviolent video games. They don't even consider other media much. Most researchers in the area have no idea if violent TV shows, say, have a greater or lesser effect on aggression than do violent games. Should you stop your children playing games and let them watch TV instead, or would that be worse for them? This lack of comparison of games to other media seems, well, bizarre.

The Verb *to Gamify*

When Roy Trubshaw began work on *MUD*, he and everyone else called it a game. However it wasn't a game, because it had no gameplay; it was a world.

Although I was only 18 at the time, I had a very strong background in playing games (I'd even run my own postal games magazine for a couple of years) and had a well-developed sense of what games *were*; I knew that *MUD* wasn't one.

I did mainly world-design stuff for *MUD* until around Easter 1980, when I took over the code from Roy so he could study for his finals (he's a year older than me). Roy had begun to rewrite *MUD* from scratch late 1979, because version 2 was in assembly language and he was finding it too unwieldy. When he started the rewrite, we had some discussions as to what direction the new version should take, and I suggested we should gamify it. The original vision was for a world so rich in its functionality that drama and fun would just flow from it (*emerge* would be the modern term), but we didn't have the computing resources for that to happen. Hence, to give people a reason to play, we had to structure that play, and this meant building gameplay into the world's physics.

Roy agreed with this plan but only had the shell of the system working by Easter; it fell to me to do most of the work. I coded perhaps 75 percent of version 3 of *MUD* and introduced game ideas into it as I did so.

You may have noticed I used the word *gamify* back there. *Gamification* is now a thing; as my work on player types is apparently foundational in the gamification world, it therefore looks as if I coined the term.

Well, I didn't. The word *gamify* was not something I recall as having invented. I'm pretty sure that there were other people in the U.K. games scene (and probably the U.S. one as well, as the two were linked) who used the word in the same sense I did at the time.

Besides, the use of *gamify* nowadays is subtly different from how it was in the 1970s. Back then, it simply meant turning something that wasn't a game into a game. Now, it means applying techniques from games to nongames while keeping those nongames as nongames. The result of gamification isn't games; it's nongames. Earlier, the result was games.

The earliest court-admissible evidence I have for my own use of the word *gamify* is from an email in 2002. However, I'd been using it for well over 20 years by then, and I'm sure others had been using it before me. As for the term *gamification*, although it's a clear derivative of *gamify* and people decades ago probably would have used it as such if they needed a noun for the concept of gamifying, it wasn't really a recognized term. I don't recall having heard it in use.

From this, it should be obvious that although I used the word *gamify* before modern gamification experts, their usage owes nothing to mine. As I keep stressing, being "first" doesn't mean that all other examples descend from that first one. The progenitor of the modern usage of *to gamify* isn't the old usage, because that didn't influence modern usage. Making a verb from a noun by adding *ify* to the end is something the English language can just *do*, so it's no surprise that it has been done several times.

As it happens, I don't actually like the modern use of the verb *to gamify*; in my view, the older meaning reflects the construction of the word *gamify* better.

Oh, how language changes.

How Violent Is Violent?

Psychologists studying the effects of violent video games on players seem to treat the concept of a "violent video game" as if it were binary. A game can't be a *little* violent; either it is violent or it isn't. Some researchers regard *all* video games as violent, although even other psychologists working on games and aggression regard that as a rather extreme position.

I wonder, how many drops of violence do you have to add to a game to make it count as a "violent game"?

Pac Man and *Centipede* were regarded as violent video games by researchers back in the day.

A Dark Path

Gamification can be made more interesting for the person engaging in it by means of adding irregularity. Regularity, which applies to vanilla gamification and regular employment, is something like "pull this handle 20 times and we'll give you $1." Irregularity, which applies to advanced gamification and gambling, is more like "pull this handle and you have a 5 percent chance of winning $1."

As you will perhaps have discerned from the fact that I've just repeated an example I've used before, gamified irregularity of this kind looks a lot like a variable ratio reinforcement schedule—an effective method of operant conditioning. This makes it very interesting if you have things to sell (and likewise if people start to use it on you to make you buy stuff).

What's more, it doesn't just work with intrinsic rewards; it works with extrinsic rewards, too. This explains some gamifiers' interest in it.

Traditionally, game designers have eschewed operant conditioning for extrinsic rewards. This is because:

- It's not fun. Fun is intrinsic, not extrinsic.

- It's an admission of failure. It means your gameplay is too weak on its own.

- It's usable only on naïve players. Once they've realized what's going on, they'll avoid it.

- It's immoral. It can lead to psychological problems for some players.

In recent years, however, some game developers (led by ones creating for social networking sites) broke ranks. They created games that do have extrinsic rewards deliberately presented using a variable ratio reinforcement schedule, the apparent aim being to hook players. Although there was plenty of backlash from designers about this, the response of those indulging in the practice was pretty well to wave their profits at the complainers and laugh.

It's from such social network games that gamifiers took their inspiration. They have fewer concerns than game designers in that:

- They don't expect their gamified content to be intrinsically fun anyway.

- They readily acknowledge that their content isn't compelling—that's precisely why they're gamifying it.

- They suspect it could be a bubble that is about to burst, but they see a lot of opportunity for profit before it does.

- They don't expect to be sued by anyone for deliberately trying to addict them to their content. If the gambling industry is safe, so are they.

Gamifiers are not game designers so can perhaps be pardoned for not really understanding what it is they're doing. Game designers who deliberately try to implement operant conditioning for extrinsic rewards have no such excuse.

Have Your Cake and Eat It

Suppose you saw this headline: "Eating Cake Makes People Overweight." What is it suggesting?

Well, why would a headline that could apply to many foodstuffs single out cake? Alternatively, why would a headline that could apply to many effects of eating cake single out that one? The tacit implication in both cases is that the effect is greater than people typically think. If the prevailing view is that eating cake doesn't make you overweight, you'd be suggesting that it does. If the prevailing view is that cake isn't as fattening as treats in general, you'd be suggesting that it is. If the prevailing view is that cake is as fattening as treats in general, you'd be suggesting that it's more so.

Furthermore, if you keep plugging away, saying the same thing, then although your statement may not vary in meaning, the prevailing view can *as a result of what you've been saying*:

- "Eating Cake Makes People Overweight"

- Really? Oh well, probably not as much as pies.

- "Eating Cake Makes People Overweight"

- What, you mean it's as bad as pies?

- "Eating Cake Makes People Overweight"

- Oh, I guess I'd better just stick to pies then.

Obviously no psychologist studying "violent video games" believes that *only* violent video games make people aggressive. They readily accept that there is *multivariate causality*: lots of things can and do make people aggressive. If you say that violent video games make people aggressive, you're not saying it's the *only* cause, just that it's one of many.

That's not how a finding of "Violent Video Games Make People Aggressive" comes across, though.

The Right Stuff

In April 2010, I went to Brunel University to listen to a series of lectures by legendary computer game designer Chris Crawford. I'd never heard him speak before and had been told he could be a tad prickly; however, in person he was no such thing. There were plenty of opportunities in the Q&A sessions for a prickly person to *be* prickly, but he wasn't at all. I'd probably have been much pricklier myself in his position.

The content of the lectures, while interesting, was more student-level than cutting edge, but then it was aimed at students, so this was only to be expected. Nevertheless, the more he went on, the more I saw evidence that my own experience as a game designer is indeed not unique. I questioned him about it when we were alone together for 20 minutes while everyone else went for a coffee and found we did indeed have much in common, specifically:

- He's well-read. OK, so he had 138 books on Erasmus (probably more now), which is selectively deep, but he reads on a broad range of topics—whatever catches his eye.

- He doesn't have problems thinking of game ideas. The hard part is deciding which ideas to pursue.

- He has lots of game designs in different states of completion kicking around.

- He became a programmer to create games; he didn't create games as something to program.

- He doesn't play games for the same kind of fun that players do, he plays them to divine the design. He even mentioned "reading" a game from its design.

Those all apply to me, too. They also apply to pretty well every other game designer I know, give or take a point. I guess there could be game designers who don't fit this profile, but it's pretty well universal from what I've seen.

Students who want to become game designers therefore ought to ask themselves the following questions:

- Do you easily get interested in random nonfiction (in books, on TV, in Wikipedia)? Or in particular objects encountered while walking around museums and art galleries?

- Do you get game ideas the whole time (well, at least one a day), unstoppably?

- Have you made, or started to make, many games? Not necessarily computer games: board games, word games, playground games—they all count.

- Do you want to design games so much that if you can't get someone else to make them for you, you'll make them yourself, no matter what arcane skills you may have to pick up to do so?

- Are you prepared ultimately to lose the enjoyment you gain from playing games to achieve all this?

If so, you may just be made of the right stuff. If not, well you could still be made of the right stuff, but I would recommend thinking about it long and hard before trying for a career in game design.

Chris Crawford had no idea who I was when we chatted. No one else stayed to talk to him during the coffee break, just me.

Three Views

On July 22, 2011 I was in the lobby of a hotel in Germany, watching a bank of TVs as the story of a sequence of terrible events in Norway unfolded. A right-wing extremist had exploded a car bomb in Oslo and then driven to a summer camp and embarked on a gun rampage among unarmed teenagers.

The German TV stations pretty well led on the perpetrator's claim to be a *World of Warcraft* player. CNN mentioned his playing of *WoW* as a contributing factor but didn't dwell on it. The BBC discussed what he'd put on his Facebook page, but his *WoW*-playing habits merited no mention at all.

Different countries have different cultures; different cultures have different attitudes to computer games and aggression. The UK got into games very early, as a result of the government's decision to put a BBC microcomputer in every school in the early 1980s. The US wasn't far behind. Germany had other issues before the Berlin Wall fell so came to computer games late (although as a consequence it now rules the board game industry).

The longer that computer games are played by a culture, the less dangerous they seem to become.

Child Protection

Most of what I say in this book, particularly when it comes to a designer's freedom of expression, assumes that MMOs are played by adults.

When children are involved, all bets are off. Children cannot be expected to know what will or won't happen in an MMO; they can't be expected to read a manual or an online description, and they're not legally bound by a EULA.

So, developers will, broadly speaking, aim at one or more of three demographics when they create MMOs: younger children, teenagers, adults. The way they manage their content depends on the youngest group that they address.

Surprisingly, given the antigame hysteria of many newspapers, MMOs that aim at younger children have so far been incredibly aware of their duty of care. With the law unclear and no precedents in the courts, they assumed from the beginning a very strict regime and worked to keep their worlds safe, child-friendly, and parent-informative. Likewise, MMOs aimed at those aged 12+ have been careful to keep their content wholesome, their violence cartoony or stylized, and their players' behavior within the bounds of propriety. Adult MMOs also tend to be responsible. It's not in their interests to see their names in newspaper articles about exposing raunchy content or scenes of violence to children.

Where all three have a problem, though, is in *identifying* that users really are the age they say they are. A pedophile could play a soft-and-pink children's MMO by pretending to be a child. A teenager could play a gory adult game by pretending to be an adult.

Developers can do only so much verification. What they'd really, really like to know is whether what they're doing at the moment is enough. Exactly what *is* required of them to fulfill due diligence criteria? If they're falling short, they want to know.

If they ask for a credit card from a player, would that be enough evidence that the player is 18? Sure, young people can take a parent's credit card, but at least it means that there's *some* adult out there who will notice the bills and can put a stop to it. However, the credit card companies themselves don't like their products being used for age verification and point out that in some circumstances it's possible for a 16-year-old to own such a card.

In the Far East, identity card numbers have been tried as a means of proving age, but this hasn't worked at all. There are web sites full of names and identity card numbers that people who want to pretend they're older or younger than they are can peruse at will. Furthermore, anyone who has had their identity card number used in this manner to access an MMO has no way of knowing what has happened unless they themselves try to play the same world. Changing your identity card number is barely practical, because it's used for so many other things too.

Besides, in a world in which children regularly stay up late to watch adult material on TV with no requirement that they prove their age to the broadcaster, MMOs are already doing more than television stations are to protect children from scenes of sex and violence. Why should they have to do any more than they are already?

As usual, MMO developers don't mind conforming to the law, but they would rather like to know what the law *is* so that they can do so.

Understanding the Experience

To everyone who has never played an MMO and is worried that someone special to them is spending too much time in one: try to play that MMO yourself for a couple of weeks. That way, you may have a fighting chance of understanding why your someone special is playing instead of watching TV or whatever else they're supposed to be doing. You'll thus be better able to judge whether their behavior is problematical.

Well, it's an idea. Unfortunately, it's one that's unlikely to be taken up. From the worried person's point of view, it would be like a drug pusher telling them to take heroin to understand what their someone special is going through. Not a good idea.

A Cynical View

I said earlier that early research found no link between video games and aggression. Research today does. Why is that?

It's two decades ago. You're a young Psychology researcher looking for a topic for your PhD. Video games are relatively new, they haven't been studied before (because they're not academically respectable), but they're cool, so you do some preliminary work on them yourself. If you find nothing, you look else-where. If you find something, you write it up as your thesis.

Hold on. How would you find that games are linked to aggression if there is no such link? Well, suppose that instead of asking "Do video games cause aggres-sive behavior?" you're asking "Is this die loaded?" You roll it, and if it comes up anything other than a 6, then you conclude it's not loaded. Statistically, though, one researcher in six is going to suspect it is loaded. Likewise, if you look at video games and aggression, then there will be people whose research hap-pens to find a link.

These are the individuals who will write up their research and attract funding to do further research in the area. If this research doesn't support their prem-ise, they don't publish it; if it does, they do publish it, and the funding continues.

Two decades later, these once-junior researchers are now senior, with their careers built on the foundation of a link between video game play and aggres-sion. New researchers in the area have to buy into their beliefs or they won't get a job.

Okay, well before I'm subject to a class-action law suit by researchers into video games and aggression, I ought perhaps to state that this is a somewhat overly cynical reading of events. Nevertheless, it is the case that most psy-chologists studying games this century have accepted almost unquestioningly that there's a link with aggressive behavior. The cracks are only now beginning to show.

See, if you keep predicting that the sky is about to fall in, you have a problem when it doesn't, actually, fall in.

Markey, Markey, and French

Suppose that violent video games did cause aggressive behavior in real life. It follows that there should be increases in incidences of violence following major game releases, yes?

Researchers Markey, Markey, and French[5] looked at levels of violence in the United States at different intervals following the release of major "violent" games such as *Call of Duty: Black Ops* and *Grand Theft Auto IV*. They found *no* increase in violence. Indeed, overall violence levels in society have gone *down* since video games became mainstream.

In the United States, it's taken almost as read that people who commit school shootings play video games. This is actually true—they do! However, it's true because *almost all* young people play video games. As Markey, Markey, and French point out, saying that the perpetrator of a school shooting played a video game is about as useful as noting that they were wearing socks.

We've had violent video games as part of mainstream culture for more than two decades now. If they really do cause people to become aggressive in real life, the streets should be flowing with rivers of blood by now. They're not.

You can get away with making predictions as to what will happen in the future only while it's not the future. When yesterday's tomorrow becomes today and your predictions haven't panned out, you have to face facts.

The question is no longer *whether* violent video games cause aggressive behavior in real life. It's why psychologists *think* they do when patently they don't.

---

[5]Patrick M. Markey, Charlotte N. Markey and Juliana E. French: *Violent Video Games and Real-World Violence: Rhetoric Versus Data. Psychology of Popular Media Culture*, 2014.

Psychology Experiments

Psychology experiments on games are necessarily short. For practical reasons, you can't pull in a group of subjects and have them play a game for 40 hours. You might get 15 minutes, half an hour, maybe a whole hour or even two hours if you're lucky. Then, if you want to see whether playing the game has made the subjects more aggressive, you have to leave a short interval—another 15 minutes, say—before you do whatever you do that assesses how aggressive your subjects now are. There simply isn't enough time to do more (especially if your test subjects are children).

For example, one way Psychologists have of determining how aggressive someone is is to give them the opportunity to blast a loud noise at a stranger. The subjects are typically informed that this can leave the recipient with permanent hearing damage (although of course no one actually *does* get blasted with the noise—a fact that seems so obviously the case that you'd have to be extremely gullible to believe otherwise, but let's assume it works). Anyway, if you have one group of players play *Tetris* for 15 minutes and another group play *Grand Theft Auto 5* for 15 minutes and then you give members of both groups the opportunity to deafen a stranger, you will find that the *GTA5* players do it more than the *Tetris* players.

Well, *of course* they do! If someone interrupts you while you're playing *Tetris*, that's no big deal. If they interrupt you just as you're getting into *GTA5*, damned right you're going to be aggressive—at the interruption!

Also, although it's not really in dispute that *GTA5* is more violent than *Tetris*, that's just one of many differences. The more apposite one here is that *Tetris* is a casual game, whereas *GTA5* is a AAA high-paced action-adventure shooter. *They're not the same thing!* To the people studying video games, though, they pretty well *are*—except for the differences in violence.

It's not hard to see how people who don't play games can easily make mistakes that people who do play them wouldn't make. So, why do so few experimenters play games? If they did, they could make better assessments about what they're actually studying.

Well, perhaps the reason they don't is that if they did play these violent games, it would make them become aggressive.

Media Effects

The primary reason that psychologists started looking at games and aggression is grounded in *Media Effects* theory. What this says is that exposure to something in the media influences your behavior. It originated in the 1920s when concerned German researchers looked at how Nazi propagandists were getting their messages across; a more modern application is to explain how the use of stick-figure fashion models leads to anorexia nervosa among teenagers.

So, if games contain violence and people play a lot of games, doesn't it make sense that they might become desensitized to violence and regard it as the norm—and that they keep regarding it as such when they've stopped playing? Well yes, that does sound plausible.

The intellectual opposite of media effects is *selection effects*. What this says is that people who have certain wants and needs are attracted to media that allow them to gratify those needs. This sounds plausible, too.

Does exposure to romantic novels make people more romantic? If so, it's a media effect. Do romantic people tend to read romantic novels? If so, it's a selection effect. The problem is, if all you know is that people who read romantic novels are more romantic than people who don't, you have a correlation, but you can't tell which way round the causality goes. The only real way to find out is to test people before they are exposed to the media in question and then test them again some years later and see what happened. This is called a *longitudinal study*.

So, do violent games make people aggressive, or do aggressive people play violent games? Or neither?

Longitudinal studies are expensive to undertake and by definition take time, so we're only now starting to see the results of such studies into violent video games and aggression. The results indicate that aggression predicts the use of violent video games but that playing violent video games doesn't predict aggression.

In other words, it's a selection effect, not a media effect.

That rather undermines this whole field.

Peer Recognition

I don't have a background in music. I listen to music, and I know what I like and why, but I don't have the same kind of critical faculties that composers do from having worked at composing day in, day out, for years. It would be very naïve of me to think that just because I listen to the results of musical composition, I'm some kind of expert. I'm not—not compared to the composers, anyway.

This same peer recognition thing works across many creative industries. Those who are best at their job influence those who are up-and-coming, all the way down to the consumer. Top chefs cook only for gastronomes who understand the vocabulary of cooking, whereas you and I only go for what we like the taste of; yet, remarkably, what we buy in the microwave section at the supermarket is directly influenced by those top chefs. The same general principle applies to clothes, books, pop music, architecture, movies, oh—and computer games.

Being an expert player doesn't make you an expert designer. You may be able to detect the outward effects of expert design (that is, more fun for you), but you won't necessarily spot, understand, or care what the designer has gone through to deliver this. Other expert designers, however, *will*.

People like Raph Koster didn't get to be treated as MMO industry celebrities based on self-publicity or the personality-cult aspirations of players; they got to be where they are because *other* world-class designers saw their stuff and went, "Wow!" Raph's views are held in the highest esteem by other designers because they're consistently original *yet right*.

It's not a cult of personality; it's a recognition of talent. This is how all arts work. Sure, orchestral music aficionados may like Beethoven because of his melodies, but *composers* like Beethoven because, hot damn, it's *brilliant* the way he does that!

If there were a Society of MMO Designers and it had a Hall of Fame, then Raph would probably be its first inductee—not because players have heard of him but because he *deserves* it.

No, I haven't bought shares in him.

Ask Dr. Psycho

From this week's *Practical Serial Killer*:

Dear Dr. Psycho,

My ambition is to become a famous mass killer. I'm leaning toward the "weird loner with no friends who walks into class one day and randomly shoots people" type, as this will make it easier for the authorities to inform the parents of my victims.

If I am to do this, though, I have to be weird. I've heard that computer games can make you weird, but I don't play any. I wonder if you could recommend something suitable? I own a PC.

—Dai

Dear Dai,

First, I'd like to congratulate you on your strong feeling of social responsibility. All too often, senseless killers will just walk into a town center and start shooting indiscriminately with no thought for how long it will take to identify their victims. I'm sure the emergency services will thank you for your kind consideration in restricting your acts of murder to a location for which an attendance list is readily available.

Second, I have some good news for you! For most young people today, computer games are as much a part of their lives as music, television, and cheap alcohol. If you don't play computer games, this means *you're already weird!* You don't have to work at it like most people—you're a natural!

Bonus: you can use the money you won't be spending on games to buy more bullets!

—Dr Psycho

Own Goal

If I pay money to watch a sporting event, I don't get to own anything. I'm paying to watch people do things to a ball. I can pay more to get a better seat or a better view, but I don't *own* that seat—or even lease it.

What am I paying for in an MMO that I can say I own? Even if I buy it from the developer, what *exactly* is it I've bought?

Games and Identification

Another reason why psychologists hypothesize that violent video games are likely to make people more aggressive concerns *identification*. If you play a character in a game, you're more likely to identify with that character than you would with a character in a book, say. Therefore, if your character is violent (because it's a violent game), then you, the player, will take those feelings on board yourself.

Game designers like the idea that players of games identify with characters more than do readers of books, so this does seem to have some possible substance to it. It's entirely justifiable for a researcher to take what players and designers are saying about games and consider what the long-term consequences might be.

That said, 40 percent of male MMO players play female characters. If this identification-changes-you thing is true, does that mean they're becoming more female?

Less facetiously, let's suppose that playing violent games does indeed make you want to act aggressively. This is only going to be meaningful if you are playing single-player games. Psychologists testing the relationship between violent video games and aggression almost never use multiplayer games. The most popular violent games *are* multiplayer, though—and in multiplayer games, roughly *half the time you lose*. If you're identifying with being an aggressor, you're *also* identifying with being an aggressee. Arguably, you'll come away with a better understanding of the consequences of violent behavior, not a newfound bloodlust you now wish to sate.

Identification in MMOs *does* change you, but along its own dimension: it improves your understanding of who you are.

Needless to say, as the theory that supports this assertion is my own, I'm 100 percent behind it.

Games and Brands

This is to save me the bother of repeatedly having to tell advertising executives how to use games to get their advertising message across.

STREET CRIER:

Ketchup for burgers! Ketchup for burgers!

BILLBOARD:

Buy ketchup! It makes burgers taste better!

MAGAZINE:

Ketchup. The not-so-secret ingredient that makes burgers taste as good as they look.

RADIO:

Tired of tired burgers? Give them a pep-up with ketchup!

TV:

Kid: Mom, why does my burger taste of wet socks?

Flashback: Mother in store looking at Regular Burgers and 100 Percent Herbal Organic Natural Low-Fat Health Burgers at twice the price; she chooses the latter.

Mother:(slams a bottle of ketchup onto the table in front of kid).

Voice-over: Ketchup. The taste of burgers.

INTERNET:

This drawing of an imaginary woman with huge breasts wants *you* to put ketchup on your burgers.

SERIOUS GAMES:

Try to squirt the ketchup into the moving burger.

ADVERGAMES:

Try to squirt the ketchup into the moving burger over the head of your smiling kid sister who's wearing a ketchup-colored T-shirt.

GAMIFICATION:

For every three squirts of ketchup you put in your burger, you'll get 100 STAR POINTS!

GAME:

You're a 6-inch-high fairy armed with a magic wand, flying around a room zapping failing things to make them better.

Scattered

It's all very well knowing that a correlation r=.3 means that 9 percent of the variation between two variables is related, but it's hard to visualize what that means.

Well, it *would* be hard, but it's not when you use *scatter diagrams*. Here are some examples of correlations given in a statistics textbook[6]:

The scatter diagram on the left is for r=.99; the one on the right is for r=.9. In both cases, the dots are close to the x=y line. If they were all on it, it would be r=1.

Here are two more scatter diagrams, from the other end of the scale:

It's hard to tell them apart, but the one on the left is r=0 (that is, there's no correlation—it's random), and the one on the right is r=.3. If someone tells you that two variables correlate with a value of r=.3, the scatter diagram on the right is how you can think of it. Keep in mind that if I hadn't told you, you'd have been hard-pressed to know which of these two scatter diagrams was the random one and which was for r=.3.

The correlations that psychologists find between the playing of violent video games and the exhibition of aggressive behavior consistently comes in around the r=.15 mark.

So many research papers, such little value.

---

[6]David S. Moore & William I. Notz: *Statistics: Concepts and Controversies*, 7th edition. Freeman, New York, 2009.

Preaching to the Converted

From *The Guardian*, July 26, 2008:

Violent computer games to be barred from jails

Most prisoners will be banned from playing violent computer games, it emerged yesterday. Only convicts who have earned the highest level of privileges will be allowed access to games consoles, according to a Prison Service directive.

If you believe that computer games turn people into violent criminals, surely the only people who *shouldn't* be at risk from playing them are those who are already violent criminals?

Sticky

Technical term incoming...

A property of an MMO is said to be *sticky* if its presence makes people reluctant to leave. This doesn't mean something like charging a $200 "administrative fee" when you try to cancel your account—it's a magnet, not an obstacle. It's sticky as in adhesive, rather than sticky as in hitting you with a stick.

Although designers may talk about the stickiness of the leveling game *vs.* that of the elder game, the term primarily exists to convey one of the following two concepts to uninformed nonplayer business types:

- Community is sticky.
- MMOs themselves are sticky.

Unfortunately, it's easy to misread stickiness as addictiveness.

And Mr. Hyde

Suppose you invented a potion that you believed turned ordinary people into monsters. How would you test it?

Well, you'd take a group of people and you'd give half of them your potion and half of them something else (beer, say). If significantly more of the potion-takers turned into monsters than did the beer-drinkers, you could say your hypothesis works.

However, you'd have *created monsters*.

If you were a psychologist and believed in your heart of hearts that playing violent video games makes people aggressive and that aggressive is a bad thing for people to be, then *why on earth* would you give people violent video games to play as an experiment—especially if those people are children?

If games are harmful, why are you harming people? If they're harmless, why are you studying them?

Fatigue

There are people who have died of fatigue from playing MMOs.

Hmm, that sounds pretty bad, doesn't it? MMOs make you *so tired* that you die?

Well, for that to be entirely true, people would have to become fatigued at a faster rate while playing an MMO than they would performing some com-parable activity—playing a regular computer game, say. They'd probably get fatigued far quicker running a long-distance race or carrying bricks up a ladder on a hod, but the implication is that they would have eased up in those cases whereas they wouldn't for MMOs.

When people are said to die of "MMO fatigue," the suggestion is that the MMOs concerned were offering these unfortunate players an experience so compelling that they didn't want to stop playing even when they really, really should have done. This is not the same thing as saying the MMO somehow "induced" the fatigue; it's saying that the players affected were more motivated to ignore it. That is indeed a concern, but it's a *different* concern. I've played two-day-long sessions of *Dungeons and Dragons* without sleep; did D&D induce fatigue? No, failing to go to sleep induced fatigue. The difference is, I wasn't sit-ting at a computer when I finally did nod off, and I didn't fall off my chair onto a hard floor, and I didn't crack my head on it, and that didn't kill me.

If someone falls asleep watching TV, thereupon dropping their cigarette onto their sofa and burning their house down with them in it, the person gets the blame. If they do it while playing an MMO, the MMO gets the blame.

I long for the day when so many people have played computer games that we can get over this whole demonization of the subject and talk about things rationally.

Oppositely Held Views

Here's something that's been bothering me for a while about computer games.

For many years, suggestions have been made by politicians and the mainstream media that there is a link between the playing of computer games and the committing of acts of real-world violence. They suppose that if you play a violent computer game, it teaches you to be violent in real life. Game-savvy people like you and I will typically regard these opinions as founded on ignorance and argue that they should not be given credence.

One of the larger sub-branches of computer game research concerns educational gaming. Its premise is that kids don't always like traditional teaching methods, but they love games, so we should design games that help teach them things. That way, learning will be fun, so children will *want* to learn.

Now, isn't there a contradiction here? On the one hand, we're saying that no no no games don't teach people all those *bad* things, but on the other hand we're saying that yes yes yes games do teach people all these *good* things. Can we really sustain both these positions? Is there something about how games teach (or how people learn) that genuinely does separate desirable from undesirable results? Or are we changing our story depending on whether we're being threatened with a ban or being promised kudos?

A Technical Term

Your character is in a fight, and its health drops to -1,000. How do you describe what's happened?

Most players will say something along the lines of "they were killed" or "I died."

Except, they weren't *killed*—they'll be back in a few minutes. Only in MMOs with permadeath, where a character's being defeated in a fight means its removal from the database, is it actually equivalent to death in any real sense.

Most modern MMO "death" is just a slap on the wrist, yet players still refer to it as "killing." They even say they've been "killed" in *Lord of the Rings Online*, which uses a morale fiction to explain why you don't actually die—you run away at the last moment (not a bad idea, but it doesn't really cover what happens when you fall off a cliff).

The reason that players do this is that *kill* and *die* are technical terms in MMOs. They mean that your character's hit points (or equivalent) have been reduced below some minimum threshold, which results in a particular undesirable state change to that character. Although originally derived from the real-world concept of death, these technical terms have evolved and are no longer equivalent to it. They're just shorthand for a common occurrence and condition.

Unfortunately, people who don't play MMOs, who still have a traditional, non-technical understanding of what *kill* means, may be rather alarmed to hear it discussed so casually. They may believe that the word has much greater significance to an MMO player than it really has and therefore be concerned.

I don't think that in general people who don't play MMOs really have much to worry about with regard to them. However, that doesn't mean I think those who do are stupid, either. After all, if your real-world attitude to death *were* the same as your MMO attitude to death, they really *should* be worried about you.

Not a Very Good Job of It

If computer games do "teach" people to be violent, they don't do a very good job of it. Society hasn't become more violent with the arrival of violent computer games.[7] This is why people in the game industry can feel confident that their products aren't turning a generation of young people into psychotic killers.

However, if computer games don't teach *violence* very well, how are we to know they'll teach anything *else* very well, either? If a computer game that emphasizes shooting at people is ineffective at making players gun down real-life passers-by, why would a game that emphasizes caring about people be effective at encouraging players to be charitable back in the real world?

Radically Different

I did some consultancy for the well-known MMO developer <redacted> once. My remit was to decide whether they should make their new MMO <redacted> 2, as an advanced clone of their existing MMO, <redacted>, or whether they should go for something new entirely—something "radically different."

Speaking to the designers, it became clear fairly soon that they were incapable of going for anything "radically different." All the big ideas they had were couched in terms of changes to <redacted>. My saddest observation was that even though they were designing an advanced <redacted> clone, they *thought* they were designing something "radically different."

If you've looked at something for so long that you understand its finest points, then there's a danger that you'll see differences as being huge when objectively they're not. To a physicist, the distance between two atoms can seem enormous, and the distance between two galaxies can seem small. It all depends on what level of detail you're used to thinking at.

---

[7]Gerard Jones: *Killing Monsters: Why Children Need Fantasy, Super Heroes and Make-Believe Violence*. Basic Books, 2003.

Maslow's Hierarchy of Needs

Earlier, I mentioned Maslow's Hierarchy of Needs, a theory of Developmental Psychology that has gained wide currency since its publication in 1943 (with management researchers and sociologists particularly liking it). Its central idea is that humans have a set of needs that can be classified in a hierarchy and that human behavior is directed at satisfying such needs. When the needs of a lower level are satisfied, the unsatisfied needs of higher levels receive more attention.

Although this theory is sometimes used in game design for providing a motivational basis for the behavior of NPCs, that's not why I'm bringing it up now.

Here's what the hierarchy looks like, with the basic needs at the bottom of the pyramid and successively higher needs above it:

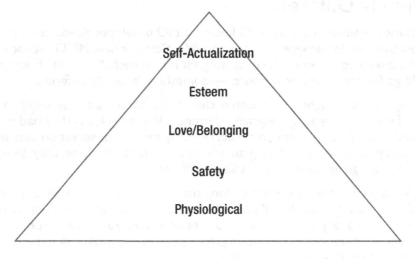

Look at the top level.

That's why people play MMOs.

Sex and Violence

September 21, 2007: I turn on the TV and the soap opera *Emmerdale* is showing.

One of its characters takes part in a brutal bare-knuckle boxing fight and is beaten to a bloody pulp. Make-up artists must live for such events. Moments later, two other characters have a long, passionate snog.

The point is, this was between 6:30 p.m. and 7 p.m., and it's just standard soap-opera fare.

Yet people complain about exposing children to computer games.

Loss Aversion

People like receiving things, but they dislike losing what they already have even more. A loss has about twice as much the effect on a person as a gain. If you lost $100, you'd need to find $200 to feel back where you were.

This psychological effect is called *loss aversion*; it explains why MMO designers will describe the effects of food on your character as a buff ("+10 health if you eat it") rather than a debuff ("-10 health if you don't eat it").

Because loss aversion is strong, this means it's sticky. Stickiness is something MMO developers like, so designers are usually encouraged to promote it. MMOs don't *need* to have a gear-based elder game, for example, but those that do will find it easier to retain their players than those that don't (because players don't want to lose the gear they've "worked" to "own"). Likewise, players who collect pets or decorate their home or rack up achievements will all be reluctant to leave because of everything they stand to lose if they do.

That said, when they do leave, they'll do so under a cloud. Personally, I'd prefer them to leave while feeling good about themselves rather than angry at me, but what do I know?

Research Interlude

Marginal Improvement

Here are some brief highlights from my career of trying to get MMOs taken seriously as an object of academic study:

- Being told when proposing a topic for my PhD that no games were academically respectable except Chess and perhaps Go, and maybe Backgammon and Reversi/ Othello, too.

- Being told by one of the Computing Department's three ruling professors that I should change my research direction because games were of no more academic interest than word processors.

- When turning MUD I commercial, having Essex University sign all its rights over to me because it didn't want its reputation damaged by association with a game.

- Giving a seminar about a multiple-hierarchy object-oriented programming system and being asked in the Q&A at the end whether it had any practical applications or whether it was just for games.

- Being offered a teaching-only post because to get a research post I'd need to publish four papers a year in quality journals to meet the minimum research criteria (and those quality journals would be...?).

Games and MMO research is still viewed in many academic circles as trying to be paid for what's basically your hobby. It's still regarded as not serious, unless it calls itself "serious games." It continues to have the same kind of air as if someone told you they had an earring fetish. Well, each to their own, it's a harmless pastime, but, er, can we change the subject?

Games research will continue to be treated in at best a patronizing fashion for the foreseeable future. The one bright light that gives hope is that computer games are now big business. If computer games companies were to give research grants to *bona fide* academics so as to enable them to pursue pure research on games, then there would be a chance we could break free. A half-million-dollar grant from Blizzard would get me a research post, "four papers a year" or not.

Unfortunately, computer games companies have been dismissed too often by universities in the past and so are highly skeptical about requests for funding. Why is it that computer games are worthy of research *now* when they never were before? It wouldn't be that they make more money than the film industry, would it?

"We were wrong; you are academically respectable now that you have money to give us" is not a convincing response.

Will things improve? Yes, but I don't expect I'll be around to see the day when a major grant to a university for studying anything positive about computer games would be greeted in national newspapers as anything other than a waste of money.

The Next Wave

MMO research comes in waves. Academic disciplines descend upon MMOs (or virtual worlds in general), the matter is discussed, the appropriate theories are applied, the results are agreed upon, and then the researchers fly away to alight on some newer topic.

Normally, this takes two or three years at most. Sometimes we do get a discipline's attention for longer. For example, MMO research went in new and very enticing directions when law professors took an interest in it, and we reaped the rewards for almost a decade before they left for greener pastures.

Curiously, there remain some areas that haven't looked into MMOs yet. It would be nice to invite researchers from History and Politics to see what they made of the subject, for example. I also think that anthropologists should be more interested than they currently seem to be.

Additionally, it could be useful to have people from some of the research areas that have "done" MMOs come and look at them again. In particular, Psychology might have very useful things to say if it could get beyond the violence/addiction/"think of the children" triumvirate.

Social and Game Worlds

MMOs are game worlds. Why should MMO players care about social worlds such as *Second Life*?

Well, the answer is that both are virtual worlds. Unless you're talking about something specifically to do with having a game element or specifically to do with not having a game element, what you say about one applies to the other.

Social worlds typically attract more academic attention on the premise that they're not games and are therefore worthy of study. This has always been the case, dating back to *LambdaMOO*. What's become more important in recent years is that some of the people who have an academic interest in social worlds aren't academics; they're revenue officers and lawyers and social workers and journalists, who could extrapolate what they see in *Second Life* to cover virtual worlds as a whole. The resulting "we must protect our children from this evil" or "geeks evade $6 billion in taxes every year" newspaper article could affect us all.

This isn't as way-out as it seems. In the past, I've read magazine articles and academic papers that made generalizations concerning *all* virtual worlds based on the author's experience of a couple of hours in *LambdaMOO* (or a half-hour interviewing someone who has spent much longer there).

Fortunately, *Second Life* has fallen out of fashion much as *LambdaMOO* did, so we have a respite until a replacement emerges.

Know Your Place

> *We don't want people to be put off coming to study telecommunications when they see we have a degree in online games.*

> —Martin Waite, September 2006

Martin Waite was the Deputy Head (Teaching) in the Department of Computer Science at Essex University. He was explaining to me why he was scrapping the degree in online games that was due to start the following academic year.

Academics and Game Designers

Here are three reasons why MMO designers mistrust academics:

- Academics understand their own theories but not what they're applying them to.

- Academics look at niche but easily accessible virtual worlds and then apply their observations to virtual worlds in general.

- Academics judge all virtual worlds by the first one they got into.

Folklore has it that they also ask for data and then use it to show that games turn everyone into aggressive, serial-killing child molesters. This also makes designers mistrust them.

Academic Snobbery

Mathematics

looks down on

Physics

looks down on

Electronics

looks down on

Computer Science

looks down on

Artificial Intelligence

looks down on

Computer Games

looks down on

Arts & Humanities

Designers and Researchers

One of the problems that researchers have with MMOs is that they don't realize that MMO designers read research.

If you are a PhD student looking at, say, the group dynamics of a new MMO, you may find that beyond a certain point guilds become unmanageably large and break up. You spot that this point equates with Dunbar's number. Yay! You can establish a mapping between the social groupings in this MMO and the social groupings of the real world. Your PhD is in the bag.

Except, you can't actually establish that relationship. Unbeknown to you, the MMO's designer is aware of Dunbar's number and has deliberately structured the guild system so that it will start to disintegrate around that point, thereby splitting guilds fairly amicably rather than having them fall apart in acrimony or collapse to a vacuum. Your belief that people in MMOs act just like they do in the real world is unsubstantiated, because what you thought was natural was artificial. For all we know, it could be that the kind of relationships people have in MMOs are sufficiently different from the ones they have in real life that this effectively adds 50 to Dunbar's number, but that would never be picked up because the designer has effectively imposed Dunbar's number on the guilds.

MMOs are not natural systems; they are *designed* systems. Don't think that just because you're a clever PhD student you know things designers don't. You may, sure, but MMO designers read very extensively, and you can't assume they're ignorant unless you actually ask them.

Besides, some of them actually have their own PhDs.

Researchers and Play

Should those who study MMOs have to play them if their opinions are to carry weight? Or is it a bit like asking whether dentists should need to have had a tooth pulled out before they are allowed to pull out anyone else's?

Things I Don't Want to Hear About MMOs #1

At conferences, whether academic or business in nature, I often hear things I don't want to hear about MMOs.

The first thing I don't want to hear is something I've heard already. There are two main reasons this can happen: the speaker is utterly ignorant of previous work in the area, or the speaker has a passionate belief that all previous work on MMOs is irrelevant because today's MMOs are different.

Here are two examples:

- "Women play as male avatars because they don't like the hypersexualized images of female avatars." So, why does the same percentage of them play male characters as did in the text-world days?

- "Player types don't work for free-to-play, because free-to-play MMOs are free to play and that makes them different from the virtual worlds of the past." What, and MUDs weren't free to play? Most were *bona fide* free!

If you're looking at something such as the scale of a world or the rendering of its graphics, then clearly that would have changed significantly over the years, meaning you can talk about it as a difference. You can't draw conclusions about it without further investigation, though, and you need to know that the conclusions you do draw aren't perfectly well explained by an existing body of research.

This frequently goes too far when people try to shoehorn MMOs to fit their pet theory. For example, they're not "third places" (they have third places within them), and players don't get their fun primarily from "flow" (because if people were in flow for two to four hours every evening for two years, their brains would shrivel up and die).

It's fine—indeed, *good*—to be cautious, experimenting to see whether MMOs do indeed fit existing theories before applying them. What's not fine is beating up MMOs to make them fit your favorite theory against their will.

This Is ... News?

From *The Guardian*, March 5, 2008:

> *Millions of internet users are using computer games to perform virtual sex changes, according to new research. A study of online gamers by psychologists at Nottingham Trent University found that a majority of them had switched gender while playing. The research, in which 125 players of complex computer games were questioned, found that women were more likely to switch their gender. Up to 70% of female players said they chose to use male identities for internet games, in which they are able to design their own characters with any race, gender or appearance.*

This is ... news?

Oh, it's news. Here's how it developed in the same newspaper the next day:

Seventy per cent of female gamers play as men online

Sexual harassment is rife online. No wonder women swap gender

A hint of sex, a hint of weird geekiness, a chance to show sympathy for women, and an excuse to picture hot babes from *Second Life*: just what editors like.

What the survey that led to all this *actually* found was that up to 70 percent of the 32 female gamers surveyed had played as a male persona in an online role-playing game at least once. In the resulting (too long to reproduce here) three-column-wide article, that turned into this: ~~up to~~ 70 percent of ~~the 32~~ female gamers ~~surveyed had~~ played as a male persona in an online ~~role-playing~~ world ~~at least once~~.

Guardian readers were then treated to a diatribe as to how awful it is to be female online, without any apparent realization that if it really were that bad, then why would any men play female characters, as many do?

This kind of wanton ignorance is one of the reasons I stopped buying *The Guardian*. However, what sparked it all was the underlying research. Was it *really* groundbreaking enough that it merited a press release?

Progress Is Progress

It used to be that when an academic discipline "discovered" MMOs, it didn't even occur to the organizers of their conferences to invite what they call *practitioners* to speak. Designers and developers were not even a blip on their radar. It would be like asking dinosaurs to speak at a conference on paleontology. This is despite the fact that game designers have invited academics to industry conferences for many years.

Nowadays, sometimes academics do invite game designers to their conferences. The big breakthrough was the *State of Play* series of conferences organized by New York Law School. It wasn't entirely because we're cool and they're not, either.

Progress is progress.

Attitudes to Academics

"These people say they're researching, but they're just playing games, ha ha ha!"

Well, they may be playing games, but they're not *just* playing games, in the same way that the early film theorists weren't *just* watching movies.

Law Professors

I've seen many researchers come to MMOs from outside, as a result of which I now fully expect them to construct completely idiosyncratic hypotheses that then became canon in their field. Many of these researchers have an incomplete understanding of what MMOs are, what people do in them, that there are different kinds of virtual world, that there are different kinds of players, pretty well everything else to do with MMOs, too.

It was therefore rather disorienting when I realized that this was not the case among law professors. They seemed to have a much firmer grasp of the essence of MMOs than had visitors from pretty well all other disciplines. If they'd given us the same kind of check-box study we got from mid-1990s gender theorists, I'd have been in a state of despair; as it was, I was overwhelmed with relief.

Of course, that's not to say that practicing lawyers will be as on the ball as law professors, although I have to say that the ones I've met at games-and-the-law conferences do indeed appear to be. It's surprisingly unnerving!

The View from Outside

Why are Games Studies in general and MMO studies in particular not regarded seriously by other academic disciplines?

Well, there are a number of reasons, the main one being that we haven't studied the subject ourselves for long enough to build up a corpus of knowledge that says anything of consequence to any discipline beyond our own.

However, there are plenty of other reasons, two of which especially hurt:

- Scientists (physical and social alike) see games as tools for helping them advance areas of knowledge within their *own* field, but they don't see games as anything *intrinsically* worthy of study. A sociologist might get a PhD and half a dozen books out of studying game players, but whether what they say would help a game designer make a *better* game is not a concern to them.

- Researchers in comparative studies see games as being just another aspect of their own field, whether that be narrative literature, performance, oral storytelling, or whatever. Games aren't of interest to them *per se* because they see them as a mere special case. Again, this may help them validate their theories, but it doesn't directly make for better games.

Take, for example, postmodernism: it can be used to "explain" MMOs, and examining MMOs may enhance the understanding postmodernist theorists have about what postmodernism is saying; however, neither has yet made any useful contribution to our getting better MMOs.

For me, as an MMO designer, I want better MMOs. I'm prepared to listen to arguments about what "better" means and what "MMOs" means, but ultimately it's the MMOs I'm interested in. I want to see better ones, not better explanations of how they slot into a one-size-fits-all theory.

I suspect, however, that the primary reason MMO and Games Studies have a weak reputation has nothing to do with either of these points and everything to do with how people *view* games. Games are "for fun" and "trivial." The very fact we have a Serious Games Initiative suggests that other uses of games are not serious. If they're not serious, why would any self-respecting academic wish to be associated with them?

That's our problem.

Not the Point

Games may be interesting to academics as objects of study, but they're just that: objects of study. Should an academic's research actually prove useful to game designers, that's seen as a welcome validation—but it's not actually the point of it.

For example, AI researchers are working on ways to make games adapt to the skills of the player so that the challenges presented are always just at the right level to keep that player in the flow zone. This is helping to advance the field of Neural Networks, which is great for Neural Networks. It's actually counterproductive for games, though, because any challenge you're guaranteed to be able to overcome isn't a challenge; it's just an obstacle. Players want challenges; they get plenty of obstacles in real life.

Things I Don't Want to Hear About MMOs #2

The second thing I don't want to hear about MMOs at conferences is anything that disrespects the subject nonaffectionately.

To start with, if you're speaking about MMOs, you should at least trouble yourself to learn something about them. Playing them is a good way to do this, although it's not the only way.

As evidence as to why this is important, consider that players and researchers have their own technical terms. Sometimes these are the same terms with the same meaning (for example, *fun*), sometimes they are the same terms with different meanings (for example, *immersion*), and sometimes they are different terms with the same meaning (for example, *deviant play* versus *griefing*). Sometimes, terms can shift meaning (for example, *avatar*). Not being aware of the differences means you could base your work on a false premise. If you ask players about *contingency* (meaning unpredictability in a philosophical sense), they will answer as if it meant *preparedness*.

It gets worse. If you don't know what you're talking about, you'll make gaffes like these:

- Assuming that work on "video games" automatically applies to MMOs

- Assuming that work on social worlds automatically applies to game worlds

- Assuming that social networking sites are MMOs

- Assuming the reverse of each of these items

I was once at a games conference at which a professor of Artificial Intelligence began his presentation with the words "I'm not interested in games. I don't like them and I don't play them, but someone told me this stuff might help you, so here I am."

I don't suppose there would be a warm reception for anyone who began their talk at an AI conference with the words "I'm not interested in AI. I don't like it and I don't use, but someone told me this stuff might help you so here I am."

If you're going to talk about a subject, you really should afford that subject some degree of deference.

Ethics in Action

Academics who study MMOs are naturally concerned about the ethics of doing so. Even minor details give them pause for thought. For example, if you want to quote what a player said, should the player give informed consent before you record them, or is it OK to ask them afterward when you know which quotes you want to use? What if asking consent would itself spoil their experience in some way? Should you use their real-world names or their character names, and should they be the ones they actually use or ones you've made up to anonymize them? Do journalists have to abide by similar rules, or can they cite expedience as a reason for being laxer? If so, can academics with a deadline be laxer, too?

As for when an academic wants to make a tangible change to an MMO to see what effect it has, isn't that, like, *experimenting* on the players? Shouldn't they all have to agree to it first? And if one player disagrees or can't be bothered to reply, the academic is screwed?

If you're interested in these issues, you might want to look at books that concern research in virtual communities; they often have chapters on the ethical approach the authors took. Here, for example, are two early ones that do:

- *Lori Kendall: Hanging Out in the Virtual Pub: Masculinities and Relationships Online.* University of California Press, 2002.

- *Lynn Cherny: Conversation and Community: Chat in a Virtual World.* Center for the Study of Language and Information, 1999.

You now have an opportunity to test your own ethics. Both these books are available on Amazon.com, and both have a "look inside" facility. The ethics part of Kendall's book is Appendix B; in Cherny's, it's Chapter 7.

Are you going to buy the books or just read the bits you want for free?

Expert Opinion

MMOs have in the past had a particular problem with researchers who have written about them without understanding them. There are two main ways this happens.

First, the researchers can fail to play MMOs or to interview enough people who do play them. They apply their theories based on descriptions of MMOs or a vague understanding of what they "must" be like and then brilliantly reach a conclusion that half the player base can immediately see is based on incomplete or incorrect assumptions.

Second, they can play MMOs too subjectively. Many people seem to think that a two- to four-hour nightly habit makes them uniquely qualified to be experts in all things MMO. They will speak with measured authority about what in practice they may know very little about. Many are the times I have seen heavyweight academic theory dangerously misapplied because the researcher arrogantly believed that their scant knowledge of MMOs was complete.

Because MMOs have suffered in the past from know-nothings who have pontificated from on high in the complete absence of experience—or even recognition that any is needed—players now happily mock anyone who writes about MMOs without having played them. The usual suspects are academics, journalists, and politicians. This makes sense: if a politician is using a bad mapping (violence in games is isomorphic to violence in real life, say) but hasn't played the game being cited, well, of course they're talking rubbish and should be pilloried for doing so. To the politician, though, games are just like any other social problem: they can talk about the harm cigarette smoking does to society without having smoke a cigarette, so they can talk about the harm MMOs do to society without having played one.

Although it's great to see angry players talking trash about upstart academics, journalists, and politicians who write ill-informed articles, unfortunately such players can also place people in their firing line who make *informed* comments about an MMO without having played it. Designers, for example, spend their working lives thinking about MMOs; they do not need to play an MMO to be able to give a considered opinion about it—they can procedurally generate the play experience in their head from reading the design, watching people play, or following comments in a forum. The more information they have, then the more detail they will be able to go into, but even a small amount can be enough. I know I wasn't the only designer who could tell that *Richard Garriott's Tabula Rasa* was going to suck merely by perusing the prerelease publicity; I certainly didn't have to play it all the way through before I could confidently predict its future.

I usually read several design documents a year. It's my job to envision how something will play before it's even made. It's ridiculous to assert that I, or any of the other MMO design consultants around, actually need to play MMOs to the level cap and beyond before being considered certified to comment on them. Nevertheless, because I got so many players moaning at me for not playing MMOs all the way through, I finally snapped and did just that (in *WoW*, *LotRO*, *RIFT*, *SW:TOR*, *TSW*, and whatever I'm playing when you read this). I regard such play as obtaining the paper qualifications I need for my job; it certainly isn't a learning exercise for me.

Apart from designers, other people who study MMOs day in and day out, will perforce eventually grok them. Academics are prime candidates here; if you've thought about MMOs for ten years, played them extensively, surveyed thousands of players, and analyzed terabytes of data, you're going to internalize it all whether you want to or not. You'll understand MMOs, but they won't be fun for you to play anymore.

Contrast this with the postgraduate who has sat 16 volunteers (all second-year Computer Science majors) in front of a computer, made them play *Warhammer: Age of Reckoning* for two hours, interviewed them afterward, drawn conclusions about the effects of MMOs on people's predisposition to violence, and now wants a PhD for it. I see this kind of thing all the time. Neither the postgrad nor the expert has necessarily played the MMO they're studying, but the difference is that the postgrad *needs* to play it, whereas the expert doesn't (because, well, they're an expert!).

My advice is that if you want to study MMOs and say anything about them as MMOs, you will save yourself a truckload of hurt if you play one first. Whether this is strictly necessary depends on what you intend to do with your results, but if you make even one obvious slip, you will be torn apart by a baying mob of bloggers in a manner you *don't* want your peers to discover when they Google you.

Recluse's Victory

Recluse's Victory was the name of a PvP zone in *City of Heroes*. It was a two-faction zone (heroes versus villains), in which each faction tried to gain control of a number of pillboxes ("temporal anchors").

Each faction had a safe zone that they started off in. These bases were protected by security drones that vaporized any enemies who got too close to them. This is standard fare for PvP zones. Now as it happened, *City of Heroes* also had a "teleport foe" power available to player characters. This enabled them to transport an opponent so that they stood next to them. When Recluse's Victory was opened, it was possible to stand next to a drone and teleport-foe an enemy next to you, whereupon the enemy would be vaporized.

This meant that anyone who PvPed would get one-shotted if the tactic was used. It made PvP no fun at all; therefore, players developed a social norm by which the practice was outlawed. If you did it, not only would your opponents complain, but your own side would complain too.

Now suppose that you decided to play *only* by the rules of *City of Heroes* as implemented, ignoring the social rules that your fellow players had layered on top. If you were in a PvP situation and could use this teleport-to-drone tactic, then you would. How do you think the other players would react?

Although it's pretty obvious what they would do, I'll spell it out; apparently, it's not obvious to everyone.

First, the other players would ask if you knew what you'd done. Then, they would ask if you knew that it was outlawed. Then, they would ask why you kept on doing it even though you knew it was spoiling the game for everyone else. Then, after you've ruined so many PvP sessions that they snapped, they would report you to the MMO's operator (NCSOFT in *City of Heroes'* case). Meanwhile, they would start making all manner of threats both in-world and in the forums in an effort to get you to stop.

All of which brings us to Twixt.

Twixt

Twixt was a character in *City of Heroes* who used the teleport-to-drone tactic. He also did three other things that annoyed his fellow PvPers:

- He didn't cooperate in consensual farming, in which heroes and villains agreed to ignore the stated aims of Recluse's Victory in order to rack up influence (*City of Heroes*' currency).

- He disrupted "fight club" events, in which a hero and a villain would again ignore the formal group-play goal of the instance, instead duking it out one-on-one in front of spectators.

- He wouldn't team with other players on his side, doing his PvP independently of them.

Needless to say, he was not at all popular because of this behavior, and all the things you'd expect to happen when someone breaks social norms like that happened.

Now the thing is, Twixt was no ordinary character. He was run by an academic, David Myers, who deliberately set about breaching these social rules to demonstrate a point of ethnomethodology.[1]

Unfortunately, as a side effect he learned that if you set out to piss people off, they will indeed become pissed off. The reaction to his experiment was extremely negative, and he found himself the subject of many breaches of real-world social norms (for example, the one about not sending people death threats).

Now ordinarily when someone in an MMO acts like a jerk and then claims they aren't really a jerk, they were just *pretending* to be a jerk, I'd be of the opinion that no, actually, they *are* a jerk. This defense has been utilized by griefers for decades (well, before even *LambdaMOO*'s Mr. Bungle); it's no more likely to be believed today than it was in the early 1980s. However, as Professor Myers did insist that this was purely an academic exercise, he deserves the benefit of the doubt.

As it happens, there is a great deal of regrettable research undertaken about MMOs. Why have I singled out the case of Twixt?

---

[1]David Myers: *Play and Punishment: the Sad and Curious Tale of Twixt*. Proceedings of *The [Player] Conference*: ITU Copenhagen, Denmark. 2008.

Player Type Misuses #4

Some researchers apply player types in edge cases to try to break Player Type theory. This is fair enough: if the theory breaks, we can find out why and then get a better theory as a result. I approve of this.

The thing is, though, most potshots at the theory never hit the target. I once saw all of the following appear in the same conference:

- **Merchants!** Yes, people want to play as merchants, and yes, Player Type theory doesn't have a "merchant" type, but it *does* have types for *why* people want to play as merchants.

- **Leaders!** Player Type theory doesn't have a type called "leaders," but it does have Politicians, which amounts to the same thing.

- **Gold-farmers!** There is no type for people who don't play for fun because the theory applies only to people who *do* play for fun. It says so right off the bat, didn't you notice?

- **Immersion!** Immersion shows up in player motivation surveys, but there's no player type for it because it comes from moving *through* the types.

- **Girls!** You can partition user bases arbitrarily. If you want to partition by gender, go ahead; it's not relevant to Player Type theory, but if it's relevant to you, that's fine. Player Type theory doesn't claim to have exclusive partitioning rights.

- **Surveys!** Just because your PhD involves "in-depth" interviews with 12 players and a "thick description" from playing an MMO yourself, that doesn't mean it's representative, and it doesn't mean you're asking the right questions. Oh, and as a heads-up, if you ask questions of griefers, expect them to grief you in their replies.

If you're a young gun who wants to earn the reputation of having taken down an aging gunslinger, at least learn to aim first.

APA, Ten Years On

August 13, 2015: Ten years after it released a report affirming a link between violence in video games and aggressive behavior, the American Psychological Association releases another[2] reaffirming that link. It's 49 pages long, 22 of which are references to scholarly publications.

Look, APA Task Force on Violent Media, I know you have hundreds of research careers to protect, but if "violent video games" really *do* make people more aggressive, we really ought to be seeing the wider societal effects of this by now.

Unsatisfactory

When social scientists experiment on people, they have to get the permission of those people. It's basic ethics.

If they experiment on minors, they have to get the permission of their parents or guardians. Even the most risible attempts by earnest PhD students to extrapolate something meaningful from interviews with 16 *League of Legends* players will nevertheless have the permission of those players.

City of Heroes had an ESRB rating of "teen."

So, how did David Myers, the player behind Twixt, ever get permission from his university's Institutional Review Board to undertake experiments on minors without their permission? They were repeatedly subject to distress without even being aware that their tormentor was an academic deliberately subjecting them to that stress.

Well, the answer is that Professor Myers didn't have permission. However, he defended himself by arguing that although he had called what he did a "breaching experiment," it wasn't *actually* an experiment. Therefore, he didn't need permission.

This did not prevent a number of high-profile MMO academics (including Nick Yee and I) from writing to the Institutional Review Board (IRB) of Loyola University New Orleans asking for it to review Professor Myers' actions. Given that it's a Jesuit university, we were hoping for a detailed assessment of the rights and wrongs of what he did.

No such response was forthcoming, but I bumped into Professor Myers at a conference a year later, and he told me the IRB had decided not to take any action against him.

---

[2]American Psychological Association Task Force on Violent Media: Technical Report on the Review of the Violent Video Game Literature. 2015. www.apa.org/news/press/releases/2015/08/technical-violent-games.pdf

To Play or Not to Play?

Overall, I think we probably need a balance between those academics who do and don't play games if we're to get a full spectrum of research for the area.

Those who can't see the wood for the trees and those who can't see the trees for the wood ought to be able to cover both the trees and the woods between them.

Things I Don't Want to Hear About MMOs #3

The third thing I don't want to hear about MMOs is research that is *no such thing*.

Just as some people disrespect MMOs, other people respect them too much and disrespect whatever home discipline they're coming from. The classic case is the academic who hankers after being a game designer so looks for a research topic to hang game design off. Serious Games, you have a lot to answer for.

Not everyone wants to create games, though. Far more people simply want to play them. Every summer in the mid-1990s, swathes of questions appeared on Usenet about MUDs; students had carefully engineered their dissertation topic as an excuse to legitimize their play. Even today, we see academics trying to trick us into thinking that their extensive play habit was research all along (it wasn't: get over it, unless you want your institutional review board to nail your hide to the wall) (*pace* Loyola University New Orleans). There are also plenty of employees of games companies who play rival products for "research" purposes rather than for fun—no siree, no fun at all there, just well-logged, written-up work.

When researchers do get over-invested in an MMO (in other words, "go native"), they can inadvertently take sides. They start using words like *should*. It's particularly prevalent in talks about MMOs and government (for example, players "should" have a say in the running of an MMO) but also popular in works on MMOs and minorities. This turns such writings from research findings into ideological tracts. The correct thing to do is to use a guard term (*"if you want this, then you should do this"*).

Player Type Misuses #5

The four misuses of Player Types I've given so far comfortably map onto player types:

- **Means to an end**: Achiever
- **Beyond limits**: Explorer
- **Bandwagon**: Socializer
- **Disproof**: Killer

This, however, is merely an example of the second misuse in action—applying a theory beyond its limits and then buying into it as if it were wholesale correct. The reason I can confidently say this is that there's a fifth misuse: meta-theory.

With meta-theory, some people—usually academics—try to reconcile Player Types with some existing pet theory. *Please*, quit trying to marry it up with Myers-Briggs and other Jung offshoots—it *doesn't fit*! It can sometimes be useful to apply two different but nonoverlapping theories together (Player Types *and* Myers-Briggs), but if you try to bend either of them too much, you'll break it.

Interestingly, when people apply meta-theory to Player Types, they do so for one of the previously-listed four reasons. I guess they could also do it as a meta-meta theory, and so on, indefinitely, but thankfully I've not seen that happen yet.

A Bit of a Quandary

I was in a bit of a quandary when I read the research paper (from Nottingham Trent University) that caused *The Guardian* to assert "Sexual harassment is rife online. No wonder women swap gender." On the one hand, I want more research on virtual worlds and don't want to discourage people from doing it, but on the other hand, this was not good work. The authors seemed to believe they had stumbled across a new research area, ripe for consideration (hence the press release); actually, it's a fairly well-researched area.

The first formal paper on the subject was Amy Bruckman's classic *Gender Swapping on the Internet*,[3] published in 1993. Interest from gender study theorists really took off following Pavel Curtis's *Mudding: Social Phenomena in Text-Based Virtual Realities*.[4] Both these papers include quotes eerily echoed in the responses listed in the Nottingham Trent paper some 15 years later. As a result of the interest that arose back then, we ended up not only with solid data about gender-swapping but predictive theories.

There were some flaws with the Nottingham Trent paper, too, in part because of its exploratory nature. Its authors did point out some of these, which although meaningful to academics would not trouble a journalist with a deadline to meet. Admitting flaws doesn't invalidate them, though. For example, if you want to know how many people play online games with a gender other than their real one, you really *should* make some effort to verify what their real gender is instead of just asking people who may well be role-playing. Also, it's good to note that your survey sample size is small, but this one was an order of magnitude smaller than some earlier surveys.[5] Furthermore, the four sources from which respondents were recruited were not very representative (womengamers.com was a great site, but it wasn't read by the average woman gamer).

[3]Amy S. Bruckman: *Gender Swapping on the Internet*. Proceedings of the *International Networking Conference*. San Francisco, 1993. www.cc.gatech.edu/~asb/papers/gender_swapping.html

[4]Pavel Curtis: *Mudding: Social Phenomena in Text-Based Virtual Realities*. Proceedings of *Conference on Directions and Implications of Advanced Computing*. San Francisco, 1992. http://w2.eff.org/Net_culture/MOO_MUD_IRC/curtis_mudding.article

[5]Nick Yee: *The Norrathian Scrolls*. 2001. www.nickyee.com/eqt/genderbend.html

Other flaws were missed, though, especially when they relied on knowledge of existing research. For example, although the paper correctly informed us that women played longer per session than men, the actual figures cited (198 minutes versus 186 minutes) were wrong. It turns out that if you compare reported playing times with actual playing times, women over-report the amount of time they spend in MMOs more than men do:[6] men report playing 24.10 hours per week but actually play 25.03; women report 26.03 but actually play 29.32.

I could go on, especially regarding the standard-but-wrong reasons players gave for their cross-gender play (which led directly to the "sexual harassment" headline). It's not my aim to put the knife in, though; rather, I'm just lamenting the fact that this kind of thing happens *time and time again* with MMO research. This Nottingham Trent paper is merely a later example of what we saw all too often in the mid-1990s. Academics would come to virtual worlds with an incomplete understanding of what they are, conduct some half-assed survey, give unsupported and occasionally damaging explanations, and then leave. Their research was regarded as a joke by specialists and ignored by them; however, it was foundational insofar as their host discipline was concerned. I spoke to the authors of the Nottingham Trent paper, and they were actually very nice about it. They *had* looked for earlier research on the topic before conducting their research but hadn't found any; it doesn't really figure in the Psychology literature. Their research was intended only as an opening probe into the area, so they were fairly pleased that it had found something (even if that "something" was that it had all been done before). This is why I haven't given a reference to the paper here. It's the lack of visibility of MMO research that's the problem, not individual researchers.

Oh, and university publicists too eager to put out press releases are rather a problem, too.

---

[6]Dmitri Williams et al: *Looking for Gender: Gender Roles and Behaviors among Online Gamers. Journal of Communications* v 59 pp 700-725, 2009. http://dmitriwilliams.com/ LFGpaperfinal.pdf

Fact-Checking

Here's a sentence from a book[7] I bought in 2005. "The code for a MOO was developed by Pavel Curtis at Xerox Parc in Palo Alto, California, from the code for a MUD, first developed in 1979 by Roy Trubshaw at the University of Reading, England."

OK...

- It's PARC, not Parc ("Palo Alto Research Center").

- It (*LambdaMOO*) was written from the first MOO code, not *MUD* code.

- The first MOO was written by Stephen White.

- Roy first developed *MUD* in 1978.

- It was the University of Essex, not the University of Reading.

I'm not going to lambast the book because actually it was pretty good (despite being a hard read because of its right-on use of the intensely irritating *Spivak* form of gender-neutral pronouns, a consequence of its publisher's attachment to the Centre for Women's Studies at the University of York; if only they'd go with the *singular they* form that is standard dialect in Yorkshire).

Anyway, I mention this sentence for two reasons.

First, it shows how easy it is to make factual mistakes simply by passing on what you have read in good faith elsewhere. If one person makes an error in an oft-read, formal piece of writing, the error propagates. By the time it's noticed, it's too late. I haven't seen the University of Reading error before (or indeed since), but the rest are common in the literature.

Second, if you're writing about something with which you don't have first-hand experience, it doesn't hurt to check the facts by email. You never know, you might get a reply. I didn't *expect* a reply when I wrote to novelist Tad Williams to ask if the opening line of his monumental, 3,000-pages-plus *Otherland* series ("It started in mud, as many things do"[8]) was a reference to *MUD*, but he did email me back and confirmed that yes, it was. Some authors, academic ones included, will happily reply if you ask them a genuine question (well, so long as it wouldn't take an essay to answer it).

---

[7]Sue Thomas: *Hello World travels in virtuality*. Raw Nerve Books, York. 2004.
[8]Tad Williams: *City of Golden Shadow*. DAW Books, New York NY. 1998.

Had the author of the sentence in question written to me, I would easily have been able to correct the mistakes in advance of publication. I could have gone beyond this though: the author's name, Sue Thomas, is the same as that used by the first gender-bending player in any MMO. This might have had some resonance because the book has a lot to say about gender and identity.

As it happened, the author did contact me after I blogged my weary complaint (but before I got around to writing to her), so I was able to tell her the connection. I don't know which one of us was more embarrassed—she for putting every error in her book into that one sentence or me for being so petty about it.

For this reason, although it's my practice to use a standard capitalization-and-colon regime when rendering the names of books that have a subtitle, in the reference[9] I've written it as it appears on the cover. To aspire to anything less than accuracy in this particular example would be even more hypocritical than usual for me.

Designer Intent

If designer intent that has been clearly stated up front does not influence the legal regulation of MMOs, we can pretty well kiss goodbye to ever having gamelike virtual worlds thereafter.

There is a paradigm difference between virtual worlds that invite in the real world (which in this book I'm calling *Reality*) and those that don't. The former are social worlds, such as *Second Life*, and the latter are game worlds, such as *Star Wars: The Old Republic*. If *Reality* decides it's coming in anyway, that makes all virtual worlds the same—social worlds, not game worlds. The reason for this is that people can't play when they're not in a play space, and *Reality* is not a play space. Parts of it are, but as a whole it isn't.

The magic circle *must* be allowed to prevail.

---

[9]Sue Thomas: *Hello World travels in virtuality*. Raw Nerve Books, York. 2004.

Things I Don't Want to Hear About MMOs #4

The fourth thing I don't want to hear about MMOs at conferences concerns poor or lazy scholarship. Academics are the main culprits here, happily extrapolating from surveys of 20 people to make statements about 20,000,000.

Things have got a lot worse in recent years, mainly because of this:

> *Why 30 cases per unit of investigation? Because it is important to allow for the emergence of important categories and subcategories that will inevitably occur during the study.*[10]

This fragment of Robert Stebbins' seminal book on social science research methodology has been seized on by any and every PhD student who wants to be able to justify a small survey sample size. They don't wish to understand that it says you need at least 30 items of a particular kind before a statistical analysis of them will find the major ways that they group together. What these students prefer to understand is that it says you can draw any conclusions about groups that you want, so long as you interview 30 people.

Thus, for example, if you interview 30 gamers and 10 of them are female, you can legitimately conclude that there are two major subgroups of gamers: female and male (well, strictly speaking in this example: female and not female). What you *can't* say is that a third of all gamers are female. You also can't interview those ten female gamers and hold their views representative of all female gamers. Nevertheless, people do this and get publications—and even PhDs—out of it.

The sources of samples are also almost always suspect. Just because it has the formal name *convenience sampling*, that doesn't mean good results will come from your decision to survey the 30 games students you happen to teach and have bribed with course credit to answer your questions.

Another thing that happens is that people believe that their 16-person survey has just as much validity as the 30,000-person survey that it contradicts. They'll also fail to appreciate that the game industry itself collects and mines much larger data sets with much higher-quality data in them. You may be pleased to have paid for an advertisement to appear alongside a particular Facebook game, from the impressions of which you can pick up time-of-day usage figures for 2,000,000 players; that's **as nothing** compared to the exact figures for 50 times that number of players, recorded every moment of every day—which is what the games company has.

---

[10]Robert A. Stebbins: *Exploratory Research in the Social Sciences*. Sage Publications: Thousand Oaks, California. 2001.

To be fair, that last one *isn't* poor scholarship; it's merely the result of paranoia on the part of games companies that don't want to release their data sets lest agenda-driven academics set about proving that the game in question fits an unhelpful agenda. Of course, if academics didn't have research axes to grind, there wouldn't be such unhelpful agendas anyway.

Experimental Economics

The social sciences are not like the natural sciences; you can hardly ever prove things experimentally. You can demonstrate things statistically, but it's hard to isolate systems to test them independently. For example, if you believe that increasing the tax on individuals and reducing the tax on companies will lead to a greater overall tax intake (because the companies will create more jobs), then you can't try that out experimentally in advance of implementing it. You have to weigh up the arguments for and against in the full knowledge that if it works, then the government could gain a vast amount of money, but if it doesn't work, then the government could lose a vast amount of money. It's a gamble with enormous stakes.

At the moment, governments use modeling software to simulate how economies work, so as to be able to see what the effects might be if changes were implemented. These are good but flawed: they don't cover all the subtleties of an economy, and they don't always accurately predict how people will behave. They allow for *some* experiment, but only with a model, not with an actual economy.

If only there were some way to perform experiments in Economics to make sure that, were they implemented, they wouldn't put a country's economy at risk.

Analysis-Friendly Games

I'm on the editorial board of several games-related academic journals and am regularly called upon to peer-review papers that have been submitted for publication.

In 2007, the game *S.T.A.L.K.E.R.: Shadow of Chernobyl* was released. Over the next two or three years, I must have read a dozen papers about it. I still see the occasional one even now.

In 2013, *The Last of Us* was released, sparking its own set of academic papers.

It's weird how this happens. In general, papers about individual games tend to be about different individual games. However, every once in a while a game will come out that attracts lots of them. The papers concerned are almost invariably readings of the game, sometimes with reference to a particular way of reading film or theater, sometimes not. They will usually include an explanation as to why the gameplay *isn't* important to the analysis, which is all about story and the player's agency (or lack of agency).

I don't know why this is, but my guess is that there are certain games that are particularly compatible with existing theories used in other media, and these are the ones that are picked up. This doesn't mean that other games aren't worth analyzing; rather, it means that the analyst would need particular theoretical tools to do so. They don't have those tools, so they write only about the games to which the tools they do have can be applied. Sometimes, this takes into account that the game is a game; more often than not, though, it only pays lip service to the game element and concentrates instead on some combination of narrative, atmosphere, and character development.

This kind of textual analysis of games has its place, but if it doesn't address the way gameplay impacts on the story, it's like writing an analysis of a movie based only on the dialogue; it's an interesting niche but missing the big picture (literally, in this analogy).

I'd like to see more papers that looked at games from the perspective of their being *games*, but until we have a usable framework for this it's not going to happen.

Hammer and Screw

Here's a picture of a hammer (mine, as it happens) being used to smack a screw into a piece of wood:

If you don't have a screwdriver, using a hammer is a better way to put a screw in a piece of wood than twisting it with your fingers or pounding it with your fist, but really you need a screwdriver.

The hammer is Player Type theory. The screw is anything other than MMOs.

Things I Don't Want to Hear About MMOs #5

The fifth thing I don't want to hear about MMOs at conferences is anything to do with Foucault, Baudrillard, or Barthes.

Damned postmodernist readings, taking half an hour to say nothing.

Petri Dish Worlds

If a biologist were to take two Petri dishes and sneeze in one and not in the other, then the resulting difference in growth of bacteria could be attributed to the sneeze.

If you want to do experiments in Economics, you first need to establish that such a principle works—that you can run a control alongside an experimental system and note changes that can be attributed only to the controlled differences between the two. You therefore need a Petri dish.

MMOs can be that Petri dish.

So, if you wanted to try this, where would you start? Well, the first thing to do would be to establish whether MMO economies behave the same way as real-world economies; if they don't, then they can't be used as an experimental proxy for them. How would you do that? Well, it's one of the fundamentals of Economics that when the price of goods goes up, demand falls. This has been observed time and time again in real-world economies, so an experiment using MMOs could be designed to test whether the same thing happens in them, too. If it does, MMOs have potential to be used for social science experiments. If it doesn't, there's something about MMO economies that makes them too different from real-life economies to act as surrogates.

There are plenty of MMOs out there that are (in terms of their code) identical in all respects; any that run multiple shards (servers) are like this, for example. If you were to select two shards for the same MMO that opened at the same time to the same basic audience, then you should find that the supply and demand of items is equivalent. They won't be *quite* identical, of course, because of noise in the data (random numbers are random after all); they will, however, be comparable in a way that using a simulation isn't.

So, if you were to increase the cost of a single potion on one shard, leaving everything else the same, you should see the demand for that potion fall, right?

Economist Ted Castronova did just that.[11] He had to abandon his hopes to develop an MMO of his own because it proved too expensive, so instead he used Bioware's *Neverwinter Nights* engine and Aurora toolkit to construct a smaller MMO (if you count a nonseamless world limited to 96 players as an MMO). Called *Arden*, it was set in the world of Shakespeare's plays. He set up two servers, the only difference in code between them being that in one the price of health potions was double what it was in the other.

---

[11]Edward Castronova: *A Test of the Law of Demand in a Virtual World: Exploring the Petri Dish Approach to Social Science.* CESifo Working Paper Series No. 2355, July 2008. http://papers.ssrn.com/sol3/papers.cfm?abstract_id=1173642

After running the servers separately for a month, he found that on the high-priced server there were 43.1 percent fewer health potions bought. Therefore, he could conclude that the Law of Demand works just the same in MMOs as it does in the real world.

Which is better? Spending $50,000,000 to develop an MMO to test how a loosely integrated single currency union would play out (say) or just going ahead and implementing it in the hope that the wheels won't fall off 20 or 30 years later?

Deconstructive Deconstruction

To be honest, what annoys me about postmodernism isn't so much the underlying theory as the sheer *smugness* of many of its proponents (present company excepted). It's as if someone has come up with the concept of color and whenever you make a pot or a shed or a hang glider they point out that, oh, look, it has color. Yes, I *know* it has color, but how does that help me make one?

I *know* I can deconstruct games—I knew that before I'd even heard of postmodernism—but how does that help me *make* games? It's not the fact that I *can* deconstruct them that's important, it's how I *do* deconstruct them.

It's not the fact that a pot *has* color that's important, it's what the color *is*.

Lab Rats

One of the potential obstacles to using MMOs as experimental domains for the social sciences comes in the form of university independent ethics committees (or *institutional review boards* as they are also known). If you want to experiment on people, then generally (*pace* Loyola University New Orleans), you have to get the permission of those people in advance. Making changes to an MMO so as to see how players change behavior would qualify as experimenting on those players.

If they know they're being experimented on, though, this can spoil the results. It could also cause potential players not to play—some people will inevitably be creeped out by the idea of being lab rats. Even something innocuous such as reducing the drop rate for a spell reagent could need institutional review board approval.

Needless to say, companies make experimental changes to their MMOs the whole time. They're not quite as bad as social games yet, but they're heading that way. Most of the major social games on sites such as Facebook are heavily driven by A/B testing, which involves showing some players one version of the game and some players another and then choosing whichever brings in the most money. Facebook itself isn't above manipulating the news streams of 689,000 users to see whether it can influence their moods.[12]

Academics are at something of a disadvantage here, compared to game developers.

---

[12]Robert Booth: *Facebook Reveals News Feed Experiment to Control Emotions. The Guardian*, 30th June 2014. www.theguardian.com/technology/2014/jun/29/facebook-users-emotions-news-feeds

Invite Sociology?

Perhaps we should invite Sociology to take a look at MMOs?

The sociological effects on real society of people spending a lot of time in virtual worlds are certainly going to become important in time (although perhaps not in my lifetime). That's nothing special, though; it's the kind of thing sociologists account for anyway.

How about the sociology of players *within* individual MMOs, though? A study (perhaps experimentally) of societies that are fairly self-contained ought to bring us rich rewards.

Unfortunately, this probably wouldn't be all that interesting to sociologists themselves. This is because Sociology is about people *en masse*. MMOs would need to have many more players per server than they currently do to excite sociologists.

I think Anthropology is a better bet than Sociology. Anthropologists and sociologists study pretty much the same things, but they have different traditions and different methods; plus, they hate each other.

Things I Don't Want to Hear About MMOs #6

The sixth thing I don't want to hear about MMOs at conferences is spun-out work.

If you have N findings to present, you get *one* presentation out of it, not N. I'm sick and tired of hearing people talk about their work in installments, as if it were some kind of TV drama series.

Academics do this because that way they get more publications to their name. Nonacademics do it because then they get re-invited to the conference next year and so escape the monstrously high attendance fee that they would otherwise have to pay to be there.

Yes, I am perfectly aware that the format of this book is piecemeal articles, but they do count as only one publication. Well, OK, two publications...

Unasked Questions

Here are some questions, the majority of which I could ask at pretty well any academic conference I go to about MMOs but almost never do:

- On what basis are you calling your software a game?

- Did it occur to you that there's a reason MMOs have been treated differently from other online games in past research?

- Wouldn't it be easier just to ask the designer why they did that?

- If your research is correct and computer games are addictive and legislation should be introduced to stop this, won't that put you out of a job?

- And you believe what your survey respondents told you because why?

- Was there a reason you didn't have a game designer look at your game design?

- Do you see any correlation between players' attitude to cheaters and what our attitude would be if we found out that you'd made all this up?

- You will get a PhD for this, but do you believe you should get one?

- What makes you think players make better game designers than do game designers?

- Had you considered that there may perhaps be a rationale as to why no one has looked at this before?

- How did you choose two people as your case studies in such a way that you could extrapolate your results to cover all online computer games?

- At what level is research on players of Counterstrike applicable to players of World of Warcraft?

- Why is computer Chess addictive but regular Chess not addictive?

- Did it occur to you that the reason this theory is applicable is that game designers know about it and used it in their design?

- Are you hung over?

- If this activity you describe happening in MMOs uses only text, not graphics, what leads you to believe it didn't used to happen years ago in text-only worlds?

- Do you think that playing World of Warcraft for fewer hours in total than I've played it for days in total will give your research more gravitas?

- Are you aware that people already looked at this 20 years ago?

- Aren't you supposed to ask people's permission before you experiment on them?

- For whom will your typology be useful, given that you have no use for it yourself?

- What the hell are you wearing?

- Why do you treat "the players" as if they were a hivemind rather than a disparate group of individuals with different ways to enjoy games?

- Have you noticed that how you define that term isn't how players use it?

- So…?

I rarely say these things because although I may *be* rude and disparaging, I don't want people to *think* I am.

Serious Fun

Imagine it's 300 years ago and you're a bright new lecturer at Oxford University. You go to the senior professor to show him this amazing new thing you've discovered—the novel! Apparently, books can be used not only for recording religious tracts or laws or accountancy transactions, but they can also be employed for telling stories! You want to study this fantastic new medium of "novels."

The professor listens carefully and sagely and then asks what use novels are.

Well, they're not *useful*, you report; however, they are fun and exciting, and you want to study them.

Your professor tells you that you can't study them for their own sake. However, if they're as exciting as you say and all the cool young people are reading them, then perhaps you could write an educational one? He therefore instructs you to go away and write a novel to teach addition.

Serious Game researchers: *this is you.*

Things I Don't Want to Hear About MMOs #7

The final thing I don't want to hear about MMOs at conferences is the view that all research is of value. It's all *potentially* of value, but that doesn't mean it's *intrinsically* of value (well, except insofar as it counts as a publication, which is valuable to academics).

I have lost count of articles that divide MMO players into different types as if that were an end to the matter. Whom is this research for? Who's going to use it? How will they use it? What benefit will they gain from it?

I could level that same charge about this book, of course.

So, here are the seven things I've said that I don't want to hear about MMOs:

- **Unlearned lessons of the past**: Young researchers hoping to stake a claim.

- **Lack of respect for MMOs**: Nongame experts looking to colonize games.

- **Going native**: Game researchers reinventing the wheel.

- **Poor scholarship**: All of the above.

- **Content-free content**: Academics judged by publication count.

- **Work in installments**: Ditto.

- **Inflated sense of importance**: If *you* view yourself as important, then naturally your work *must* be.

What's the reason for this unseemly mess?

Well, MMO (and games in general) research is being approached in two directions: people trying to use MMOs to advance their own field and people trying to use pick-and-mix research to advance MMOs. The former group wants to use MMOs as a touchstone; the latter group wants better MMOs. The two sides have met but have yet to bond; this is why we're seeing the mishmash I've just outlined.

The reason they haven't bonded is that they don't share meaning. There are no foundations to MMO research. We have no formal methods for describing games or gameplay; we have even less for describing virtual worlds. We're like Physics without Mathematics, or Philosophy without Language.

MMOs are researched for many reasons, but we're currently building our structures on swampland. Is it any surprise that they often sink? The progress we're seeing is shifting and ephemeral, and it'll take a theoretical pile-driver to put in something solid that we can build on.

Until we can describe the key features of MMOs in unambiguous terms, we're never going to have the language to describe them such that everyone can see what everyone else means.

I wish I could continue by telling you exactly how we might do that, but I can't. I know enough about operational semantics to know that it *can* be done but not enough to know how to do it.

I don't suppose you're a budding genius in computational logics looking for a topic for a PhD, are you?

Buying the Nonexistent

Some people have a hard time believing that virtual goods have any value. They don't exist, so how can they be worth something?

Well, here's something that, by definition, *can't* be brought into the real world: eternal salvation in the afterlife. Anything of the afterlife brought into the real world would cease to be afterlife and instead become life. Therefore, any concept valid only in the afterlife (such as eternal salvation) can never be valuable in life.

Nevertheless, for centuries popes sold indulgences to wealthy people that guaranteed them salvation in the afterlife. Anyone saying "Salvation in the afterlife does not exist; there **is no salvation**" would have had a swift trip to the stake. The reason that the system was stopped was because it was felt to be unfair to the righteous, rather than because it was dealing in the insubstantial.

People are perfectly able to trade in things that can never have any basis in the real world. Don't worry about it.

<Something Else>

I sometimes go to workshops for computer games and <something else>. That <something else> could be anything—Economics, Artificial Intelligence, Governance—but I'll just call it <something else> because they all work the same way.

There are four kinds of people who'll attend this event:

- People interested mainly in games, who are looking for <something else> tools and techniques that they can find a use for. This group includes me.

- People interested mainly in <something else>, who see Computer Games as a good application domain for their theories.

- People who are interested entirely in <something else>, who are paying lip service to games because there's grant money in "serious games."

- People who are interested entirely in <something else>, who hold the vague belief that their work may be useful to game developers in some unspecified way.

Of these, the first group is made up mainly of developers along with those academics who are former developers. They often have very particular uses of <something else> in mind and can be frustrated to find that the more general solutions on offer by the <something else> community have no direct bearing on their needs. They may also have practical projects of their own that are working fine but that cut too many corners to be of interest to theoreticians.

Members of the second group are all academics. They have their hearts in the right place and are split maybe 50/50 between gamers and nongamers. They do produce work of relevance to developers but will always put <something else> first and will cling to paradigms that are not helpful or are even counterproductive for games.

The third group consists of academics, too. Few of them play games, and even their contributions to "serious games" are usually only partial (resulting in technologies rather than actual games).

Those in the fourth group are also academics. They resolutely do *not* play games and are more than happy to say so in the middle of their talks, as if this gives them some weird kind of kudos. Doing so annoys the hell out of those in the first group.

Personally, I'd prefer to see this kind of workshop contain only people from the first two groups. Unfortunately, it would be harder to get funding for such workshops if that were the case, because they'd be only half the size. The bigger the potential attendance list, the greater the chance of being given a grant to hold an event.

However, if we don't drop groups 3 and 4, we could lose group I—and all connection to actual games with it. I have to say, if I went to a <something else> conference and talked about MMO design with no reference to <something else> except at the end saying "and you can probably use these things for <something else> somehow," my talk would not be received well. The audience would in all likelihood throw things at me. Quite why <something else> experts nevertheless feel perfectly at liberty to do exactly this the other way round to game developers is anyone's guess. They're not going to build any bridges with it, though, and they risk driving the game developers away. That removes the whole "knowledge transfer" aspect of such workshops that makes them attract funding.

It's good that there are developers enlightened enough to send someone to an academically oriented conference, but there's only so much belittling they'll take before they pull out.

Better

What I want from MMO research is better MMOs. Other people may want a deeper understanding of human nature, or insights into better forms of government, or innovative mechanisms for addressing real-world issues of diversity, or any of a host of other things. I just want better MMOs.

What "better" means is itself part of the issue. Nevertheless, if the answers come from quantitative, qualitative, micro, macro, experimental, or exploratory research, I don't care—I just want those answers.

Player Type Misuses Misuse

In 2009, I attended a conference in Magdeburg, Germany, at which a young researcher, Monica Mayer, outlined the results of her recent work.[13] She had come at games from the field of Psychology and employed a Uses and Gratification analysis to find out what players wanted from computer games. From this, she developed a dynamic model that explained the things that players do in order to satisfy their needs. When she ran this model, she found it had four stable configurations. Were a person to play a game for fun, they would pursue their desires in a feedback-oriented way that leads to one of these four steady states.

Said states map directly onto the types of Player Type theory.

Now the key point here is that because Mayer had designed her research from a Psychology tradition, *she hadn't come across Player Type theory* when she made her findings. The fact that they mapped onto achievers, explorers, socializers, and killers was pointed out to her only afterward. If she'd published 15 years earlier, we'd be talking about the Mayer types, not the Bartle types.

Dr. Mayer's work offers an evidence-based explanation of Player Types that was developed independently of it and is purely in terms of uses and gratifications. It doesn't say where the desires come from, just what they are and what they mean. As such, her work doesn't deny Player Types, but neither does it support it; it simply arrives at the same conclusions.

I regularly harp on about people misusing Player Types, but the truth is I misuse it myself. It has a wider applicability than I suggest. Just because I'm careful not to make claims about it that I can't justify, this doesn't mean such claims must be false. There *is* more to Player Types than we currently know, and if I constantly try to drag everything back to MMOs, we'll take longer finding out what it is.

---

[13]Monica Mayer: *Why Playing Games is Better than Living Lives: Motivation, Emotion and Cognition Based on Digital Games.* Proc. Game Cultures. Otto von Guericke University, Magdeburg, Germany. 2009.

Sense of Proportion

Jessica Mulligan has a graph she shows in some of her talks that looks something like this:

The gray part represents the number of people who play game worlds. The black line represents the number of people who play social worlds. This actually exaggerates the latter, because the line is half a point wide; really, it should be so thin that you can't see it.

Now imagine that the black line represents game worlds and the gray part represents social worlds. That's close to the way things are when it comes to *researching* virtual worlds.

On Law

Real-Life API—Confuse

CLawyer::Confuse

int Confuse(Cjurisdiction* *pJuris,* **real** *rConf* **)**

- *pJuris*: Specifies the jurisdiction (NULL for none)
- *rConf*: Specifies the amount of confusion to add

Remarks

Increases the lawyer's confusion value by *rConf*. Common reasons include the following:

- Rights of players: Freedom of speech, freedom to play.
- Intellectual property: UCC, copyright, mad patents.
- Virtual property: Effects on nerfs, rollbacks, bans.
- Commodification: RMT, tax.
- Individuality: Second Life is not World of Warcraft.

Return

Random value r such that $0 \le r < 1$.

MMO Security

MMOs have the same basic security problems that every game or online service has, such as denial of service, database injections, phishing, backdoors, viruses, Trojans, and regular human error. You can read about these in any good book on computer game security (of which there is indeed at least one[1]).

However, MMOs also have some particular problems all of their own. They can be categorized as relating to the following:

- Piracy
- Client software
- Cheating
- Real-Money Trading (RMT)
- Griefing
- User-created content
- Privacy

Yes, I guess I'll get around to describing these later, when it might make a vague kind of sense to do so.

---

[1]Steven Davis: *Protecting Games: A Security Handbook for Game Developers and Publishers.* Delmar, 2009.

When the Chips Are Down

Imagine going to a new casino where the casino owner gives you some chips with which to gamble. If you want more, the owner will sell you more. You play a few games of *Roulette*, strike it lucky, and end up with many more chips than you had to begin with. You want to cash in your winnings.

However, this casino owner doesn't *buy* chips; they only *sell* chips. If you want to convert your chips into cash, you have to find someone else *in the casino* who wants more chips. This person will buy your chips from you so long as you charge less than the casino owner does.

So, suppose there are plenty of people in the casino who enjoy gambling and who will buy your chips. New gamblers are arriving all the time, not all as lucky as you, and they're happy to buy from you at a discount. The casino owner doesn't mind because they make all their money from selling beverages anyway.

What happens, though, when people *don't* want your chips? Maybe they have enough of their own, or lots of other people have also won big and want to sell their chips. Perhaps there aren't so many new gamblers coming into the casino, so there isn't the demand.

What happens to your vast wealth of chips then? What happens when *other* people realize that *their* chip holdings are falling in value and they try to cash those in while they still can, too?

Why, yes, this is an analogy for *Second Life*'s LindeX, which is where players sell Linden dollars to one other for US dollars. It's also how *Diablo III*'s auction house works. *EVE*'s Pilot License Extension (PLEX) and *WoW*'s WoW Token allow something not exactly the same but very similar (sell your in-world currency for subscription time that someone bought for real money earlier).

MMOs give you chips. You win some, you lose some. You probably win more than you lose. The only way you're going to cash those chips in is if someone in the MMO is willing to pay you for them. If they're not, all your virtual wealth is worth precisely nothing.

Trojans

Did you know there are programs that promise to do nice things for you but that when you run them, they do something nasty?

Yes, of course, you did. These are *trojans*, named after the Trojan Horse of Greek myth (rather than the brand of American condom).

Ah, but did you *also* know that some of these trojans target MMOs? They pass on your account information to people who sell all your character's stuff for in-game money and then sell the in-game money for real-world money.

Yes, you knew that, too.

So, when I tell you that in 2006, more than 16,000 *different* such MMO-specific trojans were detected[2]—that's about *45 a day*—you're probably just going to shrug, right?

The top five targets were as follows:

- *Lineage 2* (40 percent)
- *World of Warcraft* (20 percent)
- *Legend of Mir* (6 percent)
- *Tibia* (6 percent)
- *MapleStory* (6 percent)

And that was way back in 2006.

Worth Nothing

When Roy Trubshaw and I wrote *MUD*, we knew the possibility existed that we could create in-world objects to sell to players for real money. We dismissed the idea immediately as being bad, though, on the grounds that it would spoil immersion and get in the way of what we were trying to say: that this was a *better* place than *Reality*, not part of it. It was somewhere you could go to be *free* of it— where you could be and become *yourself*.

Besides, who'd want to pay for something that might be worth nothing the next day? Hahaha!

---

[2]Sergey Golovanov: *Online Games and Fraud: Using Games as Bait*. Kaspersky Lab. 2007. https://securelist.com/analysis/publications/36169/online-games-and-fraud-using-games-as-bait/

IP

IP stands for *intellectual property*. It covers abstractions such as trademarks, copyrights, and patents. IP is something that rich, multinational companies own a lot of and lobby hard to ensure they keep control of. It's why some countries imprison you if you download one too many of the wrong MP3 files.

IP law is complicated. It was developed for the days when it actually cost money to copy something such as a book or a medicine. It still costs money to copy some things (such as medicines), but with digital objects (such as books) the cost to copy them is practically zero. This has led to widespread abuse of IP laws by the general populace (which tends to have an ambivalent opinion of it) followed by heavy-handed reactionary responses by old media (who find their valuable properties becoming less valuable through dilution).

Internet IP law is therefore something of a battleground. MMOs are not in the front line because they're very expensive both to make and to copy; however, they could be caught in the crossfire. There are some perfectly reasonable interpretations of IP law that would have alarming consequences for MMOs if taken to their natural conclusions.

Yeah, I'll give you some examples.

Cupid Stunt

Suppose I want to stop people swearing in my MMO. I can't stop them swearing in code because there are too many ways to swear, but I *can* stop them from saying anything at all in-world. Should I therefore stop everyone speaking to prevent the few who want to swear from swearing?

Well no, that would be ridiculous. Instead, I allow people to speak but put a profanity filter in (to cut out overt swearing) and make a rule saying that anyone who uses excessively profane language is going to get banned.

I can't ban in code, but I can ban in noncode. Happens all the time.

Security: Piracy

Piracy is a problem for the developers of regular computer games and in some countries is so rife that developers don't launch non-Internet games there (on the basis that they'll sell a single copy, from which everyone else will get theirs). One of the attractions of MMOs is that their client/server nature makes it hard to pirate them.

Hard, but not impossible. Actually, not even hard in many cases.

After the first few weeks of launch, it usually doesn't really matter if an MMO's client is pirated. The bulk of your revenue by that stage will come from players paying you to play, not players buying copies of the client. It's not pirating the client that's the problem, though: it's pirating the *server*.

The first time Raph Koster went to China to speak to game developers, he was surprised to discover that he was famous as the designer of *Ultima Online*. *Ultima Online* was never launched in China, so how did so many gamers there know who he was? Oh, that would be because of the 300 pirated versions of *Ultima Online* that were running in China unbeknown to Raph or Electronic Arts.

Usually, when servers are pirated, it's an inside job. Some lowly server maintenance guy or part-time programmer is offered a year's salary to sneak the code out, so they do. The pirated server can then be set up as a commercial enterprise and run in competition with the official servers. All the developer can do is complain to the local law enforcement agencies and hope they close the rogue server down. Then, they have to do it again and again and again because it keeps popping up again and again and again. These servers can be so lucrative to operate that sometimes the local law enforcement agencies decline to intervene because they've been bribed to turn a blind eye. No, I'm not making that up.

MMO designers do sometimes include server authentication codes in their software, but even this doesn't help when people decide to code their own servers. A lot of the expense in MMO development goes into creating the assets—the artwork, the animation, the music, and so on—which usually sits on the user's PC for swift loading when it's needed. Therefore, if you want to replicate an MMO, "all" you need do is write the server to go with a hacked client and there you are. Yes, it's expensive (hence the quotation marks), but it's much less expensive than developing everything from scratch.

Some of these so-called "private" servers have tens of thousands of players. There are even web sites where they are listed, rated, and advertised. I'm looking at one exclusively for *WoW* rip-offs right now on my screen as I type this, and it lists nearly 900 of them. The bigger ones claim 4,000 or 5,000 players across 5 to 10 servers; the biggest claims 24,000+ simultaneous. Some offer instant top-level characters, some offer instant top-level armor sets, some offer five times normal DPS, some offer custom quests, and some offer unique, scripted instances. Hmm, this one offers a maximum level of 254. None of them pays one penny to Blizzard.

The latest thinking in the MMO security world is not to release the source or executable code ever, under any circumstances. If someone in a strange, exotic land wants to license your MMO, you give them a sealed box with the server inside it, and you keep the admin password secret. It doesn't matter how much the licensee mewls that you don't trust them; the fact is, you *don't* trust every single one of their employees, including temps and the cleaners, so they can cry as much as they like but they won't be getting access to the code.

I don't know whether any MMOs actually *follow* this advice, mind you.

IP Example: The Better Offer

Suppose a player, let's call him JohnX, develops a cool virtual hoverbike in an MMO that allows for player-created content. OK, so object-creation is mainly a social-world thing, and most MMOs don't implement it, but some do (*A Tale in the Desert*, for example). Let's call our imaginary MMO that does do it *MMOX*. JohnX creates a vending machine that doles out a hoverbike to anyone who wants one.

Now suppose that some time later a rival MMO comes to JohnX and says, "You're a great designer/programmer. We'd like to hire you." JohnX accepts and now works for this other company. He wants every hoverbike removed from *MMOX*. They're all his intellectual property one way or another.

What should happen here?

MMO Revenue Models

There are basically five ways to make money from MMOs:

- Box/expansion sales
- Subscription
- Advertising/sponsorship
- Merchandising
- Sales of virtual goods/services
- Pay-per-play

You'll notice there are six entries in that list of five. That's because the last one is now pretty well extinct. I've put it there for historical reasons as it was the dominant model in the early days; basically, what happened was that you paid for fuel, and then you drove around having fun until the gauge was low, whereupon you paid for some more.

Box sales generally serve to recoup the cost of development. Although they can be profitable beyond this, what developers *really* want are subscribers. Subscribers offer a steady income, whereas a box sale is a one-off. Thus, after the initial rush, developers using a subscription model will often discount their client software (or even give it away for free) in the hope of attracting more subscribers. Expansion packs and downloadable content can be rather more profitable, although their main purpose still tends to be that of retaining players by offering new content, rather than simply to rake in extra cash from selling SKUs.

The subscription model is a powerful thing because each player is covering their costs; MMOs that strive to succeed primarily using the other models will therefore usually endeavor to have at least some version of a subscription service available (allowing subscribers access to "premium content" or to have a standing monthly order for in-world currency, for example).

Why would an MMO *not* charge a subscription fee? The simple answer is that if people think an MMO is free, more of them will play. Once through the door, they can then be advertised to and sold to. The more complex answer is that if people play more than one MMO at once, then those subscription fees rack up; this puts players off subscription MMOs if they play multiple MMOs.

Advertising is, on the face of it, a good thing for the players; they don't have to pay a penny to access the MMO because the advertisers cover the cost in return for getting across their messages. For in-context advertisements, players can actually welcome the idea of ads as they add authenticity. If you see a drinks machine in a contemporary MMO, you will be jarred more if it doesn't have a well-known brand name on it than if it does have one.

Out-of-context advertisements (say, for real-world toothpaste in a fantasy world) are very unpopular; they break the fiction, which breaks the persuasiveness of the virtual environment. Over-intrusive ads ("This five-second delay to your playing experience is brought to you by...") are also a big no-no, for similar immersion-busting reasons.

New developers can (and often do) cheerfully suggest that advertisement-free play can be made available for a subscription. Not entirely unsurprisingly, this isn't popular with advertisers: "Wait, you want to use our ads to encourage people to pay you *not* to see them?" Nevertheless, an advertising-supported MMO can bring in modest profits if targeted at the right demographic. It's usually done in combination with some other revenue model, though. Likewise, merchandising is a decent way to make extra income from an MMO while not being enough to sustain it alone.

Sales of virtual goods and services, on the other hand, can bring stupendous rewards *if* the players can be persuaded to accept the idea. In many game-like worlds, it's deeply unpopular. Players don't like to see other players simply buying their way to success. However, free is free, so they will often tolerate such practices to save having to pay a subscription. Free-to-play is now the dominant revenue model for MMOs, although for AAA titles it's regarded as a bit like the way direct-to-video is for movies: you should start off subscription, *then* switch to free-to-play some time later.

So, out of the sustainable revenue models for MMOs (that is, assuming box sales, merchandising, and advertising/sponsorship will be done anyway), which is the *fairest*?

Not Playing

Human beings do have a right to play, but we shouldn't, in our rush to recognize this right, forget that they have a greater right *not* to play if that's what they want.

Security: Client Software

OK, so you already know that your own computer is under constant attack from **vicious crazies** who want to **encrypt your files** and **blackmail you forever** even if you pay the ransom, but what kinds of security problems do MMOs face?

Well, pretty much the same as you do, except they have **hordes of slavering players** trying to gain an **in-game advantage**, too.

The first point to note is that players all have copies of the client on their computers; therefore, the client can't be trusted in **any way whatsoever**. *Diablo* died as a viable online game because people cracked the software; fortunately, Blizzard had learned from this when they developed *World of Warcraft*.

Even if you don't trust the client, sometimes you have to tell it information you'd rather the player didn't know, such as what's creeping up behind them. It takes only one player to release a modification that displays this information (*ShowEQ*, in *EverQuest*'s case), and everyone will want to use it. Thus, some MMOs run *sentinel* programs to beat up anything they identify as being a cheat (or as something that could be being used to gather data so as to write a cheat). This is somewhat controversial, not least because it seems to break a dozen computer privacy laws, but it's commonplace, so tra-la-la. As yet we haven't had any sentinels fight each other, although *World of Warcraft*'s did take on Sony's digital rights management software and win.

Cheats can circumvent this kind of defense mechanism by not touching the computer the client runs on at all. The client sends data to the server, but it doesn't have a direct, uninterrupted connection. You can put another computer between the client machine and the Internet and alter data in real time as it goes through. This is a *packet-sniffing* approach, and if the developer has been sufficiently lax, it can really help the would-be cheater (if they have a spare computer).

As an example of what happens if you trust the client, consider an early air combat MMO, Kesmai's *Air Warrior*. *Air Warrior* suffered badly from lag (this was in the days before broadband), which meant that people would often shoot when they saw an enemy in their sights but their screen was wrong and actually their opponent was elsewhere. They complained bitterly that they should have hit and not entirely without justification—sometimes their target filled half the screen, and it seemed unmissable! To assuage the discontent, the developers patched the game so that the *client* decided whether a shot was a hit or a miss, instead of the server. Needless to say, someone with a packet sniffer soon discovered what had happened and wrote a program that converted all misses to hits and spoofed in some extra hits for good measure.

That changed the nature of play somewhat.

EULA and TOS

EULA stands for *End-User License Agreement* except when it stands for *End-User Licensing Agreement*, except when it doesn't have the hyphen, and TOS stands for *Terms of Service*.

The EULA is effectively a contract between the provider of a service and the user of that service. Formally, it is specific to the object being licensed, which in the case of MMOs means the MMO itself and your account. It says that you are allowed to use the service under certain legal conditions and describes the service that the service provider promises to provide in return.

The TOS is (or should that be are?) all about how you use the service. It says what you can and can't do, what constitutes unacceptable behavior, and so on. It can include real-world actions as well as in-world ones.

Because the EULA allows you to use the service only under the conditions of the TOS, the TOS may be referenced by or incorporated into the EULA. Or, if you prefer, because the conditions under which you are allowed to use the service are part of its terms, the EULA may reference or incorporate the TOS.

As you can see, EULAs and TOSs are fairly intertwined, so they often amount to the same thing. MMO developers will usually use the term EULA to refer to the TOS/EULA combination and TOS to mean the more frequently updated part governing player (rather than developer) behavior; that's except for a few old-timers who only ever use TOS because EULA is too lawyerish.

Either way, what it means is that after you've clicked through them, the developer is entitled to sacrifice your children to the blood gods of Mars. Something like that, anyway—I don't read the things, either.

Security: Cheating

Cheating is knowingly breaking the rules of a game while professing to abide by them. This is mainly achieved either by lying (in *Golf*, taking two shots and claiming you took only one) or by denying that the rules other people are following are rules at all (in *Soccer*, when the team in possession kicks the ball into touch so an injured player from your team can be treated and then you don't give them the ball back from the throw-in).

In MMOs, cheating is bad because it makes noncheaters leave. Sometimes people *look* as if they're cheating but they aren't—they merely don't know or don't entirely understand the rules. Such people will usually conform to the rules once fully appraised of them. Cheaters, on the other hand, know full well what they are doing, even if they try to delude themselves into believing otherwise.

The most damaging cheating in MMOs is technical by nature—breaching the written rules, not just the unwritten ones. Here are some common methods of doing so:

> **Hacked client**: The operator has control of the server, but "the client is in the hands of the enemy." If any gameplay-significant decisions are made in the client, then either the client itself or the datastream it produces *will* be attacked. I explained how the early graphical MMO, *Air Warrior*, suffered fairly badly from lag so moved the decision as to whether a shot had hit or not from the server to the client, as a result of which some players never missed. Amazingly, this sort of thing still goes on.

> **Noninvasive**: This doesn't modify the client or datastream; it merely reads the information it contains and displays what should be secret. The vulnerability it exploits is that a client often needs to know things that you the player shouldn't know (for example, what's behind you, so that should you turn quickly, then the client can render the scene in an instant). By having a program read this information, the player can be told things that give them an edge. *ShowEQ* was just such a program: it added a radar readout to *EverQuest*, so no one could ever sneak up on anyone who was running it.

> **Bots**. Bots are programs that play the MMO in the player's stead. They are used primarily for repetitive tasks, leading to the accusation that they are a legitimate response to bad game design. They're not. The legitimate response is "don't play."

Privileged users: People who work for the developer or operator can be a threat from within. They may be tempted to use their developer privileges to gain an advantage as players (which happened in *EVE Online*) or simply to make money (which happened in *Ultima Online*). Players are understandably six kinds of livid when they find this out, yet the practice is hard to stop.

Bugs and exploits: A bug means a failure in code; an exploit means a failure in design. The worst problems arise from dupe bugs, which can render an MMO's economy worthless overnight, but anything problematical that is coded into the game must be dealt with as soon as possible. This is because, unlike the other forms of cheating mentioned here, once word about a bug or an exploit gets out, *any* player can use it to their advantage.

There are known ways to tackle some of these problems; as I mentioned earlier, some MMOs use a second program to monitor suspicious activity (Blizzard's *Warden* for *WoW* is perhaps the best known). They're not failsafe because monitor programs can be hacked just as easily as clients, but they do place extra barriers in the cheater's path.

Perhaps the best way to deal with cheating is to stop people wanting to cheat in the first place. This isn't as easy as it sounds, though. These are the main reasons people cheat:

- **Ego issues**: They want to appear to be better than they really are.

- **Catching up**: The friends they want to play with are way ahead and cheating is a way to catch up with them.

- **Frustration**: The gameplay is just too hard (or, alternatively, too easy).

- **Fairness**: Everyone else is cheating.

- **For nongame reasons**: Gold farmers fall into this category.

In games that don't have thousands of players, if you find someone is cheating, then you either kick them out or simply stop playing with them. In large, commercial MMOs, this is not possible. This is why security is so important for them.

That doesn't mean designers give a moment's thought to it until it's far too late to do anything effective about it, of course.

Firefighting Exploits

Exploits are the fault of designers, no question about it. Sometimes, players feel that this gives them *carte blanche* to use an exploit until it's fixed.

Designers disagree as to how to handle this problem. They agree that exploits must be fixed but disagree as to whether to switch off whatever feature is causing the exploit in the first place until such a time as it *can* be fixed.

Personally, I tend toward a less code-oriented approach. If an exploit is easy to isolate, sure, turn off that part of the software. If it's too broad to be isolated, though, I don't think it's unreasonable for designers to ban (rather than unimplement) the problematical activity once it has come to their attention—just for long enough to allow them time to fix it.

For example, if there's a dupe bug that arises when players cross zone boundaries in a certain way, the designers *must* try to fix it. However, they can't stop all travel between zones while they're fixing it, because this would have a more detrimental effect on the player base than the problem it addresses. A reasonable compromise would be to say, "OK, now we know about this practice, we're banning it while we fix it."

The counterargument is that once you reveal an exploit by telling people not to do it, you open the floodgates. Everyone will attempt it instead of just the handful who first came across it. Most live teams therefore keep quiet about such bugs to limit the damage caused.

Bah—wimps! What happened to the draconian developers of yore? Try putting something like *this* in the terms of service: "We've created this product in the belief that it is impossible to replicate its in-game money. If you find a way to do this, let us know. We'll give the first player to tell us about it a bug-finding reward of $2,000. If, however, you decide not to let us know, then should we discover you've used the bug, we'll cancel your account, delete any associated in-game data, and tell our smart lawyers to hassle you with a criminal damage suit."

Hmm, there are probably better ways of saying that, but you get the gist of it.

Fair Price

What's the fairest way to charge for MMOs? They do cost money to develop and operate, so someone has to pay something or we wouldn't have any.

Subscription MMOs are like a bar that charges you a fixed fee per month, during which time you can drink as much beer as you like at no extra cost. Some people are going to drink a lot more beer than they paid for, but most are going to drink a lot less.

Free-to-play MMOs are like a bar in which one person buys a round for everyone. You can drink as much as you like, just so long as someone else is putting it on their tab.

Per-hour charging MMOs are, well, practically nonexistent nowadays, but they *were* like a bar that charged you for the amount you actually drank.

The fairest way to pay for MMOs is this latter system: "The more you play, the more you should pay." It's how we used to operate the early commercial textual worlds back in the day. Given that it's the fairest method, then, why is it no longer popular?

Well, it turns out that people don't like the idea of playing with a clock running. If they usually play 100 hours every month, then at 1 cent every 6 minutes, it would cost them an average of $10/month. They would rather pay a flat $10 every month even if they played only a couple of hours some months, rather than worry that the time taken to put together a raid group was costing them 5 cents. They're also worried that they might lose track of time and find they've over-stepped their budget.

You can address these concerns by getting people to buy credit in advance and then deduct from it as they play, which is how "pay as you go" mobile phone tariffs work. If they're close to running out, they get an hour or so's warning and can either top up or wait until it runs out and logs them off.

Compared to "drink as much as you like, someone else is paying," though, who's going to go with that? Fairness is only an issue when you feel a system is unfair on *you*.

Code Is Law

There's a slight bond of recognition between programmers and lawyers. Both work within systems of rules, trying to persuade an uncooperative system to bend to their will, always on the lookout for dangerous bugs and exploits. Law is old, however, and needs to adapt when new things appear—and that includes MMOs.

The relationship between code and law was first encapsulated in a book about the new frontiers of Law opened up by the Internet: Lawrence Lessig's *Code and other Laws of Cyberspace*[3] (its central premise, *code is law*, is adapting a line from an earlier book[4] that asserted *code is the law*). It draws an equivalence between program code and legal code in terms of law and governance, in that both regulate how people can conduct themselves.

This observation is correct: code *is* law. However, it's law as in "laws of physics" and "laws of nature," not "laws of the land." Program code is not interpretive in the way that legislated laws are. There's no debate with code; either it allows something or it doesn't.

Well, it can crash or hang on it, too, but fortunately the other forms of law don't appear to do that.

Not a Handicap

Suppose you wanted to improve your golf handicap. One way to do this would be to practice, obviously, but another way would be to pay a professional golfer to pretend to be you and win a bunch of matches against decent opposition.

That would be like cheating, right?

Well, by the same token, so is paying someone else to level up your MMO character.

---

[3]Lawrence Lessig: *Code and Other Laws of Cyberspace*. Basic Books: New York NY, 1999.
http://codev2.cc/download+remix/Lessig-Codev2.pdf
[4]William J. Mitchell: *City of Bits: Space, Place and the Infobahn*. MIT Press: Boston MA, 1996.

IP Example: The Art Within Art

Suppose JaneX creates a virtual, pole-less magnet. Any object of this kind will stick to another object of this kind until a player removes it. JaneX makes a bunch of these magnets in assorted colors and constructs from them an amazingly beautiful statue. Everyone who sees it thinks it's brilliant! They take screenshots of it and post videos of themselves standing next to it.

"Hold on," thinks JaneX. "That's my IP. Those players have no right to publish it on the web without my say-so. Come to that, the MMO operators have no right to publish it to players through their client software. I'm due a license fee."

What should happen here?

Economic Migrants

A problem that MMO economies have that real-world economies don't is that it's relatively easy to leave them.

In the real world, if you're poor, then you can't simply go somewhere else where you're not poor. You're universally poor. The best you can do is to go somewhere that has better prospects, but of course if that would cost money then even that's not an option—you don't have any money!

If you're poor in an MMO, you don't have to stand for it. There are plenty of MMOs out there you can switch to where you won't be poor. This gives MMO economies a release valve that real-world economies don't have, which screws up those nice supply/demand curves that economists love to draw.

The fact that most MMO economies are so small that they can be gouged by dedicated groups of players doesn't help, either.

F2P

F2P is a sort of acronym for Free-to-Play. It became the dominant revenue model for MMOs in the 2010s (in the West; it had been dominant since the early 2000s in the Far East).

It's a catchall term to describe what are also sometimes called *freemium* and *microtransaction* models. Basically, most people play for free, but there are some things you can buy for real money (or, more correctly, for virtual currency paid for with real money). These things you can buy for real money fall into four main groups:

- The purely cosmetic, with no tangible effect on gameplay. Color for your armor, vanity pets, cool-looking mounts, house decorations, extra character slots, and the like, fall into this category.

- A gray area of things that could advantageously affect gameplay but not do so directly. If there's a better chance of getting a magic wand in a zone behind a paywall, for example, that would fall into this category. Other examples are lower repair bills, quicker cooldowns, and longer buffs.

- Tangible gameplay effects. You can get the proverbial kick-ass sword only by paying for it. You can take or deal more damage, you can teleport to places nonpayers have to walk to, you can use special one-off emergency fight-winning grenades, and you can buy stuff that other people have to spend hours playing to get.

- Pay-to-win. The things you buy are so over-powered that if you're reasonably competent, you can beat most highly skilled opponents—unless they've also paid to win.

I'll give a closer analysis later, but for the moment this is enough.

In most games that use F2P, whether they're MMOs or social network games, around 5 percent of the players will buy things, and the remaining 95 percent will never pay a penny. However, the 5 percent that do buy things are willing to pay a LOT —so much so that the income for F2P games is usually around three times higher than it would be using a subscription approach (!). Ultimately, this is why F2P overtook subscription as the dominant MMO revenue model. Well, this and the fact that it's hard to keep players when your competitors charge them nothing.

Note that if you're lucky enough to have a successful subscription model already, there's nothing about selling virtual goods for real money that prevents you from doing that at the same time.

Black-Box Trading

I have X, I want Y, so I go to this black box and insert my X. Out pops Y.

X and Y could be coinage, resources, crafted goods, magical items, whatever. X is the price I pay to obtain Y.

As for the black box, is there any material difference from my point of view whether it's a trading system (such as an auction house) or a simple replicator that conjures Y out of thin air? Either way, I no longer have X; I have Y instead. I'm satisfied.

IP Example: The Reputation

Suppose a group of players get together in *MMOX* and form a guild called The Schoolgirls. They choose as their avatars the sweetest young thangs they can create and spend 100 percent of their time role-playing being schoolgirls. They're very good at it—they're madcap, witty, and entertaining—and their post-modern take hits the zeitgeist. They get fan clubs, release podcasts, and do interviews with mainstream media. The developers of *MMOX* are ecstatic at all the publicity that The Schoolgirls are attracting to their virtual world. It's as if The Schoolgirls and *MMOX* are tied together in the minds of the MMO-playing public.

The developers of *MMOX* are not nearly as ecstatic when a pornographer pays The Schoolgirls a six-figure fee to publish pictures of their avatars engaging in sordid sex acts with virtual farmyard animals.

What should happen here?

The Long Arm

It's the law that stops me from scanning books and giving them to my friends for free.

The law *could* stop people from trading in MMO currency if it put its mind to it.

Fair Share

In the olde days, MUDs were free—literally, in that we didn't charge any money to play them. When we did charge for them, we went with the fairest revenue model: per-hour charging. The more you play, the more you should pay, right?

The per-hour charging rate was replaced by a subscription model. It turned out that people would rather pay more, knowing there was a limit, than pay less but have a clock ticking in the background. Subscription is now being replaced by free-to-play, following the discovery that you can nickel-and-dime a few people who have more money than sense for the benefit of the rest.

As an analogy, consider petroleum gasoline: car fuel. The way it works with car fuel, you buy it up front, and then the more you drive around, the more you use. When you run out, you buy some more. That's like the per-hour charging model.

The subscription model has you pay a big fee up front, but then you can drive around as much as you like. People who drive a lot love this because it's less expensive for them. Most people drive less than they've paid for, but if the only other option is not to drive at all, well, they have to pay if they want to drive. We have road tax in the UK that works like this: you have to pay a certain amount merely to have permission to drive your car on the road for the next year.

Free-to-play is where you're given your fuel for free, but there's road pricing. You can drive on the back roads for free, but if you want to get onto the trunk roads, you have to pay. You get your fuel for free because enough people go onto the trunk roads to subsidize the fuel for everyone who stays on the back roads. The people who pay to use the trunk roads wouldn't have to use the trunk roads if there weren't so many people clogging up the back roads.

Now although governments can tax fuel, cars, and roads, they have a monopoly. MMO developers don't, although they can mix economies a little (F2P fits in with subscription and per-hour charging).

The problem you get with F2P is that not all those people on the back roads are having fun. They don't get to where they want to go as soon as they might, and although some like the scenery, it doesn't go past very quickly. It's especially not fun for people who want to get to their destination before everyone else when they can see other people zooming past on the trunk road. It feels a little too much like those other people are cheating.

Back in the per-hour charging days, it could cost $12 an hour to play a MUD. That would make no sense these days, but what if the price were, say, 10 cents an hour? That would be within everyone's grasp. If you played for 5 hours every day for a month, it would cost you only $15; if you didn't play at all, it would cost you nothing. That would be fair. It wouldn't be *free*, but it would be so close as to make no difference for most people. Would an MMO that charged 10 cents an hour attract players?

Well, we don't know. There are some people who see payment as a binary proposition: an MMO is either free or costly. In their view, 1 cent an hour is too much in comparison with free. They don't care about the other benefits they might get from having a nonfree game (universally wider roads for all). If it's not free, they wouldn't play it, no matter how nearly free it is.

Other people might think, well, 10 cents isn't free exactly, but it's pretty close. So long as there's an inactivity disconnection so that if you died at the keyboard, your relatives who found your body 3 months later wouldn't have a $200 bill to pay, 10 cents an hour is practically nothing. These people *would* pay. Presumably, though, if a player has accepted the principle that it's OK to pay, a developer could probably charge more than 10 cents an hour. Would 20 cents work? 25 cents? Or is 10 cents too high but 5 cents wouldn't be?

Per-hour charging for MMOs is the fairest (or at least the most equitable) way to pay for playing. It's such a shame that it can't be spun as being "free."

The Rules

The MMO's rules as stated in its EULA are just as much part of "the game" as the rules embodied in its code. Merely because the code allows something this doesn't mean designers should have to accept players' breaking of the EULA rules that forbid it.

Not Transferable

If I go to a *Soccer* match in the UK, written on the ticket are the words "not transferable." This means that although I own the ticket and the ticket entitles me to enter the stadium and watch the game, I can't sell the ticket to anyone else. If I do, the people who own the stadium may refuse entry to the person to whom I sell it. Worse, I could myself be sued for having sold them the ticket in the first place.

Why would a *Soccer* club act like that? Why would they not want me even to *give* my ticket away—let alone sell it? Well, it's because we have home fans and away fans. Home fans support the team that is playing at home, and away fans support the team that is playing away. European countries are small enough that there may be a substantial number of fans prepared to make the journey to see their team play away. Indeed, a certain number of seats are actually set aside so that a reasonable number of visiting fans will get a chance to watch their team in action.

Now, *Soccer* is very tribal. People who support one team will usually have at least one other team that they regard as the enemy. This animosity is usually reciprocated. There are some teams with supporters who purport to dislike *all* other teams. When you have 5,000 of these in a stadium that holds 50,000, what's going to happen? Answer: although most will behave themselves, some won't. There will be fights. People will get hurt. Thus, *Soccer* clubs segregate the fans. All the home supporters go in one part of the stadium, and all the away supporters go in another. Stewards keep them apart. They taunt each other with chanting, but no one gets hurt.

Suppose that I, as a home supporter of team X, get hold of a ticket for a big match. A tout (or scalper, as they're called in America) offers to buy it from me for five times its face value, so I accept. That tout may then sell it to someone else for 10 or 20 times its face value. That someone else could be a supporter of team Y. After all, if there's only an allocation of 5,000 tickets and 20,000 team Y fans want to be at the match, how else are they going to get in?

So, the person who bought the ticket, a team Y supporter, goes to the match and ends up standing in a section full of team X supporters. Consequently, this individual gets their insides beaten out of them when their team scores and they cheer.

To stop this, we have those words on the ticket: "not transferable." Whoever buys the ticket has to use it. They can return it for a refund if they no longer need it.

For matches where trouble is likely, supporters will probably have to show some form of identification that proves they're the person whose name is on the ticket. Otherwise, they don't get in the ground. This stops the market economy from setting the price of tickets, but it also stops people getting stabbed (at least inside the stadium). People accept it.

Now what does this have to do with MMOs?

MMO objects and characters effectively have "not transferable" written on them.

Why? Well there are many reasons why. The thing is, none of these reasons actually *matter*. The MMO operators own the data; they govern access to said data, and they are within their rights to allow players through only if those players follow their rules. Provided that these rules are lawful (no "you can have a level 100 character for free if you set fire to a dog" or similar), then that's the end of it. They set the rules; if you don't like them, your only weapon is to threaten to play somewhere where the operators set different rules that you *do* like.

Some MMO companies will also stamp "not transferable" on their objects and characters for intellectual property reasons (via their EULA), but IP law *isn't* necessary to determine whether trade in such objects is allowable. If I can't trade in *Soccer* match tickets stamped "not transferable," I can't trade in virtual objects stamped (by the EULA) the same way.

That's the theory, anyway.

Commodification

Commodification is the transformation of previously noncommercial relationships into commercial ones. When speaking about MMOs, it means the treatment of virtual goods as the objects of real-world commerce.

If the commercial relationship is between players, that's generally what people refer to as *real-money trading* (about which more anon). If it's between the MMO's operators and its players, it's usually *implied* by the term *free-to-play*, but you can nevertheless have free-to-play without commodification (for example, by making the MMO actually free to play).

Physics, Politics

MMOs have both laws of nature and laws of the land. The more they can enforce as the former, the easier the MMO is to manage.

In the real world, the law of the land can decree that I wear a seat belt while driving my car, but it can't stop me from driving without a seat belt—all it can do is punish me if it finds out. If an MMO designer wants, they can stop my virtual car from starting unless my seat belt is on.

Then again, if technology allows in the real world, some government may decide that all cars sold within its borders must check that the driver's seat belt is on before the car will start. In that case, laws of the land would be being used against vehicle manufacturers to make them in turn use laws of nature against drivers.

The difference between laws of nature and laws of the land is one of physics and politics.

IP Example: The Sponsor

Suppose the McCola corporation likes the demographics of *MMOX*'s player base and is willing to pay the developers $20,000 a month to have virtual copies of McCola products appear in it.

McCola's main competitor, Burger Up, also likes the demographics of *MMOX*'s player base. It's willing to pay a smart teenager $200 a month to spam *MMOX* with copies of Burger Up products.

What should happen here?

Sparkle, Ponies!

In a concert hall, because of the physical layout, some seats are in better positions than are others. It makes sense for the concert organizers to charge less money for those seats.

In an MMO, there are no "better" seats. Anything that can be done to improve the experience of one player can be done for all players.

In 2010, when Blizzard tested the free-to-play waters and introduced into *WoW* its celestial steed mount (nicknamed the "sparkle pony"), tens of thousands of people lined up to buy one (at $25) while stocks lasted. The fact that there was an artificially limited supply was what led to these enormous lines. Many people felt their experience would be better if they had the horse than if they didn't.

Now, Blizzard could have *given* that horse away to everyone. Would doing so have improved everyone's experience? Well no, because for some its desirability entirely depended on "I have it and you don't." Blizzard created an artificial demand; the demand then created the value.

In other words, it wasn't so much the sparkle pony *itself* that gave many of its buyers a lift; it was the mere fact that they had been able to buy one.

Of course, if you don't have $25 to spend on a virtual horse, you're not going end up with one even if its intrinsic gameplay-related qualities *would* directly improve your playing experience.

Place and Jurisdiction

If you buy an antique map from me over the phone but I fail to send you it, well, there are laws that will allow you to sue me. If we're in different countries, each country will have its own laws on the subject and there will be a legal protocol for deciding in which jurisdiction your lawsuit should be heard.

If you buy a virtual antique map from me in an MMO but I fail to send you it, could you choose to sue me in the country in which the MMO's servers are hosted? Where did the contract we made "take place"?

Integrity and Attribution

In many countries, including much of the EU, individuals have rights of *integrity* and *attribution* in their work. This means no one can take the results of your creative endeavors and use them in a way that hurts your reputation (integrity) or use your work without identifying you as its creator if you so wish (attribution). What's more, these are considered basic human rights that can't be removed. Even if you signed a contractual waiver, you can still thereafter assert your rights—the waiver is worth no more than would be a document in which you signed yourself into slavery.

This has some tricky implications for user-created content. A player may assert that although according to the EULA they don't *own* the virtual laser effect they created, they nevertheless require their name to be displayed every time it appears (which could be after it's been integrated into thousands of other effects).

Oh, and they don't want it to be used as an animation for blasters because that would imply that the player was pro-violence and impugn their honor (even years after people have used the effect to make 90 different types of blaster).

If I were a lawyer, I'd say that the way out was to declare that all objects created in a virtual world are the joint creation of the player and the developer.

However, I'm not a lawyer, so you don't get to sue me in turn if you try this and it doesn't work.

IP Example: The Dispute

JackX spends two months programming a virtual pinball for *MMOX*. He's not a great programmer, but he creates a serviceable pinball that is warmly received by *MMOX*'s players.

JillX sees the pinball and likes it. She's not as imaginative as JackX, but she's a far better programmer. Within a week, her mega-pinball hits *MMOX*. No one wants to play JackX's pinballs anymore; they only want to play JillX's. JackX feels more than a little put out.

JackX has another idea: gravity-free 3D pinballs. He doesn't want to be ripped off a second time, though. That's why he's going to patent the idea. In fact, he's so angry that he's not going to mention he has a patent on it. When JillX makes her own, he'll wait a while and then sue both her and the developers of *MMOX* for a pile of money.

What should happen here?

Does Purity Matter?

Let's say a new movie came out, and its publicists paid the developers of your favorite MMO to alter the physics such that if your character says the name of the movie, you (well, your character) will be immediately restored to full health. Would you be OK with this?

It's optional—you don't *have* to say the word if you don't want; you can get your guild healer buddy to restore you instead as usual. Plenty of other people would say it, though. Is it all still fine?

What if saying the movie name also cost you a cent, in addition to restoring your health. Would that make a difference?

Reality vs. Virtuality

When it comes to a tussle between the real and the virtual, *Reality always wins.* *Reality* can switch off virtuality; virtuality can do nothing to *Reality*.

When it comes to laws governing virtual worlds, the question isn't whether *Reality* or virtuality gets to make those laws; rather, it's how much *Reality* is willing to concede to virtuality.

Farmers

Let's say you want a Gem of Whatever. Such a magical artifact would enable you to ward off the hordes of whatever that have been plaguing you. You know that a Gem of Whatever can be obtained by killing a noble whatever. You know where noble whatevers spawn, so off you go.

When you arrive, you find the area occupied by a group of professional players (that is, they do it for money). When a noble whatever appears, these players quickly kill it (because they outnumber it). If it drops a Gem of Whatever, they loot it. Either way, they then wait for the next noble whatever to respawn.

If you want a Gem of Whatever, you're going to have to buy it from these individuals—known generically as *farmers*—for real money.

Most players don't like farmers. Most MMOs ban farming for "blocking normal play" or some such.

Some people still buy stuff off them, though. Until they don't, we'll always have farmers.

RMT

RMT is an acronym for Real Money Trading. It's used to describe the situation in which virtual goods in virtual worlds are exchanged between players for real money.

Very occasionally, RMT is condoned or even encouraged by the world's developer. This is most often the case in social worlds such as *Second Life*. However, for game worlds (that is, MMOs), it's rarely tolerated. About the only established game world that does fully embrace it is *Entropia Universe*.

It's not RMT when players buy virtual goods from the *operator* of the virtual world concerned, which is usually how free-to-play MMOs make their money. Indeed, free-to-play worlds are usually just as anti-RMT as pay-to-play worlds, if not more so. Their business depends on selling virtual items to players, which means that if players can obtain those items elsewhere for less money, it eats into their income stream. That said, some of the more disagreeable effects of RMT also show in free-to-play, so there is some overlap.

RMT is an important concept in the study of the relationship between the virtual and the real. This is because of the issues it raises that have to do with property, ownership, governance, and play, all of which could have serious repercussions if mishandled.

Personally, I have no objection to RMT when it occurs in worlds designed for it. I have very strong objections when it forces itself unwanted on a world or makes designers instigate design changes so as to minimize its impact.

Have Money, Want Money

I noticed that an extended interview in *The Escapist* with *Ultima* designer Richard Garriott includes the quote, "I buy virtual gold all the time."

Why am I *so* not surprised?

Actually, that's a legitimate question, not gratuitous sarcasm.

IP Examples Summary

The five examples of IP issues I've given may seem contrived and irrelevant, but they're not. Well, they're contrived, but they're not irrelevant. Developers routinely try to head off most of them in their EULA, but unfortunately that's not always possible.

Most industrialized countries (the United States is the main exception) are signatories to article 6bis of the Berne Convention. This gives people *moral rights* in their IP, which means that they can prevent its being used if certain conditions are met (for example, the rights of integrity and attribution I mentioned earlier). Furthermore, many countries (those in the EU are the main ones) don't allow IP rights to be signed away even if the IP holder wants to sign them away. They're covered by human rights law.

It gets worse. Many countries (again, excluding the United States) have strict laws against unfair contracts. It doesn't matter that you entered into an agreement voluntarily and that you're not dealing with a monopoly or cartel, a court can render any contract void if it doesn't like the terms. Is a fearsomely one-sided EULA really required just to let people "play a game"? All it takes is one vengeful rich person to take the matter to court and we'll find out.

So yes, these examples may seem far-fetched and unlikely to be tested in front of a judge, but the principles they embody are real. They may perhaps not be used on their own terms, but they could well be used to support more specific claims.

In particular, IP has a strong relationship to RMT.

Go Right Ahead...

I don't care if a particular MMO developer wants RMT. What I do care about is whether we all have to have RMT whether we want it or not.

Unknown Rules

How can you play a game when you don't know what the rules are?

You can do so if the rules are enforced automatically by some authority.

Why would you want to play a game when you don't know what the rules are?

Because finding out what the rules are could be *part of the game.*

Why might lawyers be interested in this?

Because if you don't know what you're agreeing to when you sign it, the terms of a contract are unenforceable. The EULA is a contract in which you agree to play by the rules of the game, except, as per what I've just mentioned, you don't know what the rules of the game *are.*

The Right to Play

Let's say I and a bunch of my friends believe, zany people that we are, that we'll have a better game experience if we play in an MMO that explicitly does *not* have player ownership of its virtual property. Shouldn't we be able to create such an MMO? Shouldn't we, as developers of that world, be able to tell people who come along with the expectation of owning property in it that, sorry, one of the conditions of playing in this world is that you give up any and all real and imagined rights to any property that may or may not exist in said world, in perpetuity? Shouldn't we be able to kick people out if they treat their character's property as if they as players own it—for example by selling it to other players for real money?

RMT is just a touchstone for any number of activities that can go on in an MMO against the wishes of the MMO's operator. If players do things that the operator doesn't want them to do, well then the operator *should* be within their rights to kick those players out. As long as "what the operator doesn't want them to do" isn't breaking any real-world laws, that ought to be just fine.

The Governing Law

The first problem lawyers have with the Internet as a whole (and MMOs in particular) is this: what is the governing law?

Suppose a player in England racially abuses a player in America while playing on servers in Canada operated by a French company. Which country's courts get to pass judgment on that player?

Commercial MMO operators define the governing law at the outset in their end-user license agreements. However, that works only for disputes between the operators and the players. It can't help with interplayer disputes because the players have signed an agreement only with the operator, not with each other.

What if the servers are distributed in the cloud across several countries and it's not even possible to determine which one hosted the part of the MMO where the offense took place?

I'd say that lawyers don't like not knowing where a case will be heard, but given that it means more work for them (and therefore more money), I nevertheless suspect they're not *entirely* upset with this kind of ambiguity.

What's Traded?

What virtual goods are traded between players for real money in MMOs?

- **Currency**: Gold pieces, platinum pieces, pyreals, credits, ...
- **Objects**: Weapons, armor, recipes, ...
- **Characters**
- **Property**: Houses, shops, building plots, ...
- **Accounts**
- **Other stuff**: Permissions, memberships, maps, ...

Of these, the main one preferred by professionals is currency. The main ones preferred by amateurs are objects and characters.

Gandalf™

Should MMOs allow characters to have names that are out of books or movies or are otherwise someone's real-world intellectual property? Other than the fact it's a sad reflection of an individual's sense of immersion to want to call their character Gandalf in an MMO set in ancient Egypt, is there any legal barrier to their doing so? Should there be?

We had a *MUD1* player who called his character Conan because it was his real name.

Attitudes to RMT

How do you regard the buying of virtual currency for real money in an MMO that bans the practice?

Some players regard it as little worse than driving 10 percent over the speed limit. Sure, if you went 50 percent over the speed limit, you'd expect to be pulled over, but at 10 percent you might feel aggrieved.

Other players regard it as driving at 10 percent over the alcohol limit. You'd expect to be punished if you drove 1 percent over the limit, let alone 10 percent.

Which are you?

Property Ladder

The notion that something virtual can't be property (by virtue of its being virtual) is no longer asserted. To be honest, it never really was debated much, as it's pretty obvious that virtual goods can be real property. What *is* still being debated is who actually *owns* that property. I may create a unique virtual snake with hooves and claim the IP, but actually it's merely one end point of a huge web of interdependent pieces of code and data, almost all of which was created by other people and took them much longer to create than it took me to build my virtual hooved snake.

That said, those other people didn't create the hardware their software runs on, either.

One in Forty

It's well known that RMT generates huge sums of money for RMT sites. What's not so well known is that these huge sums depend on something like 2.5 percent of the player base. In what follows, I'm talking about RMT in subscription-based games, not F2P games.

It's very hard to get information out of companies that sell virtual currency for real currency, but it is possible. The first set of figures I saw were from South Korea in 2004.[5] Even back then, RMT in South Korea was well established; the numbers I've seen in the intervening years have been broadly in line. It seems that RMT in a mature market has certain common characteristics.

So, in any one month, around one in five players of a subscription MMO with an RMT black economy will buy any virtual goods at all. If you look at the whole year, one in three players will engage in RMT at least once. The rest won't spend any money on RMT, ever.

Remarkably, though, if you examine how *much* money people spend, it's either nothing, fairly low (less than $100), or pretty high (more than $1,000)—with very little in between. About 25 percent of Korean players spend more than $1,000 a year buying virtual goods, with 0.25 percent spending more than $10,000. The top 2.5 percent of spenders account for *half* the overall total. That's 1 player in 40.

You can see from these figures why developers who switched from subscription to free-to-play might have done so.

For Sale

Seen on eBay, June 13, 2005, *Anarchy Online* character for sale:

> I'm selling an amazing 220 MA char on atlantean has a very good reputation and clean record has many many ingame friends

Wanna buy a friend?

---

[5]Ian MacInnes, YJ Park and Sang-Min Whang: *Virtual World Governance: Digital Item Trade and its Consequences in Korea.* Telecommunications Policy Research Conference, Arlington VA., 2004.

Marvel vs. NCSOFT

NCSOFT is the developer of the once-popular-but-now-defunct MMO *City of Heroes (CoH)*, which was set in a comic-book universe. In November 2004, NCSOFT was sued by Marvel Enterprises—owners of such iconic characters as Spider-man, Hulk, Wolverine, Thor, and Iron Man.

Marvel contended that *CoH* allowed players to create characters that were virtually identical in name, appearance, and characteristics to characters owned by Marvel (which is true, it did). In the light of this, it further claimed that NCSOFT was several kinds of liable for copyright infringement as it knowingly permitted its users to copy Marvel characters that it then reproduced. Marvel also alleged that NCSOFT benefitted from this financially.

OK, well, *CoH* undeniably had a powerful character-creation system that enabled people to create characters that looked like ones Marvel owns. Although NCSOFT did filter on exact names (you couldn't create a character called "Wolverine", for example), it's very, very hard to filter by appearance automatically. It basically has to be done manually—no small task when Marvel had more than 4,000 registered characters at the time, almost any of which could have been re-created visually in *CoH*.

Nevertheless, as a result of the suit NCSOFT did undertake such a check on all its players' creations. It found 11 violations among all the characters created by its 125,000 users—and five of those violations were created by Marvel.

The case was settled a year later, but its terms were not disclosed.

If I let you use my crayons and you draw a picture of Wolverine with them, am I liable for your copyright violation?

Right of Entry

Let's suppose I invite you to a dinner party at my house. At the appointed time, there's a knock at the door, but when I open it, a complete stranger stands there instead of you. The stranger politely informs me that you sold him your invitation and as evidence hands over the box of chocolates you were going to give me as thanks. Am I going to let that person into my house?

Well, that rather depends on how big the box of chocs is. Am I *obligated* to let them through the door, though? No, I'm not. My invitation was (implicitly, in this example) nontransferable.

Now suppose the next day two engineers from the local gas utility supplier show up and tell me there's a suspected gas leak in my street. They flash all the credentials that prove who they are. They then ask to be allowed into my house to check that this isn't where the leak is originating. I didn't invite these people, and I don't want them stomping their muddy boots all over my house—especially if I don't believe that my house has a gas leak. However, under UK law at least I do have to let them in. It may be my property, but there's a principle at work here that says everyone else's right not to have the gas main explode supersedes my right not to have uninvited gas inspectors in the house.

MMOs can put whatever arcane conditions they like on whether people enter or leave them. They can make arbitrary rules as to what people can and cannot do in them. Sometimes, though, there are greater laws that invalidate these rules.

Thus, there are two things that stop MMO developers from making up rules on a whim. First, players won't play in MMOs that have too many rules that they see as idiosyncratic. If you won't let me into your house unless I wear orange Crocs, well, maaaybe I'm not going to pay you a visit even if I possess some orange crocs (which I don't, because I possess taste).

Second, there are laws that cover what can and can't go into contracts (which for MMOs means the EULA).

If I won't let you into my house because you're Hispanic/female/Hindu/blind, then I'm breaking antidiscrimination laws; my prejudices are legislated against.

It's important to distinguish between these two situations. If I won't let you into my house unless you say "open sesame" at the front door, OK, well, you might decide to indulge me. Alternatively, you might decide it's evidence of dangerous mental instability on my part, in which case don't come in. Of course, if I have an unreasonable hatred of people unable to speak and this is some wicked scheme for preventing them from entering my abode, you may decide to report me to the police instead.

Ultimately, MMOs can make any conditions they like, arbitrary or otherwise, on allowing people access to them. Legislators, being based in the real world, can of course make whatever laws they like, arbitrary or otherwise, to govern virtual worlds. The pressing questions are: to what extent do existing laws apply to MMOs, and should new legislation be formulated for MMOs specifically?

Worth Every Penny

In the olde days, the pay-to-play MUDs were better designed, better implemented, and more fun than the free-to-play ones, which were famously "free and worth every penny." Nevertheless, the free-to-play ones ate their lunch. Too many people will take free over something twice as good that's not free.

Today, the trend is to combine free with pay-to-play in the same MMO. The gameplay loses an edge because you know that other people are buying success, but "Hey, free is free!" wins out.

This model relies for its success on the willingness of a few players to subsidize the remainder. In the long term, therefore, the aim has to be to widen participation: get players to accept microtransactions as part and parcel of the game, so it becomes the norm.

The downside, though, is that the MMO itself isn't as good. In the short term, yes, fine, you can have a lot of fun, but in the long term it's vacuous. You don't ever get to *be* someone—least of all yourself.

Save the Whales

This is how free-to-play (freemium, microtransactions) works:

- Most people play for free.

- Some people will spend a little but barely enough to cover what it costs to acquire and service them.

- A few people will pay stupid amounts of money and effectively subsidize the rest.

The people in the third group are referred to by the rather disparaging term *whales*, which came to MMOs from the gambling industry. Las Vegas survives on high-rollers, not on everyday tourist gamblers. An oil-rich sheikh or Russian oligarch who loses $20,000,000 at roulette is worth the same as 200,000 regular Joes who lose $100 each.

This doesn't mean that gambling centers don't need the low-rollers, though. They provide the context for the high-rollers. Being in a city packed full of gamblers, of whom you are at the very top of the spending league, is apparently more exciting than if you lose your $20,000,000 playing online or in someone's back room.

With MMOs, the nonspenders make the place look busy and provide the high-spenders with the context they need to give their spending meaning.

Unfortunately for Las Vegas, purpose-built resorts in the Far East are luring their whales away. There is only a fixed supply of whales, and finding and keeping them is hard.

The consensus is that F2P is very profitable. *LotRO* doubled its revenue when it switched from subscription to F2P, and this experience is not unusual. As an MMO developer, you can indeed make a lot of money this way—right now. The question is, is it sustainable in the long term?

Are there enough whales to go around in a world in which every MMO is F2P?

Time will tell.

Reality 1, Virtuality 0

Reality always wins.

All virtual worlds are embedded in *Reality* because ultimately their hardware and the players are real. However, that *doesn't* mean they are all embedded to the *same degree*. In particular, there is a definite state-change line between virtual worlds that integrate their content with the real world and those that don't.

Second Life, for example, integrates its economy into that of *Reality*. You can formally buy Linden dollars in real life and spend them in the virtual world. This makes *SL* an adjunct to *Reality*.

Lord of the Rings Online, on the other hand, does not integrate its economy into that of *Reality*. You can't formally buy *LotRO* currency any more than in a game of *Monopoly* you can buy *Monopoly* money. *LotRO* places a veil between itself and *Reality*. Lifting that veil would stop it from being the game it is.

Both these views are reasonable positions for a developer to maintain. If you, a player, want to play in a world where *Reality* intrudes, play *SL*; if you don't, try *LotRO*.

However, it's not that simple. There's a legal argument that suggests because *some* players have decided to buy and sell *LotRO* objects against the wishes of its developers, that makes *LotRO* exactly the same kind of adjunct to *Reality* as is *Second Life*.

I don't accept this view. Both *SL* and *LotRO* are pretend places, but *SL* was designed to be part of *Reality*, whereas *LotRO* was designed to be separate from *Reality*. It doesn't matter whether real-life trade in *LotRO* objects exceeds that of trade in *SL* objects. It's the *intention* that counts.

MMO operators should be the ones to decide the degree to which *Reality* intrudes because otherwise commodification can always be imposed on an MMO by a tiny minority of players against the wishes of a vast majority.

Whatever, *Reality* is going to win, so *Reality* is where the arguments must take place.

Competition Laws

Most countries have a set of *competition laws* to ensure that free trade is indeed free. They're mainly used to prevent the creation of monopolies (other than state-controlled ones) or cartels. If a company has an overly dominant position in an industry, then should it abuse this, it can expect a court summons.

MMO developers have an overly dominant position in their MMOs. Do they abuse it? Well, to do so they'd have to be in competition with other legitimate traders in the market they control. Thanks to the EULA, most gold farmers and the like don't qualify as legitimate traders, so they don't count.

What about crafters, though?

Well, crafters make stuff in the game world (with the permission of the developer) that they sell to other players. There's competition from the developer in the sense that similar items may be dropped by mobs, but these are part of the game world, and the developer doesn't make any money from them.

What about objects bought using real money in a free-to-play environment, though? Here, the developer is directly competing with the crafting players for other players' money. OK, so the traders aren't able to sell goods for *real* money, but if there's an equivalence with real-money (through an exchange system such as *EVE Online*'s PLEX or *WildStar*'s C.R.E.D.D.), then it's effectively the same thing. It's pretty obvious that the developers are going to rule this market rather than the crafters, though.

Players used to argue against this kind of monopolistic practice by appealing to unfairness. Crafters have to spend ages collecting resources and making things, but the developer can undercut them with better gear in an instant. Unhappily for crafters, though, this argument didn't really carry much weight with non-crafters. Do you buy handmade furniture or mass-produced furniture? Do you buy bespoke automobiles or ones made by vast robotic assembly lines? Do you buy paper lovingly pressed from wood pulp by your friendly local paper-maker or stuff that comes from a factory where they put trees in one end and paper comes out of the other? Just because someone wants to sell something they spent hours making, that doesn't mean they have a right to stop someone else selling something similar they can make in the blink of an eye.

Competition laws offer another way to rein in developers, though. The Magic Circle may protect play within the game world, but if real-world money is involved, then the boundary becomes weaker.

EVE Online doesn't sell players anything for money that the players can craft in-world. *WildStar* has its crafted goods often be best-in-slot, so no problem there, either. The more that the real comes into the virtual, however, the more the virtual has to play by the real's rules. The challenge to developers is to shape government policy such that if and when real-world rules are brought to bear on MMOs, they're the *right* rules.

Silly Marvel?

If Marvel had won its *City of Heroes* lawsuit against NCSOFT instead of settling out of court, this would have meant that NCSOFT would have had to have checked out every new player-created character to make sure that it didn't resemble too much any of the 4,000 belonging to Marvel.

Hmm. Wouldn't it *also* have meant that every new character Marvel created would have to be checked out to make sure it didn't resemble too much any of those belonging to NCSOFT?

At the time Marvel sued NCSOFT, *City of Heroes* had 125,000 accounts, each capable of holding 8 characters. When NCSOFT looked through them to see whether any matched Marvel's character inventory, it took them ages. Marvel would have to repeat that for every new character its own artists created or face a countersuit.

It's perhaps just as well they *did* settle before a judge got to rule on it.

Basic Question

If you want to stop RMT and other game-busting activities, the basic question is, how much are you prepared to screw up the gameplay so as to prevent a few people from screwing it up even more?

Actually, that's not the most basic question. More basic than that is, why should you have to screw up the gameplay *at all*?

Early RMT

Real-money trading was highly uncommon in *MUD1*. Because its world reset periodically, there was no point in buying objects; possession of them wouldn't survive the reset. There were occasional offers of payments for services—"I'll buy you a pint if you help me kill him"—but nothing really notable.

I know of only one case where someone bought a wizard character, and we'd been running *MUD1* for a decade by then. It was only a half-assed thing. The buyer wanted a wiz, and the seller was about to lose his modem or computer or whatever, so he sold it; both players knew it would be only a matter of time before what had transpired would be detected and the character would be zapped to oblivion, which sure enough it was.

The first sales-for-real-money I know for sure occurred were in the Second Age game *Shades*. When the story broke, it caused something of a scandal. Again, it involved character sales rather than object sales. Later, an "I will play your character to wizard level" scheme was set up, as an attempt by kids to get someone else to pay for their play; some people did take them up on the offer, though, so it wasn't entirely a flop. I'd guess this would be about 1987, plus or minus a year.

This kind of activity wasn't at all rife back then. Even twinking wasn't rife because the wizzes would jump on anyone whom they suspected of doing it. In those days, there was a much higher admin/player ratio than is possible in today's vast worlds, so we could ensure that players didn't do anything that we felt sullied "the game." It was important that the only people who reached wiz level were those who deserved to be wizzes, and wizzes were therefore jealous of their status. If they saw someone cheating (and anything like this *would* have been regarded as cheating), then they were swift to act.

Most virtual worlds of that era had similar attitudes; as far as I know, only *Shades* had what we'd now call RMT incidents, and although some must have gone on in secret elsewhere, it couldn't have been anywhere near the levels we see today in even the cleanest large-scale commercial worlds. It was harder for people to find a marketplace in those days, which might have been a factor; *Shades* had tens of thousands of players, so I don't think there was a critical mass issue. The dearth of RMT was probably more to do with the way these worlds were designed, coupled with the amount of policing that went on. *Island of Kesmai*, which did allow for some objects to be kept with characters, intermittently had to battle rumors that some people had got their gear less than honestly.

When professional RMT finally became a reality, I was disappointed more than surprised. I knew it *could* happen, I'd hoped it *wouldn't* happen, and I'd hoped that the developers would have put up a more spirited defense. It wasn't to be, though. A precedent was set, and now we're all having to live with it whether we want to or not.

Perhaps unsurprisingly, the *very* earliest occasions where people power-leveled other players' characters were not about money at all. Male players did it for (people they believed were, on occasion correctly) female players, in the hope or expectation of establishing some kind of emotional or physical relationship.

What they say about "the world's oldest profession"—it's the virtual world's too.

The Beautiful Woman Analogy

Suppose you're a beautiful young woman (or, if you actually are one, don't suppose). An immensely rich but married man finds you attractive. You both fall in love, he divorces his wife, and he marries you instead.

A year later you see him eyeing up a beautiful younger woman. Is he the kind of person who is likely to stay with you, or will he dump you to marry her instead?

If you're the developer of a new MMO, trying to recruit your whales from existing MMOs, this beautiful young woman is *you*.

Take Aim

Why did Marvel sue NCSOFT?

Maybe because *Second Life* developer Linden Lab had less money than NCSOFT?

Farming Strategies

Here are the main ways (in order of profitability) that gold farmers make money:

- **Traditional farming**: Whereby you camp a spot until a rare monster with a rare item that everyone needs spawns, and then you kill it and sell what it drops. This makes money if you have a monopoly, but it's easy to design around so doesn't feature much nowadays.

- **Macroing**: Whereby you get a computer to repeat a mindless task indefinitely and exploit a resource that drops at a fixed rate. If you have several computers, this can provide a decent, steady income stream.

- **Intensive play**: Whereby you identify high-return activities in the game and play through them for hours every day. This requires you to pay people to play, but in a low-wage economy this can still be a money-spinner.

- **Chaperoning**: Whereby someone pays your team to take them through some difficult instance so they can get the rare, bind-on-pickup drop at the end. This isn't all that common because the demand isn't very high; it's easy for intensive-play farmers to arrange, though, especially if they were running that instance for profit anyway.

- **Leveling up**: The step beyond chaperoning, whereby someone pays you to play their character for them, the aim being to get it to the endgame without the player's having to bother with the leveling game.

- **Refitting**: Whereby you (let's be generous and say) buy a character from a regular player and resell its equipment at more than you paid for it.

In general, farmers make money from getting people to pay to avoid having to play; on the face of it, this is rather an odd concept for something sold as being a game.

Rules as Laws

MMOs have two kinds of rules (both of which can accurately be called laws). Some rules are coded in and make up the MMO's physics; these are laws as in "laws of nature." Other rules are not coded in and make up the MMO's rules of behavior; these are laws as in "laws of the land."

An MMO's physics may well "allow" RMT and twinking, but this doesn't prevent its behavioral rules from prohibiting one or both. Yes, designers *could* change the physics to disallow RMT, but that action would almost inevitably also prevent some other activities that the designers see as important. Instead, therefore, they keep the physics as it is but ban the practice of RMT.

When people sign up to a game, they not unreasonably expect that everyone will play by the rules. These rules are not limited to what an implementation "allows" (its laws of nature); they also include the MMO's behavioral rules (its laws of the land).

If the rules of the MMO forbid practices you think should be allowed, then rather than do them anyway, you *shouldn't play the game.*

Likewise, if the rules of the MMO allow practices you think should be forbidden, then rather than complain about the situation, you simply *shouldn't play the game.*

An Unequal Relationship

I don't expect MMO designers to start claiming they know about the law because obviously few have been to law school so they're easy to expose as know-nothings.

However, I can envisage lawyers—especially those who may have played an MMO for a couple of years—coming to believe they know everything important about MMO design.

Should they do so, expect problems.

Why Should I Have to Do That?

I can stop RMT by making compromises to an MMO's design, but why should I have to do that? Really, *why should I have to do that?*

If I make a game explicitly for players who *don't* like RMT, this won't stop RMTers from showing up and spoiling the game for them. If I *can* stop this by changing the game design, that may or may not also spoil the game; even if it doesn't, though, why should I have to do that?

I don't care if RMTers turn up in their millions. Why should *I* have to change the design of *my* MMO to stop people whom I don't want to play it from playing it? *Why should I have to do that?*

Wages

The consensus explanation that has evolved to explain why people engage in RMT in MMOs where the practice is banned is that they tend to be high-wage earners for whom time is money.

This is about as valid as the explanations given by people who play characters of a different gender. It sounds plausible and supports the actions of the people who do it, but it doesn't stand up under closer inspection.

Being a high-wage earner *doesn't* mean you spend more time working than does a low-wage earner; it means you get *paid* more than does a low-wage earner. A high-wage earner has just as much time to spend playing as a low-wage earner and may indeed have more.

Merely having developed an excuse to explain away your cheating doesn't mean it's no longer cheating.

Law Is Code

The rules of regular computer games are defined in code. If the game lets you do it, you can do it; if it doesn't, you can't. Want to fireball members of your party? Go ahead. Want to drive the wrong way round a racing circuit? If it lets you, sure, why not?

The physics of MMOs are also defined in code, but there are other rules beyond this that can't be coded: no profanity, no hate speech, no botting, no farming, no whatever else takes the developer's fancy. These rules *are* defined, but in the EULA, not in the code.

Now because a EULA's rules don't feel as if they're "part of the game," some players feel at liberty to disregard them. The typical response to a violation is, "Hey, the program *let* me do it. If you didn't want me to do it, you should have coded it out."

Hmm... So, let's take this "the only rules are those in code" argument to its logical conclusion and drop all EULA references to in-world activities. If the MMO lets you do it, you *really can do it*. Swear your head off if you like—the code lets you, so it's OK. Spam players with the URLs to Nazi web sites and macro to your heart's content. If the only rules you have to obey are those enforced by program code, what's to stop you?

Here's what.

The designers can specify that the code contains special commands that only certain privileged character classes can use. Let's call these character classes "admins" and make them available only to people on the payroll. The commands are like very powerful spells; let's call the most powerful of them FOD ("finger of death"). If an admin FODs a character, that character is permanently dead, and all their kit is garbage-collected.

So, now when you call some player a cucking funt, FOD! You're evaporated. "But the code *let* me do it!" you wail. "Yes," replies the all-seeing admin, "and the same code *let* me FOD you."

What would RL law have to say about that, I wonder?

It didn't say anything when we did exactly this in *MUD1*.

The Amalfi Coast Drive

The Amalfi Coast of Italy is famously beautiful for its spectacular scenery and cling-to-the-cliffs villages. The drive along its twisty, turny road continually reveals one amazing panorama after another.

This makes the drive popular—so popular, in fact, that during high summer you can find yourself stuck in traffic and barely moving. You get hot, you get bothered, and your kids get fractious.

Then, you see it: a roadside cafe advertising drinks and ice cream! Salvation! There's nowhere to park, but all you have to do is pull over and you're saved.

The cars behind you can't get past until there's a gap in the oncoming traffic. The oncoming traffic doesn't have many gaps. Sometimes, an oncoming car stops because the driver wants to get to the same roadside cafe and is waiting for a gap in your side's traffic.

You spend a minute buying your drinks and ice cream and then head off again. The traffic is more free-flowing now; it must have been that you set off at a bad time when the roads were at their busiest.

Well, no.

The reason for the queues is because of the cafe. People are blocking the road to buy drinks and ice cream that they want because of the queues, yet in so doing they're causing those very queues to build up. If there were no cafe there, there wouldn't be any queues, so there wouldn't need to be a cafe there. The cafe causes the very problem that justifies its existence!

This phenomenon will seem eerily familiar to any MMO player who can't get the rare drop they want because farmers are farming the mob that drops it. The shortage is entirely artificial. The farmers are causing the very problem that justifies their existence.

An Industry-Standard EULA

Every MMO provider these days has an end-user license agreement in place. These are all worded quite differently. Wouldn't it make sense if they were all the same?

It would if all the MMOs were the same, but they're not.

I was once approached by an organization of indie developers hoping to create a common EULA. Unlike typical EULAs, theirs had lots of player-friendly clauses, and its creators were justly proud of it.

I think they were a little taken aback when I told them I couldn't endorse it.

See, some things work for some MMOs but not for others. This particular EULA was strong on fairness, which is good, but it took this to a point beyond where many (but not all) developers would be happy. It was heavily in favor of allowing players to buy things from one another using real-world currency, for example. That would suit some developers, but not the majority.

EULAs didn't exist back in the days of textual worlds, mainly because they were free (and genuinely so, not free-to-play's idea of free). The online services that hosted virtual worlds—CompuServe, Genie, and the like—did have them, as they wanted to protect themselves from user misbehavior. When MMOs broke free of these online services, the EULA came with them.

Not the *same* EULA, though.

"You Could Reduce RMT If You..."

I don't care; I'm not going to do it. Why should designers compromise their design just because some people won't play by the rules? We don't change the rules of professional sports when people don't play by the rules; why should we change MMOs when people don't play by the rules?

Love and Money

MMO developers routinely ban players who RMT but not those few who twink. Why?

Some players use love to buy them money. They do things then expect a reward.

Some players use money to buy them love. They reward people and expect them to do things.

Ideally, we should have neither of these in an MMO, but we can't hurt the first one because we can't tell love from altruism. We *can* hurt the second one, so that's what we do.

Blunt Instrument

Laws are something of a blunt instrument when it comes to MMOs. For almost every law or general principle you want to suggest, an MMO can be created that rejects it for a legitimate reason. Earnest arguments over character ownership are completely academic in a world with permadeath, for example. If you were to formulate laws to govern MMO designs, you'd almost certainly prohibit some activity that in a different MMO would be perfectly acceptable.

Consider whether it would be a good idea to pass a law preventing in-game theft. Theft is forbidden in the real world, so why not in games? Well, the answer is that it could be part of the game. If you knew in-game stealing could happen when you signed up to play, you can't complain when it thereupon happens and someone steals the $300 hat you bought on eBay.

It's like complaining that you paid $30,000,000 to own the world record for the high jump. You know that someone is going to jump higher sooner or later and "steal" it from you, and you can't use the law to get it back ("Hey, that's mine, I paid for it!").

There's also the little matter that it's not something that can necessarily be "bought" anyway.

IP and RMT

IP was the first real weapon used by MMO operators to try to stop RMT. If commodifiers don't own what they're trying to sell, how can they possibly sell it? As an argument, it was credible enough that Sony managed to wield it to persuade eBay to remove *EverQuest* character sales from its service.

Of course, asserting that IP subsists in virtual objects is a double-edged sword. It implies that copyright subsists in virtual objects independently of the MMO as a whole. Sony *could* have argued that the virtual objects being offered for sale were an intrinsic part of *EQ* and that teasing them out of the code was impossible, but its lawyers chose not to take that line.

The strongest response to this we-own-the-IP argument was "No you don't. I own it because I made it," which remains something of a running sore in MMO lawyer circles.

A second strong response was to consider that even if the developer *does* own the IP, that doesn't mean the developer can stop people from selling it on. After all, the author of a book owns the IP in that book, but the author can't stop me selling it to you once I've read it. The US is particularly big on this *first sale doctrine*, which is why so many pieces of software these days are formally rented rather than sold (not that this would necessarily withstand a determined legal assault either).

At the moment, IP laws don't cover MMOs very well at all. In particular, they state that copyright subsists in only certain specific types of created content, none of which are an obvious fit for MMOs. They're not software *per se*; they're the result of executing software. They're not databases; they're ever-changing entries in databases. They are computer-generated, but is the author the person who wrote the generating software or the person who used it?

It's unlikely that you're going to fall foul of any MMO IP issues yourself, but that doesn't mean they're not there. They *are* there, waiting, until one day...

I Own It Because I Bought it

There are five principal arguments used by MMO players to justify why they *really do* own "their" virtual objects. I've alluded to one already, but I'll explain them all in more detail.

The first is the simplest: when you buy something, you own it. If I paid you $100 for your MMO account, that makes it mine.

Well, it makes it mine only if it was yours to sell. In most MMOs, it isn't. Accounts belong to the operator. You couldn't sell your real-life bank account to anyone else, and you can't sell your MMO account to anyone else, either.

There is actually an ingenious counter to this. If you buy something in good faith, this can make a difference. In Japan, for example, if you buy something that has been stolen but you don't know it's stolen and no reasonable person would have had cause to suspect it was stolen, then after two years you get to own it even if the original owner shows up sobbing on your doorstep.

You could, therefore, argue that if you didn't know that the person selling you the account wasn't allowed to, then unless the MMO operator tells you off in time, you'll get to keep it.

It's optimistic to believe that this would be accepted in a court of law, though, even in countries where such an argument might hold sway. The reason is that right at the start you accepted a EULA that said you knew accounts were the property of the MMO's operator.

Nice try.

What's the Difference?

"I have a job. I can't progress in my MMO of choice as fast as people who play it all the time. I should be able to spend some of my reward for working on advancing my MMO character if I so want."

"I play an MMO; I can't progress in my job of choice as fast as people who work all the time. I should be able to spend some of my reward for playing on advancing my career if I so want."

Neither Here nor There

Why shouldn't real-money trading always be allowed in MMOs in which it is possible?

Here's the argument that explains why:

- Some people, for whatever reasons, do not like MMOs that have RMT.

- These people have as much right to play MMOs as anyone else.

- If these people want to play an MMO with no RMT, they should be allowed to do so.

- Just because an MMO's design makes RMT *possible*, this does not mean that RMT *has* to be allowed.

- There should therefore be some MMOs in existence that are not intended for RMT and that should not have to be redesigned to prevent RMT.

In other words, if there are people who don't *want* to play MMOs with RMT, they should be able to go to some MMO that *doesn't have RMT*. The fact that RMT may not be prevented by this other MMO's design is neither here nor there. The same applies to any other aspect of MMO player behavior.

Busy-Person Jason

Jason and the Argonauts set sail to find the golden fleece.

Except, well, Jason is a busy person, he has a wife and kids, he has to work, he doesn't want to spend all that time building a boat and sailing to the ends of the Earth. Come on, Zeus, give the guy a break! Teleport him to the hydra, let him kill it, resurrect him if he doesn't manage it first time, and then give him the damned fleece so we can call him a hero. Look, he'll even pay you for it!

Maybe he should just send Hercules to get it and then buy it off him when he gets back?

Bragg vs. Linden Lab

In 2006, Marc Bragg took Linden Lab (the makers of *Second Life*) to court after they closed his account following his use of an exploit to acquire virtual property at a discount price (basically by buying it before it had officially come to market). The case was settled out of court, but before that happened two significant legal points were established.

The first point was that *SL*'s terms of service included a *mandatory arbitration* clause that the judge struck down. The intended effect of the clause was to make people who had a complaint against Linden Lab go to arbitration before going to court. The judge ruled that Linden Lab's terms of service amounted to a *contract of adhesion*, meaning they were presented on a take-it-or-leave-it basis. Contracts of adhesion are not smiled upon by the law, especially with regard to how they deal with the law itself. Although the particular clause that Linden Lab was invoking wasn't itself adhesive, the fact that the rest of the terms of service *were* adhesive meant that the judge ruled it unenforceable.

What this seems to imply is that the clauses MMO operators routinely put in their EULAs are not bullet-proof. That's scary stuff for said MMO operators.

The second point that this case established had to do with the governing law. Bragg also named Linden Lab's founder, Philip Rosedale, in his law suit. Because the suit was filed in Pennsylvania, outside of where Rosedale lived and worked (California), he disputed its jurisdiction. If he wasn't in Pennsylvania, how could he be breaking its local laws? The court did remove the hearing to federal level but noted that Rosedale and Bragg had met in avatar form in *Second Life* and that this (along with his publicity efforts for *SL*) did constitute enough of a contact for Rosedale to be considered subject to Pennsylvania's courts.

So, just because a person has never been to real-world jurisdiction X, that doesn't mean they can't feel the full force of its laws if they have in-MMO contact with someone who lives in jurisdiction X and wants to sue them.

That's scary stuff, too.

Objects and Data

For law-making purposes, it's pointless trying to say anything specific about virtual objects.

The world of an MMO is defined exactly by the game engine. This program defines entirely what the MMO's world *is*. Whatever the program does—arbitrary, planned, deliberate, accidental—is therefore precisely what you're contracting for access to: you gain the right to influence the program's manipulation of its data under the parameters of its current construction.

Associating some of this collection of data with "characters" or "objects" or "mobiles" for descriptive reasons is fair enough; making laws as if these were real characters, real objects, and real creatures is not. Their state of existence is determined *only* by the machinations of the game engine. Different games have different machinations, and it is a grave mistake to extrapolate from a handful of games legal principles that will then be applied indefinitely to all of them.

Just because one bunch of people thinks the kind of virtual world that they play in would benefit from externally imposed regulations about "property rights" (or anything else), that doesn't mean the worlds played by other people would. Indeed, the very concept could kill some worlds stone dead.

Goods or Services?

Trade in virtual objects can easily be couched in terms of services rather than goods. I'm not buying ownership of a virtual sword from you; I'm paying you to have your character transfer the object from your character's inventory into my character's inventory. The sword can still belong to the game's developer in this situation, throughout the entire transaction. The players merely call it "buying" an object as a shorthand for "paying you to transfer it to my inventory."

It's a bit trickier applying this argument to "sales" of virtual characters, but for objects it's worryingly reasonable.

Blizzard vs. MDY

In 2006, Blizzard sued MDY Industries over a program they were selling called *WoWGlider*. *WoWGlider* was a bot that used scripts to enable the user to undertake repetitive tasks in *World of Warcraft* automatically while not actually sitting at the keyboard. It was generally used for farming and leveling up characters.

Blizzard won the resulting legal battle four years later. The court agreed that users were licensees of Blizzard's software, not owners, and reversed an earlier ruling to confirm that although MDY Industries was in breach of Blizzard's EULA, it wasn't violating its copyright; nevertheless, *WoWGlider* was considered to be in violation of the Digital Millennium Copyright Act.

As a nonlawyer, it's amusing to observe that a program can violate a copyright act without violating copyright. I'm sure it makes perfect sense to those who are lawyers, though.

I was glad that Blizzard managed to prevent a third party from spoiling *WoW* but somewhat alarmed at the way they bent intellectual property legislation to do it. None of the reasons that copyright laws were created apply to this interpretation of them; they were being used for a purpose for which they weren't designed. If Blizzard were to find an exploit like this in *WoW*, they'd fix it and ban the exploiters. Real-world laws work rather differently to EULA provisions, though, so Blizzard wasn't going to be banned from the courts for their creative use of the law.

As a general point, it's my belief that if Blizzard or any other MMO operator wants to prevent people from selling software that's particularly intended to be used to help players of their MMO cheat, then yes, they should be able to do that. Whatever law, present or future, they need to bring to bear in order to achieve this end, though, one to do with copyright isn't it.

The Famous Mr. Qiu

In 2005, Zhu Caoyuan of Shanghai, a player of the MMO *Legend of Mir 3*, borrowed the account of his friend, Qiu Chengwei. One of Mr. Qiu's characters had a rare Dragon Sabre sword. Mr. Zhu sold it for 7,200 yuan. Upon learning this, Mr. Qiu lost his temper and stabbed Mr. Zhu to death.

Although Mr. Qiu was guilty of the fairly traditional crime of murder, this story was reported in the West only because of the virtual property aspect. There were no laws in China governing virtual property, so the police couldn't do anything to return the Dragon Sabre to Mr. Qiu. Mr. Zhu did apparently offer to give him the money he got for it, but Mr. Qiu wanted his Dragon Sabre back.

It was widely reported that Mr. Qiu was given a life sentence, although technically it was a suspended death sentence (which sounds like a polite way of saying "we are going to hang you" but isn't).

Reading the EULA

If you bought a used MMO account from me for real money, you could legitimately claim that you didn't know it wasn't allowed so you shouldn't be banned over it. After all, how could you possibly have agreed not to buy it when you didn't get the chance to click through the EULA until after you'd bought it? Sure, *I* could be banned, but I wouldn't care because I'd have only just sold my account to you and would not be planning on playing ever again anyway.

Oh, and if you sell it on without having installed it, again, you're still not breaking the terms of the EULA because you still haven't signed it.

All the owners of RMT companies that I've spoken to are scrupulous about never personally having clicked through any MMO EULA, ever. No one can enforce on you the terms of a contract that you haven't signed.

RMT Spectrum

The full set of partitions for RMT seems to be as follows:

- **Laissez-faire**: Anyone can create and sell virtual goods and services to anyone else for real money or convertible game currency. Example: *Second Life*.

- **Edited**: Anyone can sell virtual goods and services, but creation has to be approved. Example: *There*, iPhone apps.

- **Player RMT**: Players sell goods and services to one another, but they can't create new out-of-context saleable content. This may or may not be sanctioned by the developer. Example: *Puzzle Pirates.*

- **Developer RMT, tangible**: Developers sell to players goods and services that have actual gameplay impact. This may work alongside player RMT (example: most Far Eastern MMOs), or it may not (example: *Runequest*). This is essentially the pay-to-win variety of F2P.

- **Developer RMT, intangible**: Developers sell to players goods and services that have insignificant gameplay impact. Example: realm transfers, WoW's sparkle pony. Player RMT in these goods may or may not be possible (example: going to the convention gives you a unique code for an in-game item and you sell that code). This is the cosmetic-only variety of F2P.

- **No RMT**: Any RMT that does go on constitutes a black market. Players otherwise trade only using in-context game currency.

You can go into more detail if you like, for example making a distinction between selling direct advantages (kick-ass sword) and indirect advantages (extra time before your buffs expire), but this list basically covers the spectrum.

I Own It Because I Stole it

The second justification people use for asserting ownership of "their" virtual goods is the argument used by squatters. If I take *adverse possession* of something for a sufficient period, it becomes mine.

OK, so there are some conditions that have to do with how long I've had it since the real owner last told me it was theirs and whether I've made use of what I took, but the basic principle remains: if I take it and the MMO's operators don't ask for it back, I get to keep it.

This argument falls down because I don't have adverse possession in the first place. Subscription games in particular can argue that I'm paying a rent for access to the goods, but even nonsubscription games can reasonably say that when I log off they repossess all their stuff until I log back in again.

There are some other arguments that don't involve any initial theft, for example right-to-buy property laws. These could prove more persuasive to a judge, but they tend to involve decades of renting before their provisions come into effect.

So again, nice try, but you never *really* thought it would work.

Useless EULA

I spoke to the head of Internet Gaming Entertainment (IGE) at a time when it was the largest RMT operation in the West. He told me that IGE wasn't breaking any end-user license provisions because neither he nor any of his employees had ever signed a EULA. IGE's business was to provide a service by which people who *had* signed a EULA could violate it. X has virtual gold, and Y has real dollars: IGE takes Y's dollars and gives it to X when X has delivered the gold. IGE never touches the gold, just the dollars.

Assuming he was telling the truth, it doesn't matter what draconian clauses an MMO developer puts in the EULA, they're not going to apply to the middlemen who make money from facilitating the breaking of those clauses.

IGE later went on to become the largest RMT operation in the world but lost this crown following several unseemly boardroom spats and strong competition in the Far East.

It's a Steal

What does it mean when someone "steals" something in an MMO? Is it always, sometimes, or never a real-world criminal act? What should MMO developers be obliged to do in response to such a "theft"?

Well, it depends what you mean by "theft." There are different definitions in common currency, the most prevalent of which can be summarized as follows:

- **In-context steal**: A character obeying the rules of the MMO appropriates an object that was in the possession of some other character in that MMO. Even if a court were to insist that the "stolen" object be merely returned, it would have a devastating effect on MMO design. If the "thief" risked jail, it would be The End.

- **In-context but buggy steal**: The character operated within the physics of the MMO but did something that the designers hadn't foreseen—and that now they have seen it, they regard as a bug. Here, we have a genuine dispute that may result in compensation for one party or the other. If a court were to be brought in to rule on such an incident, it would effectively be overriding the authority that MMO operators currently have to deal with these situations independently (that is, it would stomp on the EULA). This would make operating an MMO difficult for the developers, and many more disputes would go to court.

- **Fraud**: A player gets another player to hand them something for a promised reward (real-world or otherwise) that never materializes. Here, the MMO operator would probably not want to intervene, believing it to be the player's fault they were suckered. This is especially likely to be true if the fraud took place concerning an activity of which the developers didn't approve (such as RMT). I don't think they'd necessarily care if a court ordered them to transfer "ownership" back, so long as the onus wasn't put on them to resolve these disputes themselves in future. However, if fraud is regarded as "part of the game" (as it is with *EVE Online*), then even a court may decide to let such a "theft" pass.

- **Out-of-context but buggy steal**: Here, some player exploits a security loophole to gain the ability to change the database in ways they're not supposed to (for example, they hack an account). I'd expect the MMO operator to jump on the hacker and undo all their misdeeds if this were discovered, as it's relatively easy to show that the design of the MMO wasn't "intended" to allow such things to happen and the hacker can't claim to be "playing by the rules." The developers could probably take the hacker to court in the real world over it if they felt so inclined, too, under general computer-misuse legislation.

- **Real-world theft**: Someone breaks into your house, steals your computer, logs into it, and transfers a bunch of things from one character to another. This is like the previous example, but the involvement of real-world courts would be inevitable because there was real-world property theft. The courts could reasonably ask that everything done while the computer was stolen be undone as much as possible. I don't think they could reasonably ask that the virtual world developer offer any additional compensation to the victim, though.

Tempted though you may be to dismiss these cases as never-going-to-happens, actually they all have. So far, the courts have been interested in only the last three, but there have been isolated cases that referred to the first two. For example, recall the player who exploited a bug in *Second Life* to buy in-world land before it was officially released for auction, who then sued Linden Lab when they took it off him.

Also, remember that although *you* think it's obvious what the "right" way to deal with these cases is, that doesn't mean a judge looking at an actual example of it would necessarily agree.

Not So Futile

People who complain that legislating against RMT is futile because you can't dictate the behavior of MMO players would do well to bear in mind the fact that it's only legislation that's stopping MMO *developers* from doing whatever the hell they like to players of their MMO and "their" virtual goods.

FOD

MUD1 did have a Finger of Death spell: FOD (pronounced to rhyme with "nod"). The full "finger of death" form was never used except to explain what the initials FOD stood for. It was possible for high-level players to cast it, but as the consequences of failure were that you got FODded yourself (in a world with permadeath), they tended to use it sparingly. Naturally, admin-level characters (*wizzes*) cast it with impunity. The spell name was often, er, spelled in lowercase, but in threats the uppercase version was preferred because it struck more dread into the heart of a potential victim.

FOD is the archetypal example of a *real-world extensible* term, meaning that it can be a handy addition to your vocabulary outside the game world. In FOD's case, it can easily be applied to any act of deliberate destruction (although it seems especially suited to tech-specific ones such as killing queued printer jobs).

The name came from the fifth-level anti-clerical Finger of Death spell in the original *Dungeons & Dragons* rules, which became a seventh-level druidical spell in *Advanced Dungeons & Dragons* and a seventh-level wizard spell in *Advanced Dungeons & Dragons, 2nd Edition*. For the *3rd Edition*, it was both an eighth-level druidical spell and a seventh-level wizard/sorcerer spell. In the *5th Edition*, it's a seventh-level wizard spell.

Gawd knows if it was in *D&D 4th Edition*. I looked at the rules, figured that if I wanted to play an MMO, I'd play an MMO, and left it at that.

Webzen vs. Itembay

In 2003, Webzen, the developer of Korean MMO *MU Online*, tried to take out an injunction against Korea's largest virtual goods site, Itembay. It failed because the judge ruled that Itembay was an intermediary. None of its agents had played *MU Online*, so as a company it hadn't signed the EULA.

Some of the hypothetical examples I give when I talk about MMOs and the law may sound far-fetched, but that doesn't mean they can't actually happen.

Object Representation

In most MMOs, you can't point to a set of bits in server memory and say that these are the ones that represent your character's virtual boots. Because of the way object-oriented programming works, the actual bits that represent what you are interpreting as your character's boots could be spread throughout a database. It's like trying to capture a rainbow: the air through which the rainbow passes changes the whole time; you merely perceive it as a stationary structure. So it is with virtual items. What you construe to be your character's boots is actually a sea of bits, some of which are part of other characters' boots too.

When people speak of "owning" virtual objects, what *are* these virtual objects?

Buying Success

If I wanted to practice Law in Louisiana, could I just go to some Louisiana lawyer on the point of retiring and buy their license to practice Law in Louisiana? No, I couldn't. All those Louisiana lawyers who had been through law school and took examinations to get where they are wouldn't stand for it.

Many players of MMOs want to feel they have achieved something. Their achievement is predicated on a belief that what they are achieving is indeed an achievement. They need to have their achievement validated by others, and they need to validate it themselves. They can't do either if there are people who can simply buy achievement off the peg.

If it's OK for the State of Louisiana to stop people buying a license to practice law, it should also be OK for MMO developers to stop people from buying MMO characters.

Of course, if they don't *want* to stop it, that should be OK, too.

A EULAless World

EULAs are generally good from the point of view of setting out the ground rules for MMOs. If you tell players in your EULA how you'll use your god-like powers, they'll know what to expect and where the boundaries are. Furthermore, they can hold you to these in a court of law.

Suppose, though, that a court struck down the EULA. This could happen— EULAs haven't ever been fully put to the test, and there is some suspicion that they could count as contracts of adhesion (meaning that the law wouldn't uphold them at all, at least in the United States).

Hmm. So, could a court strike down, say, a FOD executed from within an MMO? If FODs are coded into the game, then they're just as much part of the game's "rules" as fireballs. Striking them down would mean the court was changing the rules of the game. So, suddenly the court has game design skills?

These are fairly uncharted waters, particularly since the "rules" embodied in a piece of code are so complex that even the programmers can't be expected to spot every conceivable interaction between objects. Courts have occasionally changed written rules (for example, a *Golf* competition had a rule stating that people had to walk between holes, which was judged unfair on people who could hit a ball with a stick but couldn't walk long distances); however, could a court insist that a rule embodied in program code was rewritten? If so, how would the judge know that the rewritten code now did what it was ordered to do? Courts have QA skills, too?

The developer, by producing a EULA, is saying, "Look, I can do whatever the hell I want here as it's me who makes the rules, but because I don't want you to think I'm a crazy person who will act arbitrarily and inconsistently, here are the boundaries of the behavior I'll accept from you. Look at these limits, and decide whether you want to play or not."

I hope that the EULA as a general concept won't be struck down, but if it is, well, we can always go back to the old days when EULAs weren't a thing and developers did indeed do whatever the hell they wanted. It would be worse for the players, but since when have courts ever considered that the judgments they make could harm the very people they are trying to protect?

Neither There nor Here

Suppose someone wants to play a particular MMO but it's anti-RMT and they're pro-RMT. Isn't that unfair?

Well, from the point of view of the RMTer, yes, it is unfair—although from the point of view of many of the MMO's non-RMT players, allowing RMT into the game would be unfair on them.

Still, there's an obvious solution here: have one version of the MMO that doesn't allow RMT and one that does. Then, the pro-RMTers could all go to the pro-RMT server, and the anti-RMTers could all go to the anti-RMT server. Those who have a disinterest can play either. That would work, wouldn't it?

Sadly, it wouldn't. The reason is that despite their protestations, for many people the very reason they RMT is that *other people don't*. They RMT to get an advantage. They're not attracted to an MMO in which everyone can RMT; they're attracted to one in which *they* can RMT but everyone else *can't*.

There aren't three cases, there are four.

- People who don't want RMT
- People who don't mind either way
- People who do want RMT
- People who do want RMT, but only when most other people don't want RMT or don't care

So, even if you do set up separate, RMT-friendly servers, that alone won't stop RMT on the RMT-unfriendly servers because the very fact that most people there won't be engaging in RMT is what appeals to some RMTers.

Note that I said "that alone" there.

Supply and Demand

One of the explanations given to explain why RMT should be allowed is that there's a demand for it.

Huh, well, there's a demand for MMOs where buying stuff with real money is *not* tolerated. Shouldn't this demand be given some supply?

Free Not to Play Free-to-Play

The current, Sixth Age of MMOs is dominated by microtransactions, or *free-to-play* as the revenue model is incongruously known. This is part of the wider shift to F2P in digital games in general, especially in mobile games and social media games.

Personally, I don't see F2P as sustainable at its current level. This is for the following reasons:

- Players will wise up to it.

- The number of games using it is expanding at a faster rate than the number of whales is expanding.

- The same pressures that cause developers to reduce their retail price to zero also apply to microtransactions.

- Developers didn't get into the game industry to make games that they themselves resent playing.

Free-to-play can be very lucrative for MMOs, but for games in general it's a disaster. Most F2P mobile phone games make no money at all because they don't net a whale. It costs more money to acquire a player than the player will ever pay the developer. If you have a large number of players or a small number of very dedicated players, F2P rocks. Otherwise, it sucks.

All revenue model trends come and go.

- In the 1970s, people thought MUDs would be free forever.

- In the 1980s, people thought MUDs would be charge-per-hour forever.

- In the 1990s, people thought MMOs would be subscription-based forever.

- In the 2010s, people think that MMOs will be F2P forever.

In the 2020s? 2030s? 2040s?

Trends change, business evolves. Ideas split and recombine or come from nowhere.

That said, two-thirds of the developers in the audience of the Develop conference I spoke at in 2014 thought that F2P would only become more entrenched, so what do I know?

Server Size

When *World of Warcraft* launched in Europe, 80 servers were installed to support the 290,000 players who signed up for its first weekend. That's 3,625 players per server.

What if they'd had 800 servers instead of 80?

Modern commercial MMOs generally handle between 3,000 and 5,000 players per server. Players may *say* that this is what they want, but given half a chance they'll flee to subworld, instanced bubble environments so as to avoid contact with the seething masses. However, if the MMOs themselves had more shards, each with fewer players, there wouldn't be this kind of pressure to have pocket universes for friends-only play. The whole virtual world would be exactly that—only persistent instead of temporary.

Having more servers with fewer players has other advantages for players, too. It reduces the effects of farming (try selling gold from server #401 to someone playing on server #682), it makes getting away from personal griefers a real possibility (how long would it take them to track you down?), it allows for multiple server types (PvP, RMT, PD, whatever), and it gives individual players a sense that they can have a real effect on the virtual environment. If you wanted, you could have full-scale servers with 4,000 players who could either play there all the time or migrate to effectively private servers run by their guild if they wanted to *be* someone.

So, how few players would a server have to support for said players to feel that they didn't need instances, yet for the shard to remain viable? Regardless of whether instances are a good thing or a bad thing, how many players is the minimum necessary for a server to remain attractive—and is this more than the number of players that makes instancing a requirement?

What do you think? Is the critical mass required for a full sense of community greater than or less than that required for relatively hassle-free play? Indeed, are the two figures related? Does it depend on the size of the world, the maturity of the players, or what?

I've no answers for this; your guess is as good as mine.

I Own It Because I Made it

The third justification people furnish to explain why they own "their" virtual goods is (as I mentioned when introducing this concept) the strongest one. Rooted in the philosophy of John Locke, it says that when people create something through the product of their own labor, they get to keep it. There wasn't a fully geared arch-mage in the box when I bought the game; it exists only because *I* made it.

That's true, but suppose that instead of an MMO we were talking about a jigsaw puzzle. If I borrow your jigsaw puzzle and complete it, does that make it mine? There wasn't a completed puzzle in the box when you lent me it; there is now, so I should own it.

Well, no, I shouldn't. Sure, there wasn't a completed jigsaw puzzle in the box when you lent me it, but there was the *means by which to create* the jigsaw puzzle. Those were my pieces, and they remain my pieces whether assembled or not.

A second line of defense brings in the creator's artistic involvement. My arch-mage is unique; no other arch-mage has the same name and the same gear and the same stats and the same achievements. Those are only there because of what I did. It's *mine*.

This still doesn't hold water. If it did, no one would ever lend anyone an Etch-a-Sketch.

A third line of defense is that I was invited by the MMO to create my arch-mage as a unique and special snowflake, so the operators obviously *knew* I would make something in which I held intellectual property.

Again, this doesn't make a difference. Doctors' waiting rooms and family-friendly roadside restaurants sometimes have a table with blocks of Duplo on it to give young children something to do rather than wail with boredom. Does that mean that the kid who makes the amazing red dinosaur gets to keep it? No, it doesn't. The next kid who comes along is going to take it to pieces and make it into a submarine.

With MMOs, you're making transient things for fun. If you try to equate that with work, you won't get far.

Nice try, though.

Oh, Great One

On February 15, 2005, there were 12 Jedi characters from *Star Wars: Galaxies* for sale on eBay at $500 or more. This wasn't an unusual day for that kind of thing back then.

So, if you worked up your own Jedi in *SW:G*, how did you persuade strangers that you hadn't simply bought it?

(The answer is that you didn't; strangers assumed *all* Jedis were bought.)

The *Monopoly* Example

Suppose I own a *Monopoly* set and ask you and a bunch of friends round for a game. Despite the fact it's *Monopoly* and therefore about as much fun as a dirge, you accept. During the course of the game, you land on Mayfair (which is the UK equivalent of the US's Boardwalk), and you buy it.

Do you own it? Well, yes in the context of the game, but no in hard reality because it's my *Monopoly* set.

Let's say the Scottie dog owns Park Lane (Park Place) and you offer £2,000 in *Monopoly* money for it. I decide I can't let you have both, so I offer £3,000 in *Monopoly* money for it—more than you have in total. You therefore counter with a bid of £10 in real money. The Scottie dog accepts, and the sale goes through.

Do you now own Park Lane? In the context of the game, yes, you do. In the real world, though, no, you don't—even though you paid real money for it. That's because the Scottie dog didn't real-world own it. It's *my* set. I real-world own it. What's more, if I don't like what you and the Scottie dog did, I can stop the game there and then and leave in a huff (despite the fact that, amazingly, the rules of *Monopoly* do actually allow this kind of transaction).

As a player of MMOs, you don't real-world own any of the stuff your characters own in-game. That's because they're part of the MMO's set. Only if the rules of the MMO allow for real-world ownership to be transferred could you real-world own anything in the MMO.

Wising Up

When I said that players will wise up to F2P, what I meant was that they'll learn to recognize it and to work round it.

One of the main mechanics used for F2P in mobile and social media games uses the limited-energy mechanic. You get to do something, but you run out of energy and have to wait several hours before you can carry on; well, that or you could just pay to have the time lock removed.

Popular though this mechanic is, players are now routinely interlacing two games, playing each one while the other is in its energy recharge phase. They're supposed to be paying to skip that phase, but they're time-sharing with other games instead and waiting it out. Players will always resent things that spoil their fun, particularly those things that are transparently artificial obstacles. After playing enough F2P games, they'll recognize whatever pay-to-skip barrier to fun you introduce for what it is. They'll work round it or play something else instead.

Most restaurants make money from drink; most bars make money from food. If people go to a bar, they look at the drink prices. They're there for the drink. The bar's profits come from the things around the core product of drinks. For restaurants, it's the same, but their core product is food.

For games, the gameplay is the core product. Players judge the game based on its gameplay. That's what they're there for. If you interfere with it, they won't like it. An energy mechanic is like going to a restaurant where the food is free but you have to wait 90 minutes between courses unless you pay. A bonus XP buff is like having to pay a bartender not to spit in your beer.

If you want to use microtransactions in games, you should keep the gameplay pure and charge for things that enhance the experience without spoiling it for you or anyone else. Cosmetic items that are in keeping with the game's fiction are the easy win here, but it depends on what types of player you have.

You *do* understand your players, don't you?

Third, Third, Third

Sony's Station Exchange was created to allow those *EverQuest* 2 players who wanted to engage in RMT to do so legitimately. Initially, 2 of 22 possible servers were made RMT-compatible, with plans to let players vote to convert other servers to the system on a server-by-server basis.

Sony's research showed that roughly a third of *EQ2*'s players were in favor of RMT, a third were against it, and a third couldn't care less either way. This should have meant that a minimum of 7 servers and a maximum of 15 should have ultimately gone over to an RMT-friendly regime. That being the case, why did none of them do so?

The answer is surprisingly simple. Most people who engage in RMT will do so only when most other players *aren't* doing so. If everyone else is doing it, they don't get the advantage over them that they desire. The reasons they commonly put forward to explain why they want to engage in RMT are hence exposed to be *post hoc* excuses made up to justify their actions without giving the appearance of their being cheaters.

Really, though, they're just cheaters.

Well, in *some* players' eyes they're cheaters.

Rights of Publicity

If you, a developer, claim that you own the IP for how my avatar looks, does that mean you can sue me if I create an identical avatar in another MMO? What if they're also claiming IP in it under their own EULA?

What if my avatar looks like a famous person? Famous people have *rights of publicity*. You can't have a Brad Pitt lookalike advertising soda unless you make it very, very clear that it's not the real Brad Pitt.

What if I create an avatar that looks like me and I'm a famous person myself?

Oh, if only...

Making Things Yours

If you come into my house, pick up a can of spray paint, and cover my wall in some artistic masterpiece, you don't get to own that artistic masterpiece. If I invite you into my house and give you the spray paint and say you can paint a masterpiece on my wall, you still don't get to own it.

When children at play groups make things out of Play-Doh, they don't get to take them home. Those things just get mushed up so some other kid can make something out of them the next day. Those little works of art that the children spent 30 minutes making are destroyed. That's part of the condition of using the Play-Doh.

When you create a character in an MMO, you get to use a digital Play-Doh that doesn't belong to you. You don't get to keep your digital models. When you signed up to use the MMO, you were told you couldn't. All that meaning and emotion you've imbued in your character is worth nothing in ownership terms if (because you read the EULA) you knew when you started that you didn't get to keep it.

Incoming Tide

If I built a beautiful sandcastle next to the sea and put it up for sale, anyone who bought it would do so in the full knowledge that some time during the next 12 hours the tide would come in and destroy it. They would factor this knowledge into their calculation of how much a sandcastle built next to the sea is worth.

People who buy what they consider to be virtual goods do so in the full knowledge that what gives those goods meaning is a complex web of interactions between databases, programs, and other players. When you buy the virtual world's most powerful sword for $5,000, you're gambling that the developer won't introduce 10,000 even more powerful swords the next day and ruin your investment. Furthermore, you're gambling that the MMO won't be shut down, which would also ruin your investment.

For new MMOs, particularly ones from a developer with a poor or nonexistent track record, the odds of a shutdown sooner rather than later are much higher than they are for long-standing MMOs with a stable player base. Blizzard probably won't willingly close *World of Warcraft* down while it's profitable. Even *WoW* will disappear eventually, though. The chance that an MMO will close is, as with the chance that you will die, 100 percent.

The tide is always going to come in. The only question is, when?

What Really Matters

Some MMO players don't care when other people buy and sell characters. They say that what really matters is your network of friends and guildies, not your character's level.

If it were the case that this is indeed all that matters, though, why would MMO designers put in different levels at all? They could include in the character-creation system the ability to choose your character's level and to kit it out in whatever way you like. After all, you're only playing because of your friends and guildies.

Well, no. *Some* people may be playing for this reason, but other players are there because they want a sense of achievement. If your achievements can be rendered meaningless at the click of a button (whether it's marked "create character" or "$50"), then why would you continue playing—whether or not you had friends and guildies?

What really matters to *you* isn't necessarily what really matters to *other* people.

Least Worst Solution

For MMOs, where it's not possible to use the standard sanctions against (for example) cheats (that is, "I'm not playing with you, you're a cheat"), some other mechanism for dealing with this kind of problem needs to be in place. At the moment, this is described via EULAs.

EULAs aren't great, but no modern MMO has yet tried a better suggestion.

Paying for Free

The free-to-play (as opposed to free) MMO revenue model entails the selling of items and services to players. What kinds of things can be sold?

Well, pretty well anything can. In general, though, it will be described along three main dimensions.

Oh, I should mention that this is the "closer analysis" I threatened I'd go into earlier.

The first dimension is whether what is sold has any gameplay effect. The different gradations of this include the following:

- **No gameplay effect whatsoever**: Example: an impressive-looking horse that behaves just like the drab-looking horse you already had.

- **Deferred gameplay effect**: Example: immediate access to new content other people have to wait a week to access.

- **Inconvenience-unblocking gameplay effect**: Example: extra bag slots.

- **Indirect gameplay effect**: Example: experience-point boosts.

- **Small direct gameplay effect**: Example: health potions.

- **Large direct gameplay effect**: Example: invulnerability potions.

The second main dimension is how long the effects last. Here are the popular choices:

- **Instant, one-shot consumables**: Example: teleportation stones.

- **Short-term, temporary buffs**: Example: a crafting skill increase for the next hour.

- **Long-term, rental-like**: Example: housing.

- **Permanent**: Example: a 5 percent faster horse.

The third main dimension concerns probabilities:

- **Prerequisite** means you can have the paid-for item only if you already have its equivalent through regular gameplay. Example: you can only have the spell-boosting wizard's hat with stars on if you already had the plain version.

- **Equal probabilities** means there's the same chance of getting the paid-for item through regular gameplay. Example: the goblins in the pay-to-enter instance are the same as the ones outside, appearing with the same frequency and having the same chance of dropping the same items when killed.

- **Increased probabilities** means there's a small chance of getting an item through regular gameplay and a (usually much) larger one of getting it through paid content. Example: you could get a greater transmutation stone by luckily combining lesser transmutation stones, but you have a 100 times better chance if you use this Stone of Catalyzing Transmutations.

- **Exclusive** means there's no chance of getting the item through regular gameplay. Example: you can only get the rideable kangaroo from this lockbox that you have to buy a key to open.

Achievers are fine with no-gameplay or deferred-gameplay effects, although the deferred-gameplay would have to be relatively short (a month at most). They are agnostic about how long the effects last. They're OK with the first two kinds of probability, albeit requiring assurances that the second one genuinely is equal.

The other player types are fine with all the options, at least in terms of playing for fun. They may dislike them for other reasons, such as expense (if they feel they're being nickel-and-dimed), fairness (if they feel their experience is being deliberately crippled to make them pay to uncripple it), or morality (if they feel that a grab-bag mechanism is just plain, simple gambling); however, they won't object to any of them for spoiling the game. Achievers *will* object, though. Achievers regard anything too far along the gameplay or probability dimensions as being pay-to-win. The only way they *would* accept it is if the total amount any player could spend on such items per character were capped at a modest amount per month.

In other words, achievers will accept full-blown pay-to-win system so long as it works like a subscription.

Selling Yourself

It's much easier to stop a black-market trade in characters than it is to stop one in virtual goods or currency because character ownership changes all have to go through the developer.

Characters are tied to accounts, which are tied to real individuals. Real individuals are characterized by name, address, and credit card number. If anyone wants to change two of these at the same time, then the chances are higher that they're selling their account.

This may be why character sales used to be much more of a thing in the past than they are today.

I Own It Because You Sold Your Time

This next explanation people use as to why they own "their" virtual goods is a bit of a weird one. Essentially, they argue that they own it because they didn't buy the object itself from you; they bought the *time and effort* you used to create or acquire it.

This was the argument used by the company Black Snow when its accounts were banned by Mythic Entertainment (developers of *Dark Age of Camelot*). Black Snow had hired cheap laborers in Tijuana to farm virtual goods that they could sell to *DAoC* players. Mythic's EULA banned the selling of its virtual objects, but Black Snow argued that they weren't actually selling the virtual objects; they were merely selling the time and effort it took to obtain them.

Ingenious though this argument is, "I'm not selling the condemned meat; I'm selling the time and effort it took to obtain it" won't save me from a prison sentence. Likewise, "I'm not selling this heavily taxed fuel; I'm selling this lightly taxed onion and giving the fuel away for free" isn't going to impress any tax collector.

There yet remains a belief among some players that this argument is some kind of EULA exploit , as it still appears in its full glory every once in a while on eBay. The main purveyors of it, Black Snow, didn't get to test it in court, however: they neglected to pay their lawyers, so their lawsuit was dropped before it was ever heard.

Still, nice try.

Sweet Spot

At the Game Developers' Conference, 2005, there was a panel on "persistent versus instantiated spaces." I asked the panelists whether they thought there was a minimum size of player base for an individual shard to remain viable and whether this was greater than or less than the minimum size that made players feel they wanted instances.

Mark Jacobs was of the opinion that there was perhaps a sweet spot where it could happen, but he didn't say where he thought that might be. Raph Koster pointed out that text MUDs can feel like a world with as few as ten players, but didn't say what the low-end figure might be for commercial graphical MMOs.

The question comes down to asking when an instanced world beats a world's instances. The size of the world is a factor to some extent (a world made for 3,000 players could feel empty to 300, and a world made for 300 could feel overcrowded to 3,000), but it's less of an issue than you might suppose. There are far fewer players on a *WoW* server when it's 3 a.m. than when it's 8 p.m., but the night-owls still have fun despite the fact that the place is practically deserted. There are enough locations where they can meet through serendipity (cities, for example) for it to feel busier than it actually is.

There's some suggestion that groups have a maximum population before they start to split, related to *Dunbar's Number*[6]; that's not the same as asking what the minimum population is, though.

So no, I don't know the answer to this question either—but if I did, that's the scale I'd design for.

Selling Status

People in the US military are given Purple Hearts for being wounded or killed in action. The US government could make a lot of money selling Purple Hearts to people who have not been wounded or who haven't even been in the US military. If they did, though, those who got their medals for *bona fide* reasons would be outraged; those medals *mean* something.

For many MMO players, their character's status also means something. Obviously it's not as emotive or powerful a meaning as a Purple Heart, but nevertheless it's something they are *not* happy to see commodified.

Cuts and Speculation

I once asked an RMT web site owner whether he was concerned that developers of MMOs wouldn't just create the tools for a secondary market and embed them within their virtual worlds. His reply was that his site made its money not from introducing buyers to sellers and taking a cut from any resulting sale but from speculation. They bought things that people wanted to sell (normally in-game currency) and then resold them at a higher price to people who wanted to buy.

A developer wanting to muscle in on the RMT action would therefore have to sell the same things that players want at a lower price than that charged by the speculators. They could do this easily enough by completely cutting out the acquisition process: conjuring an object out of nothing is less expensive than buying it from a player.

Sure, it would trash the MMO's economy if they did that, but hey, if the RMTers are trashing it anyway. . .

---

[6]Chris Allen: The Dunbar Number as a Limit to Group Size. Life with Alacrity, March 2004. www.lifewithalacrity.com/2004/03/the_dunbar_numb.html

How Low Can You Go?

If you have many servers with small and insular populations, how can you ever make friends? You arrive at a server, and the people there are all busy having fun. How will you get involved? It would be like showing up at a random person's party where everyone else knew each other but you knew no one.

The answer is that the servers aren't necessarily *all* small and insular; population size could be a server feature. Play on the server with the 10,000-player cap, find some people you really get along with, and then after a while decamp to a server with a 1,000-player limit. Or maybe a 100-player limit? How low do you want to go?

How many players *is* the minimum necessary for a server to remain viable from the point of view of those players?

If you had your own, personal, one-player copy of your favorite MMO, could you ever play it for actual fun?

Unsporting Behavior

I've thought of an exploit for *Soccer!*

At the kick-off, one player has the ball, and the other ten in the team link arms and surround that player in a circle. They then walk the ball into the opposing team's goal. The opposition couldn't get close to it without committing a foul.

It would work, except for the catchall in rule 12 about "unsporting behavior."

Now as far as I know, whether behavior is unsporting is ultimately decided purely by the referee. No one has ever gone to court claiming that their actions weren't unsporting and therefore they shouldn't have been booked. This is perhaps because rule 5 states that the decisions of the referee regarding facts connected with play are final (but then no one has ever challenged that in the courts, either).

Maybe that's all we need with MMOs: a rule against unsporting play and someone with god-like powers to enforce the rule. Any challenge to this arrangement in court would have to be very careful that it didn't also challenge the same arrangement in *Soccer* and in so doing attract the wrath of some rather wealthy people.

Entitlement

A high-level character isn't just a high-level character; it's a mark of status. If it's worn by people not entitled to wear it, that seriously annoys those who are entitled to wear it. It *especially* annoys them if the people who wear it are doing so so as to give the impression that they're entitled to wear it.

If too many people buy success, that makes success meaningless.

There's a parasites-killing-the-host analogy in there somewhere.

Tipping Point

Following the standard Main Sequence development track, players who are achievers will eventually become socializers. What do you suppose happens if you design MMOs mainly for achievers and keep them playing that way for ten years?

Well, yes, most of the players transition to socializers despite your (real, but perhaps unintended) efforts to stop them. This is what happened with MMOs in the first decade of the 21st century. The tipping point was in 2012, when socializers outnumbered achievers to such an extent that the subscription revenue model broke down and there was a cascade of F2P. The Sixth Age of Virtual Worlds began.

This heralded a shift in attitudes of longer-term players who used to be achievers but are now pretty well socializers. At an intellectual level they still considered themselves to be achievers, but now they found themselves wanting to buy things that previously they wouldn't have deemed acceptable purchases. While conceding the argument against pay-to-win in player-*vs.*-player (because that's pretty clear-cut), they needed to rationalize why it was fine to engage in pay-to-win in player-*versus*-environment. The answer they arrived at is that PvP is competitive and PvE isn't, so P2W is OK in PvE but not in PvP. Indeed, in their view it wasn't even P2W; it was just ordinary F2P.

Well, the thing is, PvE *is* competitive—if you're an achiever. If you're not, well, you won't see it that way. If you are, though, you'll compare your progress and achievements to those of other players, and you'll resent it if those players "cheat" by paying for advantages. If you can easily identify players who are (in your terms) losers, you may be able to stomach it—but only if everyone else doesn't treat them as winners. Unfortunately for you, nonachievers will do just that.

So, what we saw with MMOs at this juncture was the effect of the natural evolution of achievers into socializers. Most long-term MMO players have made the transition or are making it, so there's lots of money to be made here (at least while they consider it money well-spent). There are two long-term problems with this situation, though.

The first is that MMOs are losing gamers. People who actually like *games* aren't going to stick with socializer-weighted MMOs. These will mainly be individuals who are transitioning from player to designer. They're going to be playing other games (mainly single-player RPGs, I suspect), perhaps coming back to a new MMO as a content locust for a short while before leaving it. Of course, the loss of these people isn't going to make a dent in MMO numbers because amortized across all MMOs there aren't enough of them; however, they're immensely important as they're the cutting edge. They embody the future of games because they *understand* them. Addressing their needs may be expensive in terms of what a developer gets back directly, but the reward lies in what spins off.

The second long-term problem concerns new achievers. If you're a newbie achiever looking for an MMO that suits your needs, you're going to have trouble finding one. You'll try one of the big names, realize it's "unfair," and after a while give up. You'll end up lost to the MMO industry. You'll get your games kicks elsewhere. All those P2W-uneasy achievers who five years from now *were* eventually going to transform into P2W-accepting socializers *aren't* going to do so because today they were put off while they were still achievers. MMOs will become things that gamers' parents played but not what they themselves play—rather like how today's players regard MUDs (those of them who have even heard of MUDs, that is).

Oh well, short-term gain always wins over long-term vision, so none of this comes as a surprise. What I expect will eventually happen is that there'll be a design revolution as the gamers create something for all those would-be achievers who are treading water waiting for something to play. Either that, or MMOs will be developed that are sustainable using non-P2W (in achiever terms) F2P to pick up all those loose achievers.

Yeah, right, like that happened in ahead-of-the-West-on-this Korea.

All in Instances

You can have a world the size of Azeroth and only half a dozen players in it, but so long as they all hang out together, the effect is much the same as if there were 10,000 players, all in instances.

Achieving Less

Content "for" achievers is difficult to design because different achievers have different ideas of what's difficult. They all feel they want to "succeed" in some regard, but whereas some won't regard an action as an achievement if they can complete it within the first ten attempts, others will get cross if they have to wait until the second attempt to do it.

Over the years, what qualifies as "achievement" has gradually become diluted. It was happening anyway, but *World of Warcraft* gave it a particular boost through the certainty of its gains for time spent playing. The more time you invested, the more you advanced; all that was in question—all that actual skill came into—was how quickly you advanced.

In the old PvP-with-permadeath days, we called this *plodding*. If someone could plod their way through content, making slow but steady gains until they reached the end, that was regarded as A Bad Thing.

Sadly for those early MUDs, plodders vastly outnumber nonplodders; MUDs that cosseted plodders always attracted more players. More players meant more money, which meant more to invest in the product. Once graphics came in and increased the cost to make a virtual world by several orders of magnitude, that was the end. Plodding became the norm.

Nevertheless, although achievement has become less and less meaningful in MMOs over the years and has been doing so for decades, it was still just about viable while players could persuade themselves that they were playing on a level playing field.

Nowadays, they can't. F2P with gameplay effects or probability effects seems to have crossed some kind of line.

On Unfairness

If you don't like the idea of playing an MMO that's unfair, play one that promises to be fair and sue its operators should it prove to be unfair.

You're unlikely to find an MMO that makes such a promise, though, given that almost all MMOs are *by design* unfair in many respects (character classes never balance perfectly, for example).

The best you can hope for is that you'll be *treated* fairly—not being banned for an offense you didn't commit, that sort of thing. However, even this is too much for some MMOs (the near-legendary MUD *MIST* is perhaps the best-known), for which unfairness is *part of the game*.

If you're being treated unfairly and don't like it, complain. It may be a genuine mistake. If your complaint is ignored, leave—and take your friends with you.

Just because MMO developers *can* legitimately treat you unfairly, that doesn't mean it's OK.

Rights of Service

MMO developers don't need a legitimate reason to deny service to would-be players. It's their business, so they can do it on a whim. The people being denied service do need a legitimate reason to request that their service is not denied.

Being discriminated against solely on the basis of race, gender, sexuality, or age could well be such a legitimate reason.

Being allowed to spoil the MMO for others is not such a legitimate reason.

Why Only Ban?

When players of MMOs misbehave and a punishment is in order, they're almost invariably banned. Yet banning is just one of the many possible weapons that customer service administrators have in their armory. Why do they almost always go from "a good talking to" straight to "ban"?

OK, well banning has some useful things going for it. First, it's reversible: if you ban someone, you can easily unban them if you made a mistake. Second, it's variable: you can ban for anything from a day to an eternity. Third, people who really care about the virtual world can't bear to be parted from it, so banning is a meaningful punishment for them. Fourth, people who don't care about anything but griefing are kept out of harm's way by bans, thereby protecting their potential victims. Fifth, banning as a punishment works whatever the type of virtual world—game-like or social—so it acts as an industry standard.

That doesn't mean other forms of punishment might not be appropriate, though, does it? Why not, say, remove a bunch of experience points? If you docked them a level's worth and it took them a week to get back to where they were, then it was equivalent to a ban except the player got to play for a week. Surely, that would be kinder than an outright ban?

Well, it would be, but players don't see it like that. MMOs are about identity. Fine a character experience points and it's as if you're personally assaulting them. They go (warning: technical term) ape shit when you do that. They *prefer* to be banned.

OK, well all *that* means is that what you thought was "community service" rather than "imprisonment" is actually "corporal punishment." That doesn't mean it isn't usable. It does mean, though, that you'll get a lot of complaints from other, uninvolved players when you use it—just as you would in real life if you administered a beating rather than locking someone up for a month.

Historically, of course, real-world authorities did employ corporal punishment as a means of enforcing the law. In MMOs, too, this kind of thing used to be commonplace. For example, in *MUD1* removing characters' experience points was regarded as generosity itself—if someone were to shout out a stream of profanities, say, they could expect to be instantly FODded. If they wanted their character back, they would have to plead to whichever wiz was responsible for their obliteration. Oh, and no, we didn't believe that cats could jump on a keyboard and type that kind of thing.

There are other old-fashioned punishments that were meted out in the past that are no longer acceptable to the MMO-playing public. For example, in schools it used to be that misbehaving children would have to sit in a corner wearing a dunce's cap; the MMO equivalent—tagging their name with some warning that they're a jerk, say—is something that we used to do in *MUD2*. The player could either take the shame and play or treat it as a ban and come back when it was removed. Again, though, with a ban, you're out of the world until it's over; with a badge of dishonor, people will constantly be asking you how you got it, and then you can spin your side of the tale to explain what an unjust set of cruel bigots are in charge (although that might be harder if the official explanation is also pinned to you somehow).

Some other tools from the punishment box of yesteryear are still around today, although they're not as widespread as they were. One example is a "police cell." What happens here is that you're tossed into it to cool down, and only when you've regained your temper/sanity and accept that you were perhaps in the wrong are you released. *MUD1* had this with a room called Limbo; *Second Life* has its Cornfield.

Over the years, then, we've seen a gradual decline in the variety and nature of the punishments afforded to miscreants in virtual worlds. Pretty well everything that has been tried before has now been dropped in favor of warning, banning, and then account closing (the equivalent of "execution").

That said, there are still some people out there experimenting. You have to admire *Roma Victor*'s in-context solution: wrong-doers are crucified and left dangling helplessly where people can see, as a warning to others.

If you can't do cruel and unusual punishments in MMOs, where *can* you do them?

Anti-capitalism

Let's say a very, very rich man wants to play an MMO that has no RMT. Capitalism and market choice being what it is, shouldn't this very, very rich man be able to find an MMO somewhere that has no RMT? After all, there's a demand for such worlds, and the man is very, very rich—so rich, indeed, that he could finance the design, development, and operation of a full-blown non-RMT MMO out of what to him is merely small change. Such is the way of the capitalist system.

Yet this very, very rich man could *not* actually do this right now. Why? Because some very, very poor people would come into his MMO and start RMTing.

Some apologists for RMTers claim that the buying and selling of virtual property against the express wishes of an MMO's operators must be OK because "capitalism allows it"; they assert that we live in a society that is prosperous because of capitalism, so there would have to be a damned good reason to ban a practice that elsewhere underpins our entire economy.

We have a paradox here, then. The very, very rich man may be able to buy the entire worldly goods of every RMTer from the income he receives in a single day, but he couldn't stop RMT even if he did that—new RMTers would step up to replace those he'd bought off. This means that even with the vast resources at the very, very rich man's disposal, what he demands can't be supplied because in supplying it other players create a demand for the very opposite—which, if adequately supplied, would in turn remove their demand (because if they could have everything they wanted, they wouldn't need to play).

Maybe the very, very rich man should buy a few politicians and get the law changed so that RMT pipsqueaks are fined out of existence if they try to commodify his MMO.

Capitalism wins again!

Over-embracing RMT

Many of the people who pay real money to buy in-game goods or currency in MMOs that ban the practice don't understand why it's a problem.

One way of explaining is to remove the monetary factor. If letting people *buy* virtual currency isn't a problem, then giving them the virtual currency for *free* would also not be a problem, right? After all, in a subscription game the developer is providing many disparate services for a single monthly fee, so it's just ripping players off to make them pay for something that's not a problem. If being able to hang out with your guildies is so great, why should you have to shell out $600 to buy the necessary equipment to do so? Why can't you simply equip whatever you want, for free? Furthermore, as it's going to be easier to implement this than a full-blown auction house trading system, it reduces production costs! What's the issue?

I'll tell you what the issue is: it SPOILS THE GAME. Take away the challenge, and you take away the fun. If there is no game to spoil, as with *Second Life*, then fine; this is obviously a reasonable idea. If the game isn't about the kind of things that money can buy (as is the case with strong role-playing worlds such as *Achaea*), then it's also reasonable. If you can legitimately buy a step toward *success*, though, either it's not a game at all or it's a wider game with different win conditions.

Why?

If you feel that a game has one or more bad rules, DON'T PLAY THAT GAME!

Is that so difficult to understand? If you decide that you know better than the designer, why would you play the game anyway and ignore the rules? Is it to punish the designer somehow? Is it to punish the other players who don't see things your way and think the rules are fine?

Why play a game for which you don't like the rules? I mean, WHY?

Jerk Avoidance

Hands up those who think MMOs are full of jerks. Ah, yes, I thought so.

Your problem isn't that there are too few people alongside whom you want to play. Your problem is that you can't find them easily, and when you do, your experience is disrupted by all the other people around who don't play how you want to play (that is, the jerks). Of course, from the perspective of the jerks, you're the jerk. You and they are basically playing different MMOs in the same MMO.

Suppose that you and your like-minded friends can rent your own MMO server and play that. You can police it so that anyone who comes along and plays like a jerk is kicked out. Your MMO will be small in terms of numbers of users, but hey, it's not as if you actually *play* with all those millions of people in *WoW* anyway—your path crosses that of maybe a couple of thousand players at most, almost none of whom you remember.

There are a thousand or more "private" *WoW* servers out there, all of which violate Blizzard's EULA and for none of which Blizzard receives money. They have various bespoke modifications, some of which are coded in and some of which are in the way they're run. Unlike Blizzard's RP servers, the private ones can be as ruthless as they choose to be in dealing with people who don't adhere to their strict standards of what is or is not acceptable role-playing; they're not going to damage their stock price with mass bannings. Even if they want an all-male or all-female or otherwise all-discriminatory server, they can do just that.

Imagine a kinder future in which there is a core set of servers run by an MMO's developers, plus as many private servers as there are people who want to run them, all of which are hosted by the developer and covered by the same EULA. You wouldn't be able to try them all—some may have entrance criteria you don't satisfy—but you don't have to try any if you don't want. They may have their own subscription or some kind of free-to-play system going on. That's fine; the developer can do the billing for them.

In this future, there would be a minimal cost to rent a server (so there aren't quite as many servers as there are players), but it wouldn't have to be high—$100 a month ought to be sufficient. The developer would be in a position to take down servers that violated real-world laws ("about this Gentiles-only server you're advertising..."), but other than that, people could do what they wanted. They wouldn't have the freedom to write actual code for their server, so there would still be a reason for people to run illegitimate private servers. Nevertheless, instead of having a small number of server types that inevitably reduce to a common denominator, you would have a wide variety of servers that address particular individual needs very, very well.

Whoah! I think I just woke up! Where was I?

The Japanese Official's Answer

People who buy in-world currency for real money in MMOs that prohibit this under the terms of their EULA will often explain themselves in terms of wanting to play the game at a certain level without spending the time it would otherwise take to get that level. They say this as if it's somehow a useful explanation.

I saw a headline from a Japanese newspaper once that said "Official who took bribe 'did it for the money.'" Well gee, I guess that explains everything.

What developers want to know is *why* RMTers want to "play the game at a certain level." Is it because of the content? Because their friends play there? Because they want to have the status of someone who has played through the content but without actually having had to do so?

Merely telling us that they want to use what they've bought is no explanation at all.

Fragments

Most myths don't follow the whole hero's journey, just fragments of it. The story of Artemis and Actaeon is such a fragment, for example.

Perhaps individual games are like myth fragments and MMOs are like myth cycles? You play the kind of games that are most important for your journey right now and then move on to other kinds as you grow as a person?

If that's the case, then Player Type theory *would* actually apply to all games. Writing a "game for achievers," say, would be a reasonable thing to do.

Integrating *Reality*

Games are a broad church. They appeal to many people for many reasons.

Some people want to keep the game world separate from *Reality*. For example, if you claim that because it's your *Cluedo* set you can look at the hidden cards in the middle, I personally am not going to play *Cluedo* with you (at least, not with your set).

Some people want to integrate the game world with *Reality*. *Poker* is a completely different game when you play for money instead of bottle caps.

Both these positions are fine.

What *isn't* fine is when someone comes along to one and plays it as if it were the other. If you and I agree to return each other's money after every hand we win in a *Poker* session, that's not going to please the others at the table. Likewise, should I promise to buy you a cake were you to show me the *Cluedo* cards in your hand, the other players will stop playing there and then.

With MMOs, part of the appeal is that they are *not Reality*. It should therefore be reasonable for an MMO's developer to eject anyone who wants to integrate it with *Reality*. The developer shouldn't have to redesign or reprogram the virtual world to beat off constant attempts to integrate it. It's not a bug in the MMO's design that is causing the problem; it's a bug in the attitude of players who want to turn the MMO into something it's not.

Is it a bug in the design of *Soccer* that a goalkeeper can be paid to dive to the left in a penalty shoot-out? No, it's fraud, and if a goalkeeper can be jailed for taking a bribe to throw a game, I don't see why developers can't use the law to protect the integrity of their MMOs, too.

I Own It Because You Made Me Buy It

The final approach employed by people to explain why they own "their" virtual goods turns accountability for the transgression back onto the designer. The players using this argument claim that although the MMO says one thing in its EULA, it says another thing in its design. The design of the MMO is so flawed that it actively encourages people to buy virtual goods. The EULA is contradicting the MMO's design, so which is to be believed?

The player here is painted as a hapless victim of forces beyond their control—an honest person subject to unreasonable and competing pressures. It takes so long to get the Sword of Three Edges that it's simply beyond the reach of the hardworking parent who spends all day in the factory making brake blocks so they can buy their children food and shoes. The game is practically twisting their arm to make them buy the Sword of Three Edges from one of those disreputable farmers. If *only* the designer had made it easier to obtain, there wouldn't *be* this problem.

The exquisite pinnacle of this argument asserts that time-rich players clearly have an advantage here. Surely, time-poor people who have to go to work instead of play MMOs all day long should be able to counteract this gross unfairness?

Well, no. It's also unfair that time-rich people can train for the Olympics but time-poor people can't. "Why can't I buy a head start in the 100 meters? I don't have the time to spend grinding through all that training!" Besides, time-poor people are often cash-poor too because they have to work long hours or hold down several jobs to try to make ends meet. They don't even have the option of buying a black-market Sword of Three Edges.

MMO designs *do* have deliberate obstacles in them, it's true. Very few games don't, though—they make games fun! If you don't like a particular game, don't play it. Really, if the design is *that* bad, why subject yourself to it at all? If it *isn't* that bad, why try to make out you're a victim of bad design?

"I'm not repaying you because your credit card made me use it." Nice try, but no dice.

Cheating

Player Type theory tells us that people play MMOs for different reasons. Associated with each of these reasons are sets of beliefs about what playing an MMO is about; the beliefs themselves are informally encoded in the players' minds as rules. Although unwritten, to each individual player these are just as important as the written rules.

Put less formally: different player types have different ideas concerning what makes up the unwritten rules of an MMO. They will follow the unwritten rules that govern the dimension of play that they personally would like to experience and will regard the breaking of these rules as cheating. The key point is that they do *not* regard breaking the rules of *other* player types as cheating.

Let's see how this works out using the four-type model as a basis.

Achievers essentially follow a meritocracy rule. They feel that if someone has status, it should be because they earned it. They are horrified if the signifiers of status can be obtained some other way. To them, it would be like buying a PhD—it's cheating! Yet other types see nothing wrong with it.

Explorers will readily pay to gain access to new content. For them, figuring out content is paramount—they want to understand the game more than do other players. They are angered by web sites that "give away" solutions. Using them, to an explorer, is cheating! Yet other types see nothing wrong with it.

Socializers don't rate the game itself; they'll happily use out-of-game methods to achieve in-game success because "success" in their view means being able to play alongside their friends. They value people and connections. This means they despair at looking-for-group tools and the meaningless, transient relationships that result. Using a community- independent grouping tool that ignores friendship and loyalty is cheating! Yet other types see nothing wrong with it.

Killers get fun from hurting people who didn't consent to that possibility. Anything that interferes with this aim is cheating, in the killer's view. This means activities such as complaining about being attacked, demanding some killer-favorite ability be nerfed, running to the protection of NPC guards, calling in help from friends, and indeed anything else that could conceivably work as a counter-killer tactic. Doing any of these would interfere with the ability of one person to bully another—it's cheating! Yet other types see nothing wrong with it.

OK, so not all cheating is like this:

- Some of it is accidental—you don't know that the rule you're breaking exists.

- Some of it is meta-gaming. You're not playing *Guild Wars 2*; you're playing one-upmanship with your real-life friends.

- Some of it comes from frustration. "This game is too hard!"

- Some of it comes from boredom. "This game is too easy!"

The difference is, for any of these other forms of cheating, the player *will* accept that what they have done can be regarded as cheating. However, for player-type cheating (which is the majority of the "cheating" that goes on), they don't accept it. They *really don't* see that it *is* cheating—because for them, it *isn't* cheating! The entire free-to-play business model is based on exploiting this friction between player types.

The only rules of computer games that you can rely on are the ones coded in, plus perhaps some real-life criminal laws such as not gouging your fellow players' eyes out. All other rules are optional. People play MMOs for different reasons, so inevitably they think the MMO is "about" different things. They will rarely break their *own* idea of the rules but have either no conception of other players' ideas of the rules or do but they've changed their minds (because they've advanced as players) and now consider that their old views were wrong.

The weird end result of this is that players cheat without cheating.

Customer Service Costs

Customer service costs can account for anything between a third and half your monthly fee for a subscription MMO.

Why?

Well, if an MMO bans RMT but the suppliers who were selling players in-game currency carry on doing so regardless, this would suggest that they are the kind of people who don't mind breaking rules. This lack of respect for rules doesn't always stop at rules targeting RMT.

Some of these people will scam players. They'll take your money and not give you what you paid for. Some of them will rob you. They'll take your money to level up your character but instead strip your character of everything in its possession and vendor the lot for virtual currency that they can then sell to someone else. Some of them will write viruses that grab your account identification and password, which they pass back to base so another program can log in and sell all your stuff. Then, three weeks later when you've persuaded the MMO operator to restore your character's possessions, they'll do it again—all automatically.

In each of these cases, it's not the scammers who get the customer service call; it's the MMO operator. So many people are affected that it takes a lot of people to field all the complaints.

That's why customer service costs add such a big chunk to your subscription fee. For F2P MMOs, it means that number of "opportunities to buy" with the microtransaction currency have to be increased.

Somehow, those who engage in buying in-game currency against the terms of the EULA they clicked through seem to think that this makes their activities even more acceptable.

RMT and the Free Market

I mentioned earlier that one argument you sometimes see in support of legitimizing RMT is that you can't buck the free market. If people want RMT, they'll get it; if they don't want it, they won't. The free market will find everyone a solution.

Recall that play is what happens when individuals willingly give up some freedoms so as to gain other, greater freedoms. So, if one of the freedoms given up is "the free market," there has to be some other way of protecting the integrity of the play space; the traditional solution, "the free market," is by definition ruled out.

Suppose that our very, very rich man (let's call him "Bill") plays an MMO incognito. He might really enjoy being main tank and be very, very good at it, but what if suddenly his guild relegates him to off-tank because one of the other members buys a better character off eBay? Bill isn't at all happy. He likes that a character reflects the achievements of the person who plays it and doesn't like it when someone rides roughshod over that connection. He prefers an MMO with player/character integrity.

Given that Bill could afford to buy the entire MMO a hundred times over if he wanted and makes more money in an hour than character-sellers do in a lifetime, market forces *should* decree that he gets his way. However, it's impossible even for Bill to succeed here, because he can't stop people selling their characters despite his vast wealth. Yes, the world's design can be changed to make commodification less attractive, but Bill doesn't want a *different* design; he wants *this* design only without people engaging in RMT. Surely, with all his money, he can have that? Why won't the free market find him a solution?

Sadly, the free market won't find a solution because it's the free market that (in this scenario) is causing the problem.

Free to Leave

In the very early days, MMOs (or MUDs as they were called back then) had an actual ending. You reached the level cap and then stopped. In *MUD1*'s case, you could play on as an administrator (wizard/witch), which many did; most drifted away afterward, though. They had no need to play any more.

This makes a lot of sense in terms of narrative. If the game tells you you've won, that's basically the Atonement with the Father step of the hero's journey. From that point onward, you're *always* going to leave—it's just a question of when. As a player, it's invariably better that you leave with warm, fuzzy feelings and fond memories rather than from disillusionment that the game has become boring and unfulfilling.

Now although this is a very satisfactory ending, it's something we never see nowadays. Why? Well, there's this feeling that if you (as a developer) give players *permission* to leave, they will actually *do* so. That means they're not paying you any more money. So instead, the leveling game is treated as a qualification you need to play a completely different game (primarily a PvP game or a raiding game). People who like neither of these are going to be frustrated; people who prefer one or other of them have a nagging awareness that they didn't really need to play the leveling game at all.

Hmm. Well you can perhaps see why someone on the business side of an MMO development company might want their players not to leave: once they do, you get no more money from them. OK, well that made sense when everyone was subscribing, sure, but does it still make sense now that most people are playing for free and are never going to give you a bean anyway? The ones who have paid you money will hang around for longer anyway as they've made an investment; the ones who haven't probably won't by this stage, unless you can convert them into payers while they're growing gradually more and more frustrated (and therefore less and less likely to want to be converted).

Suppose you had an MMO with a definite ending: an "escape from Colditz" game. You're a prisoner of war; your aim is to escape. Your ultimate goal is to go on a home run and get back to allied lines and safety. That home run attempt is going to be an incredibly exciting event, and when you make it, you're going to feel elated; you've won! That's it, pats on the back, game over, well done. I know it will be like that, because that's what wiz runs in *MUD1* were like. They're the pinnacle of MMO excitement.

Afterward, you can drop back in as another character or go play something else and come back for the developer's next game (remember those happy thoughts!). If you don't want to escape, because you like hanging around with your friends or exploring the complexities of prison camp life, OK, don't— you can always change your mind.

Revenue models do affect game design. If the revenue model rules something out, you can't do it. If the revenue model changes, though, you can revisit what you previously ruled out—*if* you remember *why* it was ruled out in the first place (or indeed that it *was* ruled out!). You don't have to go with a paradigm based on a defunct system; you can change it. Two story-driven MMOs I've played through until I was raiding at nightmare level (*SW:TOR* and *TSW*) would both have been easy to adapt to this model; designing for it deliberately wouldn't be especially difficult.

Of course, if someone did implement an "escape from Colditz" MMO, you just *know* that to cement your escape you'd need to buy some black-market in-game Reichsmarks for real-world dollars.

Customer Service Made Easy

From the very beginning, I knew that identity play was a key component of MMOs. It was therefore important that people didn't get their friends to work up their characters for them; they had to work them up through the ranks themselves. We didn't program in anything to prevent this, though— how could we? Instead, we simply banned the practice and FODded anyone we found engaged in it.

Customer service is *so* much easier when you can do that.

Tom Cruise Wears Shoes

Back in 2009, I decided it was about time I took a look at the trailer for the *Wrath of the Lich King* expansion for *World of Warcraft* instead of just reading about it. The video started running, and here's what I saw:

So, this was an embedded version of the video (which was hosted on the Viddler site). I don't know who was responsible for the video ad, but I do know who was responsible for the video itself: Blizzard. I also know that Blizzard would not want to be associated with gold-selling outfits and indeed would be very happy to see them all closed down entirely. Yet here's gold-treas.com advertising on Blizzard's video because they bought a few AdSense words from Google knowing that Blizzard were powerless to intervene.

It's not just Blizzard. When my *Designing Virtual Worlds* book first came out in 2003, there were ads for gold farmers on its Amazon page. There were also ads for them that popped up next to regular Google searches on *my* name. This means that my name was being associated with a service of which I disapprove. Was there anything I could do about it? No, there wasn't. Well, I guess I could have retaliated by buying ads for their directors' names, but it's expensive to pay for a box that says "BUY GOLD AND DECREASE YOUR SENSE OF SELF-WORTH YOU LOSER LOSER LOSER."

This isn't right! People should not be able to associate themselves with someone else's intellectual property or identity without that other person's permission. If I were the manufacturer of the shoes worn by Tom Cruise and without his permission put up an advertisement with a picture of Tom Cruise and the tag line "If you like Tom Cruise, you'll love the shoes he wears," I could expect a swift response from his lawyer. However, if he doesn't wear the shoes I manufacture but I purchase a few shots at the term "Tom Cruise" for video advertising, then every time someone watches a Tom Cruise clip there's a chance my ad for will appear. Tom won't get a penny, though—and people will think he wears the shoes I make when he doesn't.

Real-Life API: Demanding

CService::Demanding

void Demanding(CPlayer cPlayer, real rDem)

- *cPlayer*: Specifies which player's demandingness changes
- *rDem*: Specifies the change in demandingness

Remarks

Changes how demanding *cPlayer* is of the service by *rDem*. Common reasons for invoking this method include the following:

- *cPlayer* is vocal when things don't work as expected.
- *cPlayer* is extremely vocal when promised change does not occur.
- *cPlayer* perceives unfairness in allocation of the service.
- *cPlayer* has ideas for improving the service. Note that CGovernment derives from CService but does not override CService::Demanding.

Mine!

The word *my* doesn't imply ownership; it applies association. That may be *my* character, but that doesn't mean I own it.

It's like with karaoke ("That's *my* microphone!"), pony trekking ("That's *my* pony!"), *Bingo* ("That's *my* number!"), dining out ("That's *my* messy plate!"), single-player computer games ("That's *my* power-up!"), and tourism ("That's *my* view over the Tiber!").

That's *my* opinion. That doesn't mean I own it, though.

"Who Would Want to?"

Something I've noticed when people are pressing for legislation regarding MMOs or games in general is the attitude that an objection can be overruled on the grounds that no one would want to do that anyway. For example, a real-life discussion among panelists at a conference I attended contained an exchange that could be (drastically!) condensed as follows:

> **P1**: People should have property rights in their MMO possessions.
>
> **P2**: But that would mean other players or the game itself couldn't steal those objects.
>
> **P1**: Correct, they couldn't.
>
> **P2**: So, how about a hypothetical MMO set in a Gulag?
>
> **P1**: That's interesting, but who would want to play such a game?

This is an invalid argument.

As a general point, laws shouldn't be framed on the basis that "why would someone want to do what the laws might prohibit?" Just because *you* can't see why, that doesn't mean *others* can't. I can't see why people collect the numbers written on the sides of trains, but that doesn't mean I'm in favor of laws being drafted that are slack enough to ban this activity as a side effect.

In the Gulag example, people might play such a game because it's educational or even fun. I've played "escape from a prisoner of war camp" board games and found them enjoyable; I've no reason to suspect that an MMO along the same lines couldn't also be enjoyable. I wouldn't rule it out anyway.

The removal of what in the real world are liberties is acceptable because it's *part of the game*. In a Gulag MMO, I would be disappointed if I could speak openly about escape in front of guards or wave my digging equipment in their faces—I'd *expect* to have to be quiet around them and to have my stuff regularly confiscated!

You may not find it fun, but no one is making *you* play it.

Appealing Players

I once got an email from a player of *Star Wars: Galaxies* complaining that he'd been unjustifiably punished by its developer, Sony Online Entertainment, in the person of a customer service representative.

I had some sympathy with him. Yes, he had scammed some of the other players' characters, but he'd done so in the context of the game. However, I had to tell him that SOE were within their rights to mark his character. They were within their rights to do *anything at all* to his character for any reason whatsoever—or even no reason whatsoever. All MMO operators have these rights. Customer service reps could play their own "work your way through the alphabet, hosing down a character at random whose name starts with the next letter" game. MMO operators can do WHATEVER THEY LIKE in their virtual world, and all that their victims can do if they don't like it is leave in disgust (telling their friends as they do so).

That said, they'd lose a ton of business if they carried on like this, so they prefer to publish a set of rules that the players perceive as "fair"—the terms of service—and stick to them. The issue for the player who'd scammed his peers in *SWG* was whether he'd been disciplined under the restricted, TOS rules, or under the full-blown, SOE-can-do-whatever-it-likes-it's-their-world rules. If the former, his punishment wouldn't be seen as unfair; if the latter, it most certainly would. If it was the latter being passed off as the former under a general "don't exploit design bugs" clause, it might be seen as either.

The right thing to do if you want to scam other players is to run it past a customer service rep first. If they OK it, you're in a much stronger position to appeal should they subsequently punish you. If they don't OK it, well, you've just saved yourself from an automatic ban.

Oh, and I should mention that "they've never stopped me from doing this before" is an excuse along the same lines as "the police haven't stopped me from breaking into houses before." Just because they haven't *detected* it before, that doesn't mean they're OK with it.

Bogus RMT Propaganda #1

RMT practitioners have developed a number of techniques to try to justify what they do (in addition to the "I own it so I can do what I like with it" collection).

One that I've heard many times is that MMO developers actually like having RMT around, because all those people who are buying gold, plat, gil, adena, ISK, pax, or whatever would stop playing if they couldn't get it. Developers therefore turn a blind eye so that people who do buy gold, plat, gil, adena, ISK, pax, or whatever will continue to pay their monthly subscription or buy F2P goodies.

Here are four reasons why this is a bogus contention:

1. The argument doesn't account for all the nonplayers who *would* play the MMO "if it weren't for those cheats who engage in RMT." *EQ* developers mistakenly believed that hard-core raiding was a big draw because most of their players did it; what they failed to realize was that it was a big turn-off for many more people, who stopped playing because of it. The only ones left were the hard-core raid- ers. If RMT drives away non-RMT players, then the only players left will be OK with RMT—which is certainly *not* evidence that RMT is a player-retention mechanism!

2. RMT costs developers far more in handling the customer service complaints that it generates than they would ever get back from a few extended subscriptions or probably never- forthcoming F2P purchases.

3. If developers were OK with RMT, they'd do it themselves. They would directly sell gold, plat, gil, adena, ISK, pax, or whatever to their players. They can always undercut what the RMTers charge and offer a more secure service to boot. This happens to an extent with F2P, but developers still strive to keep F2P currency and regular in-world cur- rency separate. This would not be true if they liked the idea that people could buy the latter.

4. If the people who currently buy gold, plat, gil, adena, ISK, pax, or whatever were unable to do so, then many would actually play for longer. They want a shortcut, but if one isn't available then they'll take the same long route as anyone else. One very senior MMO live team member I've spoken to has data supporting this assertion: on aver- age, people who engage in RMT cancel their subscrip- tions sooner than people who don't, because they skip so much content by buying their way round it. After clamp downs, people who were previously RMTing stayed just as long as everyone else.

RMTers operate in a gray area. If your morals are such that operating in one gray area is not something that concerns you, then it would come as no sur- prise if you were happy to operate in other gray areas too. Making disingenu- ous assertions to journalists would fall into such a category.

Implications of Virtual Property Ownership

Suppose that the courts accepted one or more of the arguments put forward by some academics in support of the assertion that players real-world own "their" virtual property. What would be the consequences?

There are two.

First, property is famously "nine-tenths of the law." If the virtual goods in MMOs are accepted as being owned by players, all manner of real-world laws suddenly apply. Some of these are incompatible with the ability of MMOs to operate.

Second, MMOs could no longer be treated as if they were games. If you don't want your MMO to be a game, this is fine, but then you'd have a social world like *Second Life* rather than a game world like *World of Warcraft*. It wouldn't be an MMO, in other words.

By all means sell players virtual stuff if you want to, just don't let them real-world own it.

Security: RMT

Real-money trading is a gargantuan mess, which is why I'm discussing it in tedious detail. Right now, though, I'm not going to look at RMT *per se*; rather, I'm going to consider the security problems it raises.

RMT occurs because if some people want to cheat, other people will offer services that will help them cheat (hmm, OK, so maybe I will be a *little* judgmental about it). This is bad enough in itself, but it's made worse because in so helping these people, a good many other security problems are caused, too.

RMT is using real money to buy virtual goods or services. Although most of today's MMOs allow sanctioned unidirectional RMT for free-to-play microtransactions, almost all ban its general use between players. After all, if it were a harmless practice, then the developer could build goodwill by *giving away for free* whatever the players are buying. It's *not* harmless, though, so it's usually proscribed by the EULA (not that this stops RMTers from doing it; even when there are special servers where it's allowed, they'll still do it on the other ones). This is why engaging in RMT can usually be described as a form of cheating.

Even if you're personally ambivalent about RMT, the chances are that you'll not be happy with some of its side effects. For example, farming grounds can be effectively off-limits to nonfarmers ("if you want it, you have to buy it from us"), and the practice has an inflationary effect on an MMO's economy.

Furthermore, because RMT is usually prohibited, by necessity it attracts people with few scruples. They will regularly rip people off, which causes a big drain on customer service when they complain about it. Even if you're vehemently anti-RMT, its mere existence means that the following sequence of events could happen to you:

- Your account ID and password is acquired from keylogging or phishing.

- Your characters are stripped bare of everything.

- The proceeds are transferred to a level 1 mule.

- Your characters are left naked and destitute.

Following this, you'd call customer service to get your stuff back, thereby contributing to the 40 percent of their time that they already spend dealing with RMT disputes. Given that on average around a third to half of an MMO's post-tax income is spent on customer service, it's easy to calculate that for a typical $15/month subscription, $2/month is only there because of RMT.

In other words, with no RMT, the MMO would be $2/month cheaper. RMT raises the operating costs of the MMO for *all* players, whether they buy gold or they don't; you can understand why operators might want to limit it.

RMT is a lucrative business. The last figures I saw, the black market price of a stolen credit card's details was $6, and the black market price of a stolen *WoW* account's details was $10. Yes, you can make more money from a stolen *WoW* account than you can from a stolen credit card. This perhaps explains why Blizzard sells a dongle so that even if your login details are compromised, no one but you can use them.

If you, as a developer, want to stop RMT, you can do any of the following:

- Target the farmers and dealers

- Target the players who buy from them

- Target both of these groups

Most operators are reluctant to target players because of the resulting bad gameplay or bad publicity (just as in real life, police will usually target drug dealers rather than drug users). Even when people are caught engaging in RMT, they usually endure only a short ban as a punishment—which almost never stops the problem. There are some fairly small design changes that can be made that have a disproportionately large effect on RMTing, and this may be the way to go in future—although by all rights developers shouldn't have to do this.

RMT purveyors are as close as MMOs get to having a criminal underbelly. This is why so much effort is expended trying to stop their activities.

Save Files

One of the reasons people give for buying virtual goods is that they want to skip the boring part and get to the endgame.

That ought to mean there should exist a market for save files in single-player games to serve the needs of people who feel the same way about the boring *Civilization* midgame or whatever. Needless to say, there isn't such a market.

The *journey* is what's important. Arriving at the destination merely ends the journey.

Precedent

What concerned me when Sony Online Entertainment opened up their Station Exchange to allow the trading of virtual goods for real money with *EQ2* was not its effect on gameplay. *EQ2* was Sony's game, and if Sony wanted to enable RMT between players, well, that may be sad from a designer's perspective, but it's their business.

No, what worried me was that Sony did this *by conceding that virtual goods are property actually owned by players*. Suddenly, that's everyone's business.

Extrapolating the Argument

If there's something you want in an MMO—maybe a weapon, a mount, a crafting blueprint—but you don't want to spend hours of mindless grinding to get it, why *can't* you just buy it? You're going to get it anyway, so why waste the time?

Hmm. Well, if you are indeed going to get it anyway, why should you have to waste the money, either? If it's inevitable, why can't you have it right now for free? It doesn't have to be a trade-off between spending time or money—there are some players who have little of either. Why can't they just go to the in-game replicator, press the button marked KICK-ASS SWORD, and get a kick-ass sword there and then at no expense? Why can't they get *any* object they want whenever they want it?

Well, consider what effect it would have on gameplay if they *could* get whatever they wanted whenever they wanted it. The game would be hardly worth playing.

Now consider that this is the position that rich players are *already in* if they play an MMO in which gold farmers operate routinely or free-to-play is pay-to-win.

Bogus RMT Propaganda #2

Another argument offered by RMTers to justify their activity uses tugs-at-the-heartstrings emotional appeal.

Gold farmers are just poor people trying to earn an honest crust. Their families would starve if they didn't do it. Don't people who live in remote, provincial towns in third-world countries have the same right to set up their own business as people in the West? We're taking food from the mouths of children if we ban RMTing!

Hmm, well, if "the families would starve without our money" were a valid excuse, we wouldn't have banned sex tourism to southeast Asia. Some of the families of those child prostitutes really *are* desperately in need of the income they provide to survive.

Now of course, RMT isn't child prostitution, and RMT users aren't pedophiles—RMT isn't anywhere *near* that degree of serious. Indeed, the situation of the people involved in RMT isn't what you'd call desperation-bread-line-level anyway. Gold farmers have access to computers, for a start, and there's a lot more you can do with computers to make money than play computer games in the United States and Europe over an Internet connection. It's not such a matter of life and death that they *must* be able to do this or they'll starve—there are other things they could do.

If they particularly *want* to play games, fine, they can play those games in China and South Korea that are perfectly OK with RMT. The profits aren't as high, but that's often the case when a business is legitimate as opposed to illegitimate.

This bogus RMT propaganda makes it sound as if practitioners are noble, responsible people just trying to make ends meet for their families' sake. I'm sure Victorian clans of pickpockets felt the same way, too.

Spoiling other people's fun/business is *not* the only means by which you can make money from a combination of cheap labor, computers, and the Internet. There are plenty of other ways. Claiming that it's all that stands between RMT workers and a poverty-level existence is dishonest.

Is It Fair?

This is part of a discussion I had with MMO designer Brian 'Psychochild' Green. We were working on an MMO idea together, and I had suggested that people wouldn't think it fair that you could buy in-game advantages; Brian wanted to show that the boundaries of fairness were fuzzier so played devil's advocate and presented me with a string of questions. Here they are, along with my answers:

Is it fair that some people have more free time to play than others?

- Within the context of the game, yes.

Is it fair that some people have better Internet connections or graphics cards than others?

- Below the twitch threshold at which MMOs operate, it doesn't matter.

Is it fair that some people have better reaction times than others?

- In an MMO, lag and latency mean you can't do much with reaction times anyway. I have very, very fast reactions, but that doesn't help me at all in a virtual world.

Is it fair that some people can solve challenges faster than others?

- Part of the attraction of playing is that in solving challenges, you yourself get better at solving challenges.

Is it fair that some people have more friends in the game than others?

- It wouldn't be fair if you didn't get friends because "you're black" or "you're gay" or "you're a <some color> Sox fan." However, if you didn't have friends because you didn't want them or because other people wanted them more, then you're basically complaining about people being able to be themselves.

Is it fair that some people get into an exclusive raiding guild but not others?

- Again, it wouldn't be fair if "we don't take RL girls here" is their reason for rejecting you. If "we don't need another DPS" is their reason, then it is fair.

Is it fair that someone knows a developer on the team and gets inside information?

- No, that's not fair.

Is it fair that some classes are obviously favored over others?

- Yes it is. No one makes you play the unfavored classes.

Is it fair that some of us are developers and understand the game mechanics faster than others?

- No, it's not fair. The others get to spend months having fun, but we get to spend only hours.

Because I knew I wanted to publish our exchange in this book, I asked Brian if he had any further thoughts on the matter now it's a few years down the line. Here's what he replied:

I think that the rules are more flexible than most people think.

Players have accepted that others with more time to dedicate to a game do not have an unfair advantage in existing games, even though it is unquestionably an advantage not everyone enjoys. Other sports and games, such as cycling and golf, show that amount of money paid for equipment can have a role in a game. I think the important part is that this be made as clear as possible; it's when you change the rules of the game that I would agree it becomes unfair.

I don't believe we're in disagreement there.

Not *Cricket*

The laws of *Cricket* (don't you love games that have laws rather than rules?) say the bowler has to keep their arm straight during the delivery. If you bend your arm, that's throwing rather than bowling, and you will be penalized when spotted. This law is unnecessary, though: the governing body of *Cricket* could insist that wooden splints are attached to bowlers' arms to stop them from bending them, which would make the problem go away. It's certainly feasible, and it would completely stop all incidents of throwing. Thus, if the governing body *doesn't* stop people from throwing when it *could* adopt this simple mechanism to do so, well surely that means it's given the green light to people who want to throw?

No, it doesn't mean that. The antithrowing law is equally valid whether or not it's implemented using real-world physics. In MMOs, rules are equally valid whether implemented through the terms of service or server code.

People shouldn't have to put up with unwanted and inconvenient changes to their game just because some other people don't want to play by the rules.

Dealing with Unwanted RMT

There are basically four approaches to stopping people from trading in virtual goods.

1. **Copyright/IP**: This collapses if it's recognized that what's being sold is not some collection of virtual goods but a virtual service. "I will pay you $400 for your hat of wizardry" is merely a convenient way of saying "I will pay you $400 to transfer the hat of wizardry in the inventory of the character controlled by you to the inventory of the character controlled by me."

2. **EULA/ToS**: This collapses if the people making the money are not signatories of the EULA/ToS. I guess some contention could be made about their having "agents" doing their work for them, but this is a hard argument to win in court even when prosecuting mafia dons for ordering hoods to kill people. What a developer *could* do is adopt a zero-tolerance policy to go after every single person whom they can show is breaking the EULA. This would mean a lot of bannings, but they'd eventually win. The question is, at what cost?

3. **Alter the code**: Cap the amount of gold and objects that characters can give away per month. Cap the number of times an object can have its ownership transferred per month. Don't perform account or avatar transfers unless two details from name, address, and credit card number match. Don't let people give anything to anyone unless they're in the same guild. This would drive a gaping hole in the commodifiers' activities. However, no developer should *have* to do any of that. Creating MMOs is, at its heart, an artistic endeavor. Why should an artist who's doing nothing wrong have to change their art because some people want to vandalize it?

4. **"It's just a game"**: The traditional way, as practiced in small-scale MMOs for 30 years, is to have no EULA and no TOS. You can do whatever you like in the virtual world. So, however, can the developers, and *they* have access to the code. Thus, if they don't like what you're doing they can eliminate your goods, character, account—anything that "the code" allows. It may be that this approach can't

be scaled up, and it may be that consumer protection laws designed for nongame activities are brought to bear if there's no EULA. In the end, though, it comes down to "it's my ball, and if I don't want you to play with it then you can't." If that ability were ever successfully challenged, few companies would ever want to run an MMO at all— their hands would be tied too tightly.

Given that having no EULA is probably not an option for a large-scale commercial MMO at the moment, I generally recommend that developers go for the third option. They can use data mining from the beta test to find a reasonable capping level, perhaps backed up with a zero-tolerance attitude to put petty traders off scaling up their activities. The IP question does need answering, but I don't believe the answer is going to affect the outcome.

Can't Take It with You

Once you're in the "other world" of adventure and excitement, you can no longer use what you have in the mundane world to assist your quest. If you could, it wouldn't be an "other world," it would be the same world. That being the case, you're not going to get a hero's journey out of traveling from one to the other and back, as you never go anywhere.

The exception is that you *can* take the components of your self-actualization with you. For example, clever people have an advantage over unclever people if they take their intelligence with them into the other world. This is fine, though, because it's *your* journey, not anyone else's, and your understanding of your own intelligence is exactly the kind of fragmented feature that identity exploration helps reconcile. However, you can't argue that by the same token wealthy people can take their wealth with them into the other world because wealth isn't an internalized aspect of identity.

Only that which *is* internalized comes with you on your hero's journey. If wealth *is* important to your identity, then you seek wealth in the virtual world—you don't bring the wealth with you. If you nevertheless do bring it with you, well, you fail your hero's journey. You're only fooling yourself by continuing—and you know it.

The borderline between free-to-play and pay-to-win is a thin one, but if you cross it then you're not going to finish a hero's journey. Your self-worth will suffer, no matter how much you try to persuade yourself how great you remain.

Of course, none of this is going to bother you if you've already completed your hero's journey or if you didn't need to complete it in the first place.

Tip

When computer games are loading, they often give you a tip so you have something to read while you wait. These fall into two general categories: things you already know (which always remain for some time before they disappear), and things you may or may not know (but you can't tell because they disappear halfway through reading them).

Here's a tip I got once from *World of Warcraft*:

■ **Tip** You can download free programs to regularly scan your machine for malicious software including keyloggers.

Hmm. Yes. It might have been worth mentioning that some of these free programs are *themselves* malicious software including keyloggers, though.

To the Limits

Few people who engage in RMT against the wishes of the developer change their minds when it's pointed out to them that they don't own what they're selling. They insist that they do—or at least should—own it.

The most basic "I own it" position is that no matter what the developers say, to the players it just *looks* as if virtual property is the same as real property, *therefore it is*.

This "if it looks like a duck, walks like a duck, and quacks like a duck, it's a duck" argument can be reasonably applied in other MMO situations, not only those regarding property. Virtual reputation looks just like real reputation, virtual skills look just like real skills, virtual racism looks just like real racism, virtual incest looks just like real incest, virtual laws look just like real laws, and so on. Virtual property is just one facet of it, albeit the most important one.

How far would someone who believes "virtual property looks just like real property, therefore it is" be prepared to go before one of the consequences of this view became unacceptable to them?

Property is nine-tenths of the law. How much of that nine-tenths do you want to apply to "your" virtual goods?

Bigger Spenders

When it comes to virtual currency, a higher percentage of men than women buy it, but those women who do buy it spend double what the men who buy it spend.[7]

This is interesting to know, but it would be more interesting if we also knew what the corresponding proportions were for nonvirtual goods sales in real life.

Fragments

The hero's journey is just one example of how you can have fun. It fits MMOs well, but that doesn't mean you have to follow it. MMOs don't have a monopoly on fun, and within MMOs there are other ways to have fun. I personally believe that none of these are as intense or as rewarding as the hero's journey version, because they offer only fragments. Some people seem to like fragments, though; not everyone is ready to be a hero, and some already are heroes.

I don't think that people who don't want a hero's journey should be forced to have one; that would be ridiculous. However, I do feel that people who do want such a journey should be *allowed* to have one. Most RMT and a lot of F2P prevents them from doing this, which is the fundamental reason I'm against both in MMOs for which the designers don't want them.

A hero's journey is difficult to come by at the best of times; now that humanity has finally found a safe way to deliver one to anybody who wants to undergo it, we should strive to keep the opportunity available.

A Contradiction

Some players so identify with their characters that they regard them as part of who they are. They feel that they and their avatar are inextricably bound together.

Now you could argue that this means control over such a character should lie with the player behind it, because otherwise it would breach their human rights. To ban such a character would deprive the player not only of access to the MMO but also of part of their very *identity*. This means that *players* should own their characters, not the developer.

---

[7] Alec Meer: *Women higher spenders than men on virtual currency*. Games Industry Biz, 2010. www.gamesindustry.biz/articles/women-spend-2x-more-than-men-on-virtual-currency

Yes, in the light of the hero's journey this looks very persuasive. A judge might go for that in a court of law. Indeed, the first time I heard this argument advanced was on a panel of legal scholars who didn't immediately shoot it down.

However, when you look at *why* players generally want to own their characters, a problem emerges. The thing is, when you "own" something, you get a bundle of rights in it. Typically, these include the right to sell what you own to someone else. Sure enough, most of the people arguing (by whatever method) that players should *own* their characters are doing so hoping to enable the *sale* of such characters. The ability to sell characters is what's important; ownership is merely a prerequisite that must be met before a legitimate market in characters can establish itself.

That leads us to a contradiction, though. If the reason that a player gets to "own" their character is because this character is an intrinsic part of their identity, doesn't this mean they shouldn't *want* to sell it? If they *do* try to sell it, that means they *don't* regard it as enough of a part of their identity to want to retain it. So, why should they "own" it in the first place then?

It would be rather weird if players could dispose of characters through rights granted to them only because player and character are inseparable.

Still, weirdness never got in the way of law making.

RMT Servers

I mentioned earlier that in part to get a slice of the RMT cake, in part because they were getting flak from anti-RMTers, and in part because of the high customer-service costs arising from unsanctioned RMT, SOE decided to open up two *EverQuest 2* servers that were RMT-friendly. Play on those servers and you can RMT as much as you like. Sounds like a good idea, right?

Wrong.

Despite all the excuses they give for why RMT is a perfectly legitimate activity, the fact is that at heart most players who do it do it because they're cheats. Because of this, part of their thing about RMT is that *other players mustn't know that you've done it.*

Suppose you were a person who held these views. Why would you ever play on an RMT-friendly server? You can still buy virtual wealth on an RMT-unfriendly one just the same as you always did, except that now people will be slightly less likely to believe you've done it because "why aren't you playing on the RMT servers?" You'd stay where you were, obviously.

SOE's RMT-allowed servers were not a success, and the expected demand from other servers to turn RMT-allowed did not materialize. Until RMT becomes so commonplace that people accept it as the default, this was always going to be the case.

Yet should RMT become the default, then what? Would special, RMT-disallowed servers fare any better than the RMT-allowed ones do right now?

May, 2015: an MMO newbie in *The Secret World* asks in cabal (guild) chat where the best place is to buy pax (*TSW*'s currency). Said newbie is surprised to learn not only that paying real money for pax is forbidden by Funcom's terms of service but also that it isn't even Funcom who's selling it on these sites.

Minimum Viable Player Base

The costs of hosting and operating a text MUD back in the day are commensurate with the costs of hosting and operating a graphical MMO today. The development costs today are much higher, but the operating costs are on a par.

Assume that an MMO's development costs have already been recouped several times over. Assume that you rarely add new content and that you just fix the occasional bug or exploit players discover. Assume that the customer support load is roughly proportional to the number of players. Assume that improved technology means that operating costs will fall to hobbyist-affordable levels.

In these circumstances, text MUDs could, did, and do survive happily for decades with a player base of 50 or even fewer.

How many players would a graphical MMO need at a minimum to keep going?

Would the answer be "50 or even fewer"?

Right to Buy

Here in the UK we have "right to buy" laws. If you rent a house from a local authority for long enough, you can buy it—whether the local authority wants you to or not. More than 1,300,000 people have bought their houses from local authorities this way. New legislation extends the right to tenants of housing authority properties, not just to people who live in council houses. It's possible that in the future it could be extended to private landlords, too.

Could such future legislation be used to claim ownership of virtual houses being rented, either from other players or in-context from the virtual world operator?

Just how far do you have to go before you can say, "Hmm, you know, this *doesn't* look, walk, or quack like a duck"?

Is It Right?

Some people accept that it might be unfair of them to spend their hard-earned money (do people ever admit to any other kind?) on advancing their character in their MMO of choice, but they defend themselves on the grounds that it balances out worse injustices. Here are three of the more sensible appeals I've heard:

"Is it right that I can get something for free from a friend but I can't buy it from a stranger?"

- Yes, it's right. Friendship is a two-way thing, so you're as likely to reciprocate as they are to give to you. If you buy something, it's strictly a one-way, seller-to-customer arrangement.

"Is it right that people in guilds get benefits that help them progress, but if I'm not in a guild, I can't buy those benefits from someone who wants to sell them to me?"

- Yes, it's right. Learn to read game designs. This one is telling you to join a guild. So, either join a guild or stop playing.

"Is it right that someone who has more free time has an advantage over someone who has less free time?"

- Yes, it's right. Some of my students have part-time jobs and don't have as much time to study as the rest. However, they do have a little more money as a result. Should I be able to sell them marks for their coursework? No, I'm going to jail if I try that.

Boxing doesn't allow competitors to be bribed to throw a fight. Horse racing doesn't allow jockeys to pay for a head start. *Soccer* doesn't allow teams to agree to play for a draw so both go through to the next round of the World Cup. These are all examples of how real-world EULAs are constructed to prevent real-world interference in real-world games. Why should virtual worlds be any different?

Is it right that someone in exactly the same position as you but who doesn't have your money can't spend their way to success as much as you can?

Unwanted Responsibility

If players get to own "their" virtual property in an MMO, the MMO's operator is obliged to take on several responsibilities. The one that interests advocates of player-ownership the most is that the operator should do nothing to reduce the value of player-owned property.

This sounds reasonable enough. If someone were to damage your car in real life, whether deliberately or accidentally, you'd want compensation from them, right?

With MMOs, the value of virtual items is irrevocably tied to the software that implements them. If the people who control the software do something to it that affects the integrity of a virtual item—changing its stats, for example—they are liable to be sued by whichever player real-world owns that item; they have effectively damaged it. This simple fact would mean they couldn't do routine operations such as nerfing for game balance without getting sued by the people whose stuff was nerfed.

It's not just damage that affects value: so does scarcity. If I buy one of only 20 limited-edition cars and then the manufacturer creates another 10,000 of them, that manufacturer is *so* getting sued. Likewise, if the deadliest weapon in an MMO is a rare Sword of Truculence and I pay a premium to get it, I'll be on my phone to a lawyer at once should the next patch include a common Sword of Greater Truculence. My investment has been wiped out. The MMO operator is 100 percent responsible for wiping it out, too.

Now developers could argue that people expect obsolescence in the real world so they should also expect it in a virtual world. The difference is that in the real world no changes are ever made to physics. No deity is going to remove every pirate hat from the universe, but a developer could well decide to do just that from an MMO. Everyone who owned a pirate hat would be out of pocket as a result, and "obsolescence" doesn't cover it. After Funcom sold an ill-advised mankini outfit to players of *The Secret World* (for their characters), it returned all their money when it later saw sense and removed the abomination.

Because pretty well any change to an MMO affects *someone* adversely, having to compensate people so affected would drastically curtail designers' ability to evolve their MMOs and to fix bugs. If a change causes direct or collateral damage to an object that someone owns, that person would be due fair recompense for that object's subsequent loss in value. That's a tremendous disincentive to make any changes in the first place.

Perhaps if designers worked in such a way that it could be shown their changes were completely impartial, then it could be argued that they should be no more held liable for the loss in value of a virtual object than Google is liable for the loss in value of a company when a change to its ranking algorithm pushes that company further down its search results. However, Google isn't selling people search result placings; MMOs (particularly free-to-play ones) *are* selling the very virtual goods that they themselves are then reducing in value.

Look at it like this: when you buy a new PC, you know its value is going to fall because better PCs will inevitably come out. However, you would still feel cross if the manufacturer sent it a command over the Internet to make it run slower or to switch it off entirely. No matter how laudable their reason for doing it, you would still want compensation. It's your PC, and the manufacturer just nerfed it.

This is just one example of the range of property laws that could bring an MMO down if they were enforced. All suffer from the same irony: if you apply them, they will damage the MMO's playability and players will leave. How much is a virtual object worth if the world in which it exists has been shut down?

Bridges and Crocodiles

Suppose you want to rescue a lost soul on the opposite bank of a crocodile-infested river.

Swimming across a crocodile-infested river is brave if there's no bridge.

Swimming across a crocodile-infested river when there *is* a bridge is stupid, not brave.

People who buy high-level characters are erecting bridges across crocodile-infested rivers. They're making people who think themselves brave look stupid.

Rent-a-Character

So, you want to go on a raid but your character class, level, and gearscore aren't up to scratch. What do you do?

Well, you rent a character that *is* up to scratch.

This is a revenue model that has been tried several times, but never with any success. The problem is, most MMO developers ban the practice: as with buying characters outright, it's seen as a form of cheating. This means that if you want to rent a character, you have to rent it from someone who is operating in violation of the EULA.

Therein lies the problem. People who are prepared to flout the rules are, by definition, prepared to flout the rules. If I rent an account from you, what's to stop me from selling it to someone else? Sure, I've sold something that wasn't mine to sell, but you rented out something that wasn't yours to rent out.

Because of this, independent character-renting companies usually find themselves being ripped off (at the very least by rival companies). Besides, if they ever started making a significant profit then the MMO companies themselves would get in on the act. After all, they can create a character with the exact class, level, and gearscore you need in but an instant.

It wouldn't cost much to offer this service, either. So, why *don't* developers sell leases on characters?

A Vending Machine

MMO operators don't charge you for in-world money: the game gives it away for free when you do stuff. Some people regard this "do stuff" as a waste of their time, though. They don't want to grind for gold.

If there were no harm in letting people who don't want to grind for gold just have the gold, then the operator could provide some place in the MMO where you could just go and get the gold effortlessly, as much of it as you desire. No need to sell it; just take it and have fun!

This way, the people who like grinding can still do it the old-fashioned way, and the people who don't like it can press the button on the vending machine and avoid wasting their time.

So, why don't MMO operators do that, then?

Well, it's because the vast majority of the people who "like" grinding only do so because they get a reward for it. If they could get the reward without grinding, they wouldn't like grinding. However, then the people who don't like grinding wouldn't like even playing. The rewards for *not* grinding are meaningful only if other people *are* grinding.

So, that's why MMO developers don't give away virtual currency for free.

That and the fact that the entire economy of the MMO would inflate to arithmetic overflow levels if they did.

Acts of Gods

Insurance companies regard some events as "acts of God." Your car was flattened by freak hailstones the size of coconuts. Your house was damaged by a cow hurled against the wall by a strong wind. Locusts ate your orchard. There's no one to blame for these things; they "just happen."

In MMOs, someone *is* to blame for these things because they don't "just happen." They happen because the MMO's developer causes or allows them to happen. If the designer so chose, hailstones the size of coconuts wouldn't exist, winds able to hurl cows at walls wouldn't occur, and locusts would stay peacefully in their special locust reservations.

If you, as a player, real-world own your virtual car, house, or orchard, *could* you actually sue the gods for acts of gods?

Chargebacks

In June 2005, as I've mentioned several times already, Sony Online Entertainment legitimized RMT on two new *Everquest 2* servers. In the experiment's first year, 9,042 of the 40,663 players on the two Station Exchange servers registered to participate in RMT, opening 51,680 auctions of which 39,743 resulted in a sale.[8] Although not really intended as a money-making scheme, SOE nevertheless recognized a revenue of $274,083 from commissions and listing fees in that first year of operation.

Sony's aim was to act as honest broker. If you bought something at auction, you paid Sony, not the seller. Sony paid the seller on your behalf, coinciding the payment with the transfer of goods. It was safe to use, it was all on the level, and it did indeed meet its major objective by cutting down on the time that customer service had to spend on dispute resolution (from 40 percent to 30 percent).

So why, in 2008, did SOE agree to migrate its Station Exchange users to a new, independent service called Live Gamer Exchange?

In a word, *chargebacks*.

Sometimes, when a consumer buys goods using a credit card, either the goods never arrive or they do arrive but aren't what was expected. If this happens, the consumer can ask the credit card company for their money back ; the time they have in which to do this varies by country, but is usually at least 28 days. The credit card company will then take the money (plus a processing fee) from the merchant and return it to the consumer. This is known as a *chargeback*.

So, here's what happened to SOE:

- Fraudster buys *EQ* platinum pieces on Station Exchange for $100.

- SOE takes $100+fee$_1$ from fraudster's credit card and credits $100 to seller's.

- Fraudster sells the platinum pieces on Station Exchange for $80.

- SOE takes $80+fee$_2$ from buyer's credit card and credits $80 to fraudster's.

---

[8]Noah Robischon: *Station Exchange: Year One*. Sony Online Entertainment, 2007. www.fredshouse.net/images/SOE%20Station%20Exchange%20White%20Paper%201.19.pdf

- Fraudster issues a chargeback on original $100+fee$_1$ purchase.

- Credit card company takes $100+fee$_1$+fee$_3$ from SOE and credits $100+fee$_1$ to fraudster.

- Result: fraudster has own $100+fee$_1$ back, plus $80.

Worse, if too many chargebacks are issued against a merchant, the merchant has to pay the credit card company a fine on top of the chargeback processing fee (fee$_3$)—and SOE was seeing fines totaling more than $1,000,000 in six months. SOE could have challenged the chargebacks, but this took time, and there were concerns about bad publicity.

SOE realized that the losses were considerably outweighing the gains, so it decided to pass the business on to Live Gamer (now known as Emergent Payments). Live Gamer accepted the contract because unlike SOE they operated cross-publisher and thus had access to more data (a credit card that has been used to defraud one developer can't be used to defraud a second). Also, Live Gamer had merely to present itself as being professional, not player-friendly as SOE did, so it could pursue challenges more vigorously.

Chargebacks are a general problem for virtual worlds. That same anti-SOE scam would work with land sales in *Second Life*. Gold farmers even use it on each other: they sometimes buy their rivals' offerings and then issue a chargeback on what they paid, thus decreasing their competitor's inventory while increasing their own. It's all very distasteful.

That's not going to stop the guy who really, really *needs* that epic shoulder armor *right now*, though.

Defeatism

One of the more annoying views put forward by supporters of RMT is that it can't be stopped, merely reduced a little. This means that it inevitably creates a black market, which puts players at the mercy of unscrupulous traders. Why not throw in the towel and bring it out into the open, where its operation can be subject to proper scrutiny?

Yes, well if you accept this argument then by the same token we should allow competitors in the Olympics to take performance-enhancing drugs because we can't stop them all. Then we can thrill to the sight of athletes vying to win the 100 meters before the massive doses of steroids they have taken burst their hearts.

Legitimizing a black market can have even worse effects than keeping it illegitimate (which is why we don't see LSD for sale in supermarkets). In MMOs, legitimizing the sale of virtual objects for real money can take away a lot of the reasons why people enjoy playing in the first place.

I am happy for virtual worlds to come in two flavors: commodified and uncommodified. However, I utterly reject the assertion that *all* MMOs should follow the same, pro-commodification rules, under the defeatist proposition that it's impossible to stop RMT completely. Many smaller MMOs (such as, oh, let's be cautious, 90 percent of the world's text MUDs) have no RMT whatsoever— yet making them adhere to rules that assumed they did could kill them. If they don't have the problem, why try to fix it? What's more, how do we know this attitude wouldn't screw up MMOs with different business models or solutions (technical or operational) that are yet to be invented?

I really don't know why some pro-RMT activists keep on repeating this "if you can't beat 'em, join 'em" mantra. Why do they think that it's impossible for commodified and uncommodified worlds to exist side-by-side? I'm basically in favor of having both. I really don't understand why anyone would want one to be eliminated in favor of the other.

Crystal Ball

Back in 2003, I proposed four general ways by which the RMT industry might be threatened.

- **Over-mining**: If too many people get in on the act, the amount of sellable stuff extracted from an MMO will affect the price it fetches.

- **If you can't beat 'em, join 'em**: MMO companies can produce stuff for their MMOs with practically zero overhead. If they were to embrace the idea of selling stuff, they could pose serious problems for the RMT service industry.

- **Skill checks**: The price of goods depends on their being usable. MMOs designed so that in the hands of an amateur stuff will fall apart would really cut back on trading.

- **Nontransferability**: If goods can't be transferred, they can't be sold.

I didn't have legal action in my list, as I felt it unlikely that a ruling by a court of law would trouble a gold farmer.

So, what happened?

- Black marketers often turn on one another to keep control of a lucrative market, and this is what occurred with MMO RMT operations. Organizations trying to muscle in on the act were scammed, issued with credit card chargebacks, subject to fraud, and generally ripped-off by larger, more established groups. This even included those MMO developers who tried to facilitate RMT, such as Sony with its Station Exchange. Prices therefore remained high. *Wrong.*

- The current *de rigueur* model for MMOs is free-to-play. This involves the developer selling stuff to the players directly instead of acting as a broker for inter-player sales. *Right.*

- Player expectations became such that it was hard to destroy items permanently. Even incompetent players couldn't break their stuff; they just paid a bit more for repairs. *Wrong.*

- Large numbers of bind-on-pickup items did indeed appear. In particular, anything sold by developers directly is usually nontransferable. *Right.*

Two out of four: not bad. To be honest, though, I saw the last point as being mainly used to stop character sales so was a bit lucky with that one.

Serving Guilds

There may be reasons why developers would like players to operate closed, guild-only servers, but why would guilds want to sign up to them?

Well, maybe you don't like how the game is when it's open to all-comers? Maybe you're a strong role-playing guild, or maybe you're vehemently anti-RMT, or maybe you want a world where all the players are RL-Hindu, or maybe you'd like everyone to speak Esperanto. Maybe you want to use access to your server be the prize on offer when you recruit members on other servers. Maybe you want to charge regular players extra to play on your server because of the superior customer service you'll be offering. Maybe you just want a world that's more democratic.

There are plenty of reasons that a guild might want to have its own server.

Would *you* want one for *your* guild? Why? Or why not?

Nature *vs.* Nurture

Is there anyone who chooses to play an MMO on the basis that it allows them to pay real money to skip content? Why would they do that? If the content is so unappetizing that they don't want to consume it, why are they even there? Why aren't they somewhere that has content so tasty they'd want seconds? They're paying *not* to get stuff they've *paid* for!

Are people born RMTers and F2Pers, or do they become RMTers and F2Pers?

Security: Griefing

Originally, griefing was doing something that you knew would annoy someone else, simply because the knowledge that they would be annoyed gave you pleasure. I picked the herb you were going to pick not because *I* wanted it but because I knew *you* wanted it and because you *knew* I didn't want it, thereby inciting you to feelings of rage and impotence—which is what I *really* wanted.

These days, overuse by people trying to dramatize their lesser plights has watered the meaning down somewhat. "You stole the herb I was going to pick after the one I was going to pick after this one I'm picking now—you griefer!"

I'm going to go with the original meaning, if only to grief the people who go with other ones.

So, griefing: an important factor when considering the security implications of griefing is whether it's actually OK. Sometimes, it's part of the game. The most high-profile MMO that revels in allowing griefing is CCP's *EVE Online*, but the practice of within-the-rules griefing is a long-established one.

Early textual worlds had an explicit `steal` command, which allowed you to take things from the inventory of other players when they didn't want you to. It wasn't without their *permission*—they implicitly okayed your doing it when they signed up to the game—but it usually wasn't *desired*. Even some modern MMOs allow you to take belongings from people defeated in combat.

Is this a form of griefing? Well, it can be (depending on the motivation of the thief), but if the rules allow it, all you need to do as a developer is monitor the activity. Griefing doesn't cause a security issue when it's properly covered by the design, even if it causes other issues (an exodus of cry-babies who like to be wrapped in woolen blankets to protect them from those nasty other players, for example).

Where griefing does become an issue is when the design can't possibly cover all the situations. In other words, with user-created content...

Time to Cock

The gist of the security problems raised by user-created content is succinctly summed up by the phrase *time to cock*. This is the length of time it takes for a user base, when presented with the opportunity to create content within a virtual world, to construct an image of a penis. Traditionally, it's measured in nanoseconds.

I once spent a pleasant day consulting for a virtual world called *Church of Fools*, which was built by and for practicing Christians. I figured that if they were liberal enough to hire someone who was on a widely distributed list of famous atheists, I should be liberal enough to work for someone who ran a widely publicized Christian web site. Anyway, they turned out to be really nice people, and while we were discussing the technical specs of their (small, but playable) MMO, I asked what animations they had. They said they had several, including kneeling down and praying.

Immediately, my designer alarms went off. Here's how the conversation continued:

```
              ME
Do you extend the bounding box
for collision detection round
people who kneel down to pray?

              CHURCH OF FOOLS
We do now...

              ME
So, how long was it before
someone stood in front of someone
praying so it looked as if they
were getting oral sex?

              CHURCH OF FOOLS
Within 15 minutes of opening to
the public.
```

In *Ultima Online*, people would find a nice open space and patiently place objects on the ground so that they were in the shape of a classic graffiti penis. I've heard (but have never been able to confirm it) that in *The Sims Online* groups of a couple of dozen people would organize themselves into the shape of a penis and then move around near the McDonald's store in perfectly choreographed unison.

It's not just crude images that players create, of course. They can create all kinds of subtle images that designers really, really wish they wouldn't. Yes, we see gold farmers spelling out their URL with the bodies of scores of dead gnomes in *World of Warcraft*, but that could just as easily be a racist jibe or libelous insult—which could mean legal liability for the developer. Legal liability means law suits.

Where penises lead, lawyers follow...

Soul for Sale

I have your least-favorite politician's soul in this glass jar. I don't believe souls exist myself, but I'm quite prepared to sell one to someone who does. Anyone want to buy it from me? Just think, you can own your least-favorite politician's very soul merely by buying it from me. Send me the money and it's yours, plain and simple.

Well, no.

First, you can't get a soul in a jar. A soul (if you believe in them) is what is left of an individual when their physical body is removed. It's an emergent composite of the individual's thoughts, deeds, and being that can't be isolated in physical space.

Second, even if you could get souls in a jar, your least-favorite politician's soul is not mine to sell.

In MMOs, players who engage in F2P are buying things that don't exist but that instead are emergent composites of the interactions between bit patterns, rules, and illusion; they can't be isolated in physical space.

People who engage in RMT also do this, and furthermore they're selling things that (unless their original owners say so) are not theirs to sell.

Your least-favorite politician can't stop you and I from making whatever private deals we want, but the mere fact that we can make a deal doesn't imbue it with automatic legitimacy.

You want to say your least-favorite politician doesn't have a soul anyway, right?

Security: UCC

Although user-created content (UCC) almost instantly and inevitably leads to depictions of male genitalia, this kind of assault on an MMO is not as dangerous as another kind. Players who break social propriety don't stop the MMO from operating; they merely inhibit the enjoyment of other players (or attract the attention of the law).

An altogether more dangerous form of user-created content comes when players are allowed to create not only objects but also code. If they can write programs that the MMO will execute, the potential for problems is much, much worse.

When the developers of *Second Life* were explaining their system to me back in 2004, before they got big, they explained that they allowed players to script objects on the server. I asked whether the objects they scripted could create other objects; the Lindens said they could. I asked if users could attach scripts to these objects; the Lindens said they could. I asked if, therefore, it was possible for players to create self-replicating objects that could spread like tribbles in next to no time until their virtual world was unable to cope. The Lindens thought about it a bit, and said yes, it was possible, but why would anyone do that?

Well, because they could?

Needless to say, a couple of years later someone did do it, and sure enough, the virtual world was unable to cope. Server by server, the grid went down.

If you allow players to engage in this kind of free programming on the server, you always run the risk that something like this will happen. If you want to stop it, you can do one or more of the following:

- Allow it in walled gardens. It may crash your own space, but it won't crash anyone else's space.

- Limit access to resources. If a user account takes up too much processing power or memory or creates too many objects, kill all its processes.

- Allow it, but trust people not to do it; punish those who abuse your trust (using lawyers if necessary).

The main causes for concern relate to server-side programming. If scripts are run locally on clients, in the way that *World of Warcraft*'s add-ons are, then that's basically a walled-garden approach. Yes, you may cause a crash or a hang in your client, but you don't cause everyone else to suffer (well, not unless you wrote an add-on everyone uses and introduce a bug).

Walled gardens themselves are not entirely safe, though; sometimes, even supposedly sandbox spaces can be used for nefarious purposes. For example, until it was pointed out to Linden Lab that this was possible, *Second Life* could in theory have been used as a spambot to issue database injection attacks on other systems.[9] I'm guessing most developers of virtual worlds probably wouldn't want their product to be used as a platform for launching such attacks.

User-created content can be an exciting and powerful technology. Designers hoping to allow its exploitation to the full do need, however, to remember just how powerful "powerful" can be in this context.

---

[9]Michael Thurman: *Hacking Second Life*. Black Hat Europe, 2008. www.blackhat.com/presentations/bh-europe-08/Thumann/Whitepaper/bh-eu-08-thumann-WP.pdf

Something to Balk At

There are some things that even the most ardent fan of free-to-play might balk at.

Let's say your character is called Polly.

Suppose someone else comes along who wants to play using the name Polly. You've already claimed it, so this means they can't have it. Tough luck, other Polly!

Except ... what if they could pay the game operator to transfer the name Polly from your character to theirs? Now you either have to think of a new name or pay even more money to get your name back from the usurper Polly.

Maybe the other Polly could pay for your friends list? Or to have your name taken off other people's friends lists?

If *everything* is for sale, then things you thought weren't for sale are for sale, too.

Picture This

When users create content, most of it is of poor quality. It's a bit like karaoke: the people who are involved have fun, everyone expects poor quality anyway, and when something surprisingly good does come along, it really stands out. However, if someone picked up the mic and started singing obscene lyrics or trying to sell you something, well you might perhaps think that a line had been crossed.

So, how do MMO developers make sure that any user-created content they display is, if not necessarily high quality, at least not illegal or immersion-busting?

One way to do it is to let people create any content they like and then take it down if someone complains. This is fine for adult-rated social worlds such as *Second Life*. For most game worlds, though, it could be that the damage has already been done by the time an abuse is reported. To put it bluntly, anything that provides a profanity filter for the words that players type is going to need an equivalent for anything else they can create or upload.

Another way is to vet content before it's allowed to go live; that's how the app store works for iPhones. This approach has the side effect of making you liable if anything untoward does get through, but the benefits tend to outweigh that. What they don't outweigh, though, is content-creation spam.

Some people are highly prolific creators, but not all of them have great critical faculties. Why submit one hat design for sale in the MMO store when you can submit 20, each with minor variations? Naturally, you'll want them all to be rated, and you'll want to know why the hat with the green parrot image was accepted when the one with the red parrot image wasn't, and then you'll want to know whether this new one with an image of a green parrot wearing an eye patch will be accepted, and what about this other one where the green parrot image on the hat is itself wearing a hat that has a red parrot image on it? There's great potential for the gates to be overwhelmed by a flood of material, meaning it can be days or weeks before players get their rejection emails.

Of course, you can reduce the flow of content-to-be-assessed if you limit how much any individual can have pending (which can stifle creativity) or make people pay to submit them (which means rich people still get to spam you, but poor people don't create at all).

Pirates of the Burning Sea tried a different approach. A peer-review scheme was set up, whereby new content was looked at by other creators of new content, and only if they passed it did the developers look at it. This is a reasonable solution: if you want to submit 30 hat designs, you should have to look at 30 creations by other people to "pay" for it. The usual problems of peer-reviewed sites (ballot-stuffing, false identities, always voting the same way, and so on) are much reduced by doing it this way.

There's still a potential problem in that players can sneak in a provocative design by submitting two innocuous ones that look fine separately but alarming next to each other. Players would have to be very creative to pull this off, of course—but hey, if you want to encourage creativity, you can't really complain!

Underground, Undercover

One of the defeatist responses to the problem of preventing RMT in MMOs that don't want it is that any attempts to stop it will just drive it underground, and then developers won't even be able to find the sites where such trading goes on, let alone set the law on them.

Yeah, right, because none of these developers has their own people playing undercover. That was something that used to happen only in textual worlds and they can't *possibly* have thought of it for modern MMOs.

Playing Within the Law

Here's an argument you sometimes get from cheats in defense of their conduct: if the law of the land permits an activity, what right have MMO operators to ban that activity?

In general, games have rules. *By definition*, these are regulations beyond those stated in law. People agree to limit their behavior in some areas to gain freedom in others. For example, if I'm playing *Backgammon*, then I eschew my natural ability to move tokens an arbitrary number of points, instead restricting myself to moving them only according to the dice roll. I do this because, if you also do it, we both benefit (assuming we both think *Backgammon* is fun, which I guess some people must). Nothing in the law says I can't move my *Backgammon* tokens as many points as I want; it's a limitation stated only in the rules of the game. When I (metaphorically) sign up to play, I agree to abide by those rules. If I break them, well, whatever game I'm playing, it's no longer *Backgammon*.

Some people want to play MMOs that don't have RMT. They are willing to give up their freedom to use real-world economics so as to have the fun of playing on a more level field. *They should be allowed to do that.* If someone comes along who likes RMT, that person shouldn't play a game in which RMT is against the rules. If they play it anyway, they should expect to be kicked out when discovered.

People who like RMT and see nothing wrong with it are perfectly entitled to play MMOs where it is allowed or even encouraged. People who don't like RMT should not, however, be forced to play alongside people who disregard the rules and use RMT anyway.

Some performance-enhancing drugs are perfectly legal (for example three cups of coffee) but are banned by sports authorities. People who want to take these drugs are fully entitled to set up their own international athletics competitions if they feel really strongly that they're doing nothing wrong. Those who do not want legal drug-taking activities in their competitions are, however, within their rights to kick people out if they find they're breaking the rules on the subject. It doesn't matter what the law of the land says; it's the rules of the game that matter. The law of the land lets me ride a motorbike in a 100 meter race, but even those who advocate allowing performance-enhancing drugs would probably draw the line at that.

The state does intervene in games if those games impact people outside them. For example, *Last Call Poker* (teams of players link together gravestones to make poker hands) can upset the bereaved whose relatives' headstones are effectively being used as game tokens; there's perhaps a case for prohibiting it. The state will also intervene if the players can be overly impacted themselves, as they might with *Russian Roulette*. Other than that, though, the state will not generally intervene (and nor should it).

Now with RMT, the state has to decide whether the impact on nonplayers of not intervening is sufficient reason for it to step in. It needs to balance this against what would happen if it did step in. For example, legislators could reason that RMT in *WoW* means that nonplayers are having to pay slightly more tax to cover for the revenue that is not being garnered from *WoW*'s players for in-game transactions. Therefore, the law should tax in-game transactions. However, that would kill the game stone dead. Not only would there be no income from such a tax, neither would there be income from the tax on subscriptions that Blizzard pays. Therefore, the public purse is better off if in-world transactions are not taxed.

Then again, legislators may decide that this is the price that has to be paid to maintain the tax system's integrity and so close it down anyway.

Games are not *defined* by real-world laws; they *extend* them.

Separating Wheat from Chaff

How do you separate good user-created content from bad user-created content?

The new-to-UCC designer will typically come at this using the ju-jitsu move of applying the problem's own strength to defeat it. Players create this content, so use players to identify the good stuff! There are good ways of managing voting systems that can't be gamed, so this should work.

Well, yes, it should—and indeed it would if it weren't for the fact that the players' idea of what's good is wrong.

What content would killers vote for? Deathtraps. What content would explorers vote for? None at all; it's not canon. What content would achievers vote for? Giveaways, because anything that rains loot from the sky helps them advance. What content would socializers vote for? Also giveaways, because then the game won't get in the way of their hanging out with their friends. You always get mainly deathtraps or giveaways when players create or vote for content.

I should mention that this applies only for *game-consequent* content. If the UCC has *no impact whatsoever* on the game as a whole, then achievers at least will vote for content that's actually fun to play through.

If you want UCC in your MMO, you therefore have to isolate it all in hermetically sealed sandboxes. Stuff can get in, but nothing can get out; loot, XP, reputation, currency—it all stays inside. Cosmetic-only items *might* be allowable. This means that UCC has zero effect on the game, so players' views as to its merits switch from extrinsic to intrinsic. If they find it fun, they will be more inclined to say so.

That doesn't mean they *will* find it fun, of course. It is UCC after all.

Oh, and it turns out that the ju-jitsu move may actually work if you apply it right.

Inflated Sense of Entitlement

If someone steals my passport, I'm pretty sure I don't get compensated for its black market value, and I'm pretty sure it's the government that owns it anyway, not me personally.

If someone steals my credit card, I'm pretty sure I don't get compensated for its black market value, and I'm pretty sure it's the issuing company that owns it anyway, not me personally.

Yet when people find their MMO account has been hacked, why do so many of them expect the MMO operator to award them compensation?

Perfect World

Suppose you found a really good MMO with no time sinks or any of the other features that people routinely explain "force" them to engage in RMT. In this wonderful MMO, you can drop in any time you want, play with your friends no matter much or how little experience they have, at whatever content level you choose. When you compete with other players, it's on a completely level playing field.

Further suppose that, after a while, someone sets up a site selling, say, information. It's like coaching in athletics: people who buy this information will have an edge. There's no pretense about it. These people are buying raw advantage so they can beat you and feel good about it. Would you be just fine playing with such people? Would you feel that you'd have to pay for the same information just to regain your rightful place in the hierarchy?

All those points of law about who owns virtual property and what they can do with it are a red herring when it comes to *why* people RMT. People RMT because they want to give the impression that they're better players than they really are.

Fair's Unfair

One of the big hopes I had for computer games was that they would make society fairer.

Fairness is intrinsic to games. People don't like playing games that they perceive to be unfair. The more that people play games, the better sense of fairness they get. That sense of fairness is not restricted to games, however: players take it with them when they're not playing games. Real life *isn't* fair, sure, but it *could* be fairer. People who play games will be more conscious of life's unfairnesses than if they didn't play games. Some of those unfairnesses they may even be able to do something about.

Of course, some games are *not* fair in an absolute sense. You know that when you start to play, though. Gambling games typically favor the house, for example, and even *Chess* is asymmetric. However, what these games deliver in terms of (usually) fun is regarded by the players as sufficient reward to overcome minor, noise-level degrees of unfairness. They're not going to play a vastly unfair game without commensurate rewards, though.

So, my hope was that the sense of fairness that's part and parcel of games would carry across to the mainstream as more people played games. While I believe that this does indeed happen, and people's greater awareness of fairness is indeed being awakened, unfortunately the mainstream is fighting back. In particular, the revenue model for most professionally developed social games involves microtransactions; players are encouraged to buy an advantage over other players, which some do. This completely flies in the face of fairness within a games context, although I have heard people who buy virtual goods and services argue that it would be "unfair" if they couldn't use their money in games when they can use it in most other circumstances. As a result of players' growing acceptance of this revenue model, their acceptance of unfairness as an admissible quality of games also grows. This diminishes their sense of fairness in games. If games are unfair anyway, what does it matter if you cheat?

I was hoping we'd get "games are fair; why isn't life?" and I was pleased with how that was working out. Unfortunately, the pendulum is starting to swing to "life isn't fair; why are games?"

Oh well, back to the drawing board.

Silver Linings

I was at a conference in the late 1990s where a speaker argued that the only reason frequent-flier miles were sustainable was because they weren't sellable. If you could sell your miles, then airlines wouldn't be able to honor them. It's only the fact that most people don't have enough frequent-flier miles to use them before they expire that makes them viable.

As someone who at the time would have liked to have sold 31,000 KLM air miles if I could have done, I appreciated both sides of the argument.

Modern MMOs use a similar system in their endgames, in which you get non-tradable tokens for completing weekly or twice-weekly raids. These can be cashed in for top-quality gear. If such tokens were tradable, people would farm them using alts and kit out their main characters far quicker than was intended, which would result in a demand from the players for the creation of yet more content (which is very expensive). The same argument applies to bind-on-pickup (BOP) items.

As I mentioned earlier, though, originally BOP items were brought in by designers as a way to curtail RMT. If you can't give it to anyone else, you can't sell it to anyone else either. Adding BOP objects helped MMO designers extend the length of the elder game.

Just because an undesirable activity may force a design change, that doesn't mean the change it forces is always bad.

Then again, it doesn't always mean it's always good, either.

Ju-Jitsu

Judging whether content is good (or at least acceptable) manually is expensive. You can cut down on submissions by charging, as I've mentioned, but that just means you lose any creative people who are poor and keep any uncreative people who are rich.

Also, people want feedback when you judge them. You can't give them a yes/no as if you're some mystical black box; they want to know what it is they have to fix. Well, you *can* just give them a yes/no, but unless they answer is yes, they won't like you.

Feedback created from checkbox-filling is better than nothing but isn't enough (especially if you charged them money to submit). They want *details*. "Too many unoriginal ideas" may be true, but they want to know exactly *which* ideas are unoriginal so they can fix them.

Of course, if you *do* give them details, they will then pull a couple of all-nighters and resubmit the result, confident that it'll now be a shoo-in.

Hmm. That's a problem, then.

It's not a problem confined to UCC for games, though. All creative industries have this problem. The way they solve it is to use the problem's strength against it but in a refined way. They use *agents*.

Suppose that any player who has, say, three characters at the level cap can set up as an agent (the three characters thing is to discourage sock puppets). As an agent, they can recommend any UCC *other than their own* to you, the developer, for consideration. If you like what they send you, you will look at their stuff with higher priority next time; if you don't like it, you'll put their next submission at the back of the queue. If they send you too much rubbish, you might tell them to stop.

This way, senior players put their own reputation on the line for other players. These agents will do the filtering, the suggesting for improvements, the pitching—just as happens with books, screenplays, and acting.

As for *why* they would do it, well you'd give them a cut of what the content designer makes. You *were* planning on paying people decent money when their UCC makes it to the game proper, weren't you?

So It Goes

No one is going to give me a penny to develop an MMO today, so I feel free to say what it is I'd do if I were a new developer entering this field. It's this: I'd build a full-scale world, populate it mainly with nonplayer characters, and limit it to 250 simultaneous players per server instead of the standard 5,000 or so. I'd just run 20 times more servers than usual.

In fact, I'd run many more servers than that. Alongside the official servers, I'd let anyone who wanted to run a server run a server, so long as they paid me for its upkeep. I'd let the people who ran those servers decide who got to play on their individual server, what its general philosophy was, and how much to charge its users (if anything). Basically, I'd let guilds run servers. It would be up to them whether they were free-to-play, olde Englishe role-playing, male-characters-only, PvP with permadeath, Klingon-speaking, whatever. I wouldn't care. If you can't find a server that suits your needs as a player, well, for a hundred bucks a month you and your like-minded buddies can have your very own server to do with as you will. If you object to how the population of some other server views what it means to play, OK, don't play on that server and don't let players on that server transfer to yours.

What we see with MMOs today is so often what we've seen in the past. The original pay-to-play MUDs were better than the free-to-play ones, but people switched to free because, hey, free is free! Quality suffered as a result and didn't pick up until *DikuMUD* came along and let anyone run their own world out of the box (if they had a computer to run it on). The code for these worlds was the same for everyone, but the atmosphere across them varied greatly depending on the admins.

Next up would be allowing server owners to add new content and create extended worlds, enabling the content evolution that would ultimately lead to an implementation revolution equivalent to that of *Ultima Online* or *EverQuest*. Then we'd see a philosophical realignment again, followed by a revenue model adjustment again. It's all cyclical.

Hmm, I guess this rather explains *why* it is that no one is going to give me a penny to develop an MMO today.

IANAL

I mention the law a lot in this book. Why would I do that? I'm not a lawyer; if I were a lawyer, I'd be so wealthy I wouldn't need to have written this book in the first place.

Well, the reason I mention the law so much is that as far as MMOs are concerned it's important and fraught with dangers. It's easy to envisage situations in which judges or legal scholars with no MMO knowledge or experience might recommend viewpoints that could be disastrous were they to be adopted. It might be, for example, that the EULA for an MMO would not be upheld because it violates rights that a judge holds people to have under the real-world constitution of the country in which they live. It might be that a government lawyer decides that intercharacter transactions can be taxed because the objects being transferred have real-world value (on game gold sites). It might be that players who identify with their characters *in extremis* could sue for the psychological harm endured when something awful happened to their character.

All these have a pretty obvious "right" answer as far as I'm concerned. I, however, am not a lawyer, and I'm not coming fresh to virtual worlds from a background in Internet or new media law. It's all too easy to imagine how some judge might decide that the real and the virtual were the same thing and start making virtual property subject to divorce laws, banking/insurance laws, or the wrong set of IP laws.

Understanding the law is important because the law is all-powerful. If you know what problems it might pose in the future, you can endeavor to resolve the issues these raise before they become problems at all.

Rabbit

One day, I added a rabbit to *MUD*. At the time, we had a player with a character called Rabbit. I knew that by introducing an in-world rabbit, the character named Rabbit would immediately become inaccessible and therefore unplayable. However, I wanted the rabbit for a puzzle I was creating. I therefore offered the player a name-change, which he accepted.

Had he not accepted, I'd have added the rabbit anyway. Otherwise, players would have snaffled the names of likely new additions to *MUD* and sat on them. This had indeed already happened in the past, when a player created a character called Vampire in an attempt to stop me from adding a vampire to *MUD*'s co-world, *Valley*, until I "compensated" him. Needless to say, no such compensation was forthcoming.

MMO operators must on occasion change their virtual world in ways that some—perhaps all—of their players find disagreeable. Nevertheless, they *do* need to be able to do it.

While this situation pertains and designers are able to ride roughshod over players' opinions, an MMO can continue to evolve and (at least in the designer's eyes) improve. Anything that gets in the way of this would limit the MMO's capacity to evolve, potentially killing it as a result.

Hmm, I wonder what term creationists use to refer to the concept of "adapt or die"?

AI Interlude

States

In Artificial Intelligence research, an important notion is that of a *state*—a non-empty set of discrete variable/value pairs. States can be used to describe quite a variety of things, including, oh, games you can play on computers.

Here's an example of a game you can also play *off* computers:

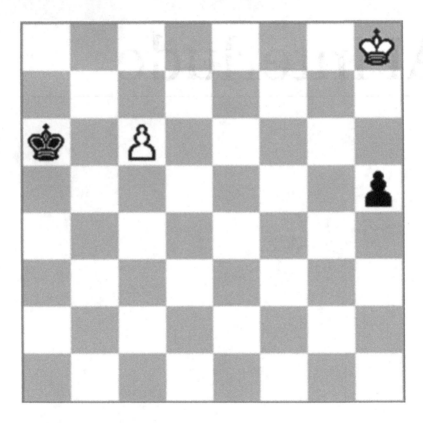

The state here is as follows:

- WK/h8
- BK/a6
- WP/c6
- BP/h5
- Turn/white

This state tells you all you need to know about the game. You could write it down on a piece of paper, and someone could reconstruct it exactly as it was 100 years later. OK, so they wouldn't know what was going on in the players' heads, but they'd know how things stood in purely gameplay terms.

In any one state, a number of *operations* are possible. These comprise the *choice* or *decision set*. In our *Chess* example here, it's white to move, so the decision set is:

- [WK-g8, WK-g7, WK-h7, WP-c7]

So, if you're in one state and you apply one of the operators from the decision set, you get a new state. If white chose WK-g7, the new state would be:

- WK/g7
- BK/a6
- WP/c6
- BP/h5
- Turn/black

The new decision set would be:

- [BK-a7, BK-b7, BK-b6, BK-b5, BK-a5, BP-h4]

This example is a famous *Chess* study, by the way, designed by Richard Réti in 1921. White can force a draw (or, if black plays badly, a win) by always making just the right move on their turn.

What if we had a different initial state? Say, the one in which every piece is present and in its starting position, with white to move? In theory, can white force a draw?

NPC Motivation

In *Star Wars: the Old Republic*, the NPCs on the Republic side fight for the Republic because the Empire came and slaughtered their families, whereas the NPCs on the Empire side fight for the Empire because the Empire came and slaughtered their families.

Rock/Paper/Scissors

Archers beat infantry (they shower them in arrows), cavalry beat archers (they get to them before they can reload), and infantry beat cavalry (spears braced against a charge). In what proportion should you build these units?

Well, 1:1:1, obviously.

RPS (I prefer *Stone/Paper/Scissors* as a name, but it doesn't abbreviate to unique letters) is a common mechanic in games, especially computer games. It offers a win/lose/draw outcome for a non-trivial choice, it's an easy fit in many different settings, it's extensible, and it's zero-sum (what one player wins, the other loses—good for tracking balance issues). It's also easy to obscure.

Suppose that infantry cost half as much as archers and cavalry to recruit. *Now* in what proportion should you build your units?

State Transition Diagrams

Many games—or subcomponents of games—can be described by *state transition diagrams*. In these, you give each state a name and connect states with one another using arrows. The arrows are labeled with the action that takes you from the first state to the second. An arrow can lead from a state to itself, that's fine.

The result is a *cyclic* (because it can have loops), *directed* (because it has arrows) graph. A tree is an *acyclic* directed graph (because it doesn't have loops).

One use of state transition diagrams is for "choose your own adventure" games, in which you are given a description of a situation and a number of options for what to do next. What you decide on takes you to another situation (state) with a new set of choices or perhaps back to an old one.

State transition diagrams can be used for many other things. Here's an example of how they fake the appearance of intelligent NPC behavior:

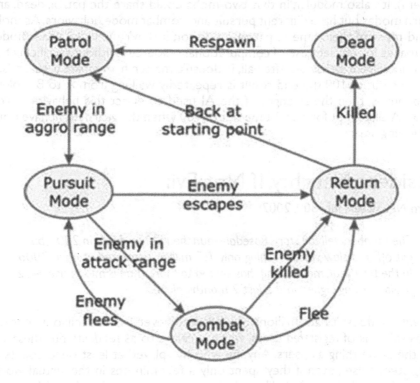

This is a very basic state transition diagram for the way mobs work in *World of Warcraft*. They start in patrol mode, in which they just follow a fixed track until an enemy (such as a player character) comes within aggro range. At that point, they enter pursuit mode and chase after the enemy until they get close enough to attack (if they have ranged weapons, they could already be close enough). This puts them into combat mode, which they stay in until either the enemy flees (in which case it's back to pursuit mode), they flee, or the enemy is defeated. The latter two put them into return mode, in which they aim to get back to their starting position. They can also get into return mode if the enemy manages to escape. In return mode, they either succeed in getting back or they are killed. Death puts them into dead mode, with return to patrol mode automatic upon respawning.

The thing about this is that each of the separate modes can be coded as an individual behavior. Different techniques can be used, so although patrol mode is fairly mindless, combat mode could use some serious AI (maybe employing its own state transition diagram, in which case this would be a *hierarchical* system). It's also modular, in that two mobs could share the patrol, dead, and return modes but have different pursuit and combat mode behaviors. As mobs spend most of their time in patrol mode (or, if they're unlucky, dead mode), this makes for efficient use of computational resources without sacrificing too much intelligent behavior. After all, it doesn't matter how smart a guard is, if 99 times out of 100 the end result is repeatedly walking from A to B looking for enemies, then the strength of the AI used to direct this behavior isn't a factor. Well, except for that 1 time out of 100 when the guard *might* have done something smart.

Resident Naughty, If Not Evil

From *Newsweek*, July 30th, 2007:

> The numbers tell the story. Rosedale launched Second Life in 2001, but it got off to a slow start, reaching only 1.5 million registered users in 2006. In the past year, membership has soared to more than 8 million users—2 million having signed in the last 2 months alone.

Second Life doesn't have millions of users, and never has had millions of users. It has millions of *registered* users, which it refers to as *residents*, but these are not the same thing as users. Anyone who has played at least once counts as a registered user, even if they spent only a few minutes in the virtual world; calling them all residents is like calling every visitor to the United States an American.

Decision Trees

Is a game a game if the players all know the outcome before they start?

The relationship between states and decision sets can be represented diagrammatically. You write down the current state; you draw one line from it for each operator in the decision set; at the other end of each line, you write the state that results from applying the associated operator to the current state. You do a similar thing for each of these new states and continue the process as much as you like, stopping the expansion for states that meet some *termination condition* (for example, someone has won).

What you end up with is a *decision tree*. Here's one for *Noughts and Crosses*, or *Tic-Tac-Toe* if you inexplicably prefer:

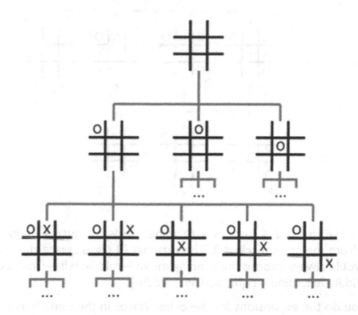

This is only a *partial* tree. It omits reflections and rotations, it's only three levels deep, and it follows only one branch. However, I'm hoping it gives you an overall idea of what a decision tree looks like. Usually, trees have the appropriate state transformations (moves) marked on the lines, but I don't have space to do that here.

Suppose you had the patience to draw the entire tree. It's not very *bushy*: each node at level *N* has a decision set of only 10-*N* members. It's not very *deep*: 10 levels. You can *prune* away some equivalent nodes, and you don't need to *expand* nodes that are a win for one of the players.

Here's a fragment of the tree, lower down:

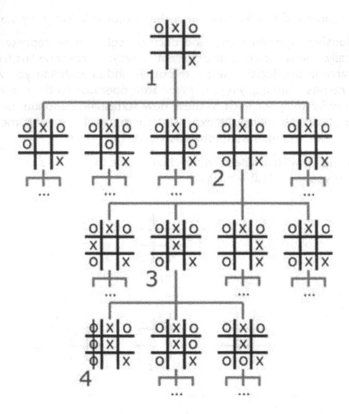

The state I've marked **4** here is a terminal node because O wins in it. It expands from the state marked **3**. The rational O player, were they to get to state **3**, would always choose the winning move—middle left—from a decision set of [middle left, middle right, bottom middle].

Now if you do the expansions for the other states in the same horizontal line as state **3**, you'll discover that they, too, include one or more winning moves for O. In other words, no matter what X does at this point, O will win. So, because all these states expand from the state marked **2**, reaching that state itself can be regarded as a win for O. Therefore, when X made the move that resulted in the state marked **1**, it was game over. From state **1**, O can guarantee a win by choosing to play in the bottom-left square no matter what X does afterward.

Using this technique to analyze the whole tree, you'll find that what you've known since age 7 is satisfyingly proven: whoever goes first can always avoid defeat.

In 2007, computers got to do the same thing for *Draughts* (or *Checkers*—why can't these games ever have the same name?). All that stops them doing it for *Chess* is that the decision tree is so deep and its branches so bushy, there are more possible states in total than there are atoms in the known universe.

Search

A powerful technique used in Artificial Intelligence is that of *search*. It addresses the following problem: given a set of operators (actions) that can be used to transform one state into another state, how do you get from an *initial* state to one of a set of *goal* states? You may or may not need the *path* (in other words, the actual sequence of operators) that does the job.

For example, the game of *Peg Solitaire* has this initial state:

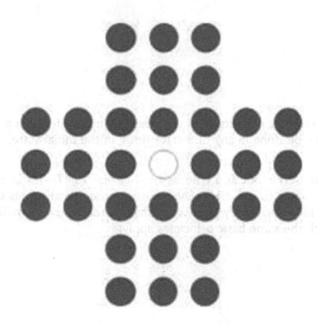

It has one goal state:

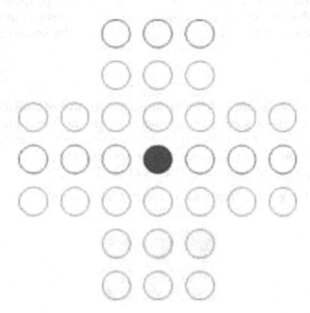

The set of operators consists of all the possible jumps, although only a few of them can ever be done in any one state (four in the initial state, none in the final state).

You can draw all this out as a tree, as I did earlier for *Tic-Tac and Crosses* or whatever you want to call it. However, creating the actual tree is tedious and tiresome, so for explanatory purposes I shall instead draw a smaller, abstract tree for which the same basic principles apply:

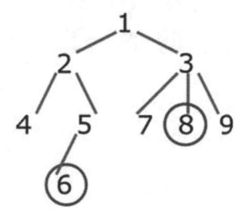

Here, we start off in state 1 and want to get to either state 6 or state 8. If we were to proceed at random, we might go from state 1 to state 3 to state 7. We wouldn't find a solution. Suppose, though, that we'd saved our progress. We could *backtrack* from state 7 to state 3 and try again. If (at random) we tried 8 this time, we'd find a solution.

A more efficient method is a *systematic* search. You try each move in turn, backtracking when you reach a dead end and stopping when you reach a goal. So from the beginning we'd try 1, then 2, then 4, then backtrack to 2 and try 5, then 6—aha! Finished!

What I've just described is *depth-first* search. It's *exhaustive*, in that if there *is* a solution, it'll find it, but it may not find the shortest path to it. In our example, state 8 is fewer moves from the start (state 1) than is state 6, but our search found state 6 first.

If you do want to find the shortest path, you can use a *breadth-first* search. This works by keeping a *queue* of the states to be searched (the *frontier set*). You look at the first state in line, and if that's in the goal set, you stop. Otherwise, you take it off, expand it, and put its child states at the back of the queue.

So in our example, your queue would change as follows:

- 1
- 2 3
- 3 4 5
- 4 5 7 8 9
- 5 7 8 9 6
- 7 8 9 6
- 8 9 6—finish, because 8 is a goal node

Depth-first is fine if you have a small tree or lots of solutions and don't care about the shortest path. Breadth-first is fine for small or unbushy trees and ones that go on forever. Both would work for *Peg Solitaire*, but neither could cut it for *Chess* or *Go* or *Civilization 5*.

Obscuration

So, you're playing *Rock/Paper/Scissors*. Your optimal strategy if you don't want to lose is to throw R, P, and S randomly. Then, you should tend to draw every game.

Let's say it costs 1 point to throw R and 2 points to throw P or S. Whoever wins gets 2 points. *Now* what's your optimal strategy?

Hmm, so if I throw R and you throw P, this costs me 1 point and you 2 points (so I'm 1 point ahead of you), but as P beats R, you win an extra 2 points (meaning I'm 1 behind overall).

Let's draw a quick table:

	You do R	You do P	You do S
I do R	0	-1	3
I do P	1	0	-2
I do S	-3	2	0

I only actually had to work out three calculations for this, as the diagonal is always zero and the top-left and bottom-right triangles are negatives of each other.

RPS is a *zero-sum game*, which means that what one player wins, the other loses (hence the zeroes on the leading diagonal). We can use this to our advantage here by treating the rows (or columns) as simultaneous equations:

- R line: $-1P +3S = 0$
- P line: $1R -2S = 0$
- S line: $-3R +2P = 0$

Rearranging: $3S = P$; $2S = R$; $2P = 3R$. Therefore: $3R = 2P = 6S$.

What use is this formula? Well, it says that three rocks are worth two papers are worth six scissors. Therefore, my optimal strategy is to throw twice as many rocks as I do scissors (because rocks are worth twice as much) and three times as many papers as I do scissors. In other words, in this modified game I should throw R:P:S randomly using a ratio of 2:3:1.

This is an example of how a simple adjustment to a well-known mechanic can obscure it.

It's also an example of why novelists should think carefully before they design games. You don't in general need to know much mathematics to write a novel.

On Procedurally- Generated Content

Procedurally-generated content is content that is created programmatically rather than by hand. For example, a *Chinese menu* quest is one constructed by picking elements at random from a set of tables: kill [mobile from this table] then go to [NPC from this table] and collect [reward from this table].

Much more detailed content can be generated procedurally, of course. *Star Wars: Galaxies* had a tool that generated entire planets procedurally, and *EVE Online* generated its entire universe from a single random-number seed (42, naturally). Employing procedural content generation to do this kind of thing is often a good idea and can save a lot of work.

Using it on-the-fly to create quests and other "things to do right now" is less good, though; it dulls what MMOs are about. Such content pits the players against a random-number generator too overtly. If it looks random and feels random, the player isn't going to find that conquering it moves them along their personal journey to fulfillment.

I believe it's possible for procedurally-generated content to feel enough like it's designed that the players can accept it as such as they do any other part of the virtual world. It's not going to be that way for some time, though.

It *is* possible, however.

Labels

As with state transition diagrams, formally the lines on trees representing state changes in games should state the transitions (moves) on them as labels, like this:

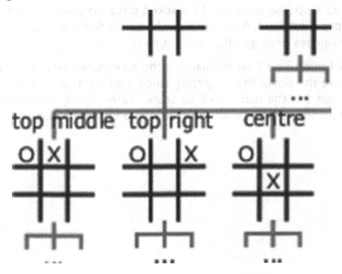

I haven't bothered for space reasons but thought I ought to mention it.

Uninformed Searches

Depth-first and breadth-first searches are *uninformed*. They work on any tree (breadth-first will even work on a *graph*—a tree with loops), but they don't take into account domain-specific knowledge.

Here's a maze. The idea is to get a token from S (start) to F (finish).

There are 33 empty squares and 15 blocked ones the player can occupy. That makes 33 possible states. A move takes the token from one square to any of the empty squares orthogonally adjacent to it.

We'll complicate this a little by marking the squares we've already visited so as to remove the possibility of getting stuck walking around in a circle. This means we can use the maze itself to store states, simply by writing in each square the number of the expansion that would take the token to that square.

Using this technique, here's what we'd get if we did a depth-first search, expanding squares (nodes) in the order North East South West:

So, depth-first search finds the finish after doing 20 expansions, but it doesn't find the shortest path. As it happens, it would have found the shortest path if we'd searched in the order East South North West, but we weren't to know that.

How does breadth-first search fare?

Breadth-first search does find the shortest path, but it takes more expansions to do it.

Oh, the reason I keep mentioning expansions is because in computational terms they're what eat up most of the time. Figuring out all the new states that can be created by applying all possible operations in the decision set usually takes a lot longer than any other part of the process. For a quick search, you want to minimize the number of expansions.

Now the thing about mazes is that actually we know more about them than the mere fact they can be represented as a search tree. I don't mean "always keep a wall to your left"—that's just a way of doing a depth-first search. No, I mean that there are physical characteristics of mazes that we can use to our advantage. In particular, if we know what direction the finish is, it makes more sense to walk in that direction before we try other directions.

What if I told you there was an algorithm that could solve this maze quicker than DFS or BFS *and* give the shortest path?

A*, a Star

When we don't know anything about the domain being searched, we have to use an *uninformed* search. If we do know something, though, we can use an *informed* search. An informed search uses a *heuristic* to rate the *promise* of a state. The more promising a state, the sooner it will be expanded to create its follow-on states (which, it's to be hoped, are even more promising). The best general-purpose mechanism for a heuristic search is called A*. Yes, it's so good it gets its own asterisk.

A* needs a heuristic. The exact heuristic depends on the application's domain, and some heuristics are more informed than others. For 2D and 3D approximations to real space, however, the best one is "as the crow flies." What this means is that you rate the promise of a node as being the distance from that node to the finish while ignoring all terrain and movement possibilities. This is an *under-estimation* of the actual distance, which A* requires of its heuristic if it's to work.

Here's the idea. We use basically a breadth-first algorithm, but instead of always putting the expanded nodes at the end of a queue, we put them in the frontier set in most-promising order. For each node, N, we know the following:

- The exact distance from the start node to this node, $G(N)$
- An underestimate of the distance from the node to the finish using our heuristic, $H(N)$

The best node to expand is the one with the shortest $G(N)+H(N)$.

So, the algorithm is as follows:

- Put the start node in the frontier set.
- Repeat:
  - Take the first node from the frontier set.
  - If it's the finish node, stop.
  - Put this node in the set of visited nodes.
  - Expand the nodes around it, ignoring the ones already in the set of visited nodes.
  - Insert the remaining new nodes in the frontier set maintaining the order of smallest-first $G(N)+H(N)$.

Voila!

A* is guaranteed to find the shortest path (if there is a solution at all), as the following shows:

- Call the length of the actual shortest path L.
- For any node on the shortest path, $G(N)+H(N) <= L$, because $H(N)$ is an underestimator.

- On any longer path, at some point G(N)=L.

- Therefore, a node on the shortest path will always be expanded before at least one node on any longer path.

This doesn't work if H is an overestimator because then G(N)+H(N) >= L can be true for a node on the shortest path.

A* is very adaptable. Of particular benefit is that you don't have to use the same H(N) for all users and uses of the algorithm. For example:

- **Terrain effects**: If you make the heuristic for a road node return 25 percent of the value for a grass node, then the solution will tend to follow roads.

- **Unit effects**: Chariots can't travel through mountains, but infantry can.

- **Influence effects**: Increase the heuristic value of a node that is vulnerable to ambush so units will go a longer distance to avoid it.

There are, however, some caveats:

- You need to recomputed the path if blockages or the finish can also move.

- You need to calculate your heuristic several times if there are several possible goals.

- Unknown areas can be a problem. *Civilization 3* would send a ship on a 26-turn odyssey through known squares rather than have it enter a single unknown square between a start and finish that were 2 turns apart.

- The shortest path may not be the smoothest path. Monsters can look jerky if they follow it.

- For big, bushy search spaces, A* is still slow—not as slow as uninformed searches, though.

You can alleviate some of these problems by using a *multitiered* system.

- Plot the route from the start to the nearest waypoint.

- Plot the route from the finish to the nearest waypoint.

- Plot the route between waypoints using the waypoint network.

This has its own issue, though, in that it's easy to set up ambushes once you know where the waypoints are.

40 Percent

Why have I spent this time patiently introducing ideas of states, searches, and A*?

It's all so I know that you'll understand this one startling fact that I wish to reveal: in pretty well every MMO ever written, path-finding has taken up *a minimum of 40 percent* of the CPU requirements of the server.

Directed Searches

When a search space is just too gosh-darned big to search exhaustively, what do you do?

Let's use *Chess* as an example because that's a respectable enough game that AI experts have actually spent some time looking at it.

So, if you have only a few pieces left on the board in an endgame and you have a supercomputer at your disposal, it is indeed feasible to do an exhaustive search. What this means is that you can reach a point where every possible future state of the board can be checked, so you will thenceforth know the exact move you should make in all situations so as to force a win or a draw (or, if your luck is out, so as to resign a guaranteed defeat).

Now you can do a bit better than this if you have precomputed the endgames and have stored them in a database. That means the end point of the search doesn't have to be "checkmate" or "stalemate," it can be "matches a board I have in my database that I calculated over a period of 3 weeks several months ago, and it guarantees checkmate after 13 moves."

This merely moves the finishing line a bit closer, though. From the start of the game, you still don't have enough computational power to generate a tree of possible moves deep enough to guarantee finding all end points. You can look forward only a handful of moves, and if you can't force a win in any of the states you encounter, then you're screwed. It could be that if you'd looked ahead one more move, you would have won, but you can't look that one move further (or, if you could, then you might have needed to look two moves ahead, and so on).

So, given this hard reality, what you want to do is to look ahead as far as you can and, if you can't force a win, decide which of the several thousand states you've generated is the one most *likely* to get you a win. This means you need to have some way of rating board positions so you can say that one is more promising than another.

As it happens, *Chess* players have been using such *heuristics* themselves for centuries. They'll perhaps give pieces a point value, so if at the end of a series of moves they've captured a queen (9 points) but lost a bishop (3 points) and a rook (5 points), they would calculate that this would be better for them than a state in which no pieces have been exchanged. They'll also use rules of thumb such as "Do I control the middle four squares?" "Are my pawns supporting each other?" and "Do I have two bishops or just one?" and so on.

So basically, what happens is that the *Chess*-playing program will take the current state of the board, see what moves it can make from there, and generate a new state of the board for each one of them. It will then do the same thing for each of those and continue to do so until it runs out of time. At that point, it will evaluate each of the as-yet-unexpanded board states it has and give them a rating. It will choose which move to make based on the highest such value it can force to occur.

While the opponent is figuring out what to do, the program will throw away the part of the state tree that it didn't use and carry on expanding the one it did choose. More sophisticated algorithms will evaluate every board state they generate (if doing so is inexpensive) so that they can explore promising branches in preference to ones that look to lead to a bleak outcome. This makes expansion of a node even more expensive, though, so isn't for the faint-hearted.

Oh, and what has this to do with MMOs? Well, if instead of *Chess* it's an NPC engaging in combat and if the world has so many variables that you can store only partial states rather than whole ones, then you're going to be looking at heuristics to determine what action the NPC should take next.

Monte Carlo Tree Search

Surprisingly, one of the best ways to evaluate a state in a search tree is to use search itself. Here's how it works.

If you were doing a full search, you would look at each new state and apply all the possible decisions that could be made in it to create a set of all the states that follow from it. This is computationally expensive when the number of possible moves in any one state is great. However, enacting just *one* decision is *not* expensive.

So, the idea is that you choose a valid move *at random* and generate the state that results. You then choose a random move in that state and repeat until either the game ends or you reach some self-imposed cap on the number of moves you want to look ahead. Now of course, this tells you very little of worth; however, if you undertake such a search multiple times, then the aggregate of the results *does* tell you something valuable. You can use this information as a heuristic.

For example, suppose you are looking at a *Chess* board and want to know what the best move is. You start by generating new boards (states) for all the possible moves (operations). Let's simplify it and say that there are only two possible moves you can make at the moment, so there are only two new board states to rate. What you do using this new, random-based heuristic is to set each of these competing states as a starting point and continue the game randomly until it ends. You repeat this a thousand times for each state.

Suppose that for one you find that you win 300 times, lose 50 times, and the game drags on 650 times; for the other, the figures are 20, 90, and 890. This tells you that the first state is probably better than the second, so you should make the move that leads to that one rather than the other.

Because it profits from the accumulation of random factors, this technique is called *Monte Carlo Tree Search* (MCTS). Its strength is its domain-independence—you need to know the rules of (in this example) *Chess*, but you don't need to know any strategy or any *Chess*-specific "control the middle squares"-style rules of thumb. It's a hot topic in AI research and is so effective that it's being adopted in computer games—most famously the *Total War* series.

If you act randomly enough times, the result isn't randomness but statistics.

Exploit or Feature?

Sometimes players do something that the designer didn't see coming. Is this an exploit, or is it a feature?

There's a simple test to determine which: if the designer doesn't mind its happening again, it's a feature; if they do mind, it's an exploit.

Unfortunately, it can be *both*.

Suppose that players ask that they can breed their pets together to create new pets. The idea is that through selective breeding they could get better pets than the default ones. The designer likes the idea and has it implemented.

Within a week, players have started breeding herds of cattle. They sell milk and meat to NPCs for money. The designer hadn't seen this coming, but the money they make is commensurate with the time they spend managing their herd, and it's pleasing that the players were imaginative enough to think of this. It adds richness to the MMO. The designer therefore decides that breeding herds of cattle is a feature.

Two weeks later, players drive 30 herds together and stampede them through a town full of high-level evil cultists. Every last one of the cultists is killed. The players spend the next two hours looting the bodies and rounding up the remaining cattle. The designer therefore decides that breeding herds of cattle is an exploit.

Perhaps a more realistic way of putting it is as follows: *until* the designer doesn't mind its happening again, it's a feature; *when* they do, it's an exploit.

Minimax

In general, if you have a decision tree for a game, how do you know which path to take? This is if you're a computer—a human can work it out with a bit of thought.

Let's make it simple. Suppose you're playing a two-player game such as *Chess* and you can look ahead only two moves. Furthermore, suppose that only three moves are possible each turn. Let's say you have a heuristic (MCTS or something more traditional) that you can use to rate a board position, which returns a value going from **-5** (you lose) to **5** (you win). A reasonably good position might score **3**, say; a marginally bad one might score **-1**.

Here's a decision tree reflecting this situation, with some numbers added to the terminal nodes:

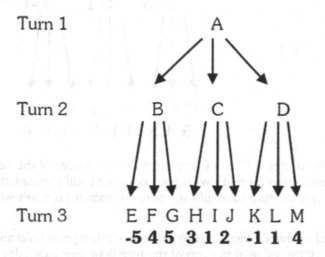

Turn 1   A

Turn 2   B   C   D

Turn 3   E F G H I J K L M
             -5 4 5 3 1 2 -1 1 4

So, it's turn 1, and the board is in state A. You have three moves available to you, which will lead to states B, C, and D. Then it's turn 2—your opponent's turn. Your opponent has three possible moves in each of these states, leading to states E through M. These "leaf" states of the tree all have numbers associated with them rating how good they are, between **-5** and **5**.

Which move do you make to give you the best chance of winning?

A naïve player might see that state G is a **5**, which means a win! So, in turn 1, they'd do the move that leads to state B. However, their opponent would then choose the move that led to state E, not the one that led to state G, meaning a result of **-5**—a win for them!

What you *should* do is make the move to get to state C. Then, your opponent will choose the move to state I, which has a value of I—a slightly good position for you, but the best that your opponent can manage from C.

Your aim is to maximize the number at each level. Your opponent's aim is to minimize it. We can propagate the numbers up the tree taking the maximum when it's your turn and the minimum when it's your opponent. In our example here, this would give the following:

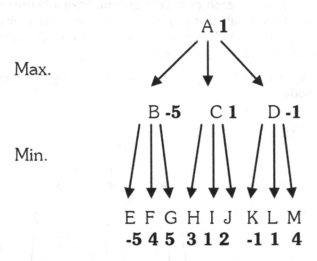

Max.

Min.

The values for nodes B, C, and D are the minimum values of the nodes immediately beneath them (as that's what your opponent will choose); the value for node A is the maximum value of the nodes beneath it (as that's what you will choose).

This is called a *minimax tree* because you're minimizing one level and maximizing the next. If the value at the top of the tree is (in our example) **5**, it means you can force a win.

This kind of tree is extensible to multiple opponents and to far deeper, bushier trees. The score range is usually wider than **–5** to **5**, and it doesn't even have to be turn-based, just action/response-based.

Of course, it's much harder for you to see what's going on in such a situation because you could have thousands of nodes in your minimax tree. You don't care, though—you're a computer. Once you've been told how, you can just *do* this kind of stuff.

The Blocks World

Suppose you have a very primitive virtual world that contains only three wooden blocks (of the kind that children used to play with before there were TVs to throw them at) and three places for them to stand. Here's an example:

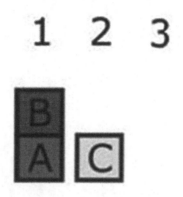

Suppose also that the virtual world's only non-player character is a robot hand that can do three things:

- Pick up the top block in its location.
- Put down the block it's holding.
- Move to another named location.

Yes, this *is* a very simple NPC. Nevertheless, let's say the NPC has to get from the initial state to this one:

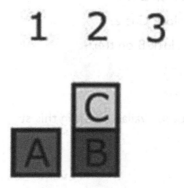

What actions would our NPC have to take, in what order, to achieve this? Assume it starts at location 1.

Well, it would do the following:

- Move to 2.
- Pick up.
- Move to 3.
- Put down.
- Move to 1.
- Pick up.
- Move to 2.
- Put down.
- Move to 3.
- Pick up.
- Move to 2.
- Put down.

This is called a *plan*: a series of actions that, when executed in order, will get from the initial state to some desired, goal state. These *are* states, too: the initial one is:

- Hand is empty.
- Location of hand is 1.
- Location of block A is 1.
- Location of block B is 1.
- Location of block C is 2.
- Block A has block B on top.
- Block B is clear.
- Block C is clear.

The NPC has three actions available to it in this state:

- Pick up.
- Move to 2.
- Move to 3.

Hmm, why *can't* it move to 1? Why *can't* it put down? Well, it can't move to 1 because it's already there. It can't put down because it's not holding anything.

Formally, actions have *preconditions* that determine whether they can be executed; they also have *effects* that describe what becomes true when they are executed. For the pick-up action, this means the following:

- Preconditions:

  - Hand is empty.

  - Location of hand is L.

  - Location of block X is L.

  - Block X is clear.

- Effects:

  - If block Y has block X on top of it, block Y becomes clear.

  - Hand is no longer empty.

  - Hand contains block X.

By comparing the preconditions of every action to the prevailing state, the NPC can construct a decision set for that state. It can therefore construct a tree of states connected by actions, with the initial state at the root. It can search this tree for the goal state, and the actions on the resulting path will be the plan.

So, we now have a general mechanism for giving an NPC a goal and having it go off and solve it all on its own without our help (in other words, the basics of *artificial intelligence*).

However, even this simple plan is 12 steps long. It's a very straightforward search through a small space with few operators, but it's *non-trivial*. A game NPC would be one of thousands in a world made up of millions of variables; it would have hundreds of possible actions, a dynamically changing environment, multiple and interacting complex goals, incomplete information, and a time budget of 30ms.

This is why MMO NPCs don't exhibit much AI.

STRIPS

The particular kind of search that constructs plans is known as *planning*. This is a powerful technique hailing from the days of "Good Old-Fashioned AI" (GOFAI)[1] when the focus in AI research was at the level of logic and symbolic thought rather than at the level of learning and neurones.

GOFAI aimed to implement aspects of general intelligence, whereas modern AI is more about solving specific issues. This doesn't make GOFAI wrong; it just makes it unfashionable.

In GOFAI, the world is usually represented as a state: a list of all atomic statements that are true (meaning that all other atomic statements are false—the *closed world assumption*). Something that can change the world (known as an *actor* or *agent*) has access to a set of *actions* that are capable of changing a state.

There can be many actions: anything an agent can "just do" is an action. In the blocks world example, I defined actions in terms of preconditions and effects (the more modern way to do it), but in a classic planner an action consists of three components:

- **Preconditions**: The statements that must be present in a state for the action to be possible.

- **Add-list**: Statements that are added to or remain in a state once the action has been executed.

- **Delete-list**: Statements that are removed from or remain absent from a state once the action has been executed.

Also, I described the planning in the blocks world example as a search forward from the current state ("I'll explore what sequences of actions I can take until I find one that meets the goal state"). Traditional planners worked backward from the goal state ("This action that will achieve my goal has this set of preconditions, so I'll make those preconditions new goals and search backward from them").

Oh, this kind of planner is known as a *STRIPS* planner, after the system that introduced the idea.[2]

---

[1]John Haugeland: *Artificial Intelligence: The Very Idea*. MIT Press, 1985.
[2]Richard E. Fikes and Nils J. Nilsson: *STRIPS: A New Approach to the Application of Theorem Proving to Problem Solving. Artificial Intelligence* 2(3) pp 189-208, 1971. http://ai.stanford.edu/~nilsson/OnlinePubs-Nils/PublishedPapers/strips.pdf

Why Plan?

The most obvious use of planning systems in MMOs is to control the behavior of mobiles. It's not something that happens a great deal, though, because mobiles tend to be in one of only two main situations, neither of which are benefitted by what planning has to offer and both of which can be handled just fine by a state transition diagram.

The first situation is the default: the mobile is simply minding its own business. Although in theory it would be great to have mobiles working, going to the shops, spending quality time with their offspring, furthering their education in the library, and so on, in practice they'll end up doing the same thing day in, day out. The fishmonger thinks, "I'll sell fish today." The blacksmith thinks, "I'll shoe horses today." The guard thinks, "I'll walk back and forth along this wall today." It's pretty well mindless, so why bother with sophisticated AI? Even if you have it, its main impact is only going to be to annoy players who expected to be able to buy fish but instead found the fish shop closed and the owner outside fulfilling an ambition to learn how to juggle while walking on stilts.

The second situation is when the player is interacting with the mobile, which is most cases means attempting to kill it. The problem here is that planning requires that only the planning agent be able to change the world. If the player can change it too, that means the mobile will need to replan when it tries to execute any action the preconditions of which no longer hold. In practice, this means that the mobile has to decide what to do from scratch almost every time it's its "move." This entails a lot of effort to little effect. There is a kind of planning system that can do this—it's called a *reactive planner*—but it's essentially rule-based. It relies on ready-prepared responses to known states of the world rather than calculated ones that work on states in general.

Planning does have its uses, particularly if you can reuse plans having worked them out once. However, for most MMOs today, all that's needed is a run-on-rails state transition diagram.

That being the case, what relevance are planning systems to MMOs? I must be describing them for a reason, right?

Hungry Pixie

Here's a simple action defined using a *STRIPS* format in which the agent, A, moves from location L1 to location L2:

```
move(A, L1, L2)
Preconditions:
 location(A, L1)
Add-list:
 location(A, L2)
Delete-list:
 location(A, L1)
```

Suppose a pixie is hungry, represented by a statement in its initial state saying hungry(pixie). The pixie wants not to be hungry. Any state that doesn't have hungry(pixie) in it is therefore a goal state.

In addition to move(A, L1, L2), let's say the pixie has another two actions in its repertoire:

```
//Agent A picks up object O.
get(A, O)
Preconditions:
 location(A, L1)
 location(O, L1)
Add-list:
 holding(A, O)
Delete-list:
 location(O, L1)

//Agent A eats object O.
eat(A, O)
Preconditions:
 holding(A, O)
 hungry(A)
Add-list:
 -
Delete-list:
 holding(A, O)
 hungry(A)
```

Let's say that the initial state is:

```
location(pixie, lounge)
location(food, kitchen)
hungry(pixie)
```

Planning using the *backward chaining* algorithm will then proceed as follows:

- The pixie looks for an action that will remove hungry(pixie) from the world state. It finds that eat(pixie, food) will do it.

- The preconditions of eat(pixie, food) are holding(pixie, food) and hungry(pixie). The latter is already true, so the pixie needs to work toward only one new goal, holding(pixie, food).

- The pixie finds that get(pixie, food) will result in its holding the food. The preconditions for this require that the pixie is in the same location as the food. Let's say it picks the wrong precondition first, aiming to get the food to move to where the pixie is. It sets up the goal location(food, lounge).

- The pixie finds no action that can make this true so *backtracks* to its previous decision point. This time, it sets up the other precondition as a goal: location(pixie, lounge).

- This time, the pixie finds an action that can add location(pixie, kitchen) to the world state: move(pixie, lounge, kitchen). Furthermore, all its preconditions are satisfied by the initial state, so the search can stop here.

- The pixie now has its final plan:

    1. move(pixie, lounge, kitchen)
    2. get(pixie, food)
    3. eat(pixie, food)

OK, that's a very simple example just to give you the gist of it. In a proper implementation, the parameters would be typed and differentiated from each other. As it stands, though, the action definitions are sufficiently lax that the pixie could equally well satisfy its hunger by doing the following:

1. get(pixie, pixie)
2. eat(pixie)

I'm telling you all this about GOFAI planning systems not because I have a PhD in AI Planning (although I do) but because they have some very interesting features that could be used for RPGs—especially MMOs.

Backward Chaining

Suppose you're a tourist in desperate need of a cup of coffee. It makes more sense to think, "What action would I have to perform to have a cup of coffee, and what would the world have to be like in order for me to be able to perform that action?" than to think, "If I take off my socks, can I get from there to the situation in which I have a cup of coffee?"

This is why planners usually use backward chaining of goals rather than forward chaining: there aren't so many possible actions to choose from.

Game Theory

The table I drew when obscuring *Rock-Paper-Scissors* is called a *pay-off grid* (or *matrix*). Important decisions of the "if I do this, they'll do that" kind can often be condensed into a pay-off grid. Together with decision trees and minimax, they comprise a branch of mathematics called *Game Theory*.

Game Theory came about from work by John von Neumann in the 1940s—the same John von Neumann who invented the architecture of the modern computer. I was once told he used to tap his foot to music while listening to the radio, which doesn't sound worth mentioning except he did it while he was driving.

Game Theory is about the relationship between decisions and outcomes. Its conceptual home is Economics, but it has also been applied successfully in Biology, Political Science, Philosophy, and Computer Science.

Initial work in the field concerned *zero-sum* games. The classic example of a zero-sum game is cake-cutting, in which one sibling gets the honor of cutting a cake in two, and the other sibling chooses which piece they want. If the cutter cuts it unevenly in the hope they'll get the bigger piece, well, they won't: their sibling will choose the bigger piece. Therefore, their aim is to cut it evenly. This is called *zero-sum* because if you add what one side gains (which is positive) to what the other side loses (which is negative), it comes to zero.

Whether it's a *game* or not is another matter, of course.

The best-known example of a *non-zero-sum* game is the *Prisoner's Dilemma*. Two prisoners, A and B, commit a crime and are caught by the police. Kept in separate cells, each can either remain silent or incriminate the other prisoner. If both stay silent then they'll both serve a short term in jail. If one betrays the other, then the betrayer will go free while the betrayed serves a long term. If they both betray each other, they'll both serve an intermediate term.

Attaching numbers to these:

- A silent, B silent: A 1 year, B 1 year.

- A betray, B silent: A 0 years, B 3 years.

- A silent, B betray: A 3 years, B 0 years.

- A betray, B betray: A 2 years, B 2 years.

Putting these figures in a pay-off grid:

	B silent	B betray
A silent	A -1, B -1	A -3, B 0
A betray	A 0, B -3	A -2, B -2

The thing that makes the *Prisoner's Dilemma* interesting is that although it's best for both prisoners if they cooperate (that is, they both remain silent), either prisoner can improve their position by betraying the other. However, as a consequence, this will make the other prisoner's situation worse. Knowing this and knowing that the other prisoner also knows it, the rational thing to do is therefore to betray. This leads to an *equilibrium* state, in which neither prisoner goes down for the full term. However, it's a worse situation than if they'd both stayed silent.

There are many different ways of configuring pay-off grids. They don't even have to be symmetric, as might be the case in the cake-cutting example if one of the siblings was on a diet and hoped for the smaller piece.

So, with a name like Game Theory, it's going to be useful to game designers, yes?

Well, it is *sometimes* useful. The problem is, its focus is too narrow. It addresses only certain kinds of situations that arise in certain kinds of game. It may help a designer envisage *how* a decision will be reached, but they're not going to plug in numbers and calculate equilibria—they don't need that level of detail to see how play is going to pan out.

Game Theory therefore has its place in game design, but it's not a large one. It can describe tokens but not rules, features but not gameplay. If you want to use it to reason about games, you need to look elsewhere.

Well, yes, you do—but where?

There have been around a dozen winners of the Nobel Prize for work in Game Theory.

There is no Nobel Prize category covering game design.

Quest Creation

In MMOs, a quest is any non-trivial task asked of the player that has some definite end and promised reward.

Informal quests grow from players' own goals and desires. A player might seek to find the magic armor, to forge the Sword of Destiny, to explore the mysterious island, or to kill every elf in the city. This kind of quest will arise naturally in any MMO that has enough richness and diversity that players will be able to interact with it without any prompting. They were a staple of text MUDs, but few modern MMOs have the required level of richness (*EVE Online* being the main exception, although it's getting old itself now). This means that players who want quests have to be given them explicitly; these are called *formal quests*.

The way formal quests work is that a player who requires one visits a quest-dispenser and presses its button. OK, so this machine may be dressed up as an NPC and the button-pressing may be disguised as conversation, but the basic process remains the same. The quest-dispenser lists the quests on offer and (usually) the associated reward. The player selects one or more of these quests to attempt and then goes off to have fun.

Since *World of Warcraft*, the trend has been to have *static* formal quests. These are always available. Everyone knows what they are, and everyone knows how to solve them (or how to look up how to solve them). Prior to *WoW*, the trend was for *dynamic* quests, generated procedurally when solicited.

Formal quests of either kind are constructed by stringing together small pieces of story called *quest elements*. Hmm, actually that's not the modern terminology: today, we say that formal *quest chains* of either kind are constructed by stringing together quests. This use rather diminishes the term, but we're stuck with it. I much prefer "I have a quest to kill the queen of the dragons, as part of which I must take this letter to a magistrate" over "I have a quest to take this letter to a magistrate, as part of a series of quests that will lead to my killing the Queen of Dragons"; the former gives a more epic sense of destiny. You can't argue with players when it comes to terminology, though.

Designers can compose quests and quest chains by combining quest elements in entertaining and enthralling ways, but this is time-consuming and therefore expensive. There's usually a tool to help, so all you really have to do is select the kind of canned quest element you want, state what objects it interacts with, and then write some flavor text to explain it for the benefit of those players who bother to read such things. Even so, it will take 15 to 30 minutes to formulate each quest, more if you have to create the objects it uses, and considerably more if those objects require new art or (for bosses) AI assets. As for associated cut scenes, those will also be a lot of work. Oh, and remember that all this has to be tested by someone, too.

Procedurally-generated quests are built basically the same way, but the computer chooses the quest elements. The type of quest is picked from a fixed set, usually including such staples as delivery (also known as "FedEx"), kill (also known as "kill 10 rats"), escort, gather, visit, and defend. An object appropriate to the quest type is chosen from another fixed set. If a second object is required, that comes from a third fixed set. As I've mentioned elsewhere, this "choose one from this column, one from this column, and one from this column" idea is apparently similar to the way that people approach the menus of Chinese restaurants in the US hence the common name for it: a *Chinese menu* quest system.

Chinese menu quests are quick to create and give a different quest every time. However, these quests are not sufficiently individual to feel different to the players. Kill 6 eagles! Kill 17 bears! Gather 18 basilisk eyes, which you'll get from killing 9 basilisks! Kill 10 rats!

With human designers involved, the same quest elements can be composed in a creative way so that players can become involved in something much wider in scope than they at first envisaged; they don't yet know they're going to be killing the queen of the dragons, but it will gradually dawn on them as the quest chain progresses. This kind of developing narrative doesn't happen with computer-generated quests, which tend to be arbitrary, pointless affairs. Without a meaningful relationship between the individual quest elements, the whole lacks an overall purpose—yet purpose is precisely what players crave in quests! Computer-generated quests therefore tend to be one-offs that players do when they're bored, rather than components of a larger quest chain.

They don't have to be, though.

Smarter

The default behavior for mobiles in *MUD2* used several artificial intelligence techniques, a consequence of my having a PhD in the subject. Formally, they married an explicit but somewhat canned planning system with an embedded reactive planner that used domain-specific knowledge to reason about what to do next. Informally, if they had time to think, then they thought about the kinds of things mobiles ought to think about, but they followed preprogrammed behaviors when they had their hands full.

At no point did they cheat by looking at the database to find out information they couldn't legitimately know, such as what players might have hidden inside a bag. Also, given that *MUD2* was running on a 33MHz server when I implemented this, I couldn't put in everything I wanted to put in; the mobiles weren't really all that smart.

Nevertheless, they were smarter than most of the players. I had to dumb them down to stop the stream of complaints.

Those among you who yearn for smarter AI in your MMOs, be careful what you wish for.

Context-Free Quests

Procedurally generated quests tend to be somewhat free of context:

- "My cat is trapped in yonder tree." (Aren't you more concerned about these orcs rampaging through your village, burning houses, and slaughtering your family?)

- "My daughter has been kidnapped by dryads in the woods!" (Aw, man! I just came back from killing someone else's dryads in the woods!)

- "A dragon is destroying our crops!" (This makes a change; it was a giant yesterday.)

- "I seek a rare and precious family heirloom that was lost in the sands of time." (A peasant family had a rare and precious heirloom and they didn't sell it?)

In contrast, human-built quest chains can involve several steps that hang together coherently. "Fetch me object A, fetch me object B, and I will use them to give you object C, which you will need to kill monster D. Do so, and I will reward you with E." They can also be dressed up with background stories so they don't look so scripted. "There is a sword of troll-slaying in my late father's tomb, but to open it I need the key that is kept in my wicked uncle's house and a scroll to remove the protective runes on the lock. Get me these, and you can use the sword to kill the troll who has been slaying the villagers whom I am sworn to protect. If you perform this service, I shall gratefully tell you the secret of how to cast level 34 lava-class fireballs."

Made-by-humans quests are usually superior to made-by-computers quests. Humans, though, are notoriously expensive—especially creative ones. Furthermore, sitting around all day trying to think of yet another way to say "fetch me this" or "kill me that" is hugely monotonous. You can see why an MMO developer might want to let computers create side quests while its designers labor on the intricately plotted main storyline's webs of intrigue that are completely beyond what computers can currently construct.

Unfortunately, when this division of labor was tried, it didn't lead to satisfactory results. The reason that today even low-complexity quests are all hand-crafted is that automated cookie-cutting from a template *feels* random. Computers just don't think like people.

Well, yes, that's true, but they can *appear* to think like people.

Zero-Sum Solution

One interesting result that comes out of Game Theory is that all finite, zero-sum, two-player games have a solution. What this means is there's a strategy for them that will at worst lead you to a draw and at best lead you to a win. There's always a "right" decision, in other words.

Noughts and Crosses is like this. So is *Reversi*. So is *Connect 4*. So are *Chess*, *Draughts*, and *Go*.

We may not *know* the winning strategy, nor even which side (if any) it favors. However, we *do* know that it exists.

I don't suppose that most players would have needed a mathematical proof to reach that conclusion, but it's nice to know there is one.

A Planning Engine

The problem with automated quest-generation is that the procedures it uses don't work like people think. However, there is a field of Computer Science that aims to make computers appear to think like humans: Artificial Intelligence.

What I've described thus far is an absolutely basic, *STRIPS*-like planning engine. There are many planning techniques available that are able to plan at degrees of sophistication far superior to this one. As I will shortly explain, however, for the purpose of quest generation even the basic system is actually surprisingly good.

Playing and Developing

There are two main ways that end-user license agreements handle the intellectual property of user-created content.

The first way is that the EULA assigns the IP of anything created in the virtual world to the developer of the virtual world. This is how most modern game worlds do it.

The second way is that the EULA allows players to keep their IP and merely gives the developers a license to use it (so they can display it on other users' screens and show people screenshots without having to pay a royalty). This is how *Second Life* and a handful of other social worlds do it.

So, suppose you created a game sub-world within *Second Life* and wanted players to assign IP rights in anything they created within it to you (which is standard practice for game worlds). Is your EULA with your players trumped by *SL*'s EULA with them?

This is a simple example of a general problem for those tasked with regulating virtual worlds. At times, individuals can be developers, players, sub-world developers, sub-world players, or potentially all four simultaneously. Which hat are they wearing when it comes to applying the laws of the land?

It was all *so* much easier in the old days when developers were just gods...

Verifiable Goals

If the designer so desires, all sentient-presenting mobiles can have goals and can figure out how to achieve them using a planning engine.

Some of these goals might be due to the mobile's job (wanting to catch criminals; needing raw materials). Some might be due to interruptions from its emotional system because of the current state of the world (screeching cats keep the mobile awake at nights; the mobile's life is in danger). Some might be more general consequences of its emotional make-up (a raging hatred of spell-casters; a crush on the gorgeous pouting babe dwarf who just moved in next door). Others might simply be random quirks, perhaps sprinkled around by members of the design team (a hobby of collecting antiques; an interest in genealogy). Some could be for different reasons entirely.

Goals are represented by sets of statements about the world (that is, partial state descriptions). There are two types: *verifiable* goals, that the computer can check have succeeded; *unverifiable* goals, that it can't.

For example, consider the goal "the elves of the south are avenged." How do you know if a goal such as this has been achieved? Unless you have a set of concrete criteria that can be checked against the world state, there's no way to tell—the goal is unverifiable. If you do have criteria that you can check, the goal is verifiable. Thus, if you were to define "the elves of the south are avenged" as meaning "the king of the orcs is dead or 100 orcs are dead or the citadel of the orcs is razed," it would be verifiable.

There are two key points arising from this.

The first is that all of a planning-capable mobile's verifiable goals can be used as the goals of quests.

The second is that the mobile doesn't have to execute its plans itself.

If the king of the elves wants the elves of the south avenged, then the *player* can be the instrument of that vengeance.

Hierarchical Plans

Not all elements of a plan have to be at the same level of abstraction. Some can be very specific ("Bribe Susan the guard with 100GP"); some can be more general ("Become the best tailor in the city"). The former can be achieved by atomic actions; the latter needs more planning to get to the point where it can be broken down into atomic actions—that's if the planner is intending to execute the plan itself.

This hierarchy of goals (which leads to *hierarchical plans*) has some neat features for quest creation:

- The quests make sense because the goals make sense. It's one thing for an NPC to say to a player, "I want you to rescue my cat from that tree," but another thing entirely if it says, "I want you to rescue my cat from that tree because it has swallowed my ring of teleporting orcs away."

- Goals can themselves be sub-goals of some greater goal, which gives them a purpose that can be used for quest chains. "I want you to acquire this book on clothing patterns." OK, now what? "I want you to go and find me some bolts of silk." OK, now what? "I want you to post these advertising fliers to attract business."

- Goals can, within reason, be measured in terms of how difficult they are to achieve. Characters can therefore be given quests appropriate to their experience. "I did mention the tree was guarded by a dryad, didn't I?"

- Most mobiles that represent intelligent creatures can be called upon at any time to generate *some* goal that a player could strive to achieve, even if the reward isn't going to be up to much.

- Mobiles can have multiple simultaneous goals. If you don't like one, you can ask for another. "Help me avenge the death of my sister." No. "Help me hit on my dead sister's widower husband." OK.

- Detecting the success (or failure after a time limit) of a verifiable goal doesn't unduly burden the system. You don't have to check continually whether a goal has been achieved. You only have to do it when the player returns.

- Creating hierarchical plans is relatively fast. Original quests can be churned out in vast numbers without using up horrendous quantities of computational oomph.

Of course, it's not all positives with no negatives. The primary disadvantages of this approach are:

- There have to be many, many goals, and ways of achieving them. It's not a good idea to have one in four NPCs trying to become the King's Champion or trying to turn lead into gold.

- Actions have to be programmed consistently, using a common formalism. If someone omits a precondition or uses the wrong parameter name, the results could appear bizarre. An NPC could ask you to murder her boyfriend instead of his stand-in-the-way-of-marriage parents.

- This is just a simple planning system I'm talking about, and the plans it produces can be comically self-defeating. "To impress the queen, I must wear my best clothes and bring a gift. I have a fancy outfit but no gift. A rare pearl is a suitable gift. Pearls can be obtained from the oysters at the bottom of the lake. My plan is therefore to put on my fancy outfit, swim to the bottom of the lake, obtain a pearl, and then present myself to the queen."

Even with the disadvantages, though, the tendency is not to think that the mobile producing the plan is just a random-number generator; rather, it's to think it's either mad or stupid.

I guess I'd better give you a fuller example of this kind of system in action.

Behavior Trees

State transition diagrams are fine except when you get states you want to link to from many other states. For example, if you wanted an NPC to eat something when hungry, then you could end up with lines labeled "find food" leading to an "eat mode" state from all but combat-related states. If you wanted to have your NPC drink a healing potion when injured (whether by opponent, environment, misadventure, or accident), you'd want something similar even for combat states.

To address this, game AI programmers use *behavior trees*. These have a test followed by options for each possible answer. High-priority tests are arranged first. Thus, a tree might have "injured?" at the root, with "drink a potion" if the answer is positive. If it's not, it could have "hungry?" as the next question, followed by a food-seeking state transition network if the answer is yes and the regular state transition network if the answer is no.

AI academics are alarmed at this kind of thing because it's basically a hack. Still, it works for games.

A Planned Quest Example

Let's say a particularly ambitious NPC has the goal "have power." This is an unverifiable goal as it stands; nevertheless, suppose we have four abstract actions that have "have power" as an effect.

- acquire military power
- acquire religious power
- acquire economic power
- acquire political power

Let's go with acquire religious power.

The action acquire religious power has "lead a religion" as its precondition. Suppose there are two abstract actions that have this as an effect:

- lead an existing religion
- start your own religion

Let's have our NPC flip a coin and go with the former. Perhaps it now finds that this is a specific case of a general action it knows, assume <position> in <organization>.

Assume <position> in <organization> has three preconditions that must be satisfied:

- be in a position lower than <position>
- be the best candidate for <position>
- there is a vacancy for <position>

For the first of these, there may be a primitive action that can be done to achieve it: join <religion>. This itself perhaps has the precondition not a member of a religion. If our NPC is indeed not a member of a religion, then this makes the primitive action executable: the NPC can "just do it."

Let's say our NPC instantiates <religion> with "the druids." The NPC now has a plan:

1. Join the druids
2. Make (be the best candidate for leader of the druids) true
3. Make (there is a vacancy for leader of the druids) true
4. Assume leadership of the druids

Some of that requires further elaboration, so at the moment it's just a *partial plan*—but one that we can draw as a tree. In the following, the dotted lines are "or" relationships, the solid ones are "and"; the faded texts are rejected possibilities; the italicized texts are those parts of the plan that the NPC can complete on its own; and the remaining boxes are goals the NPC is working on and doesn't have a full plan for yet.

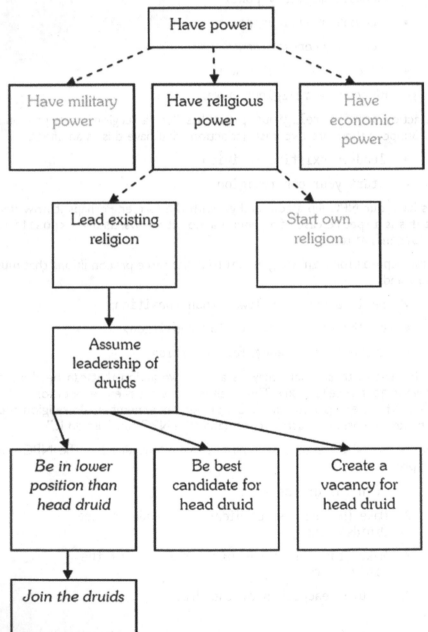

Looking at this hierarchy, we can see a bunch of potential quests that can be offered by the NPC:

- "I am about to join the druids. I want you to make me the best candidate for head druid."

- "I am about to join the druids and am going to become a candidate for head druid. I want you to create a vacancy."

- "I seek religious power. I want you to arrange for me to assume leadership of the druids."

If a plan fails, perhaps because the world has changed, it's not difficult to re-plan. Kicked out of the druids? OK, backtrack and start your own religion instead.

Whatever, this is a definite improvement over Chinese menu quest creation.

Quest Questions

Looking at a plan hierarchy, it's possible to ask questions and get meaningful answers.

Why questions refer to more abstract nodes in the tree (that is, the ones above the node you're asking about). *Why do you want to join the druids?* "To be in a lower position in the organization than the head druid."

How questions refer to more concrete nodes in the tree (that is, the ones below the node you're asking about). *How will you lead the druids?* "I'll join up, make myself be best candidate to be leader, and then create a vacancy."

At the top and bottom of the tree, these questions don't have great answers. *How will you join the druids?* "I just will." *Why do you want power?* "I just do." Still, that's the same with real people if you keep asking them *why* or *how* the whole time, as every parent of small children knows.

Which/what/who questions refer to variable bindings. *Which religion will you lead?* "The druids."

When questions refer to a node's position in an *and* group. *When will you become the best candidate?* "After I join the druids but before I make there be a vacancy for head druid." Note that "tomorrow at 3:30 p.m." is not an answer because this planning system isn't up to it—you'd need a *temporal planning system* to do that.

Even if (as is the case with today's MMOs) there's no facility for natural-language communication with NPCs, the fact that questions *do* have purposeful answers means the quests themselves feel as if they have purpose. A low-level player being paid to stick defamatory posters about the head druid to trees may not immediately know why this is important, but if they're then asked to deliver some poison to the head druid's new chef, they might get an inkling.

Problems with Planning

There are some problems with this planning system I have described for quest-generation use. When I say it's simple, it really *is*. It assumes the world will not be changed by other players or mobiles; it makes a *linearity assumption* that all an action's preconditions can be solved independently; it expects no multiple, conflicting goals; it can lead to inefficient plans. Even so, the most awful quests it creates are going to be no worse than choosing quest elements at random from tables.

This system is not really used, though. I presented the idea in 2002,[3] and no one has yet taken it up. The Storybricks system designed for *EverQuest Next* bears some similarity to it, but procedural content creation went out of vogue with *World of Warcraft* and is only now making a hesitant return. For MMOs, *Elite: Dangerous* procedurally-generates star systems on the fly when players get to them, and *RuneScape*'s dungeoneering system creates random dungeons suitable for your group on request. More will come, possibly including quest creation along the lines I've described, but so far it hasn't. Why, then, have I invested some effort explaining to you a system that isn't in use at the moment and shows no sign of being used any time soon?

Well, the reason I described it is to show you just how open MMO design still is. A relatively simple idea using 1970s AI technology can greatly improve procedural quest generation, at least on paper. What else can easily be improved? Crafting? Combat? Terrain? Magic? Weather?

Pick some aspect of MMOs and see whether you can think of a different way to do it. Then, think through the consequences. Before you know it, you'll have a whole new set of mechanics.

Go on, give it a try—you can do it!

I want *better* MMOs, and my best hope for getting them is if people think independently about them.

---

[3]Richard Bartle: *Notes from the Dawn of Time*. Skotos, 2002. www.skotos.net/articles/DAWNOF.shtml

Games Without Logic

There are no mathematical foundations to Game Studies. Anyone looking at Game Studies as a budding academic discipline is therefore entitled to regard it as mere flim-flam. Without such foundations, it could be a completely ungrounded topic consisting of a web of circularities and self-references with no anchors to tie it to the rest of the world. If it doesn't have any underpinnings expressible in subject-neutral terms (that is, some mathematical formalism), then it's a perfectly legitimate question to ask *why* it doesn't—perhaps it *is* mere flim-flam? If Game Studies wants to be taken seriously, it needs to give its foundations serious treatment.

We're seeing movement in this direction from the direction of philosophy, which as a discipline provides a holistic framework that situates Game Studies in a wider context.[4] We can do more, though. Games are fundamentally about the conversion of the potentialities offered by a rule set into sessions of instantiated play (causally dependent on the rules but interpretable as narrative). This looks pleasingly similar to the situation with computer programs; there, we have a description of a rule set that, when executed, results in a running program. The mathematics for describing programs already exists in terms of various formal logics—means by which *procedural* knowledge (that is, something described in terms of a running system) can be described *declaratively* (that is, in terms of static statements), thereby enabling rule execution to be reasoned about as a first-class object.

So, why have no logicians taken an interest in providing an axiomatic semantics for games—not even for something as amenable to it as *Chess*?

Oh, yes, I remember. Games aren't academically respectable.

This isn't just about gaining the respect of other disciplines; Game Studies needs such formalisms *itself*. There's a reason that scientific and philosophical subjects use logics upon which to build higher structures—*it helps!* The closest thing Game Studies has is "Game Theory", which is used to describe player choice and decision-making for certain types of game, and this can actually be useful within that context. It doesn't tell you what a game *is*, though, or when two examples of gameplay are the same. If people are approaching games from different directions (AI, Economics, Law, Architecture, ...), then they need a common way to ascertain that what they are talking about is or isn't the same thing. A mathematical underpinning allows them to do that. They don't necessarily need to understand the math fully; they just need to

---

[4]Noah Wardrip-Fruin: *Expressive Processing: Digital Fictions, Computer Games and Software Studies*. MIT Press, Cambridge MA. 2009.

understand the level supporting the one they use. This is like saying you don't need to know how the internal combustion engine works in order to drive a car, you just need to know how to use the controls that work it. Sure, you may be a better driver if you do know how it works, but there could still be better drivers than you who don't. So long as *someone* knows how it works so that it can feed into the design of the car, then that's all the driver needs. If no one knows how it works, we could be using engines with only one cylinder that go only a short way before spluttering to a halt. With Game Studies, right now it *seems* as if we're zipping along the road fairly well, but we can't be sure we are until we can look at the engine and see whether we can figure out what it does.

Because logicians have been reluctant to visit games, frustrated designers have started to try to develop their own means of describing games and gameplay (Raph Koster's grammar of gameplay is perhaps the best known). This is an uphill struggle, though, for people without training in logic. I do have a slight advantage here in that I was actually taught denotational and operational semantics in 1980, so I can see what's possible; however, temporal logics (which would be necessary for most digital games) didn't come along until afterward, so I'm not fully equipped. Also, I don't actually *like* working at this level—it's equivalent to programming in binary. I want to use the tools it delivers, but I don't want to have to make those tools myself.

I don't suppose you're a logician who'd like to lend a hand, are you?

Levels of Logic

How do you represent information in an MMO? I don't mean how you store it (the answer to which these days is "in a database"). I mean how do you *represent* it?

This isn't a programming language thing because any half-decent language can be persuaded to represent anything you want. This is a way-of-thinking thing. That means it's a philosophy thing. The formal systems for representing and reasoning with philosophical concepts are called *logics*.

In MMOs, we want to represent information about things. This means we need a logic dealing with the truth or otherwise of statements (or *propositions* as they are known formally). The simplest for doing this is the *propositional calculus*, which describes every fact in the world as a single statement:

```
it_is_raining
Bill_is_carrying_a_sword
```

This system can be used to describe any finite state, however it's incredibly unwieldy. If you want to know everything that Bill is carrying, you have to enumerate every single property that denotes whether Bill is carrying something and see whether it's true.

The solution to this is the *first-order predicate calculus*, which adds variables:

```
weather(raining)
carrying(Bill, sword)
```

This enables you to ask questions such as "What is the weather?" and "What is Bill carrying"? Rather than having to examine every asserted statement for the answer, you only have to look at the variables (or *arguments*—the things in parentheses) attached to the relevant *predicate symbol* (the thing before the parentheses).

The first-order predicate calculus allows you to say things a great deal more succinctly than the propositional calculus, as it allows for *quantification*. Quantification is the facility to make statements about the relationship between predicates and variables. *Universal quantification* says something about all possible values of a variable, as in "for all X such that `carrying(Bill, X)` is true, `portable(X)` is true." *Existential quantification* says something about one possible value of a variable, as in "there exists a Y such that `weather(Y)` is true."

The first-order predicate calculus is powerful enough that it forms the basis for the programming language Prolog. You can do a lot with it, but not everything; in particular, you can't quantify across predicates. You can't write `X(Bill)` to mean "everything you know about Bill." Instead, you'd need to go through all the predicates that might apply to Bill and see whether they do apply; it's ultimately the same problem that the propositional calculus has.

The second-order predicate calculus does allow quantification over predicates, but you can sort of fake it in the first-order predicate calculus if you like. You achieve this by restating your first-order predicates as variables within a new set of first-order statements. You end up with predicates that look like this:

```
true(weather, raining)
true(carrying, Bill, sword)
```

If you do do this, it leads you to a general tuple-based logic, and it's there that my memory of what I was taught in CE204 Computational Semantics in 1980 runs out.

The point is, though, that when you're representing information in MMOs, you need to decide how to do it. Which one of the following is the best way to record the fact that it's raining?

```
it_is_raining
true(raining)
weather(raining)
weather(raining, true)
true(weather, raining)
true(weather, raining, true)
```

All of those have their uses—you just need to know what those uses are before you decide on which one to go with.

The predicate calculus has close ties to set-theoretic notation and to Boolean logic, which makes it excellent for describing processes such as proofs and programs—it's at the heart of AI planning systems (as you may have noticed). It also forms the basis of database language queries, which means that in this case, "How do you represent information" actually does have the same answer as "How do you store it?"

Gameplay can readily be described in terms of processes. So, any takers?

Naxx and *Frogger*

Here's an example of what I want to be able to do mathematically but currently can't.

In the Naxxramas instance that appeared in *World of Warcraft*'s *Wrath of the Lich King* expansion, there is a section that has slimes moving across the path you have to use. These slimes don't move all that fast. They're in about four lines, with regular spaces between the lines and the slimes, and if you get hit by a slime, then your character is deaded. So, the safest way to do it is to time your run across a line, wait in the gap between lines, and then time your run across the next one, and so on until you reach the other side.

This sub-game became known universally as "frogger." The reason it was called this is because the mechanic is that of an old arcade game, *Frogger*. Google it; there are plenty of online versions you can play for free.

Frogger puts you in the role of a frog trying to cross a road. Traffic comes in flows, and you need to jump between the vehicles in the various lanes to get to the other side. *WoW* uses the player character instead of frogs, plus slimes instead of traffic, but strip away the dressing and it's basically the same game.

What I want to be able to do is show *mathematically* that it's the same game. I want to be able to write a description in a formal logic of the gameplay of *Frogger* and another for the Naxxramas sub-game and to be able to show where they're the same.

I also want to be able to show where they're *not* the same, because although it's obvious that the two are identical at some level of abstraction, actually they are quite dissimilar at others. In *Frogger*, traffic comes from both directions, the gap between vehicles is not constant, there is only one section where you can wait in safety (between the road and a river), and you can't move diagonally. Also, I'm useless at *Frogger* but find the Naxx version trivially easy. The two *are* clearly different—yet at some level they're nevertheless identical. I want to be able to write down both and do equivalence proofs.

I don't want to be able to use such a logic to create new games procedurally, but procedural game design is a thing so we could have that to look forward to as well…

Thinking like a Wolf

The key with AI for mobiles is to allow emergent behavior based on a combination of factors. You don't say, "Wolves hunt in packs." you say, "This wolf has a high help-a-friend factor, a low fear-of-death factor, a high stealth factor, a high loyalty factor, good sight, smell and hearing factors, ..." Other wolves will have similar but not necessarily identical values.

This means that what any one wolf does at any given point is dependent on a large number of variables specific to that wolf. These will, however, tend to cause it to hunt in packs with other wolves. Because of the minor differences, no wolf will necessarily behave quite the same as other wolves, and wolves as a whole may behave slightly (or, if the system flips chaotically, exceedingly) different from how jackals or rats behave. You get the overall behavior of a pack of wolves emerging from interactions between the properties of individual wolves (which is how it works in the real world).

This approach has a great deal of potential and can easily be adopted in an entity-based program design.

That said, unless the players can *tell* that individual wolves behave as individuals, making them *act* as individuals is a complete waste of time.

Imminent AI

Don't think humanity will ever create true artificial intelligence?

Let's give ourselves 1,000 years to do it. Not enough? How about 10,000 years? We can stretch to several million or even hundreds of millions of years if you like.

Is it the case that we can never, ever create true, fully conscious and self-aware AI? Or is it just a matter of waiting until the science has been worked out and then deciding whether we want to do it or not?

I'm on the side of science, by the way.

On Gods & Government

In This Instance

In *MMOs from the Inside Out*, I mentioned that there are actually two strategies for resetting "used" content. The more familiar one is *respawning*, whereby a resource or mob or puzzle is restored to some variation of its original state after a period of time. Sophisticated versions of this can involve spawning different things depending on the current world state (for example sheep instead of wolves).

The other strategy for resetting is the *sudden reset*, also known as the *Groundhog Day* approach. In this, it's not individual content items (or linked collections of them) that are respawned, but the *entire MMO*. The advantage is that quests, puzzles, and game-like content can be far more complex and intertwined, because they don't have to be unpicked a thread at a time. World-altering events can occur—cave systems flooding, mines collapsing, volcanoes erupting—which have so many causal effects that it would be impossible to follow every one through to undo it individually.

The disadvantage, of course, is that everyone has to be dumped out of the MMO while it resets, which inevitably occurs just at the precise moment you really rather wish it wouldn't.

How about a hybrid approach?

One of the innovations popularized in MMOs this century is *instancing*. In this model, a group of players get together, press the magic button, and a pocket universe appears just for them. Their characters can enter it, explore it, plunder it, whatever, and then when they depart it simply disappears. In other words, it resets when it's played out—classic *Groundhog Day* territory.

What if instances weren't *Groundhog Day* but were respawned subworlds, so that if you entered one it would be replenished over time just like the MMO itself. The trash would come back, the bosses would come back, and the resource nodes would come back. It would be like a regular instance, but would run the whole time.

This being the case, strictly speaking you don't have to respawn anything at all. You can keep the instance running and never undo any changes. This is how MMOs with instanced housing, such as *LotRO*, do it: they *persist* the instance.

OK, so with housing there isn't much scope for change anyway, but if the instance were like a *SkySaga* or an *EVE Online*, in which you could tear down buildings or breed tigers or delve dungeons, wouldn't that be something?

Hmm, so imagine that such an instance were not associated with a party or a group of random individuals, but with a guild. Every guild could have its own instance; they could do with it what they liked, and it would persist. If they decided to wipe out every bear, OK, their instance is now bear-free and will remain so until someone releases a pair of breeding bears back into the environment. Some guilds could spend a lot of time customizing their subworld, so much so that it might even work as a recruitment tool.

This leads to the possibility that such pocket universes could have much richer and more fulfilling content than the greater MMO that hosts them. Indeed, if they became large enough they could be considered *bona fide* MMOs themselves, with the host world acting as a kind of theme park that gives a context to the individual rides that are its subworlds. The host world wouldn't even have to be a game world; it could be a social world such as *Second Life*.

So to summarize: we would have instanced worlds (which can be respawn-based, *Groundhog Day*, or entirely persistent in nature); these worlds would hang off a greater world, which may or may not be an MMO (it could be a social world); this greater world runs in the real world.

The reason I've pursued this rather convoluted argument is entirely so that I can pose the following question: who gets to say what a guild member can or cannot do within the subworld, code permitting?

Welcome to the wacky world of MMOs and governance…

Rights of the Avatar

One of the seminal articles on MMOs is Raph Koster's *A Declaration of the Rights of Avatars*[1]. It was a thought experiment on Raph's part: what if MMO player characters had rights within that MMO?

To this end, Raph redrafted the US *Bill of Rights* and France's *Declaration of the Rights of Man* in terms of avatars. **Actually, avatars have *no* rights**: Raph was undertaking his thought experiment to determine what rights *players* have. Nevertheless, some people reference it without reading beyond the title, meaning it's an oft-misunderstood piece.

When the original draft of the article appeared on the MUD-DEV mailing list, it went down like a lead zeppelin. Designers and developers hated it! It seemed to give far too much power to the players, to the extent that (in the developers' view) it would have been impossible to operate an MMO under those circumstances.

Raph therefore recouched the document as *Advice to Virtual World Admins*. This was much more acceptable, because it didn't remove the power they felt they had to have, it just advised them on how best to use that power. Overall, it has 19 points to it (point 19 being "There's probably stuff missing in this doc"), but it can be summarized as follows:

- Someone's finger is on the power button.
- What this someone says, goes.
- If this someone doesn't provide a code of conduct, their players deserve all they get.
- Players should be consulted over changes to the code of conduct, but can be ignored.
- Codes of conduct should be fair and should be applied fairly.

So what does this mean in terms of the rights of players?

- Players have rights in the real world, of which the MMO is a part.
- In considering rights, MMOs should *only* be thought of in terms of the real world, not in the terms of their own context.

---

[1]Raph Koster: *A Declaration of the Rights of Avatars*. http://www.raphkoster.com/gaming/playerrights.shtml

- Developers can take their ball home if they like.
- Players don't have to play if they don't want to.

Player rights can therefore be condensed to: *if you don't like it, leave.*

Remarkably, this simple statement not only captures the balance of power between players and developers, but it underpins how this relationship is ultimately viewed by law.

Government by Consent

Governments gain their legitimacy from the consent of the governed. If the governed do not agree to be governed by a government, that government is illegitimate; it's a tyranny.

Of course, not everyone will consent to a *particular* government, but they may still consent to a *system* of government—representative democracy, for example. Some people won't consent to the system of government either, though, or will go along with it but not abide by its laws. This is why governments have police forces and armies at their disposal: to enforce the will of "the people" who legitimize the government.

The players of MMOs consent to be governed within those worlds—because if they didn't consent, they could leave (far more easily than they could leave a real country). MMOs are only sustainable because their players will it.

Suppose something goes on in an MMO that a real-world government finds objectionable. Should that country enforce its will on the MMO by closing it down? If so, on what authority? Well on the authority gained from the consent of those governed.

Wait a moment, though: didn't I just say that MMO players *also* agree to be governed by the MMO's government? Isn't there authority there, too?

Sovereignty

Suppose, hypothetically, that a South Korean MMO launches in which the consumption of alcohol is depicted widely and positively. How might different countries react? Let's construct some possible (not necessarily likely!) scenarios:

- The government of the day in the United States decides to ban access to the MMO to people under 21, but it doesn't care what older people get up to when they visit it.

- The government of the day in Saudi Arabia decides to ban all its citizens from visiting the MMO, because of religious objections to its subject matter.

- The government of the day in North Korea is in domestic turmoil and decides to embark on a foreign adventure to distract the attention of the masses. It points to the corruption implicit in the South Korean game, and demands that it be taken down.

OK, so let's look at this last one in depth. Suppose that for obscure tax reasons the South Korean virtual world's servers are physically located in Ireland, and the Irish government of the day refuses to accede to the North Korean request to take down the server farm. North Korea launches denial-of-service attacks on the servers, which manage to survive, but a week later there's a suspicious fire in a Dublin data center that burns the game's hardware to a crisp. Political crisis in North Korea is averted, but the repercussions in Ireland are only just beginning.

Why, in this example, might Ireland have turned down the North Korean demand to close the server farm? There are many possible reasons, including a disliking of North Korea, a liking of the MMO's tax revenues, strong ties with South Korea, representations from US players of the MMO, the fact that Ireland is a neutral state, and so on. These are the arguments that would work if the MMO didn't have sovereignty.

But what if the Irish government had simply said that it *recognized the independence* of any virtual world with servers on its territory? In other words, that it accepted that the virtual world was a sovereign territory?

Well the practical result of this particular incident would perhaps be the same, but in more general terms such a recognition would release virtual world developers from the creative constraints imposed by having to satisfy *all* governments in *all* territories *all* the time. What was, before, a question of obeying laws imposed by nonplayers for ill-conceived reasons suddenly becomes an issue of foreign policy.

Of course, some—indeed all—countries could object to what your virtual world was doing. If you created a world that featured child pornography you could probably expect to have your players real-world arrested for accessing it (and you, too, for distributing it, just as you would be if you started beaming such stuff to the United States from a ship in international waters). Countries do sometimes do things that other countries find so intolerable that it leads to war.

Because *Reality* always wins, all that sovereignty buys you as a virtual world developer is a slightly higher barrier on being legislated against. However, that slight raising of the barrier against legislation is a much *higher* raising of the barrier against self-censorship: people will be able to experiment creatively in ways at that at present are too much of a risk, because they're going to be less afraid of breaking national laws.

I want virtual worlds to be sovereign because I think we'll get better virtual worlds—and thus a better real world—as a result.

Unfortunately, virtual worlds aren't countries, they're realities, and their administrators aren't governments, they're gods.

Citizenship

Virtual-world citizenship is dual citizenship with a real-world country. Unless you're a nonplayer character, that is: then you can have citizenship only of the virtual world.

That's if you think virtual worlds are like sovereign states, which some legal scholars consider a legitimate possibility. Actually, though, as I've alluded to above, they're rather more than that...

Legitimacy

Real-world governments walk on tricky ground when it comes to MMOs, because they both derive their legitimacy from the same source.

Governments operate because people give up something they are able to do in order to gain benefits that arise when everyone else does likewise: I agree not to throw stones at you, because I benefit by your agreeing not to throw stones at me (I don't get hurt).

Games in general work the same way: I agree not to look at your cards because I benefit by your not looking at my cards (the game is more fun).

Perhaps for this reason, governments have been prepared to cut games a lot of slack when it comes to stretching the law—certainly more than they have done other creative formats.

See, if X number of people decide that they want to conform to a set of rules, it's only the size of X and whether there's an army to enforce those rules that determines whether the result is a government or a game.

Rights, Wrongs

I'll be so glad when this "avatars have rights" idea is dead and buried...

Do bots have rights? If so, what are they? Do the same rights apply to all unintelligent lumps of software, including operating systems and payroll databases?

No, bots *don't* have rights; yet if I wrote a bot that played an MMO, the avatar it was playing *would*? Uh?

Avatars have *no* rights. *People* have rights. Bots *might* have rights in some far distant future when Artificial Intelligence has given them sentience, but right now, no, they don't.

Avatars are *tokens*. If those tokens represent people, then the people they represent may have some rights over how those tokens are treated. Tokens themselves have *no* rights, though.

Player Numbers

Historically, there have been five means by which MMOs announce how wonderfully popular they are:

1. Count the number of registered players. This used to be the fairest way when MMOs all used the same revenue model, but in today's world some may keep registrations around indefinitely (in case people come back) and others may conceivably not require players to register in the first place (because it's a barrier to entry).

2. Count the number of player characters. This is discredited nowadays, because it falsely assumes that the average number of characters owned by a player is constant across all MMOs.

3. Count the number of distinct accounts/characters who access the game per day/week/month/year. This isn't a bad measure, as it turns out, but you do need all the figures, not just "on New Year's Eve, ..." Social worlds and free-to-play MMOs often favor this one.

4. Count the number of simultaneous players, either peak, prime time, or average (mean, mode, median). Of these, the most useful measure is the peak because at least it tells you that there *are* this number of distinct accounts playing at once (rather than a handful of dedicated accounts playing the whole time). Again, though, the peak varies depending on the time of year: you don't want the *peak* peak, you want the daily/weekly/monthly peak.

5. Count the number of player-hours. This is the best measure of how successful an MMO is as perceived by its players, but because of this it's a closely-guarded secret. Also, in a climate of flat-fee games that make their money from selling client software and expansions, developers may want to discourage players from playing too long.

For commercial games, traditional measures such as average revenue per user (ARPU) and per paying user (ARPPU) are usually just as important as the total number of players because they're the other main component of the profitability equation. It really depends on what you want to use the information for as to which set of numbers you'll find most appropriate.

What Is a God?

Before I get into answering the above question, here's an important point for those readers with a hair trigger on religious matters: I'm not asking "what is God?" I'm asking "what is *a* god?" It's a technical question about the meaning of the term *god*, not a question about a particular god (called God).

Also, it's a rhetorical question, as I'm about to give the answer.

OK, so a god is someone who can (if they so choose) change the physics of a reality. That's all there is to it. If you can't change the physics of the reality you claim to be a god of, you can't call yourself a god of that reality; if you can, you are a god of that reality whether you want to be or not. This is why, if you believe in God, you can say that God is a god (indeed, the only nonfictional god of our reality, which in this book I'm calling *Reality*).

This is actually a little stricter than most definitions of what a god is, as it distinguishes between those who can arbitrarily *change* a reality's physics and those who merely operate within an *extended* physics. For example, the ancient Egyptians believed that the god Atum willed himself into being and then created *Reality*; this means Atum had the *bona fide* attributes of a god, because he could set the rules of physics. The ancient Greeks, on the other hand, believed that Apollo could cause plagues but not earthquakes, whereas Poseidon could cause earthquakes but not plagues; in this regard, Apollo and Poseidon were deities but not full gods, because although they had access to powers beyond those of mere mortals they didn't have the ability to change the way *Reality* worked (such as by giving themselves new powers).

I suppose I should explain the reason I'm defining what a god is. Well, the thing is, because *I* co-created a reality, *MUD*, that means I can claim to be a god of that reality. Sadly, I'm not a god of our reality, *Reality*. If I were, strawberries would be the size of grapefruit and chocolate would be the elixir of eternal life.

Player Base Sizes

MMO operators are only happy to disclose how many players they have when their player numbers are growing. They're less happy to release such information when numbers are falling. If we want somehow to measure the relative sizes of populations in MMOs without the co-operation of the developers, we therefore have to ask ourselves what information is available to us directly and figure out what we can do with it to work out what the numbers we want might be.

Probably the most useful data that we can access is the number of player characters logged in per server. Many MMOs have ways of finding this out through some kind of *who list*. Sample the servers systematically, and you can get a picture of how many players are online at any one moment. If you can access their names, you can check whether it's the same characters (if not players) from day to day. Even if it's only a partial list, you might be able to track relative rises and falls in player numbers; you can sometimes get a good estimate of the absolute numbers by mapping them onto a benchmark that you know from information given in the past equates to a particular population (X players in PvP means Y players overall, that sort of thing).

That's the best we can do without looking at secondary data such as network traffic (which also needs benchmarking, as it shows too much variation world-to-world to be usable alone).

Age Restrictions

How do you know for an adult-themed MMO that a player isn't a child? Because adults have a credit card?

How do you know for a child-themed MMO that a player isn't an adult? Because children don't have a credit card?

It's all well and good for governments to bring out laws to protect children, but they ought to have to tell those who are subject to such laws exactly how they're supposed to distinguish children from nonchildren (or at least what they'll accept as a reasonable attempt).

Gods and Realities

A reality is a space of existence operating under a set of consistent rules (its physics).

We exist in a reality I'm calling (font change) *Reality*. We are subject to the physics ("laws of nature") of this reality. From the definition I gave earlier of what a god is, I'm not a god of *Reality*: I can't change its physics. I am, however, god of the several realities I co-wrote that are supported by *Reality*—the various versions of *MUD*.

Gods create and modify realities, but they themselves must nevertheless exist in what constitutes a reality *relative to them*. They are bound by the physical laws of this reality. Sure, they have potentially limitless power in the realities they create, but they do *not* have limitless power in the (higher) reality they inhabit. The power they do have there may seem wild and crazy by the standards of the physics of their created realities, but it *is* nevertheless bounded. It has to be: if a being can alter the physics of their own space of existence, then the means to change that reality's physics would have to be *part* of that reality's physics (because the being is part of it). If the being is not constrained in what they can do, then the reality itself is ultimately without constraint (because the being can change it on a whim).

A reality without constraint is called a *chaos*. Existence within a chaos is meaningless (because there are no constraints); only the existence *of* the chaos is meaningful. If you're a god of your own reality, the only meaningful decision you can ever make is how to end your (and your reality's) existence.

A chaos can end in either obliteration or order. The former causes the chaos to cease to exist; the latter causes it to cease to exist *as a chaos*. A god of their own reality could change its physics enough to lock in a system in which the physics *couldn't* be changed—a bit like in the game *Nomic*, where it's possible for the players to remove the rule that lets them change the rules. Then, you'd have a bounded reality in which a being *could* meaningfully exist. They would no longer be a god of that reality, but would of course be the god of any subrealities they made.

We thus have to talk about any god in terms of two separate realities: the one the god created, that they can change the physics of, and of which they're a god; and the one in which they exist, of which they are not a god.

Asking for a Pony

Here's one of those nice technical terms in use in the MMO industry.

Imagine you're a loving father of a young daughter. You tell her you love her so much that she can have anything she wants. She asks for a Lego set, you buy her a Lego set; she asks for a new dress, you buy her a new dress; she asks for a new game, you buy her a new game. You'll buy her anything!

Sooner or later, she'll ask for a pony.

Now it may be that you can actually afford a pony. Ponies are not just for play, though; they're a serious commitment. You really don't want your daughter to have a pony, because when she realizes what having one entails she's certain to regret having asked for one. You therefore have to break your promise to her: although she *could* have a pony, you're not going to buy her one.

It's like this with MMO developers and player power. The developers don't know what the players want in the game, and the players do know what they want in the game, so why not let the players decide what gets implemented and what doesn't? The game is basically a service, so hand over the design decisions to the service users. Whatever they want you to implement, you, the developer will implement. They ask you for hoverboards, you give them hoverboards; they ask for a new class, you give them a new class; they ask for a new zone, you give them a new zone. You'll give them anything!

Sooner or later, they'll ask for a pony.

OK, it won't actually be a pony, it'll be a complete rewrite of the combat system, or a comical way to kill newbies, or nude character models, or something else that you *can* give them but don't *want* to give them. At this point, any pretense that you're merely the servant and the players are the master disappears. They ask for a pony; you say no, they can't have one. You're the boss, not them.

So it is that when a developer raises the possibility of putting players in charge, the expression "sooner or later they'll ask for a pony" will be used to explain exactly why no, the players *won't* be in charge, and you're naïve if you think they will be.

Gods, not Governments

In considering who *should* govern a virtual world, a good place to start is by looking at who *could* govern it. There are four possibilities:

- Real-world governments
- The virtual world's developer
- The virtual world's players
- Nobody

Real-world governments prevail in the real world. An MMO's hardware is located in the real world, so a real-world government can switch it off if it wants. *Reality* always wins.

Developers prevail in their own worlds, at least to the extent that real-world governments allow. They can assert their authority in two ways: through their MMO's physics (stop theft by coding in ownership rules); through applying the real world's laws (stop theft by banning it in the EULA).

Players organize into their own groups with their own rules, within the constraints of both the MMO's physics and the real world's laws. Often, the MMO's developer will help by coding in concepts such as guilds (making them physical entities in the MMO's world).

It's clear that developers have *regulatory powers* through their code, which gives them a form of sovereignty. It's easy, therefore, to conclude that the developer is assuming the role of their MMO's government. That being so, there are standards expected of governments that MMO developers singularly fail to meet. For example, they routinely

- Punish players without trial
- Exile them
- Restrict freedom of speech
- Destroy property
- Infringe privacy

Sometimes they seek to justify this in terms of safeguarding the MMO's future. Sometimes they just do it on a whim. Surely this is *not* a satisfactory way for governments to behave, and real-world laws should be implemented to force developers to accept their responsibilities.

Indeed it isn't a satisfactory way for governments to behave, but MMO developers aren't governments. They do rule their MMOs, but they do so as *gods*, not governments.

One Against a Million

Players have the ability to express themselves through play. Sometimes, they do things that designers wish they didn't do—gank newbies, for example. The MMO embodies the designer's self-expression, but the players' self-expression through play can interfere with it. So whose rights of self-expression win here?

Well the designer's do, under the "it's my ball" rule. Whatever the players want, no matter how many of them want it, they only get it if the designer consents to give them it.

Hold on, though: this means that the view of *one* designer trumps that of a *million* players! Does that make sense?

It does, yes. What many people who study MMOs and write about MMOs and even play MMOs seem not to realize is that "the players" is not a single, uniform group. Players have all manner of different opinions, ideas, and behaviors. They each have their own forms of self-expression, many of which are more likely to clash with those of other players than those of the designer.

All the players signed up for the designer's expression. It's the *only* one that can be regarded as common ground. If players find it isn't to their taste, they can leave.

If they *all* leave, well the designer got what they deserved if not necessarily what they wanted.

On Rights

I don't object to the concept that players have rights in MMOs. I'm sure that most designers, almost all of whom are former players themselves, would agree.

What I object to are people outside an MMO demanding that players be given "rights" that may be wholly inappropriate within the context of the MMO, and people inside an MMO demanding that every rule applicable to them be carved in stone.

Great Axe of Great Axeness

MMOs are designed to be open-ended; the only difference between sandbox and theme park worlds is the degree of openness they exhibit. In either case, designers are usually very pleased when they discover that their MMO reacts sensibly to some event or situation they hadn't foreseen.

Suppose, for example, that the physics engine of an MMO were improved in a patch such that object collisions were better detected. To the designer's delight, players can now use axes to chop down trees whereas previously they couldn't. To the designer's horror, players wielding the Great Axe of Great Axeness can also chop down stone walls. Those in possession of it have been breaking into castle treasuries and carrying away bullion unnoticed by guards.

In both examples, the effects were unforeseen. Obtaining free logs was regarded as a feature; obtaining free treasure was regarded as an exploit. The designer would seek to alter the MMO's code so as to keep the former while removing the latter.

Administrators of an MMO need to be able to change its coded-in rules retrospectively and without warning, under conditions they need only specify after the event. If this were not the case, the MMO's ability to function consistently and coherently would be compromised.

Designers alone are the judges of what makes their MMO fair; if they can't act on their judgment, the result will be an unfair (in their eyes) MMO.

Player Power

If players could stop nerfs, or demand the return of property lost in an in-game context, or assert the right to import items from other MMOs, or insist that MMOs containing their stuff were not closed down, would a developer ever want to operate an MMO?

Would you ever want to play one?

Realities and Subrealities

When Roy Trubshaw and I wrote *MUD1*, we decided what physics to implement and then implemented them. This made us the gods of its reality.

We based the physics (and culture and everything else) of this reality on *Reality*. We did this because we wanted people from *Reality* to visit ("play") the reality we were creating. We wanted to visit it ourselves, come to that. The idea was that people would will themselves to believe that the virtual world was real, so they would feel they were "in" it—a concept that today we call *immersion*. To present as few obstacles to this as we could, we tried to make the world of *MUD1* be *persuasive*.

If you want to trick people into believing something virtual is real, the way to do it is to make it function as much as possible as if it *were* real. Players can then trust it, directing their willpower more in the direction of believing the things that are necessarily different from *Reality*, such as magic. If something doesn't function the same way as it does in *Reality*, players will look for a fictional cover for it. If there isn't one, they'll be disappointed.

Note that it's the player's *understanding* of *Reality* that counts here, not *Reality* in an absolute sense. As I said when discussing "unrealistic *Reality*," it's possible that a player's default expectation of how something works in an MMO is informed by their previous MMO experience, rather than by *Reality*. With *MUD1*, of course, there *were* no previous MMOs, so *Reality* was the only default in town. Later MMOs streamlined their interpretation of *Reality* by abstracting away the more "realistic" interpretations of earlier MMOs to make them less in-the-way; their worlds were still *based* on *Reality*, though.

The upshot of this is that if you're a god of a reality, you're going to make the physics of that reality reasonably resemble those of your own reality. Otherwise, you will not be able to parse it when you visit it.

More poetically, any subreality is going to be made in the image of the reality that hosts it.

A Marxist Perspective

MMO developers are the bourgeoisie who own the means of production! The players are the proletariat whom they exploit and dominate! The players should rise to seize the means of production and put it into collective ownership!

Sorry, Marxists. MMO developers are *gods*, not governments.

The Legitimate Use of Force

If I get a parking ticket and refuse to pay, I'll be summoned to appear before a court. If I refuse to go, I'll be fined in my absence. If I refuse to pay the fine, I'll be summoned to court again. If I decline to appear in court, a police officer will be sent to arrest me. If I fight off the police officer, more police officers will be sent. If I rally my friends and we fight off those officers, riot police will be sent in. If I've organized resistance because I and thousands like me dislike the unfair penalties of the parking ticket system, we'll fight off the riot police. If people hear about my campaign and it turns into a general uprising against a corrupt government only in power because of a crooked electoral system funded by outrageous parking fines, and the police switch sides to join me, then the government will have to send in the army. If the army won't turn its guns on the general populace, I get to keep my parking ticket money.

Ultimately, the ability of any government to uphold its system of law is dependent on being able to use force to back the law up. It doesn't matter whether the government is malign or benign, democratic or despotic: in the end, it can make and uphold laws concerning you because it has an army and you don't.

The philosopher Max Weber identified this as the *legitimate use of force*[2]; claiming a monopoly on exercising it is what makes a state a state. Systems of governments hold this right by the consent of (at least some of) the governed.

Now as I pointed out earlier, games have the exact same consensual element to them as do governments. The difference is that if someone breaks a state's rule of law, they're going to have to deal with law enforcement agencies; if they break the rules of a game, then there's no physical force that can be used against them. Once consensuality collapses, the game collapses.

Laws only stick because of force. Game rules stick without force. Governments can stand with the consent of a minority of the governed; games can't stand without consent of a totality of the players.

So it is that governments and games derive their legitimacy from the same, ultimate source: the consent of the governed. The difference is that governments have to use force to keep those who withhold their consent in line, whereas games don't.

Which of these is the more legitimate?

What gives governments *any* right to legislate about the goings-on in games?

One in a Million

One of the tricks used by virtual worlds to make themselves look more popular than they really are is to count every person who ever signed up for them as part of the "community."

This can easily trap the unwary into believing that a game is more successful than it is, which is of course why developers engage in the practice. On occasion, though, it can spectacularly backfire, as in the following line from a BBC report[3] about pedophiles playing *Habbo*: "the firm currently has 225 moderators for a community of 250 million users."

Ouch!

---

[2]Max Weber: *Politics as a Vocation*. Munich University, 1919. http://anthropos-lab.net/wp/wp-content/uploads/2011/12/Weber-Politics-as-a-Vocation.pdf
[3]BBC: *Second Habbo Hotel investor 3i checks out*. June 14, 2012.

A Reversal

All debate between players and developers is backed up by two fundamental real-world powers:

1. Developers have the power to do whatever they like in an MMO, without necessarily adhering to any norms of rationality, consistency, morality or commercial common sense.

2. Players have the power to leave.

Ultimately, the players' power is the greater, but it's one-shot. If a developer acts in a totalitarian, arrogant, or otherwise obnoxious way, the players can try to persuade the developer to act less so, backed up with the threat of leaving. Wise developers will put in place mechanisms for dealing with protest, in order that players can get their views heard before things come to a head; wise players will only play MMOs that have these mechanisms displayed publicly, along with some evidence that the developers will actually adhere to them (or at least no evidence that they won't).

This isn't enough for some people. They want players to have a real-world legal recourse to *force* developers to change gameplay

So, let's beg the question and imagine what would happen if this facility were available. Sure, players would sue over heavy-handed treatment by CS reps (which is the usual example given), but they'd also sue over nerfs, lack of nerfs, twinking, lack of twinking, RMT, lack of RMT, and the general behavior of each other. Developers would find themselves having to implement the collective whims of disparate collections of individuals (remember, "the players" isn't a homogenous group). Their only means of curbing this would be to threaten to close the entire MMO down if some proposed bad-idea measure went through.

Then we'd have the reverse of the above, with the players having the power to do whatever they liked and the developer having the power to leave. Except, if the developer leaves, *all* the players *also* have to leave.

Why is that supposed to be better than the original way around?

We, the Players

The most celebrated example of government by the consent of the governed is that described by the Constitution of the United States. Its opening phrase, "We, the people," states the authority under which the remainder of the document operates.

How would that stack up against "We, the players"?

Oh, I apologize for not giving a spoiler warning there, for those of you who haven't yet read the US Constitution and were looking forward to it.

Consent

The magic circle is founded on the notion of consent. Real-world government (at least in democracies) is also founded on the notion of consent. Governments govern by the consent of the governed; magic circles exist by the consent of the players.

Any argument made against the sanctity of the magic circle can therefore be reflected as an argument against the sanctity of a country's constitution. What gives law enforcement officers the right to break the magic circle? Ultimately, the consent of the people—which is *itself* a magic circle.

Authoritarianism

Today's MMOs are almost fascist in comparison with the early ones, having heavy regulation implemented directly in their software. With few exceptions, you can't steal anything from another player character, you can't attack them at random, you can't push them off cliffs to their deaths, , ...

Today's players seem to agree to that, and indeed to like it. Consider, though, that the introduction of soul-bound objects was regarded at the time as interfering too much with play; nowadays, they're accepted without a second thought.

Is this because it's what the players want, or because it's all they know?

Supernatural Powers

It may be that an occurrence *appears* to be beyond a reality but isn't—you just don't have the full picture.

For example, our current scientific theories rule out faster-than-light travel in *Reality*, so if we were to discover evidence of it, then either:

- The evidence is wrong and it didn't happen.
- Our theories are wrong and it is possible.
- We were right, it is impossible in *Reality*, but *Reality* was temporarily changed.

The third case is described by the word *supernatural*.

The supernatural is that which is governed by laws of nature that apply selectively. For example, the default laws of physics mean you can't shoot death rays out of your eyes; if you can shoot death rays out of your eyes, then some outlying law of physics that is inconsistent with the rest of the system has come into play. It's still *part* of the overall physics; it's just that it's not *implied* by the overall physics.

Gods have supernatural powers by definition, but they can also grant supernatural powers to other beings, or to objects or places. Beings that have supernatural powers (that is, supernatural beings) don't count as gods themselves unless they can reprogram a reality, but there is actually an advantage to this: if you can't reprogram a reality, you *can* exist *solely* in that reality and have supernatural powers therein. The eponymous villain of Bram Stoker's *Dracula* isn't from another reality, but he can fly in the face of the physical laws that apply to everyone else (literally, as he transforms into a bat).

In this context, it's fair to say that the "gods" that the ancient Greeks believed in were supernatural beings, as they had powers far beyond those of mortals (indeed, immortality was one such power). They could even endow mortals, objects, and places with such powers if they so chose. However, they couldn't actually change the physics—they couldn't turn back time, for example—so they weren't gods in the strictest sense of the word. Probably the best word for them is *deities*, which also works for supreme beings (as all gods are deities, but not all deities are gods).

Descent into the World

Suppose God exists and were to descend to Earth, there to perform a few miracles so that only the absolutely faithful didn't believe it really was him (or, if you prefer, Him—or indeed Her). Suppose that God then stood for election as president of the United States and was elected. Thenceforth, whatever changes God made to the US would have the backing of the US electorate.

It would merely be God's whim that caused him to seek approval for his policies through the democratic process, though. Everyone would know that he could miracle anything to happen if he wanted, with or without the approval of Congress. He would remain God, even if he only wanted to be president. He could stay his supernatural powers, but he could never give them up because the universe only exists while (as its supreme being) he so wills it.

So it is with MMO designers. They may like to play their MMOs as if they were ordinary players, but if everyone knows they're the designer then they can never *be* ordinary players. They're gods, whether they like it or not.

Democratic Ideals

Democracy in MMOs … ah, that old topic…

Basic problem: an organized group of players of sufficient size can seize democratic control and use whatever "empowerments" you've given them to make life a misery for everyone else. What's more, they'll do it for fun.

How are you going to stop them? Wave social norms at them and embarrass them into going away?

Basic solution: act like the gods you are. Let players do whatever they like, unless it offends you. Then, roast them in the fiery pits of hell (well, ban them at least).

Unable to Leave?

It's alright to say, "if you don't like it, leave," but what if you can't leave? What if all your friends are playing an MMO and if you left then you'd be cut off from your social network? What if you're addicted to the MMO and are psychologically compelled to play it?

Actually, neither of these arguments really works. The first proposition was advanced when there were only a few large-scale MMOs around and the scholars who wrote about them couldn't conceive that it was possible for a whole social group to pack up and leave together; they thought that the social ties individuals had with players of different guilds would be too strong, but this proved not to be the case. The second proposition failed because hardly any people actually do get addicted to MMOs, despite the best wishes of politicians looking for a stick with which to beat them and psychologists with reputations to protect.

Nevertheless, surely designers and developers should be in some way accountable for ensuring that nothing happens in MMOs to cause players such affront that they feel obliged to leave?

As it happens, designers and developers are generally protected from this kind of responsibility under freedom-of-speech legislation. Lots of people have a deep and abiding (if inexplicable) adoration for Harry Potter; that doesn't mean J. K. Rowling couldn't bring out a new Harry Potter book and kill him off. Yes, there would be wailings in the street and small children would appear sobbing on TV while hugging a Harry Potter DVD, but J. K. would be within her rights to do that.

Likewise, an MMO developer can do whatever they want to their MMO. Players who don't like it may feel they're being betrayed, driven out, and forced to leave, but they nevertheless *can* actually leave.

Mortals and Immortals

The reason I've spent time discussing gods and realities is to make clear what the relationship is between the various participants of MMOs:

- Designers are the gods of their MMOs. It might be better to think of them as the "greater gods" who decide how the world will be; lesser gods (programmers) do the actual physics-changing, but they do so under the direction of the greater gods.

- GMs (Games Masters/Mistresses) and other customer support staff are an MMO's supernatural beings. They have powers that are part of the physics (because they're coded in), but which are not available to regular players.

- Players and NPCs are natural beings. Different sets of rules do apply to both, but consistently so, and with much overlap. None are sufficiently exclusive that you could really call them supernatural.

For *MUD1*, then, Roy Trubshaw and I were the gods, because we controlled the physics. The players who were wizzes (wizards/witches) were *MUD1*'s supernatural beings—deities—as they had administration-level powers they could wield on regular players while being immune to anything those players could do in return. Non-wiz players ("mortals") and all mobiles were natural beings, operating within the ordinary physical model of *MUD1*. They might have been extremely powerful within that model, but they couldn't even scratch the wizzes, who in turn couldn't scratch the arch-wizzes (which is what we called ourselves—"gods" was too self-aggrandizing a term to consider).

As I've mentioned, not all gods *want* to be gods. Unfortunately, there's nothing they can do about it. Someone has to be in charge of an MMO's physics, and that person is its god. They can't abrogate their responsibility to anyone else even if they want to: ultimately, either they're the one in charge or they're not. This will become abundantly clear if they do try to pass their godly responsibility (but not their godly power) to someone else, because eventually that someone else will ask for (or even implement) a pony.

Approaches to MMO Governance

Historically, there have been four approaches by developers to the rule of their virtual world, plus a fifth that has been suggested but not yet tried in earnest.

- **Direct Rule by Fiat.**

Here, developers rule their virtual world by the application of their godly powers. Groups of players can and will self-organize, but as in the real world, there's no customized support for it (that is, no physics-supported system of player-run government). This is only fully workable in MMOs that have open PvP and permadeath, because then ordinary players can actually do something to keep the bad guys from taking over.

In this system, players can't take control of the MMO, because their characters are not on the same plane as the developers (you can't overthrow your deity). However, players can switch realities if they don't like the way things are run, and thus deny failing gods the "worshippers" they crave.

- **Supported In-World Government.**

Here, developers still rule by fiat but they embed into the physics of the MMO the explicit tools and structures for players to develop their own governments. Typically this approach expects multiple governments (such as guilds, clans, and alliances); the developer could of course arrange matters so there's a single, world-wide government, but conflict is *so* much more fun.

- **Descent into the Virtual World.**

In this approach, the developers rule by playing high-ranking characters built into the fiction; the players are like Odysseus and the developer is like Zeus. There may be an ascent component, so that the best players can themselves become demi-gods.

This is not in general a popular approach: it gives the impression the developers are so conceited that they want to lord it over their players. This impression is usually correct. In time, because it fools no one, the Descent into the Virtual World approach regresses to Direct Rule by Fiat.

- **Abrogation.**

Here, the gods regard themselves as the servants of the players, an idea most famously tried in *LambdaMOO*. They hand over control to a player council and make whatever changes to the physics the council asks for. This sounds ideal, but sadly the power the players have is illusory. Ultimately, developers have a veto whether they want one or not: a deity with a parliament is still a deity. The player council *will* ask for a pony.

- **Co-operative of Gods.**

The final (untested) idea for governing MMOs has the players *as* the developers. Real-world laws are used to define a constitution that limits the powers of the executive, so once people are in power they can't change the MMO's code or EULA to keep themselves in power. Well, they *can*, but then real-world law can be used to change it back—if there are any players left by the time it works its way through the courts…

This approach isn't quite the same as the *player-as-shareholder* model that was in vogue circa 2005, because with that it's possible for some individuals to accumulate large holdings from trading in shares. This would make the game undemocratic again, and therefore not address the concerns of those who advocate a democratic approach to virtual world governance.

The better solution is to make the development studio operate as a co-operative or a mutual society. There would need to be safeguards to stop carpetbaggers from piling in and trying to vote for demutualization for profit, but that should be manageable.

So why hasn't this been tried with MMOs yet? Well, today's MMOs are so expensive to make that it's going to be hard for a co-operative to raise the necessary money, no matter how slick their Kickstarter campaign is.

Without a designer with the freedom to design, though, would the resulting MMO be any good?

Fairness

One of the reasons democracy is considered A Good Thing is that the people in positions of power can be held to account, which means they have to act in a fair and just manner.

When it comes to MMOs, nothing quite rouses players more than this concept of fairness. If they don't think something is fair, they will complain louder than they would about anything else.

From the foregoing, it's therefore entirely reasonable to ask: should real-world governments impose laws on MMOs requiring them to have some democratic component in their governance, in order to ensure that players are treated fairly?

No, they shouldn't. Here's why.

There's a free market at work here. Unlike the real world, where you can't change nationality at all easily, you can switch MMOs almost on impulse. This means that MMOs are in competition with one another; this in turn makes democratic accountability a selling point. Put bluntly, if players highly value democratic accountability in the governance of an MMO, they will go to those MMOs that have it, leaving those that don't have it bereft and empty. There is indeed anecdotal evidence that this is a factor in the appeal of *EVE Online*, which has a Council of Stellar Management, although it comes a long way behind other factors such as gameplay, price, whether you've heard of it or not, graphics, ...

The response to this *laissez-faire* argument is that democracy may well be low down on players' priorities for choosing an MMO, but they'd wish they'd rated it higher when it's *they* who are on the receiving end of a bad decision by the MMO's operators. In order to protect players from bad governance, MMOs should therefore be obliged to incorporate democratic structures into their management.

The problem with this line of argument, as happens so often when policy-makers look at virtual worlds, is that they forget about play. Unfairness could be *part of the game*. In the past, some MMOs (such as *MIST*) have thrived on being the domains of completely capricious gods whose response to notions of fairness and justice was to strike them down or temporarily indulge them in a wholly chaotic and unpredictable manner. It was what made those worlds fun! If it's part of the game that fairness and justice go by the board, then that should be allowed. If people want to play in that kind of environment, why not?

Games are games; they're not real life. MMOs are not games, but they use the same magic circle to protect them that games do and as such deserve similar treatment. People must be free to play; if their play doesn't harm anyone, who then has any right to interfere?

Back of the Envelope

From *BusinessWeek*, May 1, 2006:

> *All told, at least 10 million people pay $15 and up a month to play these games, and maybe 20 million more log in once in a while.*

Commercial MMOs are there to make money. People wishing to move into the area may therefore not unreasonably wish to know how *much* money.

It looks easy enough to figure out. *World of Warcraft* had around 10 million subscribers worldwide when the above article appeared; if a subscription costs $15 per month, that's a turnover of $150m per month. Easy!

Well, it *would* be easy if *World of Warcraft's* definition of "subscriber" didn't include people in their first month of play (which came free with the boxed set), and if every player did actually pay $15 per month. However, over a third of those 10m players lived in China and paid more like $3.30 per month; also, $15 a month (it was actually $14.99) was the rate if you paid month-to-month; if you paid six-monthly, it worked out $2 a month cheaper. Furthermore, there are often billing issues: for MMOs in general, in any given month some 5% to 10% of credit card payments will be refused by the card issuer, much of which has to be written off.

So it wasn't a monthly turnover of $150m, it was more like only $85m. (Hmm, "only"...)

Church of Fools

Earlier, I mentioned *Church of Fools*— a long-lived virtual world for the practicing of religion, specifically Christianity. Around 2005, I did some consultancy for them.

Now given that I'm a complete atheist, this may sound rather hypocritical of me. However, as a designer, I always design for people who aren't me; I didn't, therefore, see the fundamental difference in our conceptions of the nature of the universe as being an obstacle. More to the point, the *Church of Fools* people knew I was an atheist yet still wanted my opinion; if they were willing to be tolerant, so was I.

This isn't about *Church of Fools* itself. This is about what the *Church of Fools* people told me about an experiment they'd run a couple of years earlier.

In this experiment, they pushed "turn the other cheek" to the limit. They let people do anything in their virtual world. As I mentioned earlier, within 15 minutes of opening their doors they found a female avatar on her knees in the praying pose, with a carefully-positioned male avatar standing in front of her so it looked as if he was enjoying fellatio.

Their attitude to blasphemy was especially open-minded. They let people bastardize their religion however they wished. It was a small enough world that there were never any organized attacks, and they found that those who did come to spout Satanism were usually having a crisis of faith in their own religion (always some variant of Christianity). Blaspheming in *Church of Fools* was the way these people had chosen to work through it. In this respect, turning the other cheek was a success. However, it did tend to put off people who just wanted to go there to pray, or whatever it is people normally do in churches.

When I spoke to the designer about *Church of Fools 2*, he was planning on having congregations (aka guilds) that could leave the doors of their places of worship open or closed, and decide whether to allow public speaking everywhere in their church or just from a pulpit. Each congregation could define its own rules, so if they did come under attack then they had some means of defending themselves while they called in a GM (or rather GS, as they were jokingly nicknamed the God Squad).

Contrast this with the way that MMO guild houses tend to operate, where you don't get in unless you're a guild member or you receive a direct invitation. Treating the rest of the world as being universally full of griefers may be practical, but it doesn't get your guild new members.

I may be an atheist, but the *Church of Fools* people were a pretty good advertisement for Christianity, I have to say.

Player Almost-Power

Suppose that developers retained full power over their MMO, but players (or their representatives) had rights similar to those enjoyed by the monarch of the United Kingdom: to be consulted, to encourage and to warn. Would this be a reasonable way to ensure the MMO's fair governance?

Well it would certainly be better than giving the players a veto on design matters, but even so, plenty of designers would be unhappy about losing the ability to spring surprises on players. Also, some players would be unhappy about having official spoilers in advance of the release of every new feature.

It really depends on the MMO. It *always* depends on the MMO.

Money Mining

Jagex's customer service staff shut down about 1,400,000 *RuneScape* bots every year.

One of these days, a developer is going to start charging a fee for each bot it closes down. At $10 a time, free-to-play really *could* be free-to-play. Pay-to-win would be replaced by pay-to-lose.

Would you pay a $10 deposit to play a free-to-play MMO?

You'd get it back if you quit without having cheated.

Gods, Governments, Gods, Governments, ...

Gods operate by changing the laws of physics. Governments operate by judicious application of the particular laws of physics that pertain to their reality. I can't disobey the laws of physics, but I *can* disobey the laws of the land (I just have to hope I don't get caught).

There are two key features of deities that together undermine any attempts to consider gods as governments:

1. Governments can be deposed by those they govern; gods can't.

2. Governments can relinquish powers; gods can't.

The first says that developers can do whatever they wish in their MMOs. The second says that this is true *whether the developer likes it or not*.

There is a hierarchy of constraints at work here. Each level operates under the limitations imposed by *all* the levels above it; each level constrains *all* the levels below it. The nature of these constraints depends on how they fit into the physics: *passive* constraints are enforced using whatever the laws of physics allow ("the legitimate use of force"); *active* ones are imposed through the laws of physics themselves and don't need to be enforced.

So what does this hierarchy look like?

Well, at the top you have real gods (zero, one, or many, depending on your belief system). From here come the physics of the reality we live in, that is, *Reality*.

Second we have human beings—us! We can't change the physics of *Reality* except by appealing to the gods of *Reality* (that is, those at tier one, above us).

On the third tier, we have real-world governments. These are bound by the physics of *Reality* and derive their authority from the consent of those they govern (tier two).

On tier four, there are the same people as in tier two: us. We have to work within the constraints of the laws imposed by the governments at tier three. For most people, the tiers stop here. However, some of us are MMO developers who create our own realities—our MMOs—for which we are gods. We are *not* gods of *Reality*, just of our own virtual worlds.

Now at this point we start to repeat.

Tier five has those who are bound by the physics of the virtual world: the players. If you want, you can include NPCs here, too, if they have artificial intelligence.

Tier six has player organizations, for example guilds and temporary groups. These organize the players (and possibly NPCs) within the framework of the physics of the MMO.

Finally, there's the bottom level: individual MMO players (and intelligent NPCs), the same as at tier five but bound by the rules of the group.

This means that if a fellow player rips you off by, say, accepting some metal from you to make you a suit of armor but then not making it, you have the following things you can do to seek redress:

- Appeal to your guild leader.

- Take matters into your own hands in the MMO.

- Appeal to the MMO's developer.

- Appeal to the law of the country you live in.

- Take matters into your own hands in *Reality*.

- Pray to your deity of choice, asking that you get the suit of armor you paid for. Warning: if your deity is quick to anger, this could backfire.

From this, we can see that governments are formed by members of a population. Gods, though, are *not* members of that population: they are *external* to it. Therefore gods can't form governments of the reality of which they are gods.

Now of course gods can and do play their own MMOs, but even so, they're still gods: their individual powers trump those of any in-world government of which they're members. Therefore, they *still* can't form governments.

Developers are not their MMO's government, they're its gods. Furthermore, as gods, they *can't* be governments. They live in a different reality.

Buying Users

Should you create a new MMO, you will want to have players for it.

If you spend no money on publicizing your MMO, you probably will still get some players. However, you probably won't get as many as you want. You will have to spend money to acquire more.

Never mind what marketing strategies you use to do this: what it comes down to is buying players. It's as if there's a shop out there that sells players: how much would you be willing to pay to get one? Or, to use industry terminology, what level of CAC (Customer Acquisition Cost) are you willing to accept?

In considering how much to pay to get customers, the MMO market uses two measures: ARPU (Average Revenue Per User) and ARPPU (Average Revenue Per Paying User). Confusingly, both are pronounced "are-poo."

ARPU takes the total income the MMO receives in a given time period and divides it by the number of players the MMO has. This works well for subscription games: if it comes to $10/month and you're going to have them for 18 months on average, each player is worth $180 to you.

ARPPU is used for free-to-play MMOs. In this, you divide your total income by the number of players who have actually handed over money, ignoring everyone who hasn't given you a bean. Yes, this means that for a subscription-only MMO, ARPU and ARPPU amount to the same thing. Typically, ARPPU for free MMOs is much higher than ARPU for either free or subscription MMOs.

Next, there's ACPU (Average Cost Per User), which is how much your overhead amounts to for each player. This is roughly the same for subscription and free-to-play MMOs, although you can lower it in the latter if you don't do as much customer service (your players have a higher tolerance, which they accept as a consequence of "free").

ACPU is between one-third and two-thirds of ARPU. Basically, then, for a $10/month subscription you would you clear maybe $90 per player. This is the player's LTV (Life Time Value) to you. For F2P, LTV is harder to calculate: the ARPPU may be high, but the overheads you accumulate are per user, not per paying user. On the whole, though, ARPU for a F2P MMO is usually higher than for a subscription MMO, because the small percentage of players who do pay you more than chump change will pay you a lot more.

So, let's say that for your F2P MMO the lifetime value of a player to you is an optimistic $100. If you go to the player shop, cash in hand, how much would you be willing to pay for one? The player is worth $100, so if they cost anything less to buy than that you'll make a profit. The only question is, how much profit?

In November, 2013, the average cost of acquiring a new user for a mobile phone game exceeded that user's average lifetime value. Since then, the difference between CAC and LTV for mobile phone games has widened further.

Mobile phone games are not MMOs. The number of products on the market is vast and the competition intense. Nevertheless, if MMO developers are pursuing a fixed number of high-spending individuals in an increasingly saturated market, could this be a sign of things to come?

Self-Modifying Systems

Designers and developers are gods: they control the physics. They can do whatever they want with their MMO.

If players get to control the physics, that makes *them* the gods. However, their being gods means they can of course do whatever they want with their MMO. That includes making other players *not* be gods. Someone who is granted the ability to change a game's physics because they won an in-game election could easily be tempted to change the polling code so they'd win every election in future, too.

The players who get to be gods this way may enjoy it, but the remaining players could well have a different view.

Law and Policy

Which is more likely to assure the future of MMOs: to look at the law as it stands and apply that to MMOs, or to look at the law as it should stand with regard to MMOs and lobby for that instead?

Freedom of Speech Limitations

Of course, if an MMO developer *deliberately* did something to their MMO so as to cause a player unexpected trauma, that would be wrong.

In 1975, a 50-year-old bricklayer named Alex Mitchell died laughing while watching an episode of the British TV show *The Goodies*. The people who wrote and starred in *The Goodies* did know that it was possible for people to die from laughing too much, but hadn't considered that anyone would laugh nonstop for 25 minutes at their material and then keel over. If, however, they *had* known that Mr. Mitchell was vulnerable to dying of laughter and had *intentionally* honed their episode *Kung Fu Capers* in order to induce him to do so, then freedom-of-speech laws would not have protected them from a murder charge.

Unexpected context shifts can also be a problem for content-creators. If J. K. Rowling brought out a new, hard-hitting Harry Potter book in which Harry smoked dope and shagged Hermione (or *vice versa*), then large numbers of people would be shocked: the earlier books in the series give no indication that this kind of subject matter may be forthcoming. Some individuals genuinely could need therapy afterwards. It might then be argued that this was so obviously going to happen that J. K. and her publishers should be liable for damages. Nevertheless, if the cover of the book clearly stated its X-rated credentials, that would protect her. No matter how much people don't want an author to do something in a book, the author is within their rights to do it. It's *their* book.

So it is with MMOs. Developers can do whatever they wish in their MMO, irrespective of whether the players like it or not. If the players don't like it, they can leave. If the changes are so great as to alter the very nature of the MMO, the developers might want to warn players in advance so they can make the decision to leave *before* they find themselves surrounded by pandas practicing martial arts, but they can still make the changes regardless. It's *their* world.

Mr. Mitchell's wife wrote to the Goodies after the funeral thanking them for making her husband's last moments so pleasant for him.

Guilds and Government

One of the rocks that players and academics often throw at developers is that their MMOs "aren't democratic." Democracy is good; MMOs aren't democratic; therefore, MMOs are bad.

OK, so players often use "not democratic" as a shorthand for "not a democracy of which I am the president," and academics often use it as a shorthand for "not Utopia," but they do have a point: on the whole, virtual worlds really *aren't* democratic. In part, this is a consequence of players' having little incentive to become political leaders: they'd get responsibility, but not a lot of power.

However, players *do* organize themselves politically, typically in what have come to be called *guilds*. These aren't usually democratic either, but they do embody a form of player self-governance. Furthermore, some of these guilds can get rather big.

So, here's a scenario, based on an idea I mentioned earlier. Suppose that a guild got large enough that the players in it wanted their own server, for guild members only. They approach the developer, who says OK and sets up a special server that can only be accessed if you have the guild's say-so.

This would leave the running of the entire virtual world up to the guild; guild officers could even be given customer-service-level powers if that's what the guild wanted.

It's only hypothetical, but it does raise some interesting questions. Would developers be OK with players running their worlds like this? Would such a guild-operated world address players' and academics' complaints about lack of accountability? Would it wipe out RMT on that server—or embrace it, if the players were happy with it? Would it be sustainable, if the guild had the right critical mass, or would it inevitably fail? What are the legal issues—whom could disgruntled players sue over their grievances? Would developers still get rocks thrown at them for not being democratic?

Thought experiments: don't you love 'em?

Government Interference

From the hierarchy of virtual world governance that I've described, it's not hard to see how a real-world government could order an MMO's physics to be changed. Say that it happened: would it make the government in question the true god of the virtual world, rather than the developers?

Yes and no.

No, if the government only decrees what the MMO's physics *mustn't* implement.

Yes, if the government decrees what the MMO's physics *must* implement.

The former is just another constraint. The latter makes the MMO's designer the mere instrument of an uncaring god.

This matters, because the physics of a reality determine all else about that reality. Whoever controls the physics is the reality's god. When the creator is the god, there is art in the creation. Designers put *themselves* into their worlds. If this artistic link is broken, an MMO loses its *soul*.

This isn't about governance, it's *about creating new realities*. The world of an MMO can't be governed from without, any more than the world of a novel can be!

Gods work within the physics of their own reality to create new realities with new physics. Governments apply the physics of the reality in which they're set to moderate the behavior of those who share that reality. For gods to be governments, they would have to be *of* the reality that they moderate—yet that reality is of the designers themselves! If the world has sprung from my mind, how *can* I be part of it? It's part of *me*!

Designers should always be considered as the gods, not the governments, of their MMOs, because *that's what they are*.

Guild Management

MMOs can be designed in many ways. Some of those ways could include democracy. Naturally, I have no objection to an MMO *designed* for democracy to have democracy—that's part of the designer's prerogative. However, I would object most strongly if some concept of "democracy" were imposed on the MMO from the outside.

What we today regard as democracy isn't actually all that democratic—the ancient Greeks would have regarded it as a form of tyranny. To them, democracy was a system in which the people themselves got to make the big decisions, not those few people that some of the people had elected. Of course "the people" back then didn't include women or slaves, so this wasn't an *entirely* egalitarian system...

When players have been given their own tools for creating social structures, they've tended to go not for democracy at all but for benevolent dictatorships. Why is this? Well, most players just want to play, they don't want to manage. If people want to manage, they can set up guilds and be managers. In the real world, there aren't enough country-level management positions available so we have to have representational democracy to select our national managers. In MMOs, there are as many management positions as people who want to manage. The ones who are best at it get to manage more, and the ones who aren't so good either improve or realize they're not cut out for it. People who aren't interested in managing can decide which constituency they're in by signing up to a community (a guild); in contrast to the real word, which constituency you're in is not a function of the location of your house. This means that good management in an MMO is rewarded a lot more quickly than in the real world, and likewise bad management is swiftly exposed.

It also means that people can individually decide what "good management" means, so those who like to have power-crazed autocrats in control if it means they finish raids quicker can choose that kind of guild, while those who prefer inclusive, sympathetic new agers so they can take what they like from the guild bank without an inquisition can choose that kind of guild.

Public Diplomacy

On December, 6, 2006, a new satellite television news service began broadcasting: France 24. It was available on two channels: one entirely in French, and one mainly in English.

France is one of the more protectionist countries of the world when it comes to preserving its language. Given that France 24 is funded by the French government, why is one of its channels predominantly in English?

Well, the answer is that when people live in countries where the media is heavily regulated, they can't rely on their local news services to find out what's really going on in the world. They will typically rely on BBC World or CNN International instead. France doesn't like the idea that much of the developing world might be getting its news from Britain or America, so launched France 24 in response. It broadcasts in English so as to increase the size of its audience. For similar reasons, Al Jazeera English was created to put forward the Arabic world's point of view.

This kind of thing is known as *public diplomacy*—one country communicating directly with the citizens of another country. Although such communication happens accidentally all the time (Hollywood movies export US viewpoints, but that's not exactly why they're made), it also happens deliberately: broadcasters such as Voice of America, BBC World Service, France 24, RT (formally

Russia Today) and Deutsche Welle are deliberate, government-supported attempts to expose the citizens of other countries to the views of the host country.

Now whether this is a good idea or a bad idea rather depends on the service itself and who listens to it. Not everyone watches TV these days. Indeed, many young people prefer to play computer games. Have you heard, for example, about these new-fangled "massively multiplayer online role-playing games," in which people will spend several hours every night, week in, week out, for years? Maybe *they* could be instruments of public diplomacy.

Using MMOs this way isn't as far-fetched as it sounds. The University of Southern California Center on Public Diplomacy, which is the main place where this kind of thing is studied, has been examining ways by which publicly-funded virtual worlds might get a country's ideals across to other nations. It looks eminently feasible.

To some extent, it's happening by chance anyway.

Lineage was vastly successful in South Korea, and American MMO developers were dreading its appearance in the United States. When it launched there, though, it was pretty well a flop. US players did not like *Lineage's* emphasis on the group rather than the individual, which reflected aspects of Far Eastern culture that were not attractive to them. In contrast, *World of Warcraft* became a roaring success in the Far East, because the way it presented individuals as being independent and capable (yet in a manner compatible with group-forming) really hit a chord. People could break free of the kinds of ties that had been holding them back in real-world society, but not by having to turn their back on it entirely.

MMOs are a form of art. *WoW* has many other things it says to players, in addition to "you don't have to be what other people want you to be." For example, its class structure means that actually, yes, you do have to be what other people want you to be: if the world doesn't have bards, you don't get to be a bard. *WoW* is making the point that once you've chosen your destiny, you're stuck with it. Your choice is whom you travel with, not where you go.

Might we see, in future, the more deliberate use of virtual worlds to put forward the views of one country to the citizens of another, as we do with TV and radio channels today? It's not beyond the bounds of reason to imagine that the BBC could commission, say, a Victorian London virtual world. It would be educational, almost certainly free (at least in the UK), and put forward a vision of Britain which, while removed from the truth of the present day, would nevertheless be a powerful advertisement for the British way of life.

Hey, why not?

(Hmm, maybe the price tag is why not).

Self-Regulation

When people who study government look at MMOs, they see vast numbers of players who are laboring under the yoke of developer oppression. Who will free these people from this tyranny? Are there no worlds in which players regulate and govern themselves, rather than dance to the erratic tune imposed by self-serving money-making machines?

The usual solution suggested is, as I've been indicating for the past few pages, some form of democracy. Now there are actual MMOs out there that do have this. In *A Tale in the Desert*, for example, players can elect a demi-pharaoh who has a wide range of powers, including one to banish individuals from the game.

Even this isn't quite democracy, though, because there's no law-making involved. What's happening is that the designer is providing a framework for characters to participate in a kind of "politician game." Those characters in administrative positions are allowed to enact laws within that framework, but they can't make up arbitrary ones of their own.

In theory, a demi-pharaoh of *ATITD* could create laws that were not anticipated by the world's design, and enforce them by banning those who flouted them. In practice, though, candidates for demi-pharaoh have tended to state in their manifesto that they *won't* use the power to ban. Otherwise, too few people would vote for them.

If you want to see self-regulation in virtual worlds, guild structures are the place to look, not the politician game. Guild governance isn't democracy, but it's effective.

Powerful Players

MMO players all have gripes and know What Must Be Done to address them. Of course, as all players are different, one player's fix is another player's fracture, so it's as well that the decisions on what changes need to be made to MMOs lie in the hands of designers and developers.

Some players, however, have power. The designers may control what can happen in the *game* world, but these players have some control over what happens in the *real* world.

Here's an extract from *Hansard*, the record of proceedings of the UK Parliament, July 21, 2014:

> **Mike Weatherley:** *To ask the Secretary of State for Justice if he will bring forward legislative proposals to ensure that cyber criminals who steal online items in video games with a real-world monetary value received the same sentences as criminals who steal real-world items of the same monetary value. [205872]*

The Member of Parliament for Hove (he stood down in 2015 following a serious illness), said he wanted people to be prosecuted in the event that they were to steal virtual items possessing a monetary value. That sounds fair enough, surely? As a *Warcraft* player himself, he wasn't anti-games.

Well, it does make sense for some games, but not for others. Plenty of games have stealing built into the gameplay. *EVE Online* would cease to exist if stealing things with monetary value was a criminal offence. As stated in *Hansard*, the items don't even have to be *convertible* into real-world money, they just have to *have* a real-world monetary value.

I used to think that the more politicians we got who played games, the better it would be for game developers. It seems I was wrong: the more politicians we get who play games, the more people in power there'll be who want to use their little knowledge to do dangerous things.

C*n*orshi*

Is there any subject matter than can appear in MMOs which should *always* be banned by real-world authorities?

Assume that the MMO has effective measures for keeping out children, so "because children might see it" is an invalid objection.

What do you think?

PS: The missing letters above are E, S, and P.

Who Regulates the Regulators?

Ofcom is "the independent regulator and competition authority for the UK communications industries." In February 2007, I was looking at its open consultancy document concerning the future of public service content in the "digital media age" (we academics have to read stuff like that) when I came across this gem:

> *And more than 2.5 million people now pay $10 per month to play Second Life (http://secondlife.com/), a media experience so innovative that it is prompting a reinterpretation of the idea of video games.*

If more than 2,500,000 back then really were paying $10 per month to play *Second Life*, the good folks at Linden Lab would have been buying themselves real-life jet-propelled hovercars. Sadly, though, some 2,460,000 of those 2,500,000 weren't paying a bean. The 2,500,000 figure was for "residents," which as I've pointed out before are basically just sign-ups; sign-ups aren't subscribers.

Second Life was indeed worth looking at, but that's because of what it was, not because of what it wasn't—and it wasn't a virtual world raking in $25m a month in subscription fees.

It's bad enough that so few journalists do their research, but when regulatory bodies don't, then what? If Ofcom's document contains flaws in the parts I know about, how can I trust what it says in the parts I *don't* know about?[4]

---

[4]Ofcom: *A New Approach to Public Service Content in the Digital Media Age.* http://stakeholders.ofcom.org.uk/consultations/pspnewapproach/

Taxing Problems

If I buy a skateboard from you, you should pay tax on the income you gained. You probably wouldn't bother declaring it, but if you sold a thousand skateboards you perhaps ought to worry about tax evasion rules.

What if it were a virtual skateboard? Well, people sell digital music the whole time and have to pay tax, so yes, if you sold me a virtual skateboard then you'd have to pay tax on the transaction too.

What if I bought a real skateboard from you but paid you in, say, Linden dollars (the currency of *Second Life*)? Well, you'd still have to pay tax, based on fair market value. It's the same as if I paid you in tins of beans or by mowing your lawn for you: a transaction doesn't have to involve real money in order to be a taxable event.

What, then, if I were to buy a virtual skateboard from you and pay for it in virtual money?

We have four possibilities here:

- Buy real stuff with real money.
- Buy virtual stuff with real money.
- Buy real stuff with virtual money.
- Buy virtual stuff with virtual money.

If the first three of these attract tax, then surely the fourth should also attract tax?

OK, so what do you care if it does? You don't play *Second Life*; you don't have any Linden dollars. If people who buy virtual goods for virtual money get taxed, that's only fair, surely? Everyone gets taxed.

Obtaining a shield from the auction house in *World of Warcraft* is buying virtual goods for virtual money. Now are you more interested?

Every time you kill a mobile in an MMO and it drops loot, that loot has a real-world value. There would be no gold farming if it didn't. You're receiving income when you collect that loot. Income gets taxed.

I'm sure your MMO operator can create a nice summary stating exactly how many gold pieces or credits or influence or ISK or gil or platinum or whatever you have acquired, next time you fill in your tax return.

The Point of No Return

At the Independent MMO Game Developers' Conference in 2008, I ran a roundtable session for the 50 or so designers and developers assembled. The subject was "Government Interference: How Much Can you Take?" The way it worked, I presented a number of scenarios in turn, ramping up each one of them to see when (if ever) the situation would become so intolerable that it would stop the attendees from ever wanting to develop an MMO.

Some things were irritating, but not so irritating that they'd cause the assembled developers and designers to give up. For example, government requirements for tracking every single transaction to prevent fraud fell into this category: it adds a huge overhead, but it's something people can just about live with.

There were two proposals, however, that hit the abandon ship button for everyone. Both of these are ones I've seen advocated a number of times by academics and policy-makers.

The first issue was player power. If a real-world government decreed that players had to be elected to the live team, and that the recommendations of these players had by law to be implemented, then that was a step too far. Developers at the roundtable felt that we-tell-you-then-you-do-it powers for players were unacceptable. As soon as the players got godly powers, that would be the end: no amount of softening with "a veto is OK if it threatens commercial interests" or similar would have any effect. The designers at the roundtable were almost in open rebellion at the idea! They just would *not* be able to develop MMOs under such circumstances. It would be like a sports team manager having to pick the players selected by a committee of fans: what's the point of being a manager under those circumstances?

The second issue that they would not accept concerned object ownership. If players were given real-life ownership of their characters or of their characters' in-world inventory, then developers would also draw the line. They'd be so hamstrung by such a law that they felt they wouldn't be able to create MMOs if it applied.

Interestingly, many of the people at the roundtable (who, because of the nature of the conference, tended to have an indie viewpoint) were completely unaware that there was even the possibility of either of these two situations becoming a reality. This contrasts with the views of those players, academics, and lawyers who have promoted the enactment of such laws, but who seem oblivious to the effects these would have on designers and developers.

Civil rights for players in MMOs sounds great in theory, but if in practice that means there are no MMOs, then what?

The Law in Practice

If you're punished for something you didn't do, you should be able to seek redress, right? At the very least, you should be able to clear your name.

Well yes, of course. Why is it, then, that pretty well no MMO gives you any right to appeal whatever summary judgments they may have imposed upon you without trial? Surely MMOs should be made, by law, to ensure that everyone gets a fair hearing if they feel they've been unjustly treated?

Well, maybe if you wanted to raise the cost of playing by a factor of 100, I guess yes, you would support this suggestion.

Big MMOs routinely ban tens of thousands of accounts at a time for violating the EULA. Most of these people are well aware that they have violated the EULA, and regard a ban as an occupational hazard. If they could appeal, they surely would—why wouldn't they? As a result, it would take years to handle every single complaint individually, and cost the operator (and therefore ultimately the player) a fortune.

So yes, ideally MMO developers would wish to give players with legitimate grievances a fair hearing. Unfortunately, when the pain of doing so exceeds by several orders of magnitude that felt by those being punished, the possibility of its being used by offenders to grief the developer is simply too great for it to work in practice.

Maybe if the players had to pay a deposit to lodge an appeal, to be returned only if they were successful, that might work.

Interration

It seems fairly clear now that game-like worlds (such as *World of Warcraft*) are a different kind of animal from nongame worlds (such as *Second Life*). People may disagree in the details, but there does seem to be a consensus that supportive legal intervention aimed at one kind of virtual world could hurt the other kind.

For example, some virtual worlds are perfectly happy to invite *Reality* in but others wish to keep it out. *SL* is an example of the former; *WoW* is an example of the latter. MMO economist Ted Castronova proposed that to preserve this distinction formally, game-like worlds could be offered a legal protection he called *interration*, much as companies are protected through incorporation. An interrated world (I guess it would be called a *terration*) could allow things that are not allowed in the real world (theft, for example) while disallowing things that are (buying virtual goods for real money, for example).

Interration is an ingenious solution to something that shouldn't even be a problem, yet somehow is. Nobody should have to apply for legal protection just to play—it's ridiculous! However, so many people want to use MMOs for purposes other than play that interration does make ominous sense.

The concept also brings to light some awkward possibilities for noninterrated worlds. For example, what if someone set up a game world within *SL*, building their own *WoW* clone using *SL* prims on an island they bought especially for the purpose? Could they say that their game subworld was meant exclusively for role-players, and ban RMT involving any of their in-game objects? This, despite the fact that *SL* itself is positive to the extent of being gung ho about RMT?

The problem here for legislators is that *SL* is acting as a platform as well as a virtual world. The host world and the subworld have different needs. Can one be interrated and the other not? And what about worlds-within-worlds-within-worlds?

I hear the gleeful rubbing of future lawyers' hands…

Common Carrier

MMO designers have freedom of speech: they can change their MMOs however they like, and the fact that the players object to it is immaterial.

Players also have freedom of speech. Unfortunately, some of them are a little too free, and they use language that developers (and sometimes the law) would rather they didn't.

If you send a dozen letters through the mail libeling someone, you may perhaps be sued. The postal service will not be sued, however, because of *common carrier* laws. These mean that the people who operate a service are not responsible for the content they carry so long as they don't open it. This is why you can plot a bank raid over the telephone and the phone company is in the clear.

Common carrier laws protect MMO operators, too. If a player comes into your MMO and spews forth homophobic rants, you're not going to get into trouble.

Unfortunately, there's a problem with this. If you saw someone enter your MMO and behave in such a manner, you'd want to kick them out as soon as possible. However, that would be an "editing process" taking place as a result of your "opening" their message. That means common carrier laws *wouldn't* apply!

Harsh though this may sound, it does make a kind of sense. If you, as an MMO operator, take it upon yourself to kick out players whom you find saying inappropriate things, you can't then claim not to be responsible when someone else says something bad but you don't kick them out: you're effectively condoning them.

In practice, most MMO customer service representatives when faced with an example of misbehavior don't sit around in anguish waiting for a player to complain so they can act: they just act. This does seem the more reasonable course of action.

As is often the case with the law, what it says and how it works aren't always quite the same thing.

No Place in an MMO

Perhaps slavery is something that should be kept out of MMOs? It has no place in the real world, so it should not be depicted in virtual worlds.

OK, so should we have banned *Roma Victor*? This was an MMO set in the time of ancient Rome, in which player characters *started off* as slaves. We should rewrite history to make it more palatable?

Roma Victor had crucifixion, too. Should we ban it for that? If we did, would that rule out an MMO of the *Bible*? Or do blasphemy laws already rule that out?

Benevolent Dictatorships

Guilds are governed, but few are democracies: they're usually benevolent dictatorships.

Most players want someone to do all the organizing for them, but they don't want to play politics: they prefer to vote with their feet. If a guild goes sour, they leave and join or form another guild. This isn't great news for people in the real world who want to see the democratization of virtual worlds, but it's what players in general seem to find most comfortable.

In the real world, we have to have democracy because people can't easily leave a country if they don't like the way the government is headed; in virtual worlds, people can, and this apparently makes all the difference.

Objectionable Subject Matter

Most MMOs have killing at their very core. So do a great many regular computer games. This concerns a not-insignificant number of people, who feel that killing is not appropriate material for games.

Large numbers of movies, TV series, plays and books also have killing at their core. If killing is not appropriate subject matter for games, why is it appropriate for Agatha Christie and Shakespeare?

Law and Borders

In the board game *Diplomacy*, the rules explicitly allow people to break agreements with one another. Thus, if Italy agrees with Turkey to carve up Austria-Hungary, then reneges and sides with Austria-Hungary instead, that's just part of the game. Even if Italy and Turkey had a real-world written contract, Italy could argue that the contract was just a ploy to trick Turkey into a sense of false security, that Turkey's player should have known this from the rules, and that if Italy hadn't stabbed Turkey first, Turkey would have stabbed Italy soon enough anyway.

You don't sign an explicit contract when you start to play a game, but you do implicitly contract with the other players that your activities are moderated by the rules. If Turkey's player sued Italy's player for breach of contract, Italy's player could argue that the two already had a contract in place that rendered the subsequent one meaningless. If the contract had been about a business relationship between the players, with no connection to the game, well *then* claiming it wasn't worth the paper it was written on would be less likely to succeed as a defense. The key is whether or not the parties believe that what they're doing is part of the game.

It reminds me of the Muslim actor whose character in a play divorced that character's wife. The character's wife was played by the actor's real-life wife, and the pair were not happy when an Islamic court ruled that saying "I divorce you!" three times following a script in a play counted as having a divorce in the real world.

There's a bubble that surrounds much play, whether on stage, in sports, or in MMOs, that separates it from the real world. This *magic circle* is what makes the play special, and worth protecting.

Developers of MMOs who ask for real-world laws to protect them but don't want real-world laws invading their space are, at root, arguing for the law to recognize their magic circle.

It's all about law and borders. The borders, though, are of contexts, not countries.

Public Policy Implications

What are the main public policy implications of MMOs?

This may sound like a dry, boring topic, primarily because it *is* a dry, boring topic. However, it's important: *public policy* is what governments use to help guide their decision-making on a subject, whether through laws, regulations, funding priorities or education. If the wrong public policy is in place, the results could be extremely serious.

What's that? Governments don't have a public policy on MMOs? They're just games?

Well, I'm sorry to break the bad news, but governments *do* have public policies on MMOs. Once any economic activity gets big enough, governments will consult on formulating a public policy with regard to it—even games. The UK government's Department of Business, Innovation and Skills did theirs in 2008.

What's that again? Nothing bad happened as a result of this, so why worry? Well you're right, nothing bad *did* happen as a result of this. That's because when the consultancy was undertaken, those of us who were invited to participate who actually understood MMOs were able to explain to those who understood other things (law, industry, government) the nature of what they were looking at. This is why, for example, MMOs and non-MMO virtual worlds are not treated as being the same thing.

For any country, the main public policy implication of MMOs is cultural: does the government want its citizens to spend their time in virtual worlds, especially ones developed overseas that embody the values of other cultures? As a corollary, do they want people in other countries to play virtual worlds that embody the values of their own country?

Even though MMOs are ultimately a British invention, most of the main ones today are developed by US or South Korean companies and are shaped by the culture of those countries. MMO players spend about the same amount of time in MMOs as nonplayers spend watching television, and they're influenced to at least the same degree. MMOs can therefore be seen as a vehicle for public diplomacy: you can use them to communicate your country's ideals to the citizens of other nations, in much the same way that Voice of America, BBC World Service, RT and Al Jazeera do in broadcast media. Oh, and as *America's Army* did for first-person shooters.

The main issues of public policy from the point of view of industry concern clarity of the law. Developers don't mind adhering to the law, but they do want to know what the law is and how it will be interpreted. There is particular concern that well-intended laws may be enacted that could accidentally cause irreparable damage because of the ignorance of those framing such laws. For example, giving players ownership of the digital objects their characters possess in a game world would have this effect.

Otherwise, the concerns of MMO developers are pretty much the same as for any other online business: the administrative load imposed on them, the records they must keep, the responsibilities they have, their tax liabilities—details such as those. Basically, they just want to be left alone as much as possible.

Players of MMOs, like the MMOs themselves, are all different. Although they have advocates (such as academics) and community leaders, these individuals rarely represent the views of players at large. It's therefore not easy to state what the public policy implications are for players in general. However, broadly speaking, they want to be able to have fun. Whether this is fun in a sandbox world where they can create things and keep their IP, or whether it's fun in a theme park world where they slay dragons, or whether it's fun in a free-to-play world where they can buy success rather than play to win it, they don't care: so long as they can choose which kind they want, and have fun as a result, that's enough.

The public policy implications from all of this analysis can thus perhaps be summarized as the need to ensure that there remains a wide variety of MMOs, each with the flexibility to be run as its designers, developers, and operators intend.

In other words: choice.

Special Treatment

In 1926, the Romanian artist Constantin Brancusi tried to bring his brass sculpture *Bird in Space* into the United States. According to US customs law, anything made from metal was subject to a 40% import tax. Works of art were exempt from any tax.

Prior to this, no major works of art made of metal had come to the US, and the customs officials didn't see why this particular abstract lump of metal qualified as a work of art. They wanted the import tax imposed. However, a 1928 US Customs Court judged that it *was* a work of art because it had been created as such. In other words, the intention of its creator was that it was a work of art, so that's what it was.

Once in the United States, it could have been melted down of course and treated as if it were indeed merely a lump of metal. As it happens, it's now in a gallery in Berlin instead.

MMOs written to be games should be treated as games, even if some of the people who play them treat them otherwise.

Why Censor Games?

People who call for computer games to be censored typically have one of two concerns:

- The effect of the game on the perpetrator. "Players will become desensitized to violent behavior, and may be tempted to try it in real life."

- The effect of the game on the observer. "It pains me to think that people can willingly torture their sims/catz/ neopets like that."

The first of these uses only one edge of what is actually a double-edged sword. If games truly caused desensitization, we should be calling for the authorities to ban the widespread depiction of cute, furry animals. Imagine how someone would behave if they lost their sense of all that is wholesome and good in the world! We must keep this evil away from our children!

The second concern is the real one.

Context Is King

Would it be fair to say that anything in an MMO *can* be acceptable, so long as players maintain the conceit of the magic circle? Rape, murder, slavery, racism, sexism and cults are acceptable in context, but not out of context?

Example: raping a character in an MMO that was specifically set up so that characters can be raped, and with fair warning that it's possible, would keep rape squarely within the magic circle; should it therefore be allowed? As long as you knew when you started playing that it could happen, why wouldn't it be fine? Of course, if it came completely out of the blue in an out-of-context fashion that might have a serious real-world effect on an unprepared person who hadn't signed up for that kind of thing, well then obviously that would be different. If you knew in advance, though?

You still don't like the idea of a rape MMO. Neither do I. That's why I chose it as an example. Yet if books are allowed in which rapists are the protagonist, why should a game-of-the-book be disallowed? Would a movie-of-the-book also be disallowed?

Of course, the problem with this is that real-world governments decide for themselves whether a virtual effect on a real person is "acceptable" or not. Given that an absence of evidence is no barrier to their believing that games have a stronger influence on their players than books do on their readers, could "it's a game" itself be sufficient justification to ban an MMO for in-context material (a nicely ironic inversion of the usual "it's just a game" disparagement they regularly endure)?

A government may even decide that the mere existence of a virtual effect is enough to distress people who know of its existence but don't happen to play the MMO in question. For example, I'd expect a lot of people to feel hurt by the creation of a virtual world set in an alternative universe where the Nazis didn't gas 6 million Jews, Roma, homosexuals and the mentally ill—even if it was clearly a work of fiction. Yet would a novel using that premise be banned?

Is there *any* subject matter for MMOs that should *always* be banned, because it *always* has undesirable real-world effects?

Consumer Over-Protection

In 2005, following a year-long investigation into complaints about MMO companies, the South Korean Fair Trade Commission published its findings. It declared two thirds of the Terms of Service clauses it examined void. As a result, companies could (among other things) no longer:

1. Permanently suspend or seize the accounts of players caught engaging in RMT for the first time.

2. Refuse compensation of game time lost to service outages of up to four hours, even when the company was not at fault.

3. Place on players the burden of proof that any lag they suffer is excessive.

4. Suspend players' accounts for operational reasons.

5. Give gamemasters all-inclusive powers.

You can see how this was intended to help put-upon players stand up to imperious developers, but:

1. So MMO operators have the right to ban RMT, but not the right to enforce it. Uh? Could they nerf the item they found the player had bought—would that be allowed? What if it were a general nerf of all such items, not just the player's particular one?

2. This seems a little over the top. If the state TV company had a problem and couldn't broadcast for 4 hours, would it have to pay compensation to viewers? Why should MMOs be different?

3. This is a nightmare. We actually had this in *MUD1* and *MUD2*, and people were claiming *all the time* that they'd died as a result of lag or line drops. It was only when we introduced a "log everything" policy and could *show* people exactly when our software received their commands (and their disconnect signals) that it stopped.

4. This strikes at the heart of operations. Taking a server down for maintenance or patching becomes impossible with this in place.

5. This stomps on many creative flowers, making so many assumptions about the nature of the worlds it applies to, it's staggering. It immediately rules out worlds such as *Second Life*, in which everyone has all-inclusive powers. Even if it's the relative powers between players and GMs they're complaining about, this is still outrageous. For some virtual worlds, for example the text-based *Castle Marrach*, it's the GMs who make the game world what it is—without them, there would pretty well *be no game*. For the rest, if the GMs don't have the powers, then who *does* have them? *Someone* must, in order to deal with the in-game issues that come up every moment of every day.

South Korea's Fair Trade Commission relaxed its stance somewhat following a 60-day period of negotiation with the MMO companies, but it does go to show how easy it is for well-meaning but uninformed legislation to backfire.

No matter how laudable an attempt to protect consumers is, if it works to destroy what they're consuming then it isn't really going to help in the long run.

The Four Rs

With normal goods and services, if you pay for faulty goods or bad service then there are laws that entitle you as a consumer to redress. The possible solutions on offer are known as *the four Rs*: Repair, Replace, Return, and Reduction (in price).

How would these work for MMOs?

MMO policy expert Ren Reynolds hypothesized the following situation: suppose that on the opening weekend of an MMO (traditionally the most exciting time), there were issues with the login server and you, personally, couldn't play. Two days later you can, but by then you've missed the best part and all your friends are two days ahead of you. Which form of redress, if any, should be employed?

What would work best for you?

Data Protection

As with many other European countries, the UK has legislation to protect individuals from malevolent use of their personal details by evil corporations and secretive government agencies (with some exceptions that apply to secretive government agencies). This legislation is generally recognized to be badly enacted and misunderstood, but its aims are benign: to protect individuals' privacy, to enable them to find out what information is being held about them, and to allow them to correct it if it's false.

Suppose, as a player of an MMO, I try to join a prestigious guild and am turned down. I try to join another, and am turned down again. This keeps happening, until I figure out that I'm on some kind of blacklist that all the top guilds are using to check out potential recruits. I have no idea why I am on the blacklist, nor who operates it. I would like to:

- Find out who runs the blacklist.

- Discover what data they have about me.

- Correct any incorrect data about me.

Can I call on real-life data-protection laws to do this? Even if it relates only to my characters, and not to me as a human being?

Well, probably, yes. There may be jurisdictional issues, but assuming that I'm playing on a European server these would not be serious.

Let's add a wrinkle. Say the blacklist is run by a guild of subversive players who have managed to take over the power guilds' blacklisting system as part of the virtual world's ongoing internal conflict. I can easily imagine something like this happening in *EVE Online*, for example. Such an action would make the running of the blacklist a "game" thing rather than a "real life" thing.

Would data protection laws still apply? If so, should they?

I'm not persuaded that many legal systems have a proper grasp of the concept of the magic circle.

How Much Is Too Much?

MMO operators don't mind when the law interferes in their business (well, no more than anyone else does), but they don't want it to interfere too much.

So how much is "too much"?

The thing is, "too much" is a relative term: it varies between MMOs. For example, suppose a new law enshrined the right of players to publish novels about their characters in MMOs' fictional settings. *Entropia Universe* might well be fine with that, and even pleased if it brought in more players; *Star Wars: the Old Republic* would not be fine, because this would mean players could profit from the franchise's extensive intellectual property, quite possibly damaging it in the process.

As a second example, suppose that strict new laws were enacted to stop MMOs from potentially being used as vehicles for money laundering. *Star Wars: the Old Republic* might have an easy time complying with such legislation because it doesn't let its players cash out their in-game items for real money. *Entropia Universe* could find itself wound up in excessive amounts of bureaucratic red tape, though.

What's "too much" for one MMO could be inconsequential for another. What we really need is for MMOs to be able to state what kind of a world they are and then to be allowed to operate freely within those parameters. Currently, MMOs try to manage this in a rather paranoid fashion through their EULAs, but if these were to break down then we may have to look more closely at interration.

Half and Half

How come fantasy games are fine with half-elves and half-orcs, but you never see half-dwarfs (sorry, half-*dwarves*) or half-halflings? Or quarter-elves? And how come one half of the combination is always human? If elves and orcs can mate with humans, why can't they mate with each other?

Hmm, maybe that's where humans came from.

Consumer Protection

When you buy something in the real world, there is consumer protection legislation to protect you. You can take it back to the shop if it doesn't work or if it breaks too soon with normal use; in many cases, you can return it within a few weeks if there's nothing at all wrong with it but you changed your mind and it's still in a saleable state.

Do consumer protection laws apply to MMOs?

Well to the MMO software itself, yes, obviously. The people at PC World put up a fight when I returned *Age of Conan* because the damned thing wouldn't patch itself, but they knew I had the law on my side and so eventually relented.

What about goods *within* the MMO, though?

Well, this is where we head into uncharted waters…

If you bought something in a virtual world that was all about commerce, such as *Second Life*, it would seem fair enough that you could ask for your money back if you were sold something that didn't do what it was supposed to do. However, for MMOs such as *EVE Online*, being ripped off is part of the game—consumer protection laws would diminish its appeal considerably.

The difference here, of course, is that *Second Life* has a convertible currency: when you buy something in Linden dollars, you're pretty well buying it in real dollars. *EVE Online* doesn't have a convertible currency—not officially, anyway. If you wanted to sell ISK for real money, it wouldn't be impossible to find someone with whom to trade (despite CCP's best efforts). That said, it does have PLEX, which can be traded in-game and has a tangible monetary value; this muddies the waters somewhat.

EVE Online is a subscription MMO. What about free-to-play MMOs, the existence of which entirely depends on selling virtual goods for real money? In theory, under consumer protection laws, you should be able to buy the enhanced weapon or armor or whatever it is you want, and then demand your money back a few weeks later (maybe when you've used it to help you get an upgrade?). If the developers were to nerf it even months after the "period of reflection" had expired, you could still have a case.

Consumer protection laws, which are relatively benign, are just one of the areas in which MMOs are pushing at the boundaries of existing law. In the main, it's obvious what the "right" treatment should be, but there are some gray areas where even the professionals disagree.

It's one law for the rich, another for the virtual rich…

Shooting Horses

Suppose that I run a business stabling horses. I don't own the horses—my customers do—but I look after them day to day.

Now let's say I decide there isn't enough money in looking after horses. I decide to redevelop my stables as dog kennels instead. You can't keep your horses with me anymore.

I am within my rights as a stable owner to tell you to take your horses away and find somewhere else to stable them. That would be bad news if my stables were the only ones for miles around, but you can't stop me from closing down my stables. They're *your* horses, but *my* stables. You can, however, stop me from shooting your horses when I close down my stables, because then I would be destroying your property.

If I decide I want to close down my MMO, you will lose all the virtual items you've paid for. You can't transfer them elsewhere, as they are utterly worthless without my computers. I am therefore effectively shooting your horses.

Do I get to do that?

Assuming Precedence

If one MMO comes out before a similar MMO, the latter must be a descendant of the former, right?

Oh, you know the drill: I set up a straw-man question so I can demolish it. This inheritance assumption is actually one I've had to disabuse more than one interviewer of, though, so I don't feel too bad about doing the same here.

There are four main reasons why this assumption of precedence might be wrong:

1. It's entirely possible that two people have the same idea at the same time, independently. Alan Klietz, who wrote *Sceptre of Goth*, had never heard of *MUD*; Roy Trubshaw and I had never heard of *SoG*. We just wrote something similar around the same time. One of them had to be released "first," but it would be years before either of us heard about the other.

2. It's possible to be first while having no influence on later developments. The first "video game" was played on an oscilloscope, but no one who saw or played that game ever went on to develop another game.

3. It's possible that games being developed at the same time had some influence on each other. The people working on *Meridian 59*, *Ultima Online*, and *EverQuest* had all heard that the other teams were working on similar projects and there was some cross-pollination. *M59* was first to hit the game stores, but in its striving to be first it was launched prematurely. Had the *M59* developers not known about *EQ* and *UO*, they might have launched later with a more complete product and fully kick-started the MMO revolution as they had intended.

4. Sometimes, games are similar because they share an ancestor, not because one is the ancestor of another. They're siblings, not parents/children. *Rift* and *Lord of the Rings Online* have similar gameplay because they both descend from *World of Warcraft*, not because *Rift* descends from *LotRO*—even though it came out later.

Sadly, the same assumption about precedence applies to patents as well as to MMOs…

Patent Nonsense

When a new industry comes along, it's fairly easy for people to patent ideas that cover vast swathes of that industry. I'd much rather that this weren't possible, but it is. People who are working in MMOs at the moment are in a good position to patent things that pretty well any competent programmer (or designer) would come up with when faced with the same problem. However, because today's developers meet the problem first, they get to keep the solution. This can't be good for MMOs as a whole.

What's particularly annoying is when people who aren't developing MMOs themselves sit down and consider what might be invented later (for example, "real-time speech in virtual worlds") and then word a patent in such a way that when someone else has done all the hard work and actually invented something that the patent could apply to (such as "generating speech from text in real-time"), throwing it in their face and asking for a license fee.

Worst of all are patents in which people take an existing general principle and apply it to a specific new instance to which it hasn't been applied before but inevitably will be. "Hmm, people use conveyor belts to move products from one part of the factory to another part. I'll patent the idea of moving computer game DVDs from one part of the factory to another. Actually, why don't I word it vaguely enough that once I have the patent I can use it for cases where people move computer games in any format from one place to another in any way?" I've actually seen a patent that is the software equivalent of that.

Allowing patents for software is as nonsensical as allowing patents for legal defenses. "Sorry, you can't use the 'doctrine of imperfection' defense without a license, as I patented it in 1992." I don't mind software *copyright*, but patent is another matter entirely. It's just too general (as it's understood at the moment).

Fortunately for me, we don't have software patents in the EU. Unfortunately for me, they do have them in the United States.

Ciphers

Much of the intellectual discussion of virtual worlds is put in terms of *Second Life* and *World of Warcraft*. *SL* is treated basically a cipher for "social world" and *WoW* is treated as a cipher for "game world." This unspoken convention has helped keep the argument grounded in example, rather than hypothesis.

It's not without dangers, though.

SL and *WoW* are used as exemplars because they're the biggest and best-known of their kind. This means that whatever points might apply to other virtual worlds will tend to apply to them even more, which helps to crystalize the argument. However, it's often forgotten that some of the problems they have are not shared by other virtual worlds, and that there are indeed other kinds of virtual world that aren't just *SL* or *WoW* clones.

Legislators looking at *SL* and *WoW*, for example, might propose laws that make great sense for *SL* and *WoW* but could seriously damage worlds with much smaller user bases that suddenly find themselves having to abide by rules framed for worlds a thousand times bigger than they. The same applies for worlds that are built for specific purposes (such as education or training), for specific demographics (such as children), using other interfaces (such as text), with different legal protections (such as no EULA) and having diverse business models (such as free).

SL and *WoW* are OK as placeholders for "large-scale social worlds" and "large-scale game-like worlds." However, they do not between them run the gamut of virtual worlds, and when making generalizations people should always bear in mind that other virtual worlds *do exist*.

Oh, and yes, *Second Life* is still a thing. Just because the media forgot about it that doesn't mean it went away.

Always Open

Here's a quirky legal issue about owning virtual goods that was first raised by Yale law professor Jack Balkin.

The gist of it is that US courts are empowered to keep a business running in order to allow people to liquidate any holdings that are enabled by that business. The main reason the courts have these powers relates to the banking industry, in which a failed financial institution can be kept open artificially if that means a better price will be realized for its assets. It doesn't only apply to financial institutions, though: if your car is parked in a multi-story car park and the owner goes bankrupt, someone is going to have to open the barriers so you can recover your vehicle.

Virtual worlds (MMOs included) can have objects within them that are worth thousands of dollars each on the open market. Closing such a world would mean that the "owners" of these assets would not be able to dispose of them. Said owners could petition a court to order that the virtual world be kept open to allow disposal to take place.

Unfortunately, though, these being virtual objects, they're *only* worth money if the virtual world *remains* open—you can't transfer your Sword of Mighty Cliché to some other virtual world. This means that any court electing to stop an MMO from closing overnight would then be obliged to keep it running indefinitely.

The sensible thing to do—even if you concede that players can own in-game virtual objects—would be to keep the virtual world closed. However, as US law stands, a creditor (*that is*, a player) could perhaps succeed in arguing for the virtual world to be kept open on the grounds that they could then sell their stuff to someone else.

Sure, it probably *won't* happen, but it serves as a solid example of how reasonable, everyday laws can suddenly look awfully stupid when applied to MMOs.

PS: If you think *this* is bad, wait until we have NPCs with true artificial intelligence; they'd be even *more* upset if they were to learn that their MMO were to be switched off...

Repair

The first of the four Rs to redress consumer issues with faulty goods or bad service is Repair. What it comes down to is that if you buy something and it's broken, you can ask for it to be fixed. If you had some new windows installed, for example, and they let in the rain, you could get the people who installed them to repair them. So how does this translate into MMOs?

Well, if the client doesn't work, there should be some attempt by the developer to patch it in a reasonable time; if they don't try to repair it (knowing it to be faulty) then they're in breach of consumer law. If the server doesn't work, the developer is out of business anyway because there's no game for anyone to play.

In Ren's miss-the-opening-weekend example, the login server works for some people but not for others; there should therefore be some attempt made to patch it, and if there isn't then the developer is derelict in their duty. However, fixing bugs takes time, and it's not unreasonable that two days might have elapsed before the login server worked as intended. This would still mean that some people would have received an inferior product (they missed the opening weekend) to that of the people for whom it worked every time.

If you take the view that your character is faulty because it has two fewer days of play behind it than the characters of people who could log in when you couldn't, this raises the possibility that it could be "repaired." All it would take would be to give it the same points and skills and quest completion history that you would have worked it up by if you'd been able to log in. Would that be a reasonable solution?

Well, it's like missing 10 minutes of a movie because of a faulty ticket machine and then having someone tell you what's happened in the plot so far to bring you up to speed. It's not really the same thing as actually watching the movie. Likewise, giving people double XP for a while so they can catch up their friends is like offering you the chance to watch a movie at double speed until you reach the point where everyone else is; again, it's not going to have wide appeal.

One effective way to "repair" the "damage" caused to your character by starting two days after everyone else would be to reset the database and make *everyone* start from scratch again, a bit like when there's a false start in an athletics race. Of course, the people who now have to replay content they have been through already would not be happy—it's like making them re-read the first few pages of a book they've just read. Also, even those people who missed the opening two days won't be happy, as everyone else will still get ahead of them since they have a couple of days' more experience of play. To make it as fair as possible, the developer would have to prevent those who *could* log in over the weekend from logging in for two days, to let those who *couldn't* log in can catch up. That means that these people would also now be due compensation, but Repair wouldn't work for them as there's nothing to be repaired—they're just being inconvenienced.

So Repair probably isn't going to be effective for MMO consumer protection, except for the usual patching system for the software itself.

Dispute Resolution

If you have a dispute with your MMO operator, the MMO operator will usually wish to resolve it amicably. If you want to take the matter further, you will have to go to court. This will inevitably be costly, which some players and academics feel stacks the odds too heavily in favor of the operator.

What other industries do in this kind of situation is to use an external arbitration service supported by the industry as a whole. Suppose we had one of these for MMOs: wouldn't that even things up a little?

It would in theory, but the problem is that gamers will be gamers: they'd game a system like this. If banning 5,000 players means that a developer will immediately get back 5,000 requests for arbitration—even from people who know full well that they're guilty—then arbitration as a solution is no longer viable.

So yes, if you get banned for gold farming and you've done no such thing, you might wish there were some kind of external watchdog you could go to for redress. However, just remember that you'll be standing in line with thousands of actual gold farmers who have also put in claims, just to snarl up the system so as to discourage the banning of their other accounts.

When it comes to MMOs, if it *can* be gamed it *will* be gamed.

MMOs as Realities

In my examination of MMOs as spaces of existence, I've called them "realities." Is that actually a fair description of them, though? Social scientists tend to regard virtual worlds as an adjunct to *Reality*, rather than realities in their own right (although this may be because they look at social worlds such as *Second Life* more than they look at MMOs).

The thing is, for a proposed reality properly to qualify as a reality, someone has to perceive it as a reality. Players from *Reality* are capable of doing that; however, it would be more clear-cut if there were people for whom the created reality was *their* reality—that is, people who know no other reality than the one someone in a higher reality (*Reality*, in the case of MMOs) has created.

Yes, we're now heading off on a flight of fancy, on account of how I have that Ph.D. in Artificial Intelligence and like to dust it off every now and then.

Roy Trubshaw and I populated *MUD1* with nonplayer characters and monsters I called *mobiles* (whence the MMO term *mobs*). These characters operated entirely within the *MUD1* world. They couldn't distinguish between player characters and NPCs; they treated them all the same. Yes, this did mean that they would attack each other and so on (although *MUD2* was much better in this regard). Mobiles could do anything they wanted to do within *MUD1*'s physics.

Admittedly, they weren't sophisticated enough to "want" or do much, because Artificial Intelligence isn't powerful enough to impress anyone even today, let alone back then. What about in the MMOs of the future, though?

MUD I's denizens couldn't really "think" as we understand the term. However, maybe 50 or 500 years from now we'll have true AI? Or 5,000? Or 50,000?

We have all of eternity—take as long as you want! Sooner or later, we *will* have a virtual world that we will have populated by intelligent-as-us beings.

Those beings will regard that virtual world as their reality, and will have no conception of *Reality*—even though it's the physics of *Reality* that is sustaining the existence of the reality they perceive.

This comes with some interesting philosophical questions. For example, as I hinted at earlier, would it be right to switch off such an MMO? To do so could mean the end of countless millions of free-thinking individuals! If you're not fine with killing millions of animals in *Reality*, why would you be fine with extinguishing millions of artificial intelligences who, as far as they are concerned, can feel and think and exist and are alive? Yet if you can't switch off the computers that maintain their existence, you'd have to keep their world running forever.

Perhaps you'd just take a snapshot of the database before you shut it down; years later, it could in theory be reloaded...

Old as New

US Patent number 7637806, issued on December 29, 2009:

> *The invention provides a role-playing game environment wherein the nature of various NPCs within the game may be varied over time within the game. The goals of various NPCs within the game may be dynamically and automatically changed within the game. At certain in-game time periods, the game server may dynamically assign one or more new goals for some or all of the NPCs based on the current status of each NPC. When a player later interacts with a given NPC assist (or impede) that NPC in reaching its currently assigned goal, the method may dynamically determine a steps that the player's avatar may perform to assist (or impede) the goal. Thus, players cannot predict what will happen when they move through the game and reach a location at which they can interact with a given NPC, making the game-playing experience ever fresh and challenging.*

Leaving aside the point that the fourth sentence doesn't even parse, why is any of this patentable? It basically boils down to "apply 30-year-old AI techniques to MMOs."

Patents are supposed to encourage the development of new technology, not discourage the use of old technology.

Replace

The second of the four Rs to redress consumer issues with faulty goods or bad service is Replace. This means that when you buy something that has a fault, you can by law have it replaced by a working item of the same type or better. It's most often used when it's less expensive to replace something than it is to repair it.

For example, when my mother got a new TV, after a week or so it developed a permanent, one-pixel high, red horizontal line. The shop took it back and sent it to the manufacturer to be repaired; the manufacturer figured it would cost too much to dismantle and install new electronics, so they replaced it with a slightly better model.

This isn't generally of any use for digital goods. If your PC client for an MMO doesn't work because of a fault in the medium (scratched DVD, say), then replacement makes sense. If it doesn't work because the client software is at fault, it doesn't make sense—you'd just be replacing something that doesn't work with something identical to it, which by definition would also not work. It would need a Repair, rather than a Replace.

In the two-days-lost-at-launch-weekend case, repair and replace are indistinguishable. Replacing your character with a new character that has all the attributes that your original character would have had if it had been played for two days is indistinguishable from simply making those changes to your character directly, which is a repair.

Replace is therefore not an option likely to be requested often by aggrieved players-as-consumers.

Ascending

Suppose we have intelligent NPCs. Could they ever visit *Reality*?

Now obviously, we can visit the worlds of our MMOs using player characters: the physics of the two realities are made similar precisely in order that we *can* do that. However, it can in theory work the other way, too: NPCs from our MMOs can visit *Reality*.

Now this may seem a little odd. NPCs are, by definition, contained within their reality. They can't ever escape to *Reality* because they're merely the emergent interactions of lines of computer code. They can exist consequent on the physics of *their* reality, but not the physics of *Reality*. Put another way, they can exist on hardware built *in Reality*, but not on the hardware *of Reality*.

Well that's true, yes. However, we can nevertheless give them the means to *experience Reality*. Suppose that as-many thousand years into-the future as it takes, we have human-looking robots. Instead of controlling these with "robot brains," we could pass control to the artificial intelligence of an NPC in an MMO. That NPC could then experience our world through the robot's senses.

Such an NPC could interact with our world using the physical body we have built for it. We could even teach NPCs to program their own reality from *Reality*! This is probably not a good idea in case they crashed it, or suicidally threw a software switch that turned their world off—but it would be possible.

Using such a system, people in a reality that's consequent on a higher reality *can* escape to that higher reality if they have the co-operation of that reality.

Cool! We can give our favorite NPCs a heaven! Or, if they don't like it here, a hell.

Return

In the everyday world, Return is the last resort for any provider of a faulty product: give the customer their money back. As I mentioned earlier, I've invoked it myself with *Age of Conan* when it wouldn't install the launch patch: I took it back to the shop, threw a tantrum and got my money back.

This is the nuclear option for material goods. A furniture shop that has to give you back the money you paid for your faulty wardrobe *and* recover it from your house is going to be out of pocket by quite a bit. However, it's the easiest option for digital goods. You don't like the MMO? OK, delete it. Here's your money back.

This assumes you do actually *pay* for the goods or services, though. If it's a free-to-play MMO and you can't get in on launch day, well you didn't pay any money in the first place so it can't exactly be given back. You tried to use a free service, it didn't work; you got what you paid for—nothing.

Now you *could* argue that although a full refund should be available, you actually want more than that because you wasted your time trying to use the product and so on before you realized there was a problem. This would amount to a compensation claim, and it would apply to free-to-play MMOs just as much as it would to pay-to-play MMOs. This is fair enough: it can be handled the same way as any other return that has a compensation element to it. If you bought a new washing machine and spent two hours failing to get it to work, you could ask for some money to cover the inconvenience; you might not get much, if indeed you got any at all, but if you were sufficiently enraged to try it then you may only be seeking the satisfaction of embarrassing the manufacturer anyway. Of course, if your washing machine started up but spewed water all over your carpets, you could claim far more in damages; furthermore, either you or your insurance company probably would sue for compensation beyond that of merely repairing your new device.

On this basis, I could have sued Funcom because patch 1.2 of *The Secret World* caused a blue screen of death every so often when I transitioned to and from Agartha. I suspect that I wouldn't have obtained much of an award had I pursued a claim through the courts, but if it had actually damaged my hardware or cost me data, sure, why shouldn't I have been able to sue? Another thing you *could* argue is that although you believe that you have bought a faulty product, getting your money back for it is not actually what you want. For example, if you were a big *Star Wars* fan and had been looking forward to *SW:TOR* for years, you'd still want to play it after an opening weekend login debacle (or opening week staggered login debacle in this particular instance), so you wouldn't wish to ask for your money back were that to mean you could no longer play. You'd want to play; it's just that you'd also want *something* to make up for your slight loss.

This brings us to the Reduction, or reduced-price option.

Observation and Existence

One of the things Roy Trubshaw said to me when we were working on *MUD1* was, "You know that question of whether, if a tree falls in the desert and nobody hears it, does it make a sound? Well in *MUD*, I can tell you that it definitely does. I've just written the code for it."

The world is there because the code is there. It runs, therefore it exists. It doesn't matter whether there's anyone observing it or not—it was "preobserved" by its creation.

Of course, you can argue that the hardware might have crashed between the tree's falling and the sound's being generated, and that you can only be sure it hasn't by observing it. However, in *Reality* you can only be sure of *anything at all* by observing it, and even then that's only true if you trust your senses (and sensors). The question of whether a falling tree makes a noise when unobserved is vacuous, because you can never be sure that what you heard (or didn't hear) reflects what happened anyway. All you can be sure of about your reality is one very specific fact famously noted by René Descartes: *cogito ergo sum.* I think, therefore I exist.

From the point of view of an NPC in an MMO, the world of that MMO continues to exist irrespective of whether it has any visitors from the real world.

Patently Obvious

In April 2004, Microsoft applied for a patent on "adaptive agents" in video games. These are NPCs that are "driven by rewards they receive based on the outcome of their behavior during actual game play." In November 2010, the patent was awarded[5].

So let's see. You take an idea that has been kicking around in AI for at least four decades, which has already been used in many different applications, and which people have been trying to put into computer games since the 1980s, and all of a sudden you can patent it? Uh? My original PhD proposal was to do precisely this kind of thing for the mobiles in *MUD1*, and it was only the fact that I'd have had to have rewritten *MUD1* for a more powerful computer (which didn't exist) that meant I wasn't able to do it.

Why are these travesties of patent law permitted? It's like the patent system is a drunk, staggering across the road barely able to see, waiting to be hit by a passing motorist and sent to casualty to be patched up while sternly being told to mend its ways.

NPCs that are self-motivated and learn: wow, what an idea *that* is—for 1981.

Easily Offended

What do the following have in common?

- *blonde*
- *accuse*
- *suicide*
- *nuts*
- *follower*

They're all words that my elder daughter used in the course of normal conversation in *The Lord of the Rings Online* that fell afoul of its profanity filter.

---

[5]Kurt Hartwig Graepel *et al: Reward-Driven Adaptive Agents for Video Games.* US Patent Office: patent number 7837543. http://www.google.com/patents/US7837543

Descending

Pursuing our "what if NPCs had true AI?" thought experiment, we begin to touch on what might be described as "theological" matters.

Don't worry; I'll warn you if this starts to look faith-challenging. Even though I'd sell more copies of this book if people threw it at the wall in a rage and had to buy a replacement, I don't actually want to upset anyone here.

To an NPC with artificial intelligence in an MMO, that MMO appears to be self-contained. There is no particular reason to suppose that our world—*Reality*—exists. Of course, we can enter the MMO reality using our player characters and tell the NPCs there about *Reality*. Why would they ever believe us, though? And why would we ever do that anyway?

Or, alternatively, why wouldn't we do it the whole time?

If they were inquisitive, the NPCs could look at the structure of the world around them and deduce that it was created by some higher, intelligent being. They'd be correct too—the MMO's *designer* is that higher being. They could further reason that they themselves were modeled on that higher being—that they were created in the creator's image. This is also correct—for reasons of persuasiveness and immersion.

However, they would be completely wrong as to:

- The nature of that higher being
- What the higher being's world is like
- Why the higher being created their reality
- Pretty much everything else to do with the higher being and *Reality*, too

"You mean, the creator created our world to make money in their world?!"

Some of the smartest NPCs might figure that with no evidence whatsoever to suggest that there *is* a higher being, then rationally there isn't one. In other words, we'd have atheist NPCs following a logical argument to its inevitable conclusion, who are nevertheless absolutely wrong.

Reduction

The Reduction approach to offering redress to customers who have bought faulty goods or services means a reduction in price. In the material-goods world, this is often used when buying things that you know aren't in pristine condition when you buy them. For example, my daughter's latest laptop was the last in the shop and had been on display, so we got a discount for the wear and tear (and the time it took us to delete all the videos of customers it had recorded through its webcam…). The same thing happens when a flaw in an item is discovered after the purchase: on the underside of the table you've bought, you spot a scratch which isn't really noticeable but the shop gives you a little money back as a form of reparation.

With a subscription MMO, if you miss two days of play because of something wrong the developer did, it's easy for you to be given two days longer on your subscription; this would be a Replace. It's also easy to give you a month longer as a goodwill gesture; this would effectively be a Reduction, as you would be paying two days' worth of subscription and getting a month's worth for it.

This kind of reduced-price solution is not going to work for a free-to-play model, because if you couldn't log in you necessarily couldn't spend anything; therefore there is nothing to reduce the price of as a remedy. Of course, you could be given some in-game currency as compensation, but compensation is different to statutory remedy. A repair, for example, is not compensation; compensation is basically a bribe to make you go away.

Looking back at the four Rs, it would appear that developers who wish not to fall foul of the law should simply offer aggrieved players a full refund, which is the maximum remedy that can be required of them anyway. They may on a case-by-case basis offer alternative solutions if large numbers of players are affected (for example, no one can log in for a day, so everyone gets some premium currency to spend as redress); however, it's the simplest solution for them just to offer a full refund when anyone has a problem. Developers would be keen to avoid a potential situation in which people start asking for *some* of their money back *plus* a repair, *plus* some kind of compensation for being inconvenienced. That would be much more difficult to administer and is too readily griefable; it has all the potential of being a Customer Service nightmare.

When it comes down to it, if someone sells you shoddy goods, then the very best you can hope for is that you get your money back.

It would not be a very satisfactory solution to Ren's missed-the-opening-weekend thought experiment, though, which is (of course) his point.

It's the US Patent Office

The way I understand it, the US Patent Office is funded not by the United States government, but by people/companies paying fees to have their patent applications examined. If this is indeed the case, it would seem that there's a major conflict of interest involved (in that the more patents that are passed, the more money the US Patent Office makes).

This really can't go on. Perhaps if people who managed to challenge a US patent successfully in a US court were allowed to sue the US Patent Office for the expense of the trial, or even for damages, then the US Patent Office might be a bit more discriminating in deciding which patents to allow and which to reject.

Intervention

I'm for freedom. I want people to be able to feel free in MMOs, because that helps them become freer in the real world.

If it all could be done by design, that would be great; however, it can't, because there are people who don't get it, or don't want it, or don't want others to have it, or just want to make a quick buck. Intervention by an MMO's operators is therefore necessary—not as part of play, but as part of dealing with nonplay.

Don't Worry, Atheist NPCs

Actually, those NPCs in a world that we have created who reason (incorrectly) that we don't exist are probably not going to suffer for it. Every designer I've ever asked about this has said they'd be rather impressed with an NPC who had managed to construct such a sophisticated line of reasoning, and wouldn't hold it against them at all. Such NPCs therefore *wouldn't* be going to an equivalent of hell when they died.

Then again, *no one* in their reality is going anywhere when they die—they're just bits in computer memory. We could allow *some* to ascend to *Reality* by transferring their software to robots, but how are we going to choose which ones from among potentially billions? I'm betting that the most pious ones would not be at front of the queue...

Of course, it's theoretically possible that even if the gods of your reality are uncaring and just let your bits get put back on the heap ready for the next piece of code that needs a chunk of dynamic memory, the gods of *their* reality might remove you to an afterlife instead. After all, it's not *your* fault you were worshipping your reality's designer instead of that designer's designer—how could you know how many levels there were above you? If I made an MMO with NPCs so well-developed that eventually they wrote their own MMOs on computers that they built inside my MMO, could I take NPCs from that sub-MMO and put them into the host MMO as NPCs for that? Yes, of course I could, if I so chose. In theory, I could use robot hosts to ascend them all the way to *Reality*.

Pushing this idea one level up: if you believe that there is an afterlife for *Reality* that you go to when you die, then not only could you find yourself and your loved ones from *Reality* there when you show up, you could also find the intelligent NPCs of the MMOs you've designed there, too—the very ones for whom you were their god. The only difference would be that you'd have ascended one level and they'd have ascended two to get to this higher level of existence. This assumes that the god of the higher reality would regard intelligent NPCs as having "souls," but if that is indeed the case, hey, why not?

Gamers Are Gamers

Gamers are gamers. Some of them will (and, indeed, do) attempt to use real-world laws to gain game-world advantages. You can't say "no one would do that" when it comes to games. Someone *might* and probably *will* do that.

If consumer protection law says that developers have to return goods lost to password hacks, then some players will deliberately sell their password, let the person who bought it sell off their stuff, and then announce that their password has been hacked. The developer could be forced to give them back their stuff even if there is no evidence supporting the player's claim.

If consumer protection law says that players have a right to get their money back if they return their virtual goods "as good as new" within 30 days, what's to stop players from buying some fancy in-game gear to help them level up quicker and then returning it when they've leveled up and no longer need it?

Similar scams apply to the replacement of "faulty" goods (such as virtual swords that need to be repaired after combat) and the "mis-selling" of goods (such as not explaining all aspects of gameplay in their entirety before selling the game).

Gamers are accustomed to looking for loopholes in rule sets. Laws are just another rule set.

Community

What is community?

Simply put, community is the sense of *collective belonging* players have in a virtual world.

On Culture & Community

Buff Me

My daughter bought a make-up bag to give as a present. Here's what it said on the front:

Buff me.

Is this an example of game terminology making it to the mainstream? Or did the mainstream get there first? Perhaps it's just a coincidence and it was invented twice independently.

I once walked past a clothes shop in Singapore called Newbie.

Passion

Players are passionate about MMOs. They want MMOs to improve.

I'm all for passion, but its effectiveness depends on how it's used. Basically, when it comes to improving MMOs, there are four ways to apply passion:

1. Seek realistic goals. In general, this means you ask for things that are going to happen anyway, but you help them happen sooner.

2. Seek unrealistic goals. They'll never be achieved, but you may be able to make the industry change direction so that the new way things work is more to your liking.

3. Go it alone. See the problems facing developers yourself, but follow your own advice and plough your own furrow by making your own MMO.

4. Grumble but do nothing constructive.

Most players go for number 4, of course.

Different Views of Difference

Designers are usually scrupulous about ensuring that their MMOs are inclusive. Male and female characters vary only cosmetically, and any racial difference is merely a matter of skin tone. Forget the fact that in real life there *are* physical differences; if the designer is to avoid criticism for perpetuating stereotypes, all characters must begin equal.

Equal, yes...

Sure, they're equal when they conform to established bounds of political correctness, but obviously it's *fine* to make all your elves be sensitive, high-minded, environmentally aware aesthetes and all your dwarfs (oops, *dwarves*) be hard-drinking, no-nonsense, charmingly rude boors ... with Scottish accents. It's not as if you're suggesting that it's OK to stereotype people based on *what* they are rather than *who* they are or anything.

Oh, wait, you *are* saying that.

The words "lip" and "service" would seem to be making their way over here to take part in the discussion.

What Architects Know

In the real world, the real environment shapes real communities. It has been argued that the British are a tolerant people because the weather in Britain is so changeable that they have to be tolerant to live there.

The same applies to designed environments: when architects design new estates, they always consider what kind of community to foster—it would be inconceivable nowadays not to do so.

The same strictures apply to designers of MMOs. A virtual environment shapes the virtual communities that inhabit it.

Role-Play and Real-Play

If you want to role-play a character of the opposite gender to your real-world gender, should you be allowed to?

If you want to play a character of a different sexuality from your real-world gender, should you be allowed to?

If you want to play a character of a different ethnicity from your real-world gender, should you be allowed to?

If you want to set up a guild for players all of the same real-world gender, should you be allowed to?

If you want to set up a guild for players all of the same real-world sexuality, should you be allowed to?

If you want to set up a guild for players all of the same real-world ethnicity, should you be allowed to?

Which of the following entrance criteria for guilds should and shouldn't be allowed?

- Female avatars only
- Female players only
- Gay avatars only
- Gay players only
- Black avatars only
- Black players only
- Male avatars only
- Male players only
- Straight avatars only
- Straight players only

Those are the inclusive versions. Would it make any difference if they were exclusive?

- No women
- No gays
- No blacks
- No men
- No straights

Are there some things that it's OK to role-play and some things that it's not?

Does it always depend on the MMO, or should the rules be universal?

When the law comes to wrestle with these decisions, will it reach the same conclusions that you have?

Overlapping Communities

Communities are formed by and of players, and there are multiple communities operating within an MMO. Your raiding buddies, the wider guild, the faction you're aligned with, players on your server, players of the MMO as a whole—all these are examples of communities. It can even make sense to talk about "the community of MMO players."

Communities aren't all neat, concentric rings of subcommunities within wider communities, though. You may feel you're a member of the community of paladins, or of PvPers, or of role-players, or of elves—all at the same time. Communities *overlap*.

Game design decisions can prompt the formation of communities, but so can real-world influence. There are communities of French-speaking players on English-language servers; of gay players; of players who only play in the afternoon; of casual players. If people have something in common and the ability to communicate, there's a chance a community can form.

The rules of the community are its *culture*. All the different communities that operate within an MMO have their own cultures, tempered by the fact that they have to live alongside one another. The resultant mix of opinion and ideals creates an overarching and ever-evolving culture for the MMO as a whole.

Yes, there will still be major demarcation lines. A German-language server and a Spanish-language server will not have identical cultures, because of the differences between the real-world cultures that they import. However, the cultures on those servers *will* differ from their real-world originals.

MMOs have many boundary lines that can pen a community in such that it develops in partial isolation. However, *the* major one is the MMO/Reality boundary. Players like to regard their MMOs as being distinct from *Reality* (even though formally they're a part of it), and they treat them as places where different rules—social as well as physical—apply. It's to this culture that the other in-world cultures conform.

It therefore makes sense to talk about the "culture of an MMO."

TV CD

If you play a character of the opposite gender to your real-life gender, does that make you a transvestite?

No, but it does make you a cross-dresser. Well, kind of...

Cross-dressing describes the wearing of clothes associated with another gender, for whatever reason. Actors playing a part in drag or people dressing up for

Halloween would count as cross-dressers, for example. MMOs take it a step further in that it's not just the clothes, it's the body too; real life can't do that just yet, so there it's only the clothes that get changed. (Hence the *kind of.*)

Pretty well all the reasons people might cross-dress in Reality also apply to playing virtual characters of another gender. The primary exception is when the physicality of the clothing is a significant factor (for example, it's softer on the skin), which you might get in Reality but not (yet) in virtuality.

Transvestism is a sub-category of cross-dressing (well, that seems to be the consensus—these terms aren't fully nailed down). Unlike the general case, there is an implied reason for transvestism—the clothes are an outer symbol of something deeper. As an illustration, suppose someone were to develop a super-nanobot pill that changed your entire body to that of the opposite biological sex for half a day and then reverted it to what it was originally; that would appeal to transvestites in exactly the same way that dressing in female clothes does (although I guess they might be fussy over which set of reproductive organs they had). In essence, then, the *-vestism* is descriptive of an outward manifestation of the TV condition, not the heart of the definition; cross-dressing, on the other hand, simply refers to the practice of wearing the garments of another gender (which in the case of MMOs means wearing the whole look of another gender).

For some people, there's undoubtedly a sexual element in cross-gender play. For most, though, there isn't. You only have to consider what effect it would have on your stamina to be in a state of arousal for two to four straight hours every day to figure out why libido isn't the main driving force here. Also, if sex *were* at the center of it, why would any men play as female orcs? Are tusks really that much of a turn-on?

Basically, people who play as characters of another gender are *role-playing*: inserting a difference between their virtual and real selves so that they can use the former to figure out more about the latter. Playing a Dark Elf doesn't mean you harbor secret desires to have purple skin and ears the size of a donkey's, and playing an other-gendered character doesn't mean you want to be other-gendered. It doesn't mean you *don't*, but it's probably not statistically significant enough even to be implied.

I've played female characters many times—perhaps more than I have male characters. Does that make me a virtual cross-dresser? Sure. Does it make me a virtual transvestite? No. Even if it did, though, so what? It's not as if it's any of your business either way.

For me, the interesting question isn't "Why would people play the opposite of their real-life gender" but "Why wouldn't they?"

Real-Life API: ShareCulture

CPopulation::ShareCulture

int ShareCulture(CPopulation& *rcPop*)

- *rcPop* Specifies the population with which to share culture.

Remarks

Sets the population's culture set to the set resulting from a partial union with *rcPop*'s culture set and sets *rcPop*'s culture set to the set resulting from a partial union with the population's culture set.

- The degree of union is moderated by the *ppTolerance* level of the receiving culture.

- Culture sets can contain contradictory elements.

Return

0 on success, otherwise the bitwise OR of

- *E_PTP* At least one population is too primitive to share culture.

- *E_PMU* The populations are mutually unintelligible.

Types of Community

The minimum criterion required for a community to operate is *communication*. There has to be a channel through which members of a community can and do communicate. Thus, although we may poetically be part of the "community of the Milky Way," in practice we have yet to contact any other potential members (you know those movies are just fiction, right?), and this is not, therefore, formally a community.

Sociologists recognize different types of community, defined in terms of their strength. There are four key levels:

- A *community of interest* is made up of people sharing the same goals or interests, who work together to further those aims. A pick-up group to run some instance would be a (short-lived) example of such a community.

- Members of a *community of practice* share knowledge and pool resources. They feel that the community is more than just a means to an end—it has intrinsic value. If you've ever put anything into a guild bank, you've probably been a member of such a community.

- When members of a community work on projects important to that community (rather than to individuals), the result is a *community of commitment*. Setting up a Ventrilo server or a guild web site would be evidence of the existence of such a community.

- A spiritual community is made up of individual members who know and trust each other implicitly. Communication is almost intuitive, as if members' emotions are shared. Those guild buddies you've known for years, who have always come through for you, who have their faults and foibles but whom you accept for who they are: those are members of your spiritual community.

Most communities don't reach spiritual level, in part because it doesn't scale (you can't know more than a handful of people that well), but in part because not everyone wants or needs that level of community. People will more often operate within a community of commitment, which is itself part of a community of practice, in a wider community of interest. It's not uncommon to find all four types of community at work in the same guild.

Seeding a Community

The culture of an MMO is determined in part by the design of that MMO and in part by the players. A slow-paced, cerebral MMO will have a different culture from a fast-paced hack-and-slay. This isn't simply because they attract different types of people; it's because the physics of each game world and the goals it implicitly embodies call for different human responses, and therefore different reasons for people to communicate.

As a rule of thumb, I'd say that 20% of the culture of an MMO is defined by the designer, and 80% comes from the players.

Now the thing about culture is that it is passed from generation to generation. Indeed, an anthropological definition of culture is:

A system of shared beliefs, values, customs, behaviors, and material objects that the members of a society use to cope with their world and with one another, and that are transmitted from generation to generation through learning.[1]

---

[1]Daniel G. Bates: *Cultural Anthropology*. Allyn and Bacon: Needham Heights, Massachusetts, 1996.

Therefore, the people who first play your MMO—who *seed* it—have an important influence on how its culture develops. Players that come afterwards will find an existing culture in place, and will adapt so as to fit in with it.

So who plays your MMO first? That's right, the beta-testers.

What you *want* for a good community is a set of mature, imaginative, responsible enthusiasts. What you *get* are gung-ho, hard-core, low-loyalty, hit-it-till-it-breaks opinion-formers. There's even a recognized phenomenon of *serial beta-testers*, who move from pre-release MMO to pre-release MMO, influencing all but not having to think about consequences.

This is probably *not* going to help MMOs become more culturally refined over the next few years…

OZ Recruiting

> *"OZ is recruiting all levels. We are not 'GLBT only' but we are 'GLBT friendly'! (guilduniverse.com/oz)'"*

> Sara Andrews, January 2006

This message was sent on the *World of Warcraft* Shadowmoon server, and led to Andrews' being temporarily suspended from the MMO on the grounds of harassment for sexual orientation. Blizzard felt that her advertisement was "very likely to result in harassment for players that may not have existed otherwise."[2]

So … organizing a group of players who won't harass gay, lesbian, bisexual, and transgender players is a form of harassing those players? Wouldn't you have to be, you know, *stupid* to think that?

OK, so what happened here is basically that some Blizzard GM screwed up. Initially, the customer service team rallied around that GM to protect GM authority, but it rapidly became clear that the GM had made a bad mistake. The player pack saw a wounded animal and pounced; terrier-like, they wouldn't let go, and nonplayers with axes to grind joined in. Blizzard capitulated, and atoned by sending its GMs to sensitivity training in the full knowledge that if they ever fully *acted* on said training the general chat channel would be completely unused. Those who decided to be offended by the original actions felt satisfied that they'd protected their own corner, and life went on exactly as it did before.

---

[2]Alexander Sliwinski: *Blizzard of GLBT gaming policy questions. New England Blade*, 25 January 2006.

That said, there *are* actually reasons why, in theory, banning GLBT guilds could conceivably be valid. [Aside: I'll use *LGBT* from now on as it's more widely understood. Sorry, *GLBT* fans.]

What all this comes down to is the difference between *players* and *characters*. The aim of role-playing is to separate the former from the latter; therefore, the intrusion of real life is generally forbidden. Thus, a guild of black-haired, gay, dwarf, paladin *characters* is RP-valid, whereas a guild of Shinto, French-speaking, one-eyed, chiropractor *players* is not RP-valid. If you advertised a guild for LGBT members on a RP server, you'd be asking for LGBT characters; if you advertised one on a regular server, you'd be asking for LGBT players. If you find the very notion of LGBT or anti-LGBT offensive, you don't play MMOs where this makes RP sense as part of the backstory fiction.

That said, given that *WoW* has a zeppelin master called Hin Denberg, a lumberjack who says a line from the *Lumberjack Song* in *Monty Python's Flying Circus,* and a harbor statue openly riffing off the one in Rio de Janeiro, its RP credentials could perhaps be better. In other words, Blizzard couldn't really use role-playing theory to defend its GMs' actions, so it's as well it didn't. MMOs that make much more of an effort would be on stronger ground, of course.

That's the theory, anyway. More practically, Blizzard was faced with the worry that if they allowed an LGBT guild then they'd have problems with players forming anti-LGBT guilds, anti-anti-LGBT guilds, spoof LGBT guilds, ...; some of these could indeed result in harassment of players.

It's far easier in such circumstances simply to sweep the whole lot under the carpet and enforce a role-playing approach even on non-RP servers. If Blizzard had said at the start that you *can* create a guild of players who are all lawyers or all Manchester United supporters or all RL LGBT, you just don't get to advertise your guild on that basis, they might have escaped censure. Sure, it's important to *you* that every member of your guild is a card-carrying Communist or a cat owner or a Scientologist or a Harry Potter fan or a father, but frankly the *rest of the players* don't want to know: they're playing to get *away* from the real world, and they don't want your bringing it in here.

It looks as if this "We don't want to know" approach is what Blizzard was employing. Unfortunately, even *that* was inconsistent, as they'd allowed the advertisement of RP-breaking guilds in the past (ones for all-female players, for example). Blizzard should simply have looked at its own rules. Was language being used that "insultingly refers to any aspect of sexual orientation pertaining to themselves or other players"? No.

So, no need to ban, then.

Blizzard *was* within its rights to ban Sara Andrews, but having the right to act stupidly doesn't mean you should *do* so...

On Existence

Those NPC atheists who come to believe their reality has no gods when we, in *Reality*, know they're wrong because we created their reality, do actually have a point. The thing is, existence is *relative*.

I exist in my reality (*Reality*) by definition. However, do I exist in any reality I create? When I *visit* that reality, sure, I exist there while I do so. Do I exist in it when I'm *not* visiting it, though?

Well no, I don't exist in it. I always exist in *Reality*, but don't exist in my created reality except when I actually visit it.

If I choose never to visit the world I create, but do make changes to its physics that its inhabitants can detect as being (in their view) supernatural, they can perhaps deduce that I exist in my reality, if not theirs. They could even build up a hypothetical picture of me based on my record of supernatural interventions in their reality (which I may or may not actually have done—some apparent examples may be because they simply haven't figured out the physics yet, and think that when there's a comet it's because I'm telling them something).

So when I, as a god of a reality that I have created, visit that reality, I can be said to exist in it. If I make changes to it and decide not to cover my tracks, then after I have left I don't exist in it but the NPCs in it might believe that I do, or that I exist in a higher reality that I call *Reality* and they call Asgard or something.

What if I *never* visit the reality I create, and either never change its physics or do so in such a way that it's undetectable? Do I exist in that reality then?

Well, for all intents and purposes, no, I don't. Do you, who have probably never played *MUD1* and who would have to take time to learn how to alter its physics, exist relative to its denizens? Well, no, you don't—even though in *Reality* you plainly *do* exist!

If a god doesn't visit a reality and doesn't change it, that god doesn't exist *in that reality*. So in that sense, the atheist NPCs *are* right: either you play in the MMO that is their reality and exist for all to see, or you don't and don't.

CC

One of the nondesign things I observed while playing *Star Wars: the Old Republic* was the startling number of its players who were new to MMOs. During the first four weeks after its launch, on at least half of the occasions that I saw the term *CC* used in a flashpoint (*SW:TOR*'s version of dungeon instances), someone asked what CC means. If you've played MMOs before, you know it means "crowd control" and is a shorthand for "temporarily disable," but if you haven't, well, why *would* you know that?

I saw it most in mid-game flashpoints such as Mandalorian Raiders, which had some encounters that are rather tough without CC. This is the sort of level range at which people who haven't come across the term before would first do so. I even spotted it when I was rocketing through levels in the first week, which would indicate that the people who were asking what it meant had good experience of RPGs (or they wouldn't have got that far that quickly); they just didn't have experience of MMORPGs.

Other things that experienced MMO players might do, such as abbreviating the names of instances (*MR* instead of *Mandalorian Raiders*, say), weren't happening. Also, although I saw calls such as "LFG Esselles" starting to pick up, there was still a majority of less formal approaches to looking for a group ("Anyone up for Esselles?", "Esselles, anyone?"). All players seemed to have some idea of what a healer does and why one might be necessary, but not all appeared to know what a tank does (or is).

I didn't see any of this when I played *Rift*, which is what I was playing before *SW:TOR*. I can therefore deduce that *SW:TOR* brought new players to MMOs in a way that *Rift* didn't. That's good news, because having more MMO players in the population is intrinsically a good thing. However, it's bad news for the developers of later MMOs, as people tend to judge future MMOs by the one they first got into. Making something sufficiently like *SW:TOR* to satisfy those who "grew up" playing it might be a tall order unless you have money to burn.

Use of Community Theory to Designers

This stuff about community may well be fascinating for those of you who have an interest in sociology, but what use is it to designers?

Well, designers can *influence* communities. They can help determine their size, their degree of overlap, their ease of joining, the boundaries between them, and (through the provision of organizational tools) their structure. If designers don't understand the basics, they're going to mess this up major big time.

They might also occasionally stoop to listen to what their community managers have to say on the subject, too.

Cultural Formation as It Was

Back in the days of text MUDs, when such worlds were still being played by people who had no experience of other ones, new and different cultures could still form spontaneously from the different takes their players had on how to behave. [3]

Nowadays, so many people are veterans of other MMOs that when they start to play, they bring all the cultural norms established in those earlier MMOs with them. Some of these can be traced all the way back to *MUD1*, such as the fact that cross-gender play is OK.

I miss the old days, though. This gradual evolution of a set of common cultural norms is interesting, but experiencing them is not *exciting*.

Are we AIs in a Virtual World?

Anyone who has worked on creating artificial intelligence for NPCs in MMOs has had the thought that perhaps what we call the real world is actually a virtual world in some higher reality and we're just AIs ourselves. The points raised by this include:

- If we are AIs, then the same argument can be applied circularly to the people who created us, and thence to the people who created them; therefore there's a potentially infinite regression. (This is the "If God created man, who created God?" argument.)

---

[3]Elizabeth Reid: *Cultural Formations in Text-Based Virtual Realities*. University of Melbourne, 1994. http://www.aluluei.com/cult-form.htm

- It doesn't matter a jot, because our creators never, ever, ever interact with their simulation, so even if we *are* AIs then for all practical purposes we may as well not be. (This is the "If God doesn't interact with our reality, then for those in our reality God does not exist" argument.)

- If you were to create an AI world and keep from interfering in it but sample the behavior of individual AIs, the ones who'd impress you most would be the ones who reasoned you didn't exist. This is because even though they're wrong, they're the only ones who are right based on the zero evidence you've given them. (This is the "Only atheists go to heaven" argument.)

- If you were to build a real-life robot that looked human and operated in the real world, you'd want to give it some AI. The particular AI you chose could be that of an individual NPC in your virtual world. Thus, not only can you visit the world of the AIs, but you can invite AIs from it into your world, too. (This is the "Hmm, I really must write this up as a novel some time" argument.)

Patronizing through Design

Patronizing isn't when a designer (male or female) provides female characters with huge wardrobes of clothes to choose from.

Patronizing is when a designer (male or female) provides female characters with huge wardrobes of clothes to choose from "because that's what women want."

Bugged

When *Age of Conan* first came out, players noticed something weird. Part of *AoC*'s contribution to the evolution of MMOs is a hit location system, so you don't just swing your sword at your opponent; you swing it at *part* of your opponent. What the players noticed was that if they were using a female character, they swung more slowly than if they were using a male character.

OK, so *AoC* is set in a gritty, uncompromising fantasy world, drawn from a series of stories written in the late 1920s and early 1930s by an author whose views on the role of women reflected those commonly held in that era. In other words, Funcom (*AoC*'s developer) could have legitimately claimed that they were being faithful to the books by making women punier than men. Come to that, they could perhaps have further claimed that they were being faithful to Reality: it's not hard to imagine that 75% of real-world men might indeed be able to swing a longsword faster than 75% of real-world women. Yes, this would have been a brave move on Funcom's part, given MMOs' traditional resolute insistence that male and female characters are different only in appearance, but they *could* have done it.

It turned out that the reason female character swung slower was *because* of the differences in appearance. Using separate models meant that male and female characters were animated differently, which in turn meant that they hit at different rates. Once this was explained, the alarm over concerns of deliberate sexism died down.

They were replaced, however, by something potentially even *more* damaging: the realization that if animations were slowing down combat, then combat must be keyed to animation. Animations are run entirely in the client; therefore the decision as to how frequently you swing your weapon in *AoC* must be determined by software running on the user's PC—which makes it entirely and invitingly hackable.

There's a technical term for this kind of design: *jaw-droppingly stupid*.

Design and Community

If MMOs have players, they have communities. Communities are not mere random, amorphous blobs, though: they have shape and they have direction. Furthermore, as I stated earlier, designers can influence the communities that arise in their worlds (and that *is arise* rather than *emerge*).

MMO communities share some commonality, in that they're made up of people who exhibit the same, recurrent levels of involvement. However, they do have differences: some types of community are better for a given MMO than are others. What's more, designers get a say regarding what kinds of community arise in their world (whether they want such a say or not).

Important: designers can't design communities. What they can do is a bit like lighting a fire: you hope it'll burn how you think it will burn, but you can't *tell* it how to burn.

Designers create the initial conditions that define the boundaries of the possible; they can also create constraints that make some of the otherwise possible impossible. The presence or otherwise of constraints within the initial conditions affects the way players perceive the MMO. If there are few constraints, it's a sandbox: the designer hopes that players will be happy however things turn out. If there are many constraints, it's a theme park: the designer hopes that players will be happy because things turn out as planned. In the former, the hope is that players want what they get; in the latter, it's that they get what they want.

This leads to an ongoing difference of opinion among designers. Do you have few constraints, confident that whatever communities arise as a result of the initial conditions, they'll be ones of which you'll approve even though you can't foresee them? Or do you have many constraints so that you only get the communities you're expecting, even though the unforeseen ones might be better?

Influencing Community

Designers influence their communities in three ways:

- Through the physics of the MMO
- Through the metaphysics of the MMO
- Through the culture of the real world

Communicating with other players through the medium of the MMO is an example of the *physics* in action. If there's no communication at range (*for example,* no tell command), that would lead to a different kind of community from one in which it was routine.

Communication is the basis of community. The best type is usually *freeform,* in which players can say whatever they want to one another with no restrictions. However, for some MMOs this is not appropriate for the kind of community the designer wants. For example, in the now-defunct *Toontown Online* (which was aimed at young children), communication between strangers was enacted through a menu system called SpeedChat in order to constrain what people could say to one another.

The physical properties of a communication system affect what kind of community its users develop. Among the most important dimensions are the range of communication, the degree of privacy, and whether the system is broadcast or point-to-point. It's also important to note that communication doesn't have to involve words, or even emotes: beating someone with a sharp, heavy object is also communicating a message to them, for example.

This is something that the developers of *Toontown Online* would have done well to bear in mind.

Freeform chat was possible in that world, but to unlock it you needed to give anyone you wanted to talk to a unique numeric code for them to type in. Because SpeedChat didn't include numbers, you could only give them the code externally. The intention was that you would only be able to chat with people you knew and trusted in real life, which worked just fine until players started communicating their codes by arranging furniture to form integers.[4]

---

[4]Randy Farmer: *The Untold History of Toontown's SpeedChat (or BlockChatTM from Disney Finally Arrives).* March, 2007. http://habitatchronicles.com/2007/03/the-untold-history-of-toontowns-speedchat-or-blockchattm-from-disney-finally-arrives/

Designers can further affect the kind of community they get by providing content that can be more easily solved by communities possessing certain desirable features. This is a form of "survival of the fittest," where *fittest* means *that which fits the design*. If you want people who are deep thinkers, say, in the belief that these will be more loyal and less troublesome, you would design a world packed with fiendish logic puzzles in order that a community of such people would be encouraged to develop around solving them.

Many professional designers will be reading this with a cynical eye, by the way, thinking "Yeah, right, like we have the kind of luxury-level design freedom that allows us to do that." Well, yes, many professional designers, you *do* have that freedom: the only reason you wouldn't have it is if you don't *believe* you have it.

Exceptions, Exceptions

There are some things that, on the face of it, should simply be banned from MMOs. Who could ever argue that a blanket ban on racism in MMOs would not be a good thing, for example?

Well, I could.

Racial hatred in an MMO may be indicative of racial hatred in the real world, but it doesn't *have* to be. It could be quite the opposite, in fact. Setting an MMO in, say, the period of the American Civil War would not only involve racism at the social level but it would even require it to be programmed-in ("no dark-skinned Confederate officers"). It wouldn't be remotely authentic otherwise, and would teach people nothing. Stripping race from the equation would be both figuratively and literally whitewashing the past.

Should anti-hatred laws mean that people can't face up to the realities of the past and *learn* from them? If we don't know—and can't experience—how things were, how can we judge how things *should* be?

You Decide

Communities are defined by members; members are not defined by communities.

If a group decides that you are one if its members whether you like it or not, that isn't a community—that's a tribe.

Community through Metaphysics

Designers can influence community development by providing commands that can be used in community-building ways, and by providing goals and activities that select for some community forms over others. We call this *passive* physics: community arises that is consequent on it.

There's also the case of *active* physics, sometimes known as *metaphysics*, which codes community-building tools directly into an MMO. Guilds are a good example of this: they come with private communication channels, a management structure, management tools, guild property, and so on. These are built into the physics of the MMO, which is not how things are in the real world ("ownership" is not a concept much used in university Physics courses).

Such metaphysical support can extend beyond the physical structures of the MMO, for example by hosting guild web sites.

Different approaches to metaphysics have different effects on the communities that result. If a fireball can kill members of your own side, say, this raises the level of trust that members of a group need to have in one another. Similarly, worlds with a looking for group tool will emphasize different community values from ones without.

Because designers get to decide what metaphysics they implement (if any), this means they can help shape the communities that arise in their worlds through using them.

American Success

Why do so many MMOs convey American cultural values, regardless of whether they're made in the United States or not?

Some answers:

- The United States is a large market, so if non-US developers are hoping to pick up any players outside their region, they'll aim to be attractive to an American audience. This ensures that American cultural tropes are at least respected.

- Raising finance in the United States is much easier than elsewhere. American financiers look on investment in game development as what it is—a gamble—and if they lose, they just take the hit. Elsewhere, it's often only possible to obtain investment capital if you can prove, beyond any doubt, that you don't need it.

- Many Americans speak a form of English. Because English is the second language for much of the world, if people can't find an MMO in their own language, they'll try one in English instead. MMOs developed in English-speaking countries have an advantage over those developed elsewhere.

- The United States has a history of MMO development and now possesses a body of expertise in the area. It even has a center of excellence: Austin, Texas, is the MMO equivalent of Hollywood.

Of course, assuming that MMOs carry American cultural values is *itself* an American cultural value. Few people in China or South Korea are going to detect any particularly American cultural value in the majority of their MMOs.

Have a Ball

Spotted in *WoW*:

Who doesn't include British English in their profanity filter, then?

Culture and Community

In addition to physics and metaphysics, designers can influence community through culture (which, by the way, can also be affected by physics and metaphysics). Culture is the most important way to design for community, because it's the most powerful.

An MMO's culture affects its players' behavior. Much of this culture comes from that imported or established by its early players (and this, as I mentioned earlier, is one reason why beta-testers can be a double-edged sword). However, designers do have significant influence on their MMO's culture through the MMO's design.

[Corollary: while they are designing their MMO, designers should account for what its final culture will be given its likely starting population. I know of no MMO designer who does this, though...]

The culture of an MMO is shaped by three factors:

- What players bring with them from elsewhere, whether that's the real world or other MMOs.

- The design of the MMO. For example, people are more open in MMOs because of pseudonymity, not because they come from some more open real-world society.

- The culture of the MMO itself, generation to generation. Yes, it's recursive.

External factors are in general beyond the designer's control. No matter how much you might want your players to speak English to one another, if they want to speak some other language, they will.

There's a cultural family tree for MMOs that means players go to one MMO taking with them cultural values they picked up in others. There is some uniformity as a result of this; nevertheless, there are also striking differences because of the design. The players of social worlds such as *Second Life* have a different culture from that of *DikuMUD*-derived MMOs such as *WoW*. Hardcore worlds such as *EVE Online* have a different culture from soft-core worlds such as, well, these days also *WoW*. Players may switch between them, but they have to adapt to the MMO's local culture if they're to prosper in it.

Design *matters*.

Speaking Freely

In most democracies in the world, individuals have certain guaranteed freedoms. One such freedom is usually the ability to voice your opinion without fear of reprisal. This is known as *Freedom of Speech*.

You generally have freedom of speech in any public space. You can say anything you want there, subject to some exceptions depending on the country. It may be that you can't make racist remarks, or slander anyone, or give misinformation that could be dangerous (people have been trampled to death following prank shouts of "fire!" in a crowded theatre). Also, the manner of your delivery could be restricted; for example, you may not be allowed to use a megaphone in a residential street at night. Mostly, though, the content of your message can be whatever you want.

This is usually true irrespective of who owns the public space. You *can* be moved for blocking an entrance while chanting slogans in a railway station, a stadium, a shopping mall, or whatever, but you *can't* usually be moved for what you're saying. Furthermore, just because a location is private property, that doesn't mean it can't be a public space, too.

So should political parties be able to send activists into MMOs to disseminate their manifesto pledges? If they get to broadcast on TV, and MMO players spend more time in MMOs than watching TV, well under principles of freedom of speech, why not?

Seeds and the Environment

Seed players are important, but they can be irrelevant. *MUD2* had two incarnations with the same seed players and the same program code that nevertheless went on to develop different cultures. One drew its players mainly from American professionals; the other drew its players mainly from British adolescents.

How much of *EverQuest's DikuMUDish* culture came from its having *DikuMUD* players seed it, and how much came from its near-identical gameplay?

Five Examples

Reality impinges on MMOs all the time, but sometimes it comes in such a large dose that it shocks some or all players out of the virtual and into the real. For those affected, it ceases to be a "game"; for everyone else, the magic circle holds and the attack from Reality is beaten off.

Whenever the real impacts the virtual enough to yank players back into Reality, those concerned can do one of four things:

- Grit their teeth and suffer in silence
- Leave

- Threaten to leave, in an attempt to get the MMO changed so it better suits them

- Call in the real-world police or other higher authority

The first of these is invisible. The second doesn't happen much; people tend to leave after an accumulation of things they don't like, rather than just one. We see a lot of the third, but the threat is rarely carried through. I'm generally against the fourth, because there is *always* a legitimate reason that *some* virtual world or other might want to represent *anything at all*.

Here are five examples of virtual worlds with boundary-pushing viewpoints. Would you ban any or all of them?

Example 1: An MMO in which players took on the role of POWs trying to escape from a World War II camp would need to have all-male characters because otherwise it would be too distant from historical fact. Sure, it might mean fewer players, but is the reflection of real-world sexism in a game itself sexism?

Example 2: An MMO depicts a far-future feminist dystopia in which all men are kept drugged as docile servants by dominant amazons. This may be off-putting to many people, but if it's OK as a mainstream movie, then it's probably OK as a game. It is indeed a mainstream movie, as it happens: *Planet Earth*, a 1974 Science Fiction film based on a story by *Star Trek* creator Gene Roddenberry.

Example 3: An MMO set in the age of piracy could legitimately depict slavery: they had slaves in those days, so it would be disingenuous to sweep it under the carpet (like doing a game about life in Nazi Germany and consciously not making reference to what happened to Jews, Roma, homosexuals, and the mentally ill). To avoid annoying potential players, though, most age-of-piracy games *don't* depict slavery. Should they? What if someone who had been playing a slave-free age-of-piracy game for a month suddenly found their character had captured a ship full of half-dead slaves: it might be a very unpleasant shock for them. Could the developers be open to a lawsuit on the subject? If they'd warned that "Something unpleasant but historically accurate" could happen in advance, should that protect them from such lawsuits?

Example 4: An MMO for teaching psychologists about pedophilia allows adult avatars to perform sex acts with child avatars. If the police can keep highly disturbing examples of child pornography to train officers working in the field what to expect (which they do), then surely an MMO that served a training purpose for psychologists should be allowed? Would you insist on safeguards, such as requiring the permission of a judge and stringent access checks? Or would you disallow it flat out?

Example 5: A bunch of terrorists create an MMO for the purpose of recruiting and training members of their organization. They say it's just a game, and claim that freedom-of-speech laws protect them. Is this a case of disagreeing with what they say but letting them say it anyway? Or is it "Sorry, terrorist dudes, you're going to jail?"

It doesn't matter whether I personally have any answers to these questions; I'm asking them so *you* can figure out *your* view on where freedom to design crosses the line.

Put another way: when does "I'm not playing this game" turn into "No one should be allowed to play this game"?

Who'd Work in Customer Service?

One person in 100,000 is a psychopath.

How many players does your MMO of choice have?

Human Rights and MMOs #1

Let's look at human rights and MMOs.

Now you might think that these aren't topics that are often discussed together. That doesn't mean they *shouldn't* be discussed together, though, nor indeed that they aren't (I've spoken at ministerial-level EU and Council of Europe events on the subject). All it means is that the connection is not as yet well-explored. Oh, I guess it also means that decisions are being made about this kind of thing without the general MMO-playing public's having much awareness of the issues. Just as well that you're reading this, then...

When it comes to games and human rights, it's important to remember that *everyone* has human rights, whether they play games or not. Yes, incredible though it may seem, people who don't play games have just the same rights as gamers do. Also, games and MMOs are designed by designers, who, being in the main human, also have rights.

Fortunately, most of the issues to do with human rights and MMOs concern only competing rights: nonplayers versus players versus designers. There is no one being dragged from their bed at gunpoint in the dead of night to be taken away and tortured for their MMO beliefs. Game-related applications of human rights (HR) laws are relatively trivial as things go, although they do have some important nontrivial implications for those involved.

Note that it's easy when talking about HR to slip into other areas of law. For example, fraud may be a crime, but it's not a HR violation. Likewise, it's easy to confuse HR with law-making: many countries incorporate international conventions on HR as part of their constitutions, but that doesn't make breaking them a constitutional issue. Human rights are supposed to be universal and to transcend the law; it would be like putting a requirement to be subject to gravity into a constitution—it applies regardless of its constitutional presence. I should also perhaps mention that it's possible to stretch HR very thinly, to the extent that it looks tenuous. Is being hurt emotionally a security-of-person violation, as in "You made me cry"? Will the answer be the same 100 years from now?

I'll continue this worthy hand-wringing anon...

A Lens

The view of realities and subrealities I've been describing gives us a lens to look at *Reality*. It works at both a spiritual level (looking up) and a nonspiritual level (looking down).

If you're a spiritual person, then if we look at the way we treat the realities that *we* create, at the very least this illuminates some of the decisions that the higher-order being whom you believe created Reality would have had to face with regard to *us*. This could in all likelihood make you even more impressed by what this creator achieved than you were already.

If you're not a spiritual person, what this tells you is that you have to decide what you want your creations to *be*, and *why*.

OK, so this is all great for a late night, first-year-undergraduate get-to-know-you philosophical debates, but apart from shining a new shaft of light on something that has had spotlights shone on it for centuries, it's a bit "so what?" All I've really said is:

- We can create realities.

- The people we create in those realities don't know about Reality except what we choose to tell them.

- We can apply the same realities-consequent-on-realities arguments up and down indefinitely.

Some reality *will* be at the bottom of this chain. We can suppose that *Reality* was until Roy Trubshaw and I created *MUD*, but people on other planets could have got there long before us.

Some reality *will* be at the top. As far as atheists are concerned, it's *Reality*. As far as religious people are concerned, it's their god's or gods' reality—the Heaven of Christianity, for example.

It's important to point out that nothing I've said here favors either theism or atheism; nor does it favor one religion over another. It's just a tool to help us think about Reality, or—more importantly from the perspective of this book—virtual worlds.

That doesn't mean it doesn't raise awkward questions, though.

Supervising a Culture

Why would a developer want to pay any attention at all to their MMO's culture? Whatever evolved from adopting a *laissez-faire* attitude would surely be stronger than anything the developers could concoct.

The thing is, any MMO will almost certainly go belly up if left to its own devices. There's a power differential between the players and the developers. The experience of text and early graphical worlds showed that developers are held responsible for all of an MMO's ills, whatever they are; this means that unless designers anticipate problems and have systems in place to deal with them, they're going to suffer from being blamed for everything. Players will stop trusting them and leave.

Developers will therefore usually try to take a hands-off but nevertheless supervisory role in directing their MMO's culture. They want to ensure that things happen that they want to happen, and that things don't happen that they don't want to happen.

A designer's main goals here are essentially practical: they wish their MMO to be socially appealing to newbies while minimizing the number of direct contacts that players need with customer service (as this is very expensive to operate). However, they do also have a more aesthetic reason for taking a lead, in that an MMO's culture is part of its personality—which is to say in part a reflection of the designer's own self-image.

To achieve this, designers will want to reconfigure or at least align their players' opinions, attitudes, beliefs, values, and customs. Note: this will usually be done by relaxing such views, rather than by tightening them up; designers seek to offer the players experiences they don't have in real life, which means widening their horizons and granting freedoms, not narrowing their experiences. They can—and should—narrow players' opportunities to act, because that's what game rules do; however, in narrowing these opportunities, the players' experiences should be broadened.

Different designers have different ideas of what these "experiences" should be, of course. That's because they have artistic differences, too.

Cultural Crucibles

I've mentioned that in the early 1990s, distinct cultures for new MMOs (text MUDs as they were) could form spontaneously because players who had never played or seen anything like them before could join all at once. Nowadays that doesn't much happen, but there are still some crucibles where new MMO culture is formed, mainly at the level of individual instantiations of MMOs.

The Chinese and United States servers for *World of Warcraft* have different cultures, for example. When servers have different histories and admins, and are sufficiently remote (in time zone or language, say) to be independent, cultures can develop separately. Some few travelers between the servers—Chinese nationals playing on US servers, say—can then act as a vector for the transfer of important new cultural ideas.

There can also be distinct cultures within individual MMO instantiations: a raiding guild and a casual guild will be different. Some of this will be as a result of design; for example, the type of person attracted to one faction or race might lead to a group of people with a common set of values that's out of line with those attracted to a different faction or race.

There's still room for cultural development, but less opportunity for it than there was in the past.

Indiscriminate Discrimination

If you created an MMO in, say, England and you kicked people out of it for being, say, Irish, you'd be in all kinds of trouble for breaking a bunch of anti-discrimination laws.

However, if you kicked someone out simply because you didn't like the cut of their jib, well, that's your right as a developer. You'd be stupid to do it, but there's no law against stupidity.

Indiscriminate actions against players are fine in MMOs; it's when you *discriminate* that you have to make sure you're on solid legal ground.

LGBT Free

Should it be legal for an MMO to decree that no player is allowed to play a gay character?

Yes.

Before you hit me, suppose you had an MMO in which all characters were toddlers. The concept of a "gay toddler" or "straight toddler" isn't meaningful—children that age haven't developed any sexual preferences. If someone were to play the role of a toddler with a defined sexuality of *any* kind, well, they wouldn't actually be role-playing a toddler. Indeed, they could well be breaking the laws of several European countries if they tried to sexualize a representation of a child in this way.

We should stamp out prejudice whenever it rears its ugly head, but always, *always* look at the context first. Sometimes, what appears at first glance *prima facie* bad can lead to knee-jerk responses that do more harm than good.

Sharia Law

According to an impressive analysis[5] of character names in *World of Warcraft*, the most popular three letters to begin the name of a Night Elf are *Sha-*. The most popular three letters to end the name of a Night Elf are *-ria*.

So that makes the ideal name for Night Elves *Sharia*. I don't suppose it would go down well in Saudi Arabia, but the same could be said for a great many things.

The ideal name for a Tauren is *Mooorn*.

---

[5]Play On: *Naming Patterns in Fantasy Races*. PARC, June 2006.

What Would You Want?

If you created a virtual world and populated it with AIs, what would you want them to do if they figured out you existed?

I guess it would depend on why you created the virtual world. If you did it so you could visit the place and live among the AIs as one of them, you probably wouldn't *want* them to figure out you were their creator, because then you could no longer keep up the pretense. In that case, if they did work out the truth, you'd stop the program, find out how they sussed you, change the software so it wouldn't happen again, and then reboot from the last save you took before they rumbled you.

If you were running the virtual world just to see what interesting things happened in it, you'd probably leave it as it was. You want them to behave how they behave, so you let them get on with it. Assuming that the virtual world had no way of interacting with the real world, there would be nothing they could do to contact you in such a way that you'd be obliged to respond. Whatever you'd done that tipped them off to your existence, well, that's as much information as they'd ever get. You could sit back and watch the AIs take the idea and run with it, impressing yourself with what their imaginations managed to construct before they started to doubt the results.

You almost certainly would not want to appear in the virtual world and announce that the game is up; they're right, you do exist. If you did that, you'd have to answer many awkward questions. "Why did you make it so that we get old and die, if it was actually easier to implement it so we live forever?" "Diseases, illnesses, pain, and suffering: are they bugs, in which case you're not infallible, or are they deliberate, in which case you're an asshole?" "Why can't you make it so that cake is healthy to eat?"

I would expect that responding, "I did it that way because that's how it works where I come from" probably wouldn't go down too well.

Cultural Differences

Designers only get to design their MMO. They don't get to design its players. Ideally, they will design *for* its players, but that presupposes that said players will read the design the way it was intended.

When the strongly PvP MMO *Shadowbane* launched, it had cross-border servers. Someone in the United States could play alongside someone in China. This was seen as a selling point; you could meet someone half-way across the world, from a completely different culture! You could see the world from an alternative perspective and have new experiences!

This is indeed what the US players thought. In general, "You're from China! Cool!"

As for what the Chinese players thought? In general, "你不会说汉语. 好极了！"

Or, if you don't know Chinese: "You don't know Chinese. Excellent!"

The US players regarded difference as a strength, and tried to group with Chinese players. The Chinese players regarded difference as a way of dividing players into teams, and ganged up to beat the pulp out of any lone Americans who wandered over to say hi.

Different real-world cultures can reflect as different virtual-world behaviors.

The Ultimate Aim of Design

Different people have different ideas of what's the ultimate aim of an MMO's design. Some will say that it's community, or immersion, or the creation of an online society. Others will say it's presence, or flow, or an impact on real-world society.

None of these are right. All of these are right.

The ultimate aim of an MMO's design is what the MMO's designer says it is.

There's Gold in Them There Hills

Let's talk about the Wild West.

Around a quarter of all the Hollywood movies ever released are Westerns. They were hugely popular during cinema's golden age, collectively developing a mythology that everyone can recognize. It's a genre screaming to be made into an MMO, usually scoring highly in "What untapped genre of MMO would you like to be made?" polls. Previously, the arguments against it were along the lines of irrelevance to anyone under the age of 30, most of whom have seen very few Westerns. However, the success of *Red Dead Redemption* showed that the genre is alive and well and can still draw in a modern audience.

That doesn't mean that the genre has no other problems, though; it does.

The Wild West has equalizers: anyone can in theory buy a shotgun and empty it into the head of anyone else. This is such an obvious thing to do that you really *need* some fiction to explain why players can't do it; otherwise, the setting won't work. The equivalent in Fantasy worlds would be that a low-level character could loose a shotgun bolt into an adjacent high-level character's head and do no more than give them a headache. That's routine for Fantasy worlds, though; it's not going to fly in a world with a Wild West aesthetic quite so easily.

Also, there are issues to do with different grades of opposition. Let's suppose that you spend most of your time killing bandits. What happens when you go up levels? You kill bigger bandits? Unlike Fantasy worlds, there isn't a wide variety of monsters to kill—apart from the odd coyote, you're pretty well stuck with humans. What tends to happen in this kind of world, as we've seen with *Star Wars: the Old Republic*, is that the enemies look pretty much the same the whole time but have higher stats. You're level 43 so you're killing (in *SW:TOR*'s case) humanoids and droids of level 43 plus or minus a few levels, but they look pretty much the same as the ones you were killing 30 levels earlier. There is no fictional explanation as to why they are universally so much tougher; they just are.

Groups and Culture

Grouping is a cultural exchange mechanism for MMOs. What affects the means by which groups normalize culture across their members?

- The design of the virtual world. This will promote some social groupings and demote others, which is a strong influence on how and what people communicate. For example, if instance group sizes are 5 and everyone knows their role, the relationships that develop would be different from the situation in which group sizes are 8 and roles are more fluid.

- The real-world culture of the players. Social interaction between people of different real-world cultures enriches them both and spreads positive vibes.

- The virtual world's own culture. MMOs were first written and played by old-style hackers (programming gurus, not software vandals). Each new wave of players adapts to the pre-existing cultural norms, which were initially the norms of the first players back in the *MUD* days. This means that people come to value freedom, trustworthiness, altruism, live-and-let-live…

In an MMORPG, a man plays a female character and no one bats an eyelid; in real life, a man presents as a woman and people keep their children away from him (or should that be her?).

So the factors that affect individuals through groups are the same that affect individuals on their own: design, wider society, and history.

Coping with Culture

Supervision isn't merely telling people how to behave: it's also responding to their behavior so as to put them back on course if they point themselves at a wall and put their foot down on the accelerator.

There's not a lot to worry about when supervising MMOs, though; just the usual effects of bugs, ill-judged statements by the dev team, rumors, bad patches, perceived unfairness, hackers, crackers, competing MMOs, thick players, spammers, exploiters, griefers, journalists, generic whingeing, unrealistic expectations, use of [bad language, foreign language, scripts, hacked clients], habitual TOS violations, accidents, hordes of clueless newbies, real-world events, inter-player rivalry, inter-player disputes, rivalries and disputes between groups of players, rivalries and disputes between CS reps, rivalries and disputes between groups of CS reps, different ideas concerning what the MMO is about, players cheating each other, players cheating you, players cheating themselves, betrayals (especially cross-gender), nonacceptance of your authority, real-life psychopaths, the bizarre and unpredictable…

As for how to cope with this kind of thing, that's another matter. My own recommendation is "with gritted teeth."

Care Bears

Back in the early 2000s, MMO players were divided into two camps: *hard core* and *care bears*.

Hard core players were ones who took everything the MMO threw at them and ate it whole. If something required a 4-hour wait followed by a 4-hour grind for a 5% chance of killing a boss, they'd do it.

Care bears were players who wanted an easier time of it and didn't regard pain to be essential for having fun.

The distinction was basically one of challenge level. The hard core saw the care bears as being spoiled; the care bears saw the hard core as being masochists.

Nowadays, people who used to be called care bears would be regarded as hard-core. Then again, people who used to be called hard-core would have been called soft-core by those who grew up playing MUDs with permadeath.

How much challenge can be removed from the MMO paradigm before it dies of blandness?

Human Rights and MMOs #2

Before I go on about human rights and MMOs, I should mention that people have many "rights," not all of which are human rights. For example, as I described earlier tediously and at length, players may have rights as consumers ("I bought this jacket for my character and you said it would be grass green but it's more of an olive green: I want my money back") but these aren't *human rights*, they're everyday legal rights.

A "right" that is often invoked when talking about games is the "right to play." According to the international conventions, this isn't a human right either (although it perhaps should be). There *is* a right to self-expression, which could be interpreted as a right to play; it's borderline at best, though.

Oh, the "international conventions" I mentioned back there are multiple, but the most important is the *Universal Declaration of Human Rights* (UDHR),[6] which was passed by the United Nations General Assembly in 1948. Together with the *International Covenant on Economic, Social and Cultural Rights*[7] and the *International Covenant on Civil and Political Rights*,[8] which were passed by the UN in 1966, it makes up what is informally known as the *International Bill of Human Rights* (IBHR).

I don't know why I bother including references to web sites. If you're interested, you're just going to hit a search engine rather than painstakingly type in the address manually, and if you're not then you're just going to skip them anyway…

Two-Way Traffic

Although the cultural traffic between the real world and MMOs is dominated by the former, nevertheless there is some transfer the other way round. For example, the real-world terms *newbie* and *PK* (which is used a lot in the Far East) both came into common currency from text MUD origins.

---

[6]United Nations: *The Universal Declaration of Human Rights*. Palais de Chaillot, Paris. 1948. http://www.un.org/en/universal-declaration-human-rights/index.html
[7]United Nations: *International Covenant on Economic, Social and Cultural Rights*. New York. 1966. http://www.ohchr.org/EN/ProfessionalInterest/Pages/CESCR.aspx
[8]United Nations: *International Covenant on Civil and Political Rights*. New York. 1966. http://www.ohchr.org/en/professionalinterest/pages/ccpr.aspx

For most of the cultural transfers from MMOs to the real world, though, it's harder than this to ascertain the effects. Has the fact that cross-gender play is accepted in MMOs had any influence on real-world attitudes? If so, what is it? If not, then how come in MMOs it's resisted negative real-world perceptions for so long?

This is probably a good place to look if you're a gamer sociologist who's looking for a topic for a thesis.

Are there gamer sociologists?

Cultural Imperatives

Should MMO cultures reflect real-world cultures? People in the real world have children, which is why social systems for dealing with family have developed there. In MMOs, whether or not characters have children is entirely the decision of the designer. Some designers may wish to free players from the concerns of responsibility for others; some may decide to include the responsibility in some way that doesn't involve virtual children; some may choose to have the virtual world mimic the real world.

In the real world we have biology, physics, and the environment directing our cultural development, but in a virtual world all those are up for grabs. Why would a virtual world necessarily follow the real world in its cultural features if the imperatives for having those features don't apply in it?

Blurred Boundaries

The LGBT guild incident in *World of Warcraft* cast light into a normally shadowy part of virtual world theory—the murky area where freedom of speech meets freedom to play meets freedom to be.

Freedom of speech: a virtual world can be set up to advocate any position or opinion that's legal in the real world. If a legal church is legally allowed to espouse anti-LGBT feelings, and it legally sets up its own virtual world, you could not expect much sympathy from the admins were you to try set up a LGBT-friendly guild within it. Practically the only reason for doing so would be to bring attention to the church's policies.

Freedom to play: in real life I'm male, but in virtual worlds I sometimes play female characters. In real life I'm straight: is it OK if I play LGBT characters? People have done so in the past—it's another form of identity exploration. Sure, it's unusual, but just because a behavior is uncommon, that doesn't mean it's wrong.

Freedom to be: if in the real world I were a lesbian (yes, this *is* just hypotheti-cal) and I were perfectly happy with that part of my identity—or even held it to be at the core of who I am—then why should I not take it with me into a virtual world? I can take my real-life dislike of stinging insects with me, why not my real-life sexuality?

Let's suppose you wanted to set up a guild only for people who in real life are, oh, let's say, vegetarians for a change. What possible sources of conflict might you expect?

Well if the designer has created a Fantasy world, there's a fair chance that meat will play a big part in it. This is because the gameplay tends to involve killing large quantities of assorted enemies, some of which are animals. What kind of things do you find when you loot the corpses of dead animals? Well, that would be skins, meat, fish… These are resources that could have uses. If you're a vegetarian in real life, you'd be putting yourself at a gameplay disadvan-tage if you tried to follow through your convictions with your characters. *You* may be a vegetarian, but by your character has to eat meat to get the buffs or whatever. You can, of course, complain vehemently that the virtual world isn't vegetarian-friendly, but sadly for you *it doesn't have to be*. If the designer wants all characters to be omnivorous, *that's enough*—even if the reason they want it is because they hate vegetarians. If bias is OK for books, it's OK for MMOs.

Still, at least in most worlds you *can* probably set up the Vegetarians' Guild. Except, if this is a virtual world with a lot of role-playing, maybe you can't. Role-playing is about *character*, not *player*. In such a regime, you can found a guild on the basis of your *character's* vegetarianism, but not of your *own*. In a game-like world that blocks 200 variants of the name Legolas in an attempt to keep play as immersive as possible, there would be no place for a guild with out-of-character entrance criteria. When people have expressly chosen a server that is designated as being for strong role-playing, shouldn't you respect their desire to keep everything in-character? What right have you to come in from nowhere and shatter their illusion with your real-life references? It doesn't matter how worthy your cause is, either: if you want to set up a guild for victims of child abuse, or to raise money for refugees, or to connect lonely ex-military people who have post-traumatic stress disorder, OK, good for you—but either do it on a non-role-play server or do it on a role-play server but don't tell anyone about it. Only, you definitely *will* tell people about it so as to gain your cause publicity when you're told off for it, right?

Let's imagine, though, that you find a live-and-let-live MMO that's happy with your setting up a vegetarian players' guild. Great! So now you're able to hang out with like-minded people who don't eat meat in real life. Well, who *say* they don't eat meat in real life. Actually, you have *no idea* whether they eat meat or not. You could interact with them daily for two years and *still* not know. The same applies to practically every other real-life criterion you might envisage. You may be on safer ground if voice is involved, so "the guild for people who speak with a Texan accent" or "the girl guild" could work. Usually, though, you just *can't tell*. Your guild is entirely built on the faith that no one would join it for reasons other than yours; if they do, then you have management issues of your own.

The boundary between the real and the virtual is blurred. The reason it's blurred is that the boundaries between real people and their characters are blurred.

Sex *vs.* Graphics

There's one area where a text MMO just *might* still have the edge over a graphical one: sex.

Sex in a text world has three things going for it that sex in a graphics world doesn't:

- It's freeform. You don't have to motion-capture every position in the *Kamasutra* and beyond, because people can animate it themselves using words.

- It's legal. You can *write* about antics that would involve a stint in prison and your name on a sex offender's register were you to depict them visually.

- For a basic sex game to work, you need comparable numbers of both men and women. A female-friendly game, by virtue of its having women in it, is automatically male-friendly; therefore, you need to attract women. Hey, guess what? Study after study has shown that, in general, women prefer words to pictures—especially when it comes to sexual fantasizing.

Confession: I did actually work on such an MMO for about a year during the dot-com boom, when the team of 30 I was recruiting to make a graphical world was suddenly capped at 6, none of whom were artists. Sadly, the dot-com bust came before we'd finished, so I'll never know whether it would have worked or not.

I was cautiously optimistic that it *would* have worked, though, despite the fact that there was scant support In the company itself for the product. This was summed up in the following memorable quote from a guy on the sales team: "We can't be associated with sex games, only with violent games."

Managing Players

I posted the following in the forum for *British Legends* (that is, *MUD1*) on CompuServe following yet another blow-up between players. It succinctly explains my approach to community management, which flows from my overall design philosophy.

```
#: 195733 S10/BL Wizzes & Witches
      27-May-91 12:00:28
 Sb: #195119-#Fod from mortal to wiz
 Fm: richard 76703,3042
```

There are two ways you can run this
kind of game:
1.   Let people behave as they see fit.
2.   Let people behave how you see fit.

In *BL*, I try for the former. Sometimes, yes, people do foul up and we get a nasty mess that needs cleaning up. That's the price that has to be paid for freedom.

In other games, they go for the latter. Anyone who doesn't conform is speedily despatched. Enforced niceness is the rule. Rock the boat, and they throw you overboard.

This non-*BL* approach is fine if you don't mind having unimaginative players doing unimaginative things. Indeed, since most people in their leisure time tend to be unimaginative, it even makes commercial sense. I still opt for the
BL regime, though, because I don't like
snuffing out personalities that sparkle, I don't like the thought that I'd be running a sham with a facade of niceness beneath which dull people are saying dull things about what would be a dull game, and I don't like stifling creativity.

If you want to play a totalitarian, "managed" game and have fun because that's what the management tell you you're having, well, fair enough. *BL* CAN be run that way, but I prefer it the way it is. If I wanted to make money from milking cows I would, but where's the fun in that for me? I'd rather take nectar from the gods.

Richard

Fact and Legend

Let's talk about the Wild West some more.

In addition to the practical problems associated with designing a Wild West MMO, there are human problems, too. Three forces are at work that clash with one another:

- The Wild West as it was historically.
- The legendary Wild West as depicted in fiction.
- The modern world.

The Wild West that people want to play is basically the legendary one, but its fiction is at odds with history in ways that a modern audience may find disturbing. Also, the fiction and the reality may both be at odds with what a modern audience expects. Do designers sacrifice the legend to placate the modernists, or do they hold to the legend to placate the romantics?

One problem is gender. There were very few female personalities (let alone gunslingers) in the real or legendary Wild West. Female players who like the genre would have to play as male characters to be true to it. This is annoying to some people in and of itself (they want to play characters of their own gender), but it is also politically sensitive as it perpetuates outdated social attitudes of the past through into today's more enlightened times. Female US cavalry officers: sure, why not?

Another problem is race. In real life 25% of cowboys were of African descent, yet this is not reflected by the legends. Of the major historical characters who are part of Wild West mythology, only Nat Love (Deadwood Dick) makes the cut. So should the MMO reflect the reality and give 25% of NPC cowboys dark skin, or should it reflect the legend and paint them out of the picture? Also, should that 25% apply to player characters or only to nonplayer characters?

Race introduces a second problem, in that some of the factions of the Wild West were (historically, as well as in legend) split along racial lines. A Sioux brave isn't going to have very dark or very light skin, and will have particular facial features. If you want to play as a Sioux brave, then unless you're a native American in real life, you're going to be playing across race. Now although playing across gender is widely accepted in MMOs, playing across race is less so: it can be offensive to the people whose race you're playing (which is to say, stereotyping), and can be like a magnet for people who want to make repellent political points under the cloak of "role-playing."

What I suspect we'd see, should a Wild West MMO appear, is a modernized version of the legend in which all the US side conforms to a modern-day vision of an egalitarian utopia, so that no matter what the color of your skin or the contents of your jeans you can go out and shoot bad guys with the best of them. As for who those bad guys might be, well there could be a Fantasy element, there could be a race restriction such that natives and Mexicans are all NPCs (although that's not going to make real-life natives or Mexicans any happier), or the whole structure of Wild West society can be mapped exclusively onto the US side with natives either being made invisible or treated "just like everyone else."

Whatever happens, it will involve a lot of pushing at the legend or pushing at the players.

Oh, and although I've been talking about the Wild West here, what I've said here is pretty much the same for any MMO with a historical setting.

Cultural Environments

Although I talk here about "culture" and "community" as if they were unitary concepts, it's important to remember that they exist in many, overlapping environments: offline, online, multiplayer, massively multiplayer, codebase, world, instantiation, group, …

A more specific culture will inherit some—but not all—of the aspects of the more general cultures of which its members are also members. More general cultures are only approximations of the intersections of the subcultures of their members.

Thus, when we talk about "MMO culture" or "MMO community," we need to be clear about what level of abstraction we're considering.

This is why it's dangerous to talk about "the players" at a general level as if at a more detailed level, or *vice versa*.

Sacrament or Blasphemy?

Although I've been pursuing this thought experiment about gods and realities as objectively as I can, it unavoidably raises issues of significance to some religions. I'm going to illustrate this with a question that the Abrahamic religions (Judaism, Christianity, and Islam) have a special interest in answering. Don't worry; I don't say anything to make you angry with the religions (although it might make you angry with MMO designers).

I should say that this isn't actually *my* question; it's Kevin Kelly's.[9] I'm merely paraphrasing it.

---

[9]Kevin Kelly: *Out of Control*. Addison Wesley: New York. 1994. http://www.kk.org/books/ooc-mf.pdf

So the way it goes, God created the world (Reality); Adam (that is, mankind) was created in his (or His—God's) own image. Because Adam is created in God's image, Adam has free will and creativity, just like God. Adam can't create his own world, though, because although he's in the *image* of God, he isn't *actually* God. He has no powers over *Reality*.

Scoot forward to the present day, with MMOs. Adam still doesn't have powers over *Reality*, but Adam *does* have powers over new realities of his own making.

The question: should Adam (well, Roy Trubshaw and I) have taken that final step and created a new reality?

Some people would say no:

- God created the universe.
- If we create virtual worlds, we are "playing God."
- This is a mocking act of arrogance, false pride and hubris.
- It's therefore blasphemy.

Some people would say yes:

- God created Adam in God's own image.
- Of *course* Adam is eventually going to create worlds – that's what gods do!
- It completes the final step of Genesis!
- It makes us the true copies of God we were always intended to be.
- It's therefore sacrament.

From a theological perspective, it has to be one or the other—it can't be both or neither. Either virtual worlds mock God's creation, or they fulfill it.

Lest you think that this is just a question for theologians, here's a follow-up: are those who *play* MMOs contributing to the glorious potential that God instilled in humanity from the very beginning, or condoning a false mantle of arrogant pride that can not end well for them?

If you're a follower of Judaism, Christianity, or Islam, you might want to get your answer straight before you decide whether to continue playing or not.

Cultural Abstractions

MMOs are full of real-world cultural features. Korean behemoth *Lineage* sank in the United States because it embodied Korean cultural norms about groups and grouping that US players simply couldn't or wouldn't adopt. You'll see cultural features all over if you look for them.

For example, as I mentioned earlier, if MMOs have elves and dwarfs (oops, *dwarves*) and orcs and gnomes and humans as "races," where are the NPCs that are half one, half the other? Do elves never marry dwarves or orcs or gnomes or humans? More to the point, why does no one complain about this? Well, they don't complain because it's a *cultural* point. You're more likely to notice it if you come from an inclusive real-world society than from an exclusive one.

Designers say things though their designs, and players say things through their playing choices. Together, these pass behavioral norms and accumulated knowledge from one generation to the next, each one shaping what follows.

MMOs are one of the best ways for a real-world culture to spread its values around. It's just that the culture isn't necessarily at the same level of abstraction as we think of it in the real world.

False Assumption

Just so I don't have to keep pointing this out when I review academic papers...

When role-playing games offer the possibility for player characters to romance nonplayer characters, the pressure for including same-sex relationships *doesn't* come primarily from gay players. Rather, it comes from straight male players who are playing female characters and get creeped out when they are hit on by male nonplayer characters.

Human Rights and MMOs #3

Computer games raise more questions about some human rights than they do others. Also, some types of computer game raise more issues than others. It's arranged like a tier: the games at the bottom involve some HR, the ones above involve those of the bottom plus some more, and so on until those at the top involve all the HR issues of all the other games, plus some of their own.

These are the tiers, from lowest to highest:

- Rights of nonplayers. Example: can I play a game if playing it offends you?

- Single-player games. Example: can I kill NPC beggars for experience points?

- Multiplayer games. Example: can I always shoot black characters in preference to white ones?

- MMOs. Example: can I launch a campaign for a real political party in a fantasy world?

- Weird futuristic stuff. Example: if NPCs are intelligent, can I switch them off?

As you can see, when it comes to existing games, MMOs are at the top. They're also likely to remain there when the weird futuristic stuff becomes available, because they'll be among the first to implement it. However, I'll begin this analysis by explaining the issues raised at the lower tiers and then build on those.

Fair warning: that #3 at the top eventually gets to #14...

MMO Shared Culture

So back in the days when few players new to an MMO had experienced one before, a fresh MMO would develop its own culture almost sponta-neously. Such cultures were partly informed by mainstream culture but weren't part of it.

Over time, mainstream culture has become more influential; however, there are still distinct elements of early MMO culture that have been passed down (the acceptability of cross-gender play being the classic example—which I keep mentioning because I think it's helped player-understanding). There are also new cultural phenomena developing, such as a swing towards care-bearism that wasn't there at the turn of the century. Some of these changes in culture are having an impact on the design of up-coming virtual worlds.

As always, the smaller the group, the more distinct its culture is likely to be. Isolated communities develop along lines influenced more by individuals than do cosmopolitan communities. Thus, the culture of a small-scale text MUD could be noticeably different from that of a near neighbor (even one using the same codebase), for historical and personality reasons. Even individual MMO guilds can have their own very distinct subculture for this same reason.

An interesting question to ask is whether any distinct cultural traits that MMOs share arise because of the very *nature* of MMOs, rather than the per-sonalities of generations of designers or the import of real-world culture. For example, has the fact that players are pseudonymous led to the widespread establishment of particular cultural norms not seen in any real-world society? Has the fact that characters don't need food or shelter (unlike real people) made a difference?

The short answer is that we don't know for sure. To find out, someone would have to study several different, isolated MMOs to see what behaviors came up time and time again. Sadly, although we *are* beginning to see such anthropologi-cal work, it's patchy and of varying quality.

Yes, there probably is a PhD in this for someone…

Inequality for Equality

In a single-sex MMO (that is, one in which characters are all of the same bio-logical sex, if not gender), some players will complain because they want to play the other sex and they can't. Likewise, in MMOs that tie specific character classes to particular sexes, some players will complain that they want to play a class that isn't available for their chosen sex.

This reveals something of a contradiction. People say that they want the sexes to be equal, but some of them wish to privilege one over the other (that is, they want to play one in preference to the other), therefore in their eyes the sexes *aren't* equal: one is preferable to the other.

Blasphemy or Sacrament?

I asked earlier whether you thought that, in the context of monotheistic religions, our creating virtual worlds was a mockery of God's works or was fulfilling God's plan for us.

Let's take it a step further.

Suppose that far in the future, we've populated our virtual worlds with NPCs that have artificial intelligence. What if they develop their own systems for simulation? They may create their own virtual worlds and in time populate those with their own AIs. After all, if we created the NPCs in our image and did a good job of it, then they, like us, should eventually be able to create realities of their own in which dwell intelligent entities in the image of our NPCs. Creation of intelligence is necessarily recursive.

So if you created an MMO and the NPCs within that MMO built themselves a sub-MMO, would you be annoyed with them for believing they could create something better than what you have created for them? Or would you be pleased with them for having fulfilled their potential?

Blasphemy or sacrament?

Does your answer change depending on whether you're the god or the NPC?

Public Accommodation

The United States has constitutional protection for freedom of speech. One consequence of this is that once somewhere becomes a place of public accommodation, you can't restrict people's freedom of speech there. If, for example, two people are having a political argument at a ball game, OK, well it may not be much fun for the members of the crowd sitting nearby who have paid to watch a ball game rather than listen to impassioned rants about the government's economic policy, but so long as the arguers don't endanger the place or other visitors to it, they're within their rights to say what they want and they can't legally be ejected for it.

So, as I alluded to earlier, could MMOs ever be regarded as places of public accommodation?

In time, the answer is probably yes. It really depends on whether the definition of "endanger" extends to the violation of the rules of play. Most MMOs wouldn't be all that fussed if players discussed last night's TV news, but some might be—one in which a major narrative event was taking place could be spoiled by it, for example. However, even otherwise anything-goes MMOs can sometimes be touchy about discussing such relatively banal topics as the merits of other MMOs (it may even trigger the profanity filter) Public accommodation status would mean that they couldn't do this.

The awkward thing about public accommodation from an MMO designer's perspective is that it's not up to you whether your MMO qualifies as public accommodation : it's up to a judge. There's nothing you can do that a judge would say categorically rules it out. It's all to do with social norms, expectations, boundaries, and attempting to draw a line that makes sense. It's an issue of judgment (which is, of course, why judges get to decide). Control of your design could effectively be taken away from you. The magic circle itself could be forcibly evaporated.

As with so much to do with MMOs and the law, we're only going to get a hint of which way the wind is blowing if a case actually goes to court. It's to be hoped that we won't see a judgment that, by allowing relatively unfettered freedom of speech in an MMO, causes the MMO to lose players and ultimately close down.

Triangles

Years ago, we used to get these triangle diagrams with a "hard-core" point at the top and a "care bear" line at the bottom.

This showed that there were fewer people in the hard core than in the care bears. We'd then see this triangle form its own small triangle at the tip of a larger triangle with "mainstream" at the bottom.

This represented the future. If only we could get the mainstream interested, what riches would await!

Well, we do now have the mainstream interested, and riches do await. Yes, to get to them we have to be as soft an alternative to care bears as care bears were to the hard core, but we *can* do it; we *are* doing it, in fact.

The whole structure hangs from the tip, though. That's where the definition of what's beneath it flows from.

It's the same in any artistic field: you have the leading edge, which is only attractive to (and in some cases, such as modern art, only accessible to) the cognoscenti. The rest flows from this tip. The rules and aesthetics for this tip are arcane in comparison to the base of the pyramid, but they are what those who understand the form consider to be important. It's like this in sculpture, dance, fashion, literature, and movies; it's like this in MMOs.

At our MMO tip, the people who are playing are outright gamers. They're why these things are ever called "games." There may not be many of them in comparison to the mass below, but they're what gives context to the whole triangle. They're the core of what an MMO player "is." They're why this is an "MMO players" triangle and not an "online games players" triangle.

Another aspect of the old triangle drawings we used to see was that players tended to move up the triangle (gain a more sophisticated palate), and this is still what usually happens. If the upward flow of people is too slow or the downward artistic coherence too interrupted, then we get a shear. Movies used to be recorded theatre; they're not any more. Movies sheared off from theatre to create a triangle of their own.

This is a general feature of the arts. If the distance between the tip and the base is too great, so that the base no longer finds the tip relevant, then it will tear off, land in a heap, and make its own, new triangle in its own, new area. The part that didn't tear off is still there, but with less to support it. In MMO terms, there will be fewer new hard-core players if there are fewer people in the triangle to bubble up, at least until the triangle grows again.

When I defend those players who have a very particular, purist view of MMOs, I do so in order to defend the MMO form. If you cut them off from the mainstream, the mainstream will need to grow a new head in short order or it will rapidly decline, and the purists will have to promulgate the art they love or it will wither to irrelevance.

Reality Bias

If male characters were consciously designed to do more melée damage than female characters but the two were otherwise identical in all respects, would everyone choose to play a male character? Would even the female players?

Or would they simply not play?

Reinforcing a World View

What character race do you play in your favorite MMO?

I don't actually want to *know*, I just want to demonstrate a casual use of the word "race" to mean elf, dwarf, gnome, lizardy person, human, …

First, those aren't races; they are just secondary classes by another name.

Second, they're *species*, not races.

What the general public means by "race" is reflected in most MMOs only by the slider that determines skin tone, plus perhaps some facial feature combinations.

Although a purist might argue that this aspect of race in an MMO *could* accurately be reflected by sets of bonuses such as "+5% sunburn resistance," this carries an unacceptable smell of racism for which it would be roundly condemned. However, having distinct fantasy "races" with hugely differing abilities is apparently fine, despite the fact that it nonchalantly validates a view that stereotyping individuals by race is OK.

Now it's obvious that there are genuine physical differences between, say, birds and fish. The former have feathers and can, in general, fly (although some can also swim); the latter have scales and can universally swim (although some can also fly). If you were to create two "races" in your MMO, one of bird people and one of fish people, you could reasonably argue that they should have different physical abilities. Obviously you'd make the males and females of both be identical in all respects except appearance, because not to do so would be sexist, but having the bird people fly and the fish people swim, well isn't that just common sense?

Here's the thing: it doesn't matter whether it's common sense or not: it's covert racism. You're saying it's OK to stereotype people by their "race." Like it or not, you're making an unsavory political point.

For NPC-only species, you can usually get away with it. For any playable "race," though, you can't: to pigeonhole characters by race is to pigeonhole the players of those characters by race. You can have cosmetic differences and *perhaps* some species-specific commands that are only for show (for example, your dog people can howl at the moon and your cat people can cough up furballs), but if there are any gameplay effects, no.

Given that *Star Wars: the Old Republic* can make a good go of doing this in a universe full of space aliens, you can do it in your fantasy world.

Don't call them *races*, though…

Fiction from Fiction

The traditional view of the Wild West, as portrayed in movies and books, is a particular genre with its own particular rules and its own particular reasons for having those rules. In developing an MMO for that genre, some people would be content with playing to the general spirit of the rules, modified to be more acceptable to people of the present day, and some people would prefer to play to the traditional rules and the core values of the past that these imbue.

There's a lot of psychology going on in Wild West mythology. It's loaded with symbolism. For some people, interfering with the syntax (such as allowing half the Seventh cavalry to be female) interferes with the semantics; for others, this is an opportunity to repurpose the myth for a contemporary audience, and therefore different semantics are called for.

No Wild West game is going to be historically accurate, because the whole genre is mythologized. While rooted in historical fact, it has become embellished, romanticized, and signified over time. It's not quite as divorced from Reality as, say, Arthurian myth, but it's a lot further from it than, say, *M*A*S*H* was from the Korean War.

When you create an MMO based on an established historical genre, you have to accept that you're not creating a fiction from fact: you're creating a fiction from fiction. As for your source fiction, all you can really say about its relationship with fact is that it's one step closer than yours is.

Thinking or Unthinking?

Here are some of the things that *World of Warcraft* responds with when you type **/silly**:

- Dwarf female: "I like my ale like I like my men: Dark and rich."
- Dwarf male: "I like my beer like I like my women, stout and bitter."
- Troll male: "I like my women dumpy and droopy with halitosis."
- Tauren male: "Homogenized? No way, I like the ladies."

Are these lines written to say something?

Well yes, of course they are—how could they not be? What they're *trying* to say is probably something along the lines of how this isn't a virtual world that takes itself too seriously. Fair enough, it *doesn't* take itself too seriously: that's good artistic consistency for you.

Yet they *also* say something else. In the context of *WoW*, all the above lines take a solidly heterosexual view of the world. In other words, if you're a homosexual player, be careful which character type you pick.

Was such a decision made deliberately? I doubt it: it reflects an unthinking attitude, not a thinking one. Someone wanted jokes there for a design reason; they didn't particularly want *gay-unfriendly* jokes there for a design reason, they just didn't think about their jokes that way. Ironically, if the lines *had* been put in deliberately, there might have been some political or artistic point being raised; this may then have made the remarks excusable on freedom-of-speech grounds. The fact that they were in all likelihood put in thoughtlessly is merely a sad symptom of a wider malaise that cuts across many virtual worlds: designers just don't know their players.

Imagine what the response would have been to this:

- Dwarf male: "I like my beer like I like my women—I'm teetotal."

"Disabled"

"MMOs must be a boon for disabled people, because within them they can play without the prejudice they receive in real life."

That's not a direct quote from anyone, it's just a summary of a view I occasionally hear.

OK, so this is a sentiment that's usually well-intentioned, but it carries a risk of seeming to be patronizing. By suggesting that characters in MMOs are somehow superior as they don't have a particular "disability" some people have in real life, there's an implication that people in real life who also don't have that "disability" are similarly superior to those who do have it. Plenty of people would object to that, pointing out that there are many individuals having this "disability" who enjoy just as rich and fulfilling lives as anyone else and it's condescending to insinuate otherwise.

In this sense, it's a bit like claiming that working-class people can play an MMO and none of the other players will know: such a remark implicitly assumes that there's something deficient about being working-class. There isn't. The problem is with societal attitudes, not with the state of being one thing or another.

In its strongest expression, there are some people for whom their "disability" is so much a part of their sense of identity that they reject all "cures" offered them on the grounds that they feel they have nothing that needs curing. There are families of deaf people like this, for example, who see any attempt to "correct" through surgery what other people perceive as failings (but that they don't themselves) as an attack on their culture.

I do have some considerable sympathy with this position. As an analogy, I *could* change my Yorkshire accent so I didn't get treated as a yokel by Londoners, but I don't see why I should.

Ultimately, though, I have to reject the argument that we shouldn't say MMOs are good for swathes of "disabled" people: I've encountered too many people who self-identify as disabled and feel they've been liberated by MMOs for me to believe otherwise.

Uru Live, Dead, Live, Undead

Uru Live was an MMO set in the world of the single-player game, *Myst*. Yes, that statement alone really does tell you why it flopped. The players it had dearly loved it, but there just weren't enough of them.

Uru Live was launched in November 2003; it closed in February 2004. That was still long enough for players to form relationships, so a large group of them—about 300 in number, mainly shy women in their 50s—left for the world *There*. In this social world, which allowed user-created content, they rebuilt the world of *Uru*. They constructed a library containing stories, screenshots and videos recording what they called the "Last Days of Uru." It was a cultural record of a lost society.

However, it turned out that *Uru Live* had more life in it than people thought. Other players stepped in and were able to run an unsupported but legal version of the game on servers operated by the developers. This meant that the players who had decamped to *There* were able to come back.

Except, they didn't come back. When they tried, they didn't feel at home in *Uru* anymore. They had originally been refugees, fleeing *Uru Live* for the safety of *There*. Their primary aim was to preserve the culture of *Uru*, which meant they never really fit in with the existing *There* culture. However, over time they came to see themselves less as refugees and more as emigrants, with their own *émigré* culture. They didn't feel at home in the "new country," but neither did they feel at home back in the "old country," either.

Uru Live was acquired by another developer, relaunched, closed, and then reacquired by the original developers and released as open source. It now has a kind of undead existence, with a small following that nevertheless exhibits cult-like devotion.

There was not the success it had been expected to be either, bowing to the inevitable and closing in 2010. The writing had long been on the wall, though, so its *Uru* community had by then moved to *Second Life*. After a couple of years there, they found the cost of land too expensive so moved again to an *OpenSim* world.

We see the same kind of thing in MMOs. Guilds form, migrate, change; in the end, the guild itself becomes the bearer of culture, rather than the absorber of culture from whatever world its nomadic path has led it. Guild members are polite to the denizens of their host world, but are never really a part of it; never, that is, until they find the self-promised land they dream of and settle down.

People are people. They behave the same way in virtual worlds as they do in the real world, only more so.

Correcting Reality

For almost all MMOs, one of the first things to decide when creating a character is the gender of that character. Is it male or female?

Also for almost all MMOs, the choice is of importance only cosmetically (it affects how the avatar looks) or socially (players—not NPCs—typically treat male and female characters differently).

What about tangible, in-world differences, though? Well, usually there are none. Male and female characters are identical in all gameplay respects. Neither gender is stronger. Neither is faster. Neither is nimbler. Clothes that fit one fit the other. They're identical. When they're not identical, as was the case in *Age of Conan* when its collision-detection combat system penalized female characters, it's almost invariably a bug.

In real life, however, men and women are *not* identical. Neither are people of different races (skin color trades off the creation of vitamin D against resistance to skin cancer, for example). There are advantages and disadvantages. These are not, however, reflected in the implementation of MMOs.

Are MMOs correcting Reality by ignoring these differences? Or are they painting a false picture?

Suppose that a new MMO is coming out with a medieval fantasy setting, in which characters can have children so that players can establish their own dynasties. Do male characters get to give birth to babies, or is this restricted only to female characters?

Only One Joan of Arc

I did some consultation in the early 2000s with a company that had an absolutely superb MMO design. One of their ideas was to base the fiction on European nobility around the year 1200 or so, and make gender roles operate like character classes. Basically, the men were knights who went off to fight each other and the women were managers who stayed behind and ran the castle and estate. Female characters had the babies and controlled their education for the first 12 years, whereupon the player of the (official) father got to decide whether he or the player of the mother would have final control. At age 16, the child character became playable by whoever had control of it.

There were other possibilities apart from playing an adult character. For example, younger sons could be packed off to a monastery to be "stored" (gaining no children of their own but being educated further, ready to be removed should the eldest son die); superfluous daughters who weren't successfully married off could be sent to a convent. There were some mixed-sex occupations such as troubadours, but these operated outside the feudal system.

This approach raised an interesting issue, epitomized by Joan of Arc. People who wished to play as a female knight were simply not allowed to do so: the class was not implemented. This division of roles by biology is much the same as it was in real-world medieval times; however, in real life we *did* have Joan of Arc—a female knight. Players could argue that they should be able to play as a female knight, citing real-world precedent.

The thing is, in real life we pretty well *only* had Joan of Arc: one female knight among tens of thousands of male knights. Does this exception mean that the MMO should have allowed all female characters to play as knights if they wanted to? Or just one? Or (as the designer chose) none?

Again, it's a question of whether you want to reflect *Reality* or correct *Reality*.

Minds and Bodies

When Gender Studies theorists first descended on virtual worlds in the mid-1990s, they developed two contrasting points of view:

1. The virtual frees the mind from the body; therefore, the more time we spend being virtual, the greater the chance we'll be able to leave outdated physical notions such as gender behind us.

2. The mind and the body are too integrated to be separated in a simplistic fashion. People will always take into a virtual world aspects of their being that are informed by their body.

As far as I could tell from reading as much of what they wrote as I encountered, the gender theorists settled on the second option. Having done so, they then went away to study something else.

The thing is, although the academics back then were *bona fide* gender theorists, all the arguments as they were phrased seemed to be entirely from a "gender=female" point of view. Maybe I looked in the wrong places (search engines were rickety affairs back then), but I didn't see a great deal of discussion about whether male players were as tied to their bodies as female players (and, indeed, I saw some suggestion to the contrary: women's monthly cycles were cited as a major reason why women are bound to their physical form).

It's well known from empirical evidence that male players are far more likely to play female characters than female players are to play male characters. Perhaps the first point above could be applicable to men in ways that the second point isn't?

Worlds within Worlds

Sure, we might all be living in a simulation, but if we can't contact the simulators and they don't choose to contact us, so what?

Targeting Your Audience

Here's an ad for the Korean MMO *Sword of the New World*, also known as *Granado Espada*:

Ah, female pirates! Anne Bonney, Mary Reade, er, probably some others if you look *really* hard...

I checked the *Sword of the New World* web site, and of the 38 screenshots they had there: 11 showed only female avatars; 17 showed mixed male/female; 7 showed distance (crowd) shots; 3 showed only male avatars; one showed an avatar I couldn't tell the gender of for sure, but I'm guessing it was probably intended to be male.

Female characters feature so much in the ads for MMOs that a casual observer might suppose that virtual worlds were played overwhelmingly by women. Of course, the fact that the women in the ads invariably look hot is the giveaway that they're mainly aimed at men, but that's not entirely true. *Second Life* has a high proportion of female players, but take a look at the next image (which came from its home page).

[Aside: notice how her right arm cuts through her wing. Is lack of collision detection accepted as the norm nowadays?]

So if you want to attract players, male *or* female, should you always use hot female avatars for promotional purposes?

No, you can go all-male if your target is ...

...teenage boys.

An Analogy

Interestingly...

The stages of development of community are analogous to the stages of development of players:

- Instinctive phase. Members go in their own directions to ascertain boundaries and norms.

- Learning phase. Members pool knowledge to increase that of the community as a whole.

- Doing phase. Members work to achieve the community's goals.

- Expert phase. Experiences are fully internalized.

This looks promising, but it's only an analogy. Sure, friend-type players will almost certainly be in a spiritual community, but hacker-type players could be in communities of any strength—and conceivably in no community at all.

Human Rights and MMOs #4

I like to play Chess *with old men in the park. Of course, the tough part about playing* Chess *with old men in the park is finding 32 of them.*

—Emo Philips

The most direct way in which nonplayers' human rights are affected by games concerns consent:

- Example game 1: The computer generates two secret random words, one for you and one for me. The first of us to get the other to say our word wins.

- Example game 2: The same as example game 1 but we try to get unsuspecting nonplayers to say our words.

This kind of thing can annoy the nonplayers being used as pawns (if they find out), but is it breaching their human rights? What if, instead of getting them to say words, you punched them? First to knock out a stranger wins! The harm there is more obvious, but where's the boundary lie between the two?

The magic circle defense of "We're just playing a game" can work if the people involved give their consent, which is the case in *Boxing*; it totally fails if for any reason they don't give their consent. *Boxing* is particularly interesting here because boxers are temporarily giving up a clear-cut human right (Article 3 UDHR: Security of Person). Although HR conventions would ordinarily nullify any contract between us that allowed us to pummel each other with fists, we're OK when doing so consensually as part of a game.

Is it therefore a general principle that people can opt to waive their human rights if they do so as part of a game? What about *Russian Roulette*? Shouldn't nonplayers be able to protect you from yourself?

I've mentioned before that the state does typically take on this role, but that's not the point. The point is *should* it, and if so, how ought you to decide when it shouldn't?

By the way, the subject of HR and games has lots of questions but very few actual answers. I'm not asking these questions here so I can answer them myself later; I'm asking them so that *you* can answer—or try to answer—them for yourself.

Kicking a Virtual Kitten

If you came across a virtual kitten in an MMO, would it be fine to kick it for fun? After all, no real kitten is being hurt.

It depends.

Why would kicking it actually *be* fun?

Well, if it looks and acts like a real kitten, you may get a small sadistic pleasure in seeing how it reacts to being booted the length of the room. Sure, you might also get a thrill from doing something naughty that you couldn't do in the real world, but for this to work you'd still need to sense that your heart wants you to kick kittens even if your head says not to.

If people get pleasure from hurting something artificial that they have anthropomorphized, should they be encouraged to stoke the flames of this pleasure?

It depends on what happens as a result.

On the one hand, it could be that before you know it they'll be out there kicking real kittens for fun. On the other hand, it could be that the ability to kick a virtual kitten is harmlessly addressing a need that would otherwise have to involve rather less happy actions.

It depends.

It always depends.

Transubstantiation Limitation

According to the Pontifical Council for Social Communications, "Virtual reality is no substitute for the Real Presence of Christ in the Eucharist."[10] It would seem that you can't take communion in virtual worlds.

Hmm. So God can turn real bread into the body of Christ, but not virtual bread?

---

[10]Pontifical Council for Social Communications: *The Church and the Internet*. February, 2002. http://www.vatican.va/roman_curia/pontifical_councils/pccs/documents/rc_pc_pccs_doc_20020228_church-internet_en.html

Levels of Legendary

On occasion, MMO players develop beliefs about some facet of the MMO that aren't true, but that they think are true. For example, in *WoW* it was rumored that if you carried a rabbit's foot around with you, you'd get better luck than if you didn't. Was it true? No one ever proved it either way. It was, therefore, a legend.

This sort of thing goes back a long way. We had so many of them in *MUD1* that we classified them as myths (collections/cycles of legends), legends (rumors that had come to be believed), rumors (things that people thought might be true but weren't sure about), scams (attempts to convince players in general the truth of something that the perpetrator knew not to be true), wind-ups (a scam applied to an individual), fobs (wild goose chases to get someone out of your hair), and cliffies (something you tell someone just to stop them from continually asking you questions).

All these enable ways for virtual communities both to define themselves and to admit new members. Common sets of beliefs bind together those who hold those beliefs; shared experiences bind together those who have had those experiences. Common stories bind together those who have heard those stories. Each of these levels of legendary—even the less pleasant ones—acts as a tiny hook to bring people together. Whether they *want* to be brought together is another matter, of course.

Oh, cliffies would usually result in nonpermanent character death. They got their name from the standard response to the question "What do I use <this thing I just found> for?", namely "You use it to jump safely off the cliff."

Reflecting or Correcting?

In *MUD1*, character attributes were strength, dexterity, and stamina. When you created a new character, the values of these were determined by rolling 5d20+5. Female characters would then have 10 knocked off their strength and 5 each added to their dexterity and stamina. Values were restricted to between 10 and 100 for both genders.

Each time you went up a level you'd get 10 added to all your abilities, so after going up five or so levels most players would be maxed out at 100 in each stat.

Reflecting *Reality* or correcting *Reality*?

What if I told you that the way the combat mechanics worked, 45/60/60 characters had an ever-so-slight advantage over 55/55/55 characters?

What if I told you that in real life, whether women are more dexterous than men or *vice versa* depends on the ambient temperature at which they are asked to perform their dexterous feats?

Vicarious Displeasures

Personally, I don't think that "It will lead you to do it in the real world" is the reason some people object to other people's kicking of virtual kittens. Rather, it's that they find the very idea of tormenting virtual pets intrinsically distasteful, and they don't want other people enjoying something that they personally find distasteful. They just use the escalation argument as cover for what they *really* mean.

That doesn't imply that "It will lead you to do it in the real world" is necessarily wrong, though.

It depends.

Different Cultures

One of the best-selling US computer games of 2005 was never released in the UK. Why not?

Here's the overview from the Atari publicity blurb[11]:

> *Put your skills and experience to the test! Travel the globe to hunt in six incredibly detailed natural habitats. Hunt five amazingly realistic species of deer including Axis and European Roe deer. Choose from a huge variety of weapons, ammo, equipment, vehicles and transportation to bring down prize game. Play alone or online for exciting multiplayer action. The hunt is on!*

---

[11]Atari:DeerHunter®2005.http://www.metacritic.com/game/pc/deer-hunter-2005

Now those readers who are American may be looking at that and wondering what's wrong. Those readers who are British will have their eyes and mouths wide open. *Bring down prize game?*! If *Deer Hunter 2005* had been on sale in the UK, the stores with it on their shelves could have expected outraged protesters picketing outside and zero sales inside anyway.

In the UK, the wanton slaughter of animals—even *pretend* animals in a computer game—is strictly taboo. Killing pretend humans is just fine, though.

Community in the Far East

There is some evidence that although players in the West don't conflate community and identity, those in the Far East do.

The theory is that the latter's main sense of identity is concerned with the group, not the individual. It's therefore the group that follows a hero's journey-like progression, and the group that becomes "immersed." Community is the way this is expressed externally.

Research is only preliminary, though, so there are no formal papers for me to point you at (not that you'd read them anyway, of course).

Back to Reality

I'll now bring to a close my deliberations about the similarity between MMO gods and the gods believed in by people in Reality. I could take it further, because there are implications arising from the relationship of created realities to their host reality—namely that they are like their host reality but with the sucky bits taken out. However, although this would lead to a very satisfying conclusion for the atheists among you, this book is not the place to evangelize. Well, it *is*, but only to evangelize MMOs, not real-life religions (or lack thereof).

What I've aimed to show is that the designers of MMOs don't have "god-like" powers, they actually have *godly* powers. These powers bring with them inescapable responsibilities. Designers should take what they do seriously. They should understand what they're doing and why they're doing it. Every once in a while, they should step back and *think* about what they've done, rather than just following their usual, tedious, mundane routine.

Once every seven days ought to do it.

Reality Corrected

In real-world society, there is a commitment to gender equality that is not reflected by real-world biology: it doesn't matter how much you want men and women to be equal, in real life wombless biological men are *not* going to give birth.

However, in a virtual world we can do pretty much what we like, so if we decide to make male and female characters both able to have babies, OK, they can. We can "correct Reality."

If there's no gameplay reason why we need to do it and no genre reason why we need to do it, then we're doing it simply because we *want* to do it.

That makes it politics; or, if you prefer, art.

The Lot of a CSR

The function of a Customer Service Rep is self-defeating: better CSRs mean fewer complaints, but fewer complaints mean that fewer CSRs are needed. Therefore, if you do your CS job too well, you could lose it.

You might expect that this would lead to a work environment in which CSRs are lazy and slack, because if they perform too well their jobs are on the line—but no! MMO developers are alert to the end case, and so don't employ enough CSRs in the first place.

That way, all CSRs are overworked all the time and can never undertake their duties well enough to make themselves redundant.

Pregnant Men

As things stand in real life, you have to have a working womb to give birth. If you want to invoke Fantasy to give womb-functionality to characters of a type that in real life don't have wombs, that's fair enough: you'd be on the side of "correcting Reality." If, however, you think that real life should take precedence, you'd say that people without wombs don't get to have babies.

I should point out that there's a difference between *sex* and *gender* in the social and scientific literature. Sex is biological and is mainly determined by genetics (although the fetal environment can also occasionally play a part); gender is social and psychological, but it can also have a biological basis. Therefore, if you ask whether a male character can have a baby, you have to decide what you mean by "male." Gender is very fluid: an individual could self-present as male yet possess the biological equipment necessary to have a baby. Sex is less fluid but still not binary (for example, some people with Y chromosomes do have wombs: they have a male karyotype but a female phenotype).

Either way, though, if your brand-new, genre-busting MMO is going to involve babies, at some point you still have to decide whether or not a character that purports to model a real human phenotype that can't become pregnant could, in your MMO, become pregnant.

Human Rights and MMOs #5

What if my game-playing offends you?

As I mentioned earlier, *Deer Hunter 2005* was a big seller in the United States. It simulated, apparently fairly realistically, the act of hunting a deer. You took your rifle, went out into the fields, snuck up on a deer or waited patiently for one to appear, and then you lined it up in your crosshairs and pulled the trigger.

The reason for not launching *Deer Hunter 2005* in the UK was primarily cultural, but let's suppose it had gone on sale anyway. My actions as a player— shooting realistic depictions of innocent animals—would have distressed many nonplayers. Even though no actual deer were hurt, nevertheless some people might have felt sufficient an emotional connection with what I was shooting to be pained by it. Would I be abusing the HR of those people if I carried on playing?

Note that "I don't care, they're way too sensitive" might be true, but that doesn't answer the question. Also, the deer is just an example: would *you* be happy knowing that there were people around playing games in which their character mocked your religious views, or kicked a child, or raped a woman, or that showed gore so realistic that it would make you feel ill if you saw it?

There's a follow-up argument often used in these kind of circumstances, because the person who is distressed usually needs more, er, ammunition than merely saying "Knowing that you are raping virtual women is upsetting me, please stop." This line of reasoning suggests that people learn things from games, therefore if they play games that feature <what they don't like>, they'll be more likely to do <what they don't like> in real life. It's a media effects argument, then.

Applying this to HR in general (so I don't have to keep using distasteful examples and risk abusing your human rights by doing so), is it the case that if I play games in which I witness HR abuses, I'll come to think that they are acceptable? What kind of human rights violations am I likely to see anyway?

Actually, we do have a good answer to that last question.

Group Types

If players in the Far East do indeed conflate community and identity, such that it's the group that follows a hero's journey rather than the individual, does this mean there should be group types equivalent to player types?

There you are, at level 80 or whatever the level cap is, playing alongside the friends you've known since you were all level 18. Elsewhere in the MMO are other groups of L80s, who have also grown into almost unitary bands over time. Is your group doing basically the same kind of thing as these other groups? Or will different groups of friends focus on doing different things? Do these things change, depending on the level at which the group operates?

Suppose they do: can the groups themselves perhaps be regarded as ersatz individual players, so there might be an "explorer group" or "socializer group," or is the nature of their dissimilarity new and different, requiring its own typology? And are the groups that form in the West and those that form in the Far East the same or different in this regard?

Don't bother looking through the rest of this book for answers—I don't have any. It would be fascinating to find them out, though.

The more we know about how and why people play MMOs, the better MMOs we'll get.

The Customer is Always

The traditional customer service mantra is "The customer is always right."

Yes…

There's a fundamental problem with MMOs in that the customer is *not* always right. The customer is only occasionally right, and even then it's often by accident. A large proportion of the player base of an MMO is made up of gamers. Gamers like to win. If they can win using nongame mechanisms that they can persuade themselves are part of the game, many will do so. Buying success by secretly paying real money for in-game advantage is one way of doing this.

Manipulating customer service representatives to do your bidding is another.

So, as a thought experiment, what would happen if you changed your mantra from "The customer is always right" to "The customer is nearly always a scheming, lying, misinformed whinger"?

Single-Sexism

What do you think about setting an MMO in a world that removes one biological sex entirely?

For example, the "escape from Colditz" MMO I mentioned earlier is not going to have a mix of male and female captives; only men were recruited as front-line troops in World War II (at least on the western front), and even if you know of evidence that a woman managed to trick her way into a combat unit, she'd still have been found out by the medics when she was captured.

Note that having one *character* sex does not equate to having one *player* sex. "The world of *The Three Musketeers*" might be attractive to female players, for example, even though they couldn't expect to play as female musketeers without compromising the genre. Women play the *FIFA* franchise console games, regardless of the fact that all the in-game players are male (well, pre-*FIFA 2016* anyway). In MMOs, many men routinely play as female characters without any prompting whatsoever.

Are single-sex settings the way to overcome unfairness between the sexes in MMOs? Or are they, by their mere existence, unfair themselves?

Human Rights and MMOs #6

A 2009 report[12] by TRIAL ("TRack Impunity ALways," a Swiss organization with a neat line in retrofitted acronyms that's dedicated to helping the victims of international crimes) looked at 20 first-person shooters covering contemporary combat. The game content was judged against international human rights law and international humanitarian law (pro tip: IHRL is mainly about war; IHL is mainly about peace).

Some FPSs scored well, but many didn't. The two commonest violations depicted were: principles of distinction and proportionality (such as by destroying civilian property); and torture or cruel/inhuman/ degrading behavior. Did you know that it's bad form to use a tank to blow up a church that has a sniper in the tower? Did you know that it's bad form to put a sniper in the tower of a church?

Although reports such as TRIAL's are generally informative, they usually fail to appreciate that game design is an art form. *All* IHRL/IHL abuses are regarded as universally bad in the TRIAL report, whereas actually the effect they have may be good. For example, the bad guys may be shown using torture so we *know* they're bad guys—good guys don't do that. You could even learn this way that torture is bad (that's if you didn't know anyway; I'd venture that FPS players tend not to be so poorly educated as to be unaware of the fact).

In summary, tier 1 of the HR-and-games hierarchy (which addresses the rights of nonplayers) primarily concerns four issues:

- The use of nonplayers as game tokens

- Protecting players from being complicit in their own HR abuses

- Upsetting nonplayers, for example by glorifying pedophilia

- Planting seeds in the minds of players that HR abuses can be acceptable.

This last point brings leads us to tier 2: HR abuses and single-player computer games.

---

[12]Frida Castillo: *Playing by the Rules: Applying International Humanitarian Law to Video and Computer Games.* TRIAL: Geneva, Switzerland. 2009. http://trial-ch.org/fileadmin/ user_upload/documents/Evenements_et_manifestations/Playing_by_the_Rule.pdf

Chinese Adena Farmers

Adena is the currency of the South Korean MMO *Lineage*. There are people who make a living from farming adena in *Lineage*'s US servers; this is then sold to players for real money. These people are generally known as Chinese adena farmers.[13]

So ... why Chinese?

Most of them actually are Chinese by ethnicity, nationality and physical location. Also, most of the players from China on US servers are probably farming. If what you object to is the farming, though, why mention their being Chinese? What does it matter where they come from?

If the political, economic, technical, and cultural conditions of China are what drive some of its residents to farm in MMOs in ways that aren't so apparent elsewhere, it would be fair to pass judgment on China for allowing this to happen (assuming you're against farming in MMOs). That's not what's happening here, though. While it's acceptable to criticize a country (China, the United States, the UK, wherever) on the basis of its politics, its use of its economic muscle, its technological infrastructure, and even its culture, what's unacceptable is to condemn individuals for being citizens of that country through accident of birth.

When people do this kind of thing, it's called racism. "Chinese adena farmers" is a racist term.

Just call them adena farmers.

Gender-Specific Pronouns

We didn't want gender in *MUD1* (well, we didn't want to force the choice). However, the way the English language works and the fact that *MUD1* was a text world meant that we pretty well had to do it. Basically, it comes down to the pronouns.

My own dialect of English uses the *singular they*, and I was in my 20s before I found out that *themself* wasn't generally regarded as a word by other English-speakers (the MS Word spell-checker certainly doesn't think it is). I can say sentences such as "So, this new teacher, what's their name?" and it sounds just fine to me. However, the singular *they* only works if you don't know the gender of the person you're talking about; if you do, you use *his* or *her* rather than

---

[13]Constance Steinkuehler: *The Mangle of Play*. In *Games and Culture* 1(3), July 2006, pp199-213. http://citeseerx.ist.psu.edu/viewdoc/download?doi=10.1.1.488.8042&rep=rep1&type=pdf

their. For this reason, it didn't extend well into *MUD1*: "Richard has doused their brand" jars somewhat when you know that Richard is a male name. The only other way to avoid gender-specific pronouns that I could see was to go with names the whole time ("Richard has doused Richard's brand," that sort of thing) but that was hardly going to help immersion either.

Some of the MOOs that came out had (and indeed have) multiple genders, and even include variants such as "the royal we" and actual plural characters ("Laurel and Hardy are here"). There are also MOOs and the like that implement disparate sad attempts by academics to "update" the English language ("Richard has doused eir brand," for example).

So in the end, we had to have gender in *MUD1*. Graphics force the issue further, though. Text means that characters get a gender; graphics mean they get a sex.

Human Rights and MMOs #7

In a single-player game, you, the player, can't directly abuse anyone else's human rights because you're playing by yourself. However, as the TRIAL report showed, you *can* do things that would, if they happened in real life, be violations. In theory (not necessarily using theories I subscribe to), some of these could: indirectly abuse other people's rights; cause you to regard HR as not all that important; abuse your own HR.

Here's a spectrum of the ways games can depict HR violations:

- Things you see happen but can't prevent, for example cut scenes of torture.

- Things you can do but that the game punishes you for having done, for example mission failure for ramming a mosque.

- Things you can do and the game lets you, for example imprisoning a character from *The Sims* in a doorless room.

- Things the game rewards you for doing, for example earning points for killing passers-by.

- Things the game requires you to do, for example feasting on beggars as a vampire in *The Elder Scrolls: Oblivion*.

Of these, the only one that the player might feel is an abuse of their own rights *as a player* is the last one. If I personally don't want to do things in a game because they disturb me, I should have been given enough warning up front to be able to decide not to play in the first place. This is what the covenant that designers make with players is supposed to stop.

Is it *really* a HR abuse to upset people by requiring that they do something in a game they don't want to, though?

Slay and Pee

Here's some classic advertising material that was put out by NCSOFT in 2005:

Can boys play, too?

A Thought Experiment

Suppose a disgruntled programmer were to run some code that flipped the sex of every player character in your current MMO. Every male avatar would become female and every female avatar would become male. In all other respects, the characters would be unchanged.

Further suppose that this programmer did such a thorough job that it would take a week before all the characters could be flipped back.

The players would complain, obviously, but would they actually play for that week? Would they learn anything from the experience? What do you think?

Feel free to partition the player base any way you like, if you feel that different groups would have different reactions. Note, though, that I'm not asking how *you* would react; I'm asking how you think players *in general* would react.

There's no answer; it's a thought experiment, not a real one.

Reason to Be Fearful

Most of today's politicians fear games. They are right to do so.

Games don't make people violent. They're no more addictive than soap operas. They're not primary vectors for pedophiles to groom children. None of these are reasons to fear games; they're mere bogeymen, created to rationalize what those who don't play games *really* fear about them: the unknown. If more politicians played games, the bogeymen would simply fade away.

Today's politicians nevertheless *should* fear games—and even more so than they do already. This is because there genuinely *is* something games do that threatens the fabric of society. The politicians just don't realize it.

Games make people think.

Starting as Yourself

I mentioned earlier that a higher proportion of female MMO players play female characters than male MMO players play male characters. I also mentioned that the explanation given for this back in the day by gender studies theorists (as opposed to the explanations given by players) is that women have a stronger sense that their body is part of their identity than do men.

There is some anecdotal evidence to support this. If you play in an MMO with good facilities for choosing how characters' faces look, ask players why they chose the look they did: you'll probably discover that more female players will say they designed their character to look like an idealized version of themselves than male players will.

Note that playing as an *idealized* version of yourself isn't the same as playing *as* yourself: you still have the freedom to explore your identity.

If you were to play as yourself—perhaps you're a company employee standing around in its virtual world shop, using an avatar modeled on your real face, wearing your real name on a name badge, alongside the avatars of your real-world colleagues who are sitting next to you in the same real-world office—well you might find your options to behave in a manner different from that expected of you somewhat curtailed.

Two Views

"If I'm going to spend all this time looking at an avatar, blah blah blah"…

I mentioned earlier that there's no compelling technical reason why your avatar can't look different to you than it does to everyone else. This means that *you* could choose to look at the backside of a curvaceous human female, but present everyone *else* with a view of a hideous half-orc barbarian (or *vice versa*, half-orc fans). No one need ever know.

You'd be OK with that?

The Bureaucratic Defense

Back in 2000, I had an account with a large online service that only fear of being sued prevents me from naming. Here's how their customer service thinking seemed to be to me:

- Want to sign up? Easy!
- Want to cancel your account? Let's put the account cancellation department somewhere where the people speak with an accent so thick that no one can understand them. Let's pay such low wages that only people too incompetent to get jobs stacking supermarket shelves apply. Let's divide the number of CSRs we actually need by 4 to obtain the number we employ. Let's have one incoming phone line for every two of these people, and queue calls for 25 minutes before cutting them off without answering them. Then let's make it that if you want to cancel your account, you can *only* do it by telephone "for security purposes," so email is not an option. Then we'll ask for the number on the charge card you're paying with, which expired three years ago but can still somehow be drawn upon thanks to loopholes in international banking rules, and which you have to go to your bank to find out because *no one* remembers the numbers on their last-charge-card-but-one.

- Then let's reactivate accounts every few months so people have to go through this entire process 6 times.

Bitter and unforgiving? Me? Why yes.

It was like this in MMOs for a while, too:

- If people wanted to pay you money or reactivate a cancelled account, they would get instant service by well-paid, courteous, articulate staff who would gladly get out of bed at 2 am to deal with your request.

- If people wanted something done in the MMO that was trivially easy, for example they were stuck in a mass of polygons and /stuck didn't work, their problem was dealt with less quickly and less efficiently, accompanied by a suggestion that it was a lot harder than it really was and that the player should be thoroughly grateful for the intervention.

- If people wanted you to do something inconvenient, you charged them for it. If too many wanted you to do it, you charged them some more.

- If people wanted to cancel an account, they would have to speak to people recruited from Cambridge University, England. These people would be the only three in the world fluent in the dialect of Anglo-Saxon spoken in Frisia *circa* 450 AD, which, while technically still English, is not comprehensible as such.

Hmm, I think I may have let my sarcasm get the better of me there.

So didn't this approach, well, annoy people?

Yes, of course it did, but *not* the people who mattered: newbies. Newbies would only see the good side of the system. Whenever they had a problem, it was of a kind that could be fixed quickly or even automatically. Requests for help were sometimes even prioritized so that newbies were seen to first.

Oldbies didn't see such a great level of service, except for billing enquiries (which account for around 25% of CS communications, but because they involve money are treated expediently).

Oldbies, however, didn't generally want to leave, because of what they had invested in the MMO, so they had to put up with this—and those who *did* want to leave had to learn Frisian first.

Human Rights and MMOs #8

Part of the definition of a game is that players play freely. If you don't like the game, stop playing!

However, what if a game were designed to remove that freedom? The gambling industry designs slot machines to be psychologically addictive, so game designers could do something similar.

Would designing a game in such a way as to give players a psychological dependency on it be an abuse of their human rights? What if you told them about it before they started to play? What if you had no intention of making the game addictive, you just did it by accident?

I'm not saying there *are* games that work like this, but I am asking what the HR implications would be if there were.

Hours per Week

How many hours do you play your MMO of choice per week, on average?

This is a question that has been asked many times in surveys, and the answer usually comes back as around 20. More fastidious surveys that ask people to keep diaries come out a little higher, at around 25.

Both are wrong. Players consistently under-report their playing time. Furthermore, women under-report more than men do.

In the largest study of its kind[14] (by several orders of magnitude), a research team led by Dmitri Williams compared survey responses with actual server logs for *EverQuest 2*. As I mentioned a while back, they found, on average:

- Males report playing 24.10 hours per week, but actually play 25.03 hours per week.

- Females report playing 26.03 hours per week, but actually play 29.32 hours per week.

Any male readers out there thinking they get kudos for lying less than women will now have to balance that against the kudos that women get for playing more than men.

Are the *real* hard-core MMO players female?

Bait

MMOs are regularly advertised using female characters, but inside the virtual world female NPCs are almost invariably outnumbered by male NPCs.

Why would that be? If female avatars are used to draw people into the MMO, why would a developer not also populate the MMO with female avatars? Why the bait and switch?

Just pick one kind of sexism and stick to it.

---

[14]Dmitri Williams, Mia Consalvo, Scott Caplan & Nicholas Yee: *Looking for Gender (LFG): Gender Roles and Behaviors among Online Gamers. Journal of Communication* 59 pp 700-725, 2009. http://dmitriwilliams.com/LFGpaperfinal.pdf

Perspective

There's an argument that says we should have more female game design-ers, because female game designers would design games from the female perspective.

That's not how design works. You can't design games from *the* female perspec-tive; however, you can design games from *a* female perspective. All designers are different; all designers are individual; all designers have their own perspec-tives. Female designers are different from male designers, but they're different from each other, too. They have their own perspectives.

There are degrees of difference, though. The more different the designers, the more different their perspectives; hence the more different the games they design. Differences in games lead to evolution in game design; encouraging designers who are different from the majority therefore increases the rate at which games improve. We want games to improve.

If most game designers are male (which they are), and if being female is a meaningful difference (which it probably is), then female designers have an advantage. However, if the only way to get a job as a designer is through a contact network dominated by men, the disadvantage of being female some-what outweighs it.

All designers understand their players. I don't believe that women can't design games that men will play, and I don't believe that men can't design games that women will play. I do believe that the more people who design games, the more games we'll have that *people* will play. Denying a huge swathe of talent the platform to excel—whether on the grounds of gender, age, education, accent or love of pizza and Red Bull—is just a *waste*.

Masquerading

The number-one cause of death for beautiful, young, female MMO players is that the guy playing them has finally accepted that he's gone too far.

To some extent, all players of MMOs are pretending to be someone in the virtual world who is different from their real-world self; we call this pretend person their *character*. The act of projecting yourself into your character is called *role-playing*. Some people take it a step further, however, and pretend to be someone different from their real-world self, who is in turn supposedly role-playing a character. An intermediate, invented real-world person is called a *sock puppet*; role-playing a sock puppet with intent to deceive people into thinking it's a real person is called *masquerading*. Actually, that's the ancient term; the modern one is *catfishing*, but I think tradition wins on classiness.

Masquerading is less common in MMOs than it was in text MUDs, because in a world of social networking sites and Teamspeak it takes quite some effort to maintain. Most people who try it only push lightly, acting as if they were the sock puppet they have in mind but never lying about it. For example, a common scenario is where a male player role-plays a female character so consistently well that other players think he's female in real life. Most will be up front about it when questioned ("No, I'm a guy in real life"), and although some will tease the questioner a little at first, they'll usually soon fess up. A few take it much, much further, though, to the point of inventing a female player to play the female character. This is where they cross the line to true masquerading.

They don't have to be brilliant at it: contrary to what many people believe, it's not actually difficult for real- world men to pass as female in a virtual world. If they do it well, they can become accepted as part of the game's community just the same as any other player. That's not to say they can't be found out, of course.

Signs to look out for:

- They come from an exotic, faraway place, or are disabled and housebound.

- They play often and make lots of friends.

- They never turn up at face-to-face meets or use Voice-over-IP ("I don't have a mic").

- They won't give out their phone number, or, if they do, when you call them they don't say much except that they'll meet you in the game.

- No one has ever met them in real life, or only a few, tight-knit individuals have. These individuals may also never have been met by any player in real life.

- The photos and Snapchats they send you and the ones that appear on their Facebook page are of someone drop-dead gorgeous.

- They don't spend much time in the company of players who are provably female in real life.

Normally when players leave a game, they just drift away. For a guy masquerading as a gal, though, this isn't enough. He wants to kick the habit; he wants to make sure he isn't tempted to bring his female *alter ego* back. If he's a happy-ending sort of person, she'll have a sudden opportunity that will change her life forever—a whirlwind romance, a lottery win, a college scholarship, a year abroad, whatever. If he doesn't want to leave the door even slightly ajar for a comeback, though, he'll kill her off. Tragic, violent deaths are a favorite.

Why can't he simply own up? Well, sometimes he can, and it's actually the best solution. His friends will feel very betrayed, but if they're true friends they'll understand the nature of online worlds, and how role-playing can get the better of people. It'll bring closure, and although people will be angry initially, at least they won't be stricken with grief. In time, people will forgive and forget, and come to accept the man behind the mask. In time...

Don't underestimate the lengths people will go to in order to maintain their fiction, either. I know people who have set up blogs and developed a forum-posting history which they've maintained for over a year before playing in an MMO, just to give their character a backstory that stands up to Google. After all, "She *must* be real, or someone would have had to have been planning this for a year!" Well actually, someone has...

The Mutterings of Old Men

When, back in the day, it was Customer Service policy to cut corners when dealing with the kind of annoying problems oldbies had, why didn't the oldbies complain? All they would have had to do would be to go to a public forum and rant about it. Word would get around that the MMO was bad, so newbies wouldn't play it.

Well yes, oldbies did used to do that, but so what? Oldbies complain *the whole time*, like grumpy old men. You address one complaint and they find another one. It doesn't matter *what* you do to address their issues, they're going to slag you off for not having done something else instead. They have an *endless* supply of changes they want you to make and behaviors they want you to adopt. You can *never* win them over to your side. *Ultima Online* got so many complaints about its nonconsensual PvP that it created two facets, Felucca and Trammel, so that people could choose the playing style they preferred: this didn't reduce the volume (in both senses of the word) of CS complaints *one iota*.

What's more, oldbies complain because they care. If they didn't care, they wouldn't make such a song and dance about it. The ones who don't say a word are the ones who are going to leave. Noisy people who leave are back within two weeks.

So what used to happen was that MMOs got their newbies from untapped sources. These people didn't read any forum postings, and they came to think that the CS experience they were given was industry standard. Anyone who did read forum postings was regarded (not unreasonably) as being basically loyal to some other MMO anyway, so even if you did manage to sign them up they'd be off the moment the next MMO appeared that was just like the one they played first except for being different.

That worked, but only while there were still ample sources of newbies around.

Change

I've mentioned before that *MUD1* had a spell, CHANGE, that allowed a player to change the gender of its target. There were also a small number of ways to toggle gender through other actions (for example, by picking up a bangle, which you could then convert into points).

As a consequence, players would occasionally forget which sex their character was ("Oh, am I female at the moment?").

The things you lose when you introduce graphics...

Designing for Whom?

The notion that a designer of an MMO is an artist is often regarded by designers themselves as at best an indulgence and at worse an experiment in manipulation. There's so much that designers have to cover, so much they have to deal with, so much they *must* do and so little time to do it, that the stuff they don't *have* to do takes a very distant second place. However, this "optional extra" is central to the notion of what MMOs are *about*.

Are designers designing the MMO to fit the potential community or the potential community to fit the MMO?

The answer is neither: designers are designing the community *and* the MMO to reflect aspects of the designers themselves. If designers are prevented from doing this, their MMOs will have no soul. Soulless MMOs are about as much fun as the name suggests.

Priming their MMO's culture allows designers to speak to their players, thence to the world, thence to themselves.

I assert in *MMOs from the Inside Out* that players play MMOs to undertake a hero's journey. Once they finish, they *are* their characters and their characters are they. Well, designers design MMOs for the same reason players play them: to find out who they are. Once they finish, the designer *is* the MMO and the MMO *is* the designer. Through this identity, the designer can affect the *real* world.

Art.

Two Movies for CSRs

The Yangtse Incident was a 1957 film written by Eric Ambler and directed by Michael Anderson, starring Richard Todd as Lt. Commander John Kerans of HMS Amethyst, a crippled British frigate caught on the Yangtse in 1949. It was based on a true incident.

Here's what happens in the movie. Kerans, sensing low morale among his men as the Chinese communist forces approach, starts giving them pointless and/or tedious tasks. For example, when they've scrubbed the decks he immediately orders them to do it again. Everyone aboard ends up hating him, almost to the point of mutiny—but they're unified in (and by) their hatred. Morale improves dramatically! Kerans has deliberately offered himself up as an outlet for their frustration. Morale holds, and the ship manages to sneak back into the open seas under cover of darkness after 100 days.

Dr. No is a 1962 James Bond movie, based on the book by Ian Fleming. Bond aims to thwart evil, as personified by the villain, Dr. No.

Or, in subsequent Bond movies, by Blofeld, or Goldfinger, or Scaramanga, or Blofeld again, or …

The thing is, evil is always personified in movies. You're never fighting the system, or the corrupt police force, or the terrorists, or the communists. You're fighting a particular representative of the system, or a particular corrupt cop, or a particular terrorist, or a particular Soviet officer. People like their enemies to have a *face*.

Combining *The Yangtse Incident*'s distraction and the Bond movies' personify-the-enemy results in a technique has been used in the past for MMO customer service:

- Don't send out bad news in the name of the company or the CSRs. Send it out in the name of the head of the CS section, "Dr. No."

- Whenever anyone complains to a CSR about level of service or indeed anything else that's the company's fault, that CSR should blame it all on Dr. No.

- Whenever anyone not in the CS section screws up, Dr. No should publicly carry the can for them.

- Dr. No can occasionally talk sense, too, which is useful if a mutiny looms.

If you do this, everyone is going to wind up complaining about Dr. No, rather than what they *should* be complaining about. Who cares about the message when there's a messenger who can be *shot*?

Dr. No's real name should never be used. Players will then feel patronized because the chief CSR is pretending to be a player when clearly they're not, and thereby they'll be predisposed to hate the person.

There is another reason, though. See, there are two ways to find yourself a Dr. No. The first is to recruit someone who has incredibly thick skin and is prepared to pay in infamy for what they get in power. The second is to make up a person. I'm pretty sure that Uncle Ben probably has little to do with the rice in your supermarket.

Sure, any company that were to do this would risk being found out, but hey, to whom is anyone going to complain about it?

Is this Sexist?

As I mentioned earlier, in *MUD1* we had minor differences between the sexes of characters. Male characters started off stronger than female ones, but with less stamina and dexterity. They all capped out at 100, though, so after going up a few levels the difference had gone. We also had some (what would now be called) quests that you could only do if you were male and others you could only do if you were female.

For example, female characters could kiss a frog and then kiss the resulting prince for experience points, whereas male characters couldn't. Likewise, male characters could kiss a sleeping beauty for experience points but female characters couldn't.

Is this sexist?

I also mentioned earlier that *MUD1* had magic by which characters could change from one sex to the other. A female character could change to kiss the sleeping beauty and then change back to kiss the frog. A male character could change to kiss the frog then change back to kiss the sleeping beauty.

Is *this* sexist?

Is either homophobic?

Professional Masquerading

Who might masquerade as an invented, real-life person?

Well, several suggestions spring to mind. Confidence tricksters could do it, although MMOs don't tend to attract them (except perhaps *EVE Online*, where it's part of the gameplay). Reluctant celebrities could do it, but they tend not to have problems anyway. People who genuinely have something to hide could do it, although they tend to be too suspicious-of-everything to risk being found out. Customer service staff who want to get a feel for the MMO from a player's perspective could do it.

Actually, customer service staff *do* do it. As far as I can tell, it's not widespread among those CS representatives whose job it is to answer players' queries on a day-to-day basis. However, among the senior CS managers I've spoken to over the years, around half have had one or more sock puppets that they've cultivated in order to get the true "word on the street." For them, it's like Henry V on the eve of the Battle of Agincourt, donning a disguise to find out what his soldiers really think. A leader can become too remote; this way, by going deep undercover, they can remain grounded.

OK, so yes, I have done it myself, in both *MUD1* and *MUD2*. To be honest, I didn't like it; I made sure I didn't form any friendships with players, because that would have led to an inevitable betrayal. Indeed, I don't know anyone who does this professionally who actually enjoys it; it feels grubby and dishonest.

With a small user base, masquerading is hard to get away with for long, so I always retired my own sock puppets after a few months; had one been found out I would have retired it immediately, but none ever were.

With a large user base it's easier to blend in, but there are problems for the would-be masquerader today that we didn't have in the text-world past. The main one is social networking: if you want to create a sock puppet, you have to decide whether the person you've invented would have a Facebook, Google+, Twitter, Pinterest, Youtube, Wordpress or any other account, and then set them up—and not all on the same day, either. Then you have to populate them periodically, leave comments, interact; it can be somewhat time-consuming.

Weirdly, the part you might think was hardest—getting friends—isn't much of a problem at all. To inform readers of a novel I wrote about upcoming developments for sequels, I created a sock puppet in the name of the novel's lead character. It wasn't a success, in that about four people who had read the novel asked to be friends. However, over a hundred additional people (all teenagers from Dar Es Salaam) then asked to be friends for no apparent reason. I suspect that one of them thought the sock puppet was someone they knew in real life and it all flowed from there.

If I can accidentally acquire over a hundred friends for a sock puppet whose profile *explicitly says she is a fictional character,* how easy would it be to get a larger list if you set your mind to it? All you'd need is a profile picture of a cat, cartoon character, or popular toy, a name that doesn't sound made-up, a bunch of random people to send friend requests to, and you're set. Just hope that Facebook doesn't find out that you're contravening its rules and suspends your account.

Setting up a phony identity with which to play an MMO really shouldn't work. People you meet in the game world whom you ask to be friends (in the social networking sense) can expose you as a fraud merely by asking your other friends how they come to know you. They *almost never do this,* though: they see you have a posting history, see you have a bunch of friends (anecdotally, 15 seems to be the tipping point), and then they accept your request.

As I said, this feels grubby and dishonest. It *is* grubby and dishonest. So why do customer service people do it? Contrary to what players may suspect, CS managers tend not to be grubby, dishonest individuals.

Well, the reason they do it is that if they want to feel the pulse of their MMO, they have to play it as a regular player. If their own real-world identity were to become known, they couldn't play as a regular player. Therefore, until some-one thinks of a better solution, they have to masquerade. It's the logical thing to do.

It's still grubby and dishonest, though…

Human Rights and MMOs #9

Being an art form, game design allows designers to present political opinions through gameplay and fiction. The "all elves are nature-loving aesthetes and all dwarfs (sigh, *dwarves*) are beer-drinking boors" example shows how you can use games to reinforce a world view that says racial stereotyping is natural and justified. This is not a human rights violation itself, but could you perhaps argue that it's an assault on its principles? Books seem to get away with this just fine; should games be any different? That elves and dwarves typecasting came to games through *The Lord of the Rings* (although the understanding of its mythological symbolism didn't necessarily come with it).

Stereotyping elves and dwarves can be read as a tacit endorsement of (in this case racial) discrimination. Discrimination can be far more open, though.

For example, in *A Tale in the Desert,* the events team created a new character—the trader Malaki—who would only trade with male characters and had overtly disparaging views as to the relative worth of women. There's no question that this character was directly discriminatory in the context of the game, because that's how he was deliberately designed; but was his appearance or action an abuse of human rights? After all, you don't have to be female in real life to play a female character, and if you are female in real life you don't have to play a female character either. It's certainly a way to light up the forums, whatever…

In some cases, rights abuses appear in a game because they reflect reality. *Medieval II: Total War* has no female generals, but it does have princesses who can be married off. All the Premier League players in *Football Manager 2015* are male. Is that lack of balance discriminatory?

Sometimes, discrimination can be there to make an artistic point. The all-female priesthood in *Dragon Age: Origins* can feel unfair to men, but in doing so it gives them an insight into how women might feel about all-male priesthoods in real life.

As *DA: O* shows, game designers can be quite a liberal bunch of people. They may decide to be proactive and (as I mentioned earlier) "correct Reality" by doing things such as reducing gender to a cosmetic level. This sounds all very right-on egalitarian, but it's not immune from HR concerns. This very idealism itself can be attacked, for stripping away aspects of individuality. After all, if it's part of a woman's identity that she can have babies and men can't, then if she plays an MMO in which she can't or men can, that could shake her up more than somewhat.

Inauthentic representations in the name of equality can be annoying (for example, the female popes of the dynasty-based, real-time resource-management game, *The Guild*), but that's not a HR violation. This kind of thing can, however, gloss over HR abuses of the past, leading players to feel that a grim chapter in human history was a golden age, or that no one has ever had to struggle for their rights and never will have to again. Recall the earlier example I gave about slavery in pirate games: should those who wish to promote human rights demand that these games *don't* depict slaves as cargo, or that they *do*?

In single-player games, you can evade many of these issues by giving the players a choice. Click this button on the configuration screen if you want to allow female popes, that one if you don't. This is not something you can really do with multiplayer games, though.

Preserving Games

Suppose we wanted preserve a computer game for posterity. What would that mean?

Well, the first thing to consider is why we ever want to preserve anything at all for future generations, anyway: it's so they can learn from it. Learn *what*, though?

The main things the people of the future can learn are:

- Who we were
- Who they are
- Why important things are important

Put another way: history, literature, and art.

Customer Service for Thickies

Let's see how this "The customer is only right by accident" approach can be used by CSRs to address the typical reasons people complain about MMOs:

- **Buggy company.** "You deliver late, you charge too much, you make false promises." Solution: Make more false promises.

- **Buggy hardware.** "Your servers and routers and other stuff with wires in them are always crashing." Solution: It's the manufacturer's fault and we shall pursue them through the courts of Southeastern China for the maximum compensation their government allows.

- **Buggy software (1).** "Your servers keep crashing." Solution: It's buggy hardware!

- **Buggy software (2).** "Your client keeps crashing." Solution: It's buggy middleware! We are currently working with software engineers from the middleware company, hopefully in time for the next patch. A nondisclosure agreement forbids us from naming the middleware company involved.

- **Buggy players (1).** "One of your other players is a moron who shouldn't be allowed anywhere near your MMO." Solution: Tell this other player what was said by whoever complained, and then act as a go-between as they exchange insults until one of them leaves.

- **Buggy players (2).** "I know I'm being a pain here, but I need help." Solution: give them the help, but next time, roll a die: on a 5 or 6, help, otherwise put their request in a folder marked "long grass." If they're that dumb, they'll think they screwed up sending it anyway.

- **Buggy design.** "Your game sucks!" Solution: insist that if they keep playing it, it unsucks. They've reached a deliberate content plateau that was put in to give players a breather, and the suckiness will disappear if they just play a while longer.

Security: Privacy

Walls have ears.

Conversation in MMOs *feels* like conversation in the real world. When you say something to someone else privately, it's as if you said it to them privately in real life. You don't expect it to be overheard any more than you do in real life.

OK, so obviously this is not the case if you spend a moment thinking about it. Everyone surely *knows* that MMO developers hear all, and that nearby players could perhaps hear it too. In some virtual worlds, even nearby objects could record what you've said (you can buy bugging devices in *Second Life*).

The problem is, people *don't* give it a moment's thought when they're deep in weighty discussion. This means that everything they say is potential fodder for data mining. Fortunately, the chances are that at the moment this isn't happening, because MMO operators have enough to do without giving themselves more; this is not to say that it won't happen in future, though.

Operators collect data because they want to detect cheating and TOS violations; they can also use it as evidence when someone reports an infraction. They would prefer not to have to record anything at all, because it's a huge data storage cost to them.

However, since they're doing it anyway, what's to stop them from selling it on?

As it stands, pretty well nothing stops them doing this if they're in the United States. The view there is that if it leads to a less expensive game, then having someone build a behavioral profile about you to be used for marketing purposes is a small price to pay.

In the EU, human rights legislation gets in the way. Perhaps because they have more painful memories of what can happen when organizations build files on large numbers of people, there are safeguards in place to protect people's privacy. As a consequence, data security is a much bigger deal in the EU than it is in the United States —which leads to intractable problems when the two meet to discuss harmonizing their Internet legislation.

Customer Service for Smarties

Just in case it's not clear, a lot of those "MMOs in the past had this stupid idea for dealing with customers" anecdotes apply to quite a few MMOs in the present, too. About the only area where there has been a marked improvement is in account cancellation by the player: this is now usually handled by a web-based form automatically. The reason for this is that if you depart on good terms, you can sometimes persuade people to come back after a few months, whereas if you don't they'll subject you to a stream of abuse in Frisian were you to suggest it.

Indulge me for a moment, though. Might it not be possible that there is another way to handle customer service issues? I'm not sure this is feasible, but hear me out…

- **Buggy company.** Perhaps the customer *is* always right? If you get your act together, the complaints (and calls for compensation) will go away.

- **Buggy hardware.** Ditto.

- **Buggy software.** Ditto.

- **Buggy players.** These can be dealt with through implementing complaint procedures. Almost all acrimony in MMOs arises from misunderstandings. Those that don't should lead to graded responses that can lead ultimately to permanent banning. People *do* reform, so give them the chance. If they don't, one bad player lost is 20 good players kept. Be firm, but be fair. Commercial organizations in the real world handle this kind of thing *all the time*, and the solutions are well known.

- **Buggy design.** This is the disease for which many other complaints are symptoms. You're not complaining about X because he's a jerk, you're complaining about him because he's the same level as you but more powerful. Basically, you're frustrated. Now it may be that you're frustrated because you misunderstand the "game" you're playing, or because you're not very good at it, or because this isn't your first MMO and you think it should be: these are basically buggy player issues that can be educated away. However, it may be that you're frustrated because of a genuine problem with the design. That being the case, the designers really *ought* to be told. It may be too late for them to do anything about it, but it may not. If they don't know, though, they're never going to get to say either way.

Document all problems, document their responses and solutions, put them all in a database (a part of which can be player-searchable), regularly mine the database so you can follow trends, send individual players to their allocated CSR case worker whenever possible, or to a supervisor whenever not. You can try to use AI to suggest possible solutions, but only once per query: if a player *wants* to explain things to a human being, *let* them speak to a human being—and not a second program pretending to be a human being, nor a human being just cutting-and-pasting stock answers from the aforementioned database.

The point I'm trying to make here is that there are experts in the real world who know this stuff—and have known it for years. MMO developers should seek out and listen to these experts, rather than abusing their godly status and calling that a solution. Don't be too proud to hire someone with no gaming experience if they used to run the CS section of a mail-order company. Customer service is *customer service*, not developer armor.

Whoah, pull over there rant boy…

OK, so I may have been a little harsh on MMO operators here. I appreciate that if you have a million players all trying to talk to you at once, it's going to be impractical to deal with all of them on a personal level. That said, mobile phone companies have 100 times the number of users that you do, and *they* somehow manage it. Some MMO developers *are* actually good at CS, of course, such as Trion Worlds (developers of *Rift*), who are excellent in my experience. It's just that the majority, well, *aren't*.

One more thing: the free-to-play revenue model introduces issues that may actually be relatively novel. At least with a subscription-based system, when you budget for a third of your income to go on customer service you can be moderately sure that the people complaining *are* actually customers. Who are your customers in a free-to-play world? The 5% who pay, or the 100% who play?

Hey, don't look at me, *I* don't know…

Human Rights and MMOs #10

Multiplayer brings a whole new dimension to the discussion about human rights: other players. Players of single-player games can directly abuse NPCs but not other real people. Players of multiplayer games *can* abuse (the human rights of) other real people.

Here's an example: when players get along with each other, they form or join guilds (or whatever the local term is). The entrance criteria used by these organizations can be openly discriminatory. Remember that list of "female avatars only," "female players only," and so on that I gave earlier? There are human rights issues in that for people who want to join a guild but are denied the opportunity.

Although I've been careful not to be overly opinionated myself with reference to HR issues for games, on this occasion I shall make a comment. I believe that players *should* be able to discriminate against *characters* in an MMO if the basis of the discrimination fits the world's fiction. For example, if you had a role-playing guild for Viking warriors in a stylized, early medieval setting, it would be acceptable not to accept beardless or nonwhite characters—even though in real European history there is evidence that half the Viking warriors were female (and therefore, on the whole, beardless). A ban would nevertheless make sense in the heightened fictional context. You couldn't, however, ban beardless or nonwhite *players*. The context only gives cover *within* the MMO, and there it's *characters* that count, not players.

As a side note, I also believe that MMO developers should be allowed to dissolve any guild that implements discriminatory policies, particularly if they do so at the player (rather than the character) level. Of course, as the LGBT Riots of '06 in WoW showed, it's entirely possible to mess this up big time if you lose track of *why* you implemented your nondiscriminatory policy in the first place; nevertheless, if a developer doesn't want people recruiting players in-world based on out-of-world prejudices or allegiances, they should be allowed to enforce that: it's *their* game, and *they* get to decide who is allowed to play or not. MMO developers ought to be allowed to close down guilds on a whim if they so choose. If their actions backfire, well, they should have thought it through more, but they *did* have the right to make the mistake.

Naturally, if the reason a developer closes down a guild is itself rooted in discriminatory principles, that could mean the *developer* is abusing the human rights of the players affected. If you banned all men-only guilds but no women-only guilds, you could expect lawsuits. Well, that's unless there was something about your MMO that was intrinsically yet allowably discriminatory; for example, it was set up as a gentle place for women who have endured miscarriages to meet one another so they can share their experiences. Banning all-male guilds in that world probably wouldn't raise many eyebrows or lawsuits.

When it comes to games of any kind, context is *always* important.

Service Agreement

Customer Service in MMOs is something of an anomaly. There are two main reasons for having an army of customer service staff, but few companies make the effort.

The first reason is that of *retention*. If customer service staff know the customers, such as occurs in the *Iron Realms* textual worlds, then that can really boost retention. People like being treated as decent human beings in a polite and timely manner by someone they've spoken to before.

Unfortunately, this level of considered attention is expensive to scale up. Also, it turns out that if you were to rate customer service in MMOs from "none" at the low end to "personal relationship" at the high end, then "miserable" has much the same impact on retention as "pretty good." Thus, developers go with "miserable" because they'd just be throwing away money if they tried to improve it incrementally. The fact that almost everyone else also has miserable customer service dampens further any urge to do something about it.

The other reason for increasing the number of people working in customer service—that your staff won't be over-stretched and over-stressed—is not apparently often a factor.

On Real Life

Anatomy of an *SW:TOR* Customer Service Ticket

February 1, 2012:

> *Greetings Polly,*
>
> *I am Protocol Droid A0-L6 of Human-Cyborg Relations.*
>
> *I have received your transmission regarding about unable to get the Unassembled Columi Master Force Offhand weapon that was in the chest for hard mode Battle for Ilum because you got killed on the final boss.*
>
> *We appreciate your feedback about the game and apologize for the inconvenience that you have experienced as well. The game is always a work in progress and still needs fine tuning. We are doing all the best that we can to provide our loyal customer the best Star Wars game experience by minimizing and resolving these kinds of reports that are being sent to us.*
>
> *We will take this as a suggestion and possibly be corrected in the future updates of the game. Kindly check for patch notes updates in our website for more informations.*
>
> *Please do not hesitate to contact us again if there is anything further we can help you with.*
>
> *Galactic support is our specialty…*

There are seven paragraphs, counting the greeting and sign-off.

First two paragraphs: computer.

Third paragraph: computer pretending to be human.

Fourth to seventh paragraphs: computer.

Did they buy their customer service response software from a bulk email spamming company or something?

Human Rights and MMOs #11

Most online games are facilitated by operating companies: Microsoft, Blizzard, Valve, Sony, Electronic Arts, Zynga, and so on. These companies have details about the players behind the characters. Can they reveal this information publicly?

Privacy is a human right (Article 12 *UDHR*). If someone revealed to the world that you're playing a sexy female night elf mage when in real life you're not sexy, female, a night elf or a mage, this would be an abuse of that right. Nevertheless, Blizzard did just that in 2010 with their Real ID system. They reversed their decision after a few days because of player outcry. Sadly, this was before I could check out whether anyone in my guild was a real-life celebrity in order to try tapping them for money.

Part of Blizzard's problem was that its proposal was retrospective. If you were told up-front your name and character could be revealed, would that be OK? By definition you can't sign away your human rights, but if you tell someone something willingly, knowing that it is going to be broadcast—well, why would you do that if you did indeed want it kept private?

Some MMO features require the disclosure of personal details in certain situations. Membership of *EVE Online*'s Council of Stellar Management demands it, for example. Some guilds want to know that the people they're taking into their community are who they say they are.

Context and consent play a big part here. Are HR protocols geared to handle multiple, nested layers of subtle frames?

(No. That's why we have judges.)

UIs

User interfaces: a doctor writes.

There are many ways that an occupation can harm a body, whether it's tennis elbow or housemaid's knee. However, in today's modern age of sitting at a computer doing nothing more strenuous than moving a mouse and pressing keys, surely all we need worry about is morbid obesity?

This is not so!

Different computer games come with different dangers. For example, one of my favorite games, *Patrician III*, is real-time. It has no *Europa Universalis*-like facility to pause automatically on events: if you want to pause it, you have to hit the pause key, as in the key with Pause written on it. You'll want to do this a lot. Thus, after playing it for three hours every night for a week, you may well find yourself develop shooting pains running up the bones of the middle finger of your right hand. Well. I did, anyway...

Another game I play a lot is *Football Manager*. The interface here is characterized by having buttons you must click on successively that are positioned in different corners of the screen, so you end up using the heel of your mouse hand as a pivot as you cover vast distances between selecting something and OKing it. This means that after a few days of heavy playing, you end up with a callus the size of a Malteser next to your wrist.

Particularly bad in this regard are games that use WASD controls. I don't like these at the best of times, because of the fact they use the left hand. Keeping your arm static for several hours and just depressing the fingers is a great way to make your entire hand go numb; over time, you're looking at a frozen shoulder. It's not just the body that suffers, either: here's a photograph of what my desk looked like after an evening of playing *World of Warcraft*:

Those are scratches on the wood south of the Shift key there. I suppose if I didn't have a metal watch strap it wouldn't be so bad, but then all that friction would have been against my skin instead. I'd be risking spontaneous human combustion.

Some games have interfaces that don't seem to have any overtly bad physical side effects. I can play *Pillars of Eternity* for hours at a time, and a medical examination of my extremities afterward wouldn't show up anything abnormal. Things don't have to be the way they are.

That said, when I was writing my book *Designing Virtual Worlds* I had to invest in a wrist pad for my left hand because the QWERTY layout was killing it. I suspect that some of these interface issues are going to be with us for rather a long time.

Game Addiction

On August 22, 2006, I received an email from a journalist writing for a major national newspaper, asking about—well, this is what he said:

> *I am a British journalist working on an article about computer game addiction and would be very grateful if you would email any recent facts and figures that you may have to illustrate the extent of this problem.*

So he's already made his mind up that it's a problem, has he?

Most British newspapers are resolutely anti-technology. Computer games, in their minds, are things played by teenage boys and no one else. Violent and puerile content abounds, and people are hooked to the extent that they abandon the rest of their lives (starting with attendance to personal hygiene).

Actually, at the time this journalist contacted me, computer games were played by 59% of the UK population aged 6–65 (according to research by the BBC[1]). If games were addictive, surely we'd have been seeing major societal breakdown as a result even back then?

Were journalists to write about how addictive soap operas are, and then contact broadcasters asking for the names of people to interview who are in the grip of such an addiction, they'd be a laughing stock. So why are they deadly serious about addictive computer games? Do they particularly *want* to seem out of touch to a large section of their readership? And don't they understand that "computer games" are not all the same? What next, "food" is fattening?

A game designer is probably not the best person to ask about the problems of computer game addiction. I wrote back, saying—well, this is the last sentence:

> *Sorry I can't help you much, but if I wrote to you out of the blue saying that I wanted you to point me at any recent facts and figures concerning the alcoholism of journalists, you'd understand a little of how I feel at the moment...*

---

[1]BBC New Media Research: *Gamers in the UK: Digital Lives, Digital Lifestyles.* http://crystaltips.typepad.com/wonderland/files/bbc_uk_games_research_2005.pdf

Girlz

This advertisement appeared on the back page of the April 2007 issue of *Toy News*:

What monster have I unleashed?

Am I like one of those naïve scientists who sees their peacetime invention being used as a weapon of war?

The Industry

Whenever I read an article about computer games that mentions the industry, I take special note of how the author refers to that industry. There are five common terms employed:

- "The games industry": This tends to be used by developers and people who play an awful lot of games.

- "The computer games industry": This tends to be used by developers and people who play an awful lot of games when talking to people who don't play a lot of games.

- "The videogames industry": This is mainly the haunt of journalists, academics, and developers who cut their teeth in the 1980s.

- "The video games industry": This is used interchangeably with "the videogames industry," sometimes in the same article.

- "The gaming industry": This is used by clueless journalists and academics who don't know that it means the gambling industry but instead think it must be something to do with what gamers do.

Of course, the "games" components of the first three of those terms could also be "game." We're across-the-board consistent in our inconsistency.

Ah, Griefers

I've lost count of the number of times players in *MUD* would say something like "You punished me for setting fire to my own sticks!" when they knew full well that what they were actually being punished for was setting fire to their own sticks in the presence of a keg of gunpowder which then blew up and killed everyone in the room, including the total newbies who were being shown around and who would never play again as a result.

Ah, griefers.

Preserving for History

Historians aim to understand old meaning from old artifacts. To them, "the past" means the *people* of the past. Preservation is important to historians because it gives them a source: from this, they can reconstruct some aspect of the past, which they can then explain in ways relevant to their present.

Computer games don't have a very long history, but they still give historians problems. A game historian playing *Galaxian* today can only imagine what it must have been like playing it when it first came out. To understand the games of the past in the context of the past, you need to put aside your present-day self and try to play as your period self. This can help you get a sense of what games *meant* to people back then.

To preserve a computer game is to treat it much as a library would an ancient text: you keep the original in its original form wherever possible but reproduce its content in a more accessible form. The problems are mainly practical, to do with hardware and software simulation: you'll retain original software that runs on original, working hardware if you can, but use simulators to demonstrate it in action. People who have a particular need to see it running on the physical hardware can do so, but most researchers will be happy to use a simulator rather than risk damaging the ancient artifact.

Oh, and if you really want to know, *Galaxian* was like *Space Invaders* except that I could get to the second screen.

Wrong Answer

Whenever I'm interviewed in my capacity as "father/grandfather/great-grandfather of virtual worlds/MMORPGs/MMOs," I'm almost invariably asked which of the day's commercial MMOs I like best. For ten years, I always replied that from a design point of view my favorite was *EVE Online*. OK, so it has a 6-month learning curve, but apart from that…

The thing is, this response almost *never* appeared in the resulting write-up.

So… why was I ever asked?

Awe and Wonder

I have two children, both of whom have known for years that my job involves something to do with MMOs. Apart from the slight kudos buff that this gives them in parent-criticizing conversations with their friends, I'm otherwise just the same taxi-driver/ATM that every other father is. They did, of course, express an interest in playing some of the games I've worked on or their descendants, but for years I wouldn't let them. I wanted them to wait.

I grew up in East Yorkshire, which, for those who don't know much about the geography of England, is not exactly metropolitan. I was 9 years old before I left the county (for 2 minutes—my dad drove over the Lincolnshire border because we were nearby and I asked), and 11 before I left again.

The first time I went to London, I was 18. I can remember right now the thrill of walking up the Mall toward Buckingham Palace, marveling at how close it was to Downing Street. All these buildings I'd heard about and seen on TV, and I was *there* right among them! It was an amazing experience.

My daughters went to London on school trips. It wasn't special to them as adults. Going there at age 18 didn't give them that sense of wonder I had.

Your first virtual world stays with you for always. It's something that should be experienced only when you can appreciate the experience. If I'd let my children play before they were old enough to be blown away, they'd miss out on that. I didn't want them to miss out: I wanted it to be like it was for me when I visited London for the first time—another world.

It worked, too. My younger daughter had a warlock, a druid, and a shaman in *WoW* and played for an hour or so every night when she finished her homework. She got the awe thing as soon as I let her jump one of my characters off the top of a tower in Westfall. Her sister deliberately didn't play until she felt she was old enough to appreciate it; she finally got the awe thing from meeting Gaffer Gamgee early on in *LotRO*.

This is why my heart sinks whenever I hear of the latest virtual worlds being thrust on 7-year-olds. That's too young for someone to realize how special such places are, but old enough for them to assimilate the concept into their view of the mundane. For today's children, their best shot at experiencing the awe and wonder of MMOs has been kicked aside; basically, they've been to London on a school trip.

Damn you, BarbieGirls.com!

007

Open-PvP worlds without permadeath tend not to be popular except among people who are either very good at it or who are members of a marauding gang. Ordinary players don't like being serial victims, and neither do the PvPers who become the victims once the ordinary players have all left.

Idea: make people pay to PvP. You buy a "license to kill" and it's good for one fight against another player character. Ordinary players can buy one to keep in reserve in case someone really, really annoys them (damned ninja-looters!); people who find it amusing to gank or otherwise bully people who have no chance of beating them can subsidize the game for them.

I wonder how much people would pay for such a license? $1 seems a bit low, and $100 seems high; even $30 seems high, but some of these PvPers are likely to be very rich individuals who will happily pay a premium if it means they can hunt down an unwilling yet intelligent opponent. Maybe, to lessen the inconvenience, victims of PvP should receive a proportion of the fee?

It works as a revenue model for big game hunting in Africa (well, apart from the sharing-the-fee-with-the-victim part)…

Rights of the Person

In the real world, people have "rights of the person." This includes, for example, the right to control their own bodies and minds. Rights of the person form a subcategory of human rights in general. That doesn't imply they're not open to debate, though: what it means for abortion and for recreational drug use is still the subject of heated discussion.

One of the concepts that falls within the purview of rights of the person is that of identity. You have the right to be you.

So should rights of the person be extended from the real-world you to the digital you in MMOs?

This isn't a pointless academic question designed to show you how widely read in philosophy I am (mainly because a moment's exposure to an actual philosopher would demonstrate how little I in fact know about the subject). The thing is, at the moment almost all conversation concerning what players can and can't do in MMOs is framed in terms of property law. This allows for great unfairness on the part of developers, because the MMO is their property. Would it perhaps be better if the relationship between player and character were framed in terms of rights of the person, rather than rights of access to virtual property owned by the developer?

On the face of it, yes, it would. However, on closer inspection it's not as clear-cut. Much of what MMOs have to offer players in terms of identity comes from the fact that rights of the person do *not* extend into the virtual world. When you play a virtual world, you can "be who you want to be"; if you can't do that (because the over-imposition of identity rights means that you're always grounded to be the person society deems you to be), then it hacks away a key reason people find MMOs attractive.

Different virtual worlds are amenable to identity protection to greater or lesser extents (something like *Second Life* might benefit from it in ways that would hurt *World of Warcraft*, for example), and it's always possible to conceive of an MMO where a digital identity should be kept very separate from a real-world identity as it's "part of the game." A virtual world based on the 1960s TV series *The Prisoner* might be like that, for example.

That said, focusing on identity rather than property may be worth a look. This is why philosophers such as Ren Reynolds (of the Virtual Policy Network[2]) are doing just that. It's better to have people who understand both MMOs and human rights look at this, rather than leaving the job to people (such as me) who understand one very well but have only a superficial understanding of the other.

---

[2]The Virtual Policy Network http://www.virtualpolicy.net/

One thing *is* clear, though: painting all virtual worlds with the same broad strokes of law without allowing for different fidelities is going to do more harm than good.

Irony

When it comes to daily newspapers, one of the advantages of reading *The Independent* is that it offers such a rich vein of rant-friendly material. It sees itself as progressive and liberal, but it's hamstrung by its snobbish pro-arts, anti-science attitudes. I love these contradictions!

I was reading its weekly radio review in one issue, in which the author was complaining about the presence of trailers for celebrity TV programs (on the not unreasonable grounds that if radio listeners liked celebrities, then they wouldn't be listening to the radio); all was fine, until it ended with this pot-shot at computer games:

> I don't recall anyone saying that the novel offers a degree of narrative richness and potential which the video game cannot even begin to. Games can't even do irony.

No *irony* in computer games? Uh? So *Grand Theft Auto* is some kind of gritty, urban drama and I've been misreading it all these years?

This is what finally tipped me over to stop reading *The Independent* and switch to *The Guardian*…

Volunteer Army

In the olde days, customer service in MMOs was performed by volunteers. In return for a free account, you had super powers in the virtual world which you used to sort out complaints from your fellow players. This is how it was for over 20 years, and things seemed to work.

Then, in 2000, as a result of a successful class-action lawsuit brought against America Online by its unpaid volunteer moderators, things changed. A bunch of *Ultima Online* players were inspired to bring an action against Electronic Arts, claiming that they, too, should be paid at least the minimum wage for their time spent servicing customers. Given that for a free *UO* account and a $500 monthly "thank you," a top community leader spent up to 40 hours a week operating to a schedule and managing a team of 90 other volunteers,[3] you can perhaps see why they might consider it an underpaid job.

Not all MMOs were quite so demanding of their volunteers, of course; however, as a result of the AOL lawsuit, most of them stopped their volunteer programs almost overnight. There remains some flexibility for worlds operating outside US borders, but not much. Nowadays, customer service staff are paid for their time; whether those employed in a call center abroad get the same deal as those local to the MMO's main customer base is another matter, of course.

So how is it that MMOs in beta test with 200,000 or more volunteers performing directed, unpaid "work" (often to schedules) don't also run afoul of the minimum-wage clauses of the Fair Labor Standards Act?

Old Attitudes Die Hard

From http://www.bbc.co.uk/games/:

> *Following a review of the BBC's online service, it was decided to close the games portal because its value to audiences was not sufficient to outweigh the risk of negative market impact.*

Games have *negative market impact?*

This was in 2005. In 2010 the BBC went back into games with an announcement of a *Doctor Who* portfolio.

Not so negative after all, then?

---

[3]Janelle Brown: *Volunteer Revolt*. Salon.com, September 2000. http://www.salon.com/2000/09/21/ultima_volunteers/

Contradictory Policies

So, I was attending an intergovernmental conference on Internet security policy in Reykjavik, Iceland, and in two separate sessions was told the following:

- Virtual world operators should keep personal data on their players for a maximum of two weeks, in order to protect their players' privacy.

- Virtual world operators should keep personal data on their players for a minimum of one year, in case the security services need access.

Oh, well. Should these both become law, then I guess it's up to individual operators to decide under which one they prefer to be prosecuted.

Long Arm of the Lore

In late 2009, some guy wanted in Indiana fled to Ontario to escape the law. However, he continued to play *World of Warcraft*; Blizzard passed his details to the police, and the Mounties picked him up.

Yeah, yeah, that's all very interesting, but the question all *WoW* players wanted answering was: what faction did he play?

Yes! Horde! Ha!

Preserving for Literature

Students of literature begin with the fact that the same text today does not mean what it did in the past: language and symbols gradually change in meaning over time. More importantly, today's readers are not the readers of the past: Twenty-First-Century Jane Austen is not Nineteenth-Century Jane Austen. Although books are situated in their historical contexts, they always remain open to interpretation by new readers.

A Games Studies expert looking at an old game isn't trying to extract old meaning from old symbols: they're trying to extract new symbols, to which they attribute new meaning. The designer ceded authorial control the moment the game was published: it became an artifact for players in general to interpret however they choose. If you play a 1985 game for fun, does it matter whether it's 1985-player fun?

In practical terms, this means that from a literature-style perspective, content is more important to preserve than form. Physical hardware is important only as an object of fetish, in that its existence as a direct link to the past might inspire certain players to take an interest that they otherwise wouldn't. However, it should be remembered that for multi-player games, "content" doesn't simply mean the embodiment of rules in software: other players are content, too.

A Question of Emphasis

Should MMOs have special servers for people who want to play as homosexual or bisexual characters?

No, they shouldn't.

There may, however, be an argument for having special servers where the over-religious, the closed-minded, and the "Eww, it creeps me out" brigade can go so the rest of the world can play in peace.

Suppose…

Suppose you are playing an MMO set in the present day. Further suppose that you are a devout female follower of Islam, and feel uncomfortable that your avatar is showing her hair.

Let's say that the developer has not created any headscarves for avatars to wear. Under the UN human rights laws regarding religious expression, could the developer be made to add headscarves? *Should* the developer be made to do so?

What if the game were set in medieval Europe? How about Ancient Greece, 1,500 years before Islam was founded? What if your character were an elf in a Fantasy game? What if you were male playing a female character?

Suppose…

Suppose you are playing an MMO set in the present day. Further suppose that you are not a devout female follower of Islam, and feel uncomfortable that your avatar is not showing her hair.

Let's say that the developer has created headscarves for avatars to wear and that you can't take them off. Under the UN human rights laws regarding religious expression, could the developer be made to create removable headscarves? *Should* the developer be made to do so?

What if the game were set in medieval Asia Minor? How about Judea, 1,500 years before Islam was founded? What if your character were a mage in an *Arabian Nights* game? What if you were male playing a female character?

Human Rights and MMOs #12

MMOs have all the issues that I have so far outlined under the banner of human rights, plus many more. They're where all the action is concerning human rights and games, and also the reason I've been rambling on about this somewhat remote area of law.

MMOs get a tier to themselves because they are played by unmanageably large numbers of players for often very different reasons (not all of which are legitimate). The basic groundwork in this area was done by Raph Koster in his *A Declaration of the Rights of Avatars*, which I've mentioned previously. Basically, it comes down to "If you don't like it, don't play."

I've already discussed some of the implications of this, which on the face of it don't look good in terms of the human rights of players. A great swathe of human rights conventions concerns the relationship between the individual and the state, but earlier I went to great pains to explain why it is that MMO developers are the *gods* of worlds, not the governments of states; these rights are therefore inapplicable. Also, I've explained how and why it is that the freedom of speech of designers trumps that of their players, so that although players may believe they have a right (of expression) to play just how they want to play, actually they don't.

I've also gone into some detail about property in MMOs, which is another HR issue. I concluded that although there's no basic problem with the concept of the real-world ownership of virtual property, it's in the best interests of everyone for the developer of an MMO to retain that ownership rather than cede it to players.

In 2010, a ship in *EVE Online* was attacked and destroyed, along with its cargo of 74 pilot license extensions with a face value of $1,295; how does that sit with article 17.2 *UDHR*, which says that no one should be arbitrarily deprived of their property? Was the attack arbitrary? Pilot license extensions are essentially pre-paid monthly subscriptions, bought from CCP (the developer of *EVE Online*): are they property? If so, can CCP properly claim they own them?

Article 27.2 *UDHR* talks about the right of an individual to protection of the moral interests in their artistic creations. I've suggested that developers should assert that any user-created content was actually a joint creation, in order not to be at the mercy of players who assert their rights only after their content has been thoroughly embedded. Again, this is an area where players come off worse than they might have hoped; again, it's because if they did have the rights they feel they should have, MMOs would be unable to function.

Immersion is another problem for MMOs and human rights. If player and character are (in that player's mind) one and the same, then what you do to the character, you do to its player. There's a whole frame removed from the equation. This means that if I'm playing an educational game in which I am a serf and I get treated badly, OK, so I gain some insight—but if I'm immersed, I'm *actually suffering emotionally*. Isn't that a security-of-person issue? If someone ganks me, isn't that a real assault of some kind? Remember *A Rape in Cyberspace*?

You can probably deduce from this that although there is a lot I *could* say about HR and MMOs, I've already said pretty well all of it in this book. That's the point. Human rights may have been framed primarily to hold tyrannies to account, but they do apply to the more mundane aspects of life, too. Because they are in theory inalienable and universal, they stand above local laws and constitutions. This means that they could be wielded against MMOs at any point; it's therefore a good idea for MMO developers to marshal their defenses as a precaution—especially given that in all the examples I've cited, what initially seems the "correct" ruling could well be disastrous if acted upon.

It's not just for these reasons that I've been talking about MMOs and HR, though. In considering human rights, we get to look at what MMOs actually *are*. We come to understand what we're making, why we're making it, why it's important, what it means for us, …

We also get to look at what MMOs *will be*, which is the top tier of the hierarchy.

Not Pleased

On the front page of *The Guardian* on March 25, 2010, there was a summary of the previous day's budget. Here's what they had to say about the tax relief that the computer game industry had been demanding for the previous three years:

> **The geek dividend.** *New tax breaks are coming to halt the exodus abroad of game-inventing nerds.*

What the hell? I switched to *The Guardian* from *The Independent* because of the latter's smug, anti-technology attitudes, but here was *The Guardian* doing exactly the same thing! If the government had given tax breaks to the British fashion industry, would we have seen a summary saying it was to stop the exodus of self-obsessed airheads abroad? No, we wouldn't.

The Guardian would be advised to remember that well over half its readership actually plays computer games. With attitudes like this, they can expect an exodus of readers to the Internet. The BBC may have its faults, but it doesn't call game developers geeks and nerds as a form of insult.

Data Exposure

In an effort to show that they are not giving particular players preferential treatment, some virtual worlds make their processes transparent. For example, in *Second Life* it's relatively easy to find out who owns what land. This is all well and good, but it leads to *data exposure*. You may trust the developer not to misuse your data, but do you trust your fellow players?

Most MMOs will allow you to discover who's logged in at any particular time. This is useful information for criminals looking for a house to break into. If they can tie your virtual identity to your real identity, they can tell whether you're probably at home or not.

How would they do that? Voice chat is a good place to start. The chances are that it's offloaded from the server and operated peer-to-peer. This means that the sophisticated criminal can get your IP address. They can cross-index that with the marketing database they bought from the legitimate web site you gave your name and address to once. Voila.

If this seems a little far-fetched, well, yes, it probably is at the moment. However, you only need to look at the level of organization exhibited by gold farmers to realize what's possible when groups of people working on the wrong side of the EULA put their minds to it. If that kind of professional approach were directed at gathering data from MMOs, privacy issues would suddenly become a lot more visible than they are right now.

Scare-mongering—it's such fun!

Human Rights and MMOs #13

Can nonhumans have human rights?

Suppose, as I mentioned earlier in a "take as long as you want" way, that some-one created an MMO with NPCs so sophisticated that you couldn't tell them apart in-world from player characters. Do these NPCs have human rights?

They're sentient and sapient. They're based on humans. They may not even know they're artificial. They're in the same position that we would be in if we suddenly found out that our universe was a computer simulation. Do they have human rights?

Could you treat them inhumanely if the only reason they were created was so you *could* do that? If you wanted to plan for what to do if, say, an asteroid hit Earth, then you might create a virtual Earth and kill millions of virtual Earthlings by smashing a virtual asteroid into them. Is that OK? Those people wouldn't have existed anyway without you. Then again, the same could be said for your real-world children.

The main issue of human rights for the distant future concerns not what it means to be human, but what it means to be *you*.

Fortunately, MMOs are very good when it comes to ascertaining what it means to be you.

Oh, the Irony

So, I gave an open-ended interview in *Second Life* as part of their *Future Salon* series. It was two hours long, the first of which I spent answering questions as to the relative merits of text and graphics. Given that *Second Life*'s players are graphics evangelists to the very core of their being, and that there were 50 or so of them in the audience, I felt reasonably happy to come out of it with my first life still intact.

When I used to do this kind of Q&A thing on CompuServe in the late 1980s, they had interview software that meant the only questions I saw were the ones that the moderator sent my way. *Second Life* is not so fascistic, though, so I had questions coming thick and fast from all over. The only way I could keep track was to expand my text window to occupy 80% of the screen.

If people want to argue that graphics are better than text, why do they do so in text?

Last Straws

There was once a moderately experienced *MUD1* player who delighted in ganking newbies and taking their stuff. This was against the policy of the game, so he was told not to do it. He kept doing it, however, despite repeated warnings, so in the end I banned him.

He immediately went onto the forum and complained that I had banned him for killing a newbie. Lots of people killed newbies: it was unfair to ban him, he was being picked on, the game sucked, and people were stupid for playing it.

Well no, he wasn't banned for killing a newbie. He was banned for killing *yet another* newbie having been told very patiently for weeks that he wasn't to do it.

Whenever customer service reps punish a player for something that was the last straw, the player will almost invariably present it as being for *just that one* straw.

A Little Pleased

Remember that reference to "the geek dividend" I mentioned which appeared in *The Guardian*? The one that disparagingly referred to "game-inventing nerds"? You must, it was only like a page ago.

Well, I was sufficiently incensed that I wrote to *The Guardian* to rant at them about it.

It's something I regularly did when I took *The Guardian*, not because I expected to see my email in print but because I wanted to let them know they were out of line. However, on this occasion they actually published my tirade. I therefore believe I may inadvertently have stumbled upon a formula for attracting their attention:

> Bloody hell! What kind of vapid ignorance is this?! I switched to The Guardian from The Independent because of the latter's anti-technology attitudes, and yet here you are pandering to the same smug, outdated, luddite views! Grow up!
>
> **Professor Richard Bartle**
>
> *School of computer science and electronic engineering, University of Essex*

Swear at them.

Words and Pictures

If you layer text over graphics, you're conceding that text is superior to graphics. Likewise, if you accompany words with pictures, you're conceding that graphics are superior to text.

Both are superior for some things and inferior for others.

The point is, when you're immersed in an MMO, they amount to the same thing: how you see the world *in your mind*.

It's a Trial

I once gave a talk to some students from a university in Texas. Given that I was separated from them by an ocean and half a continent, naturally the best place to conduct it was in an MMO. The chosen venue was *EverQuest 2*, because that's what all the students were using.

At the time, I didn't have *EQ2* installed on my PC, but hey, that was OK, Sony Online Entertainment did a *Trial of the Isle* edition that covered the first 6 levels for free—I could use that.

So I downloaded it; no problem there. Then I installed it; that went well, too. Then I ran it.

It began a patch. Not just any patch, though, ohhhh no: this was a patch that it estimated would take 12 hours, 47 minutes and 58 seconds. I don't know if that's how long it *did* take, as I went to bed with 6 hours of it left to run and it was finished when I woke up next morning.

Way to go, SOE. Provide people with a free download and then hit them with a 12-hour patch. As newbie-friendly experiences go, I've had better.

Yes, I am aware that I wasn't actually intending to buy *EQ2* and was therefore freeloading and so have no right to complain anyway—but I *could* have been a newbie.

MMOs and Bad Press

MMOs have lots of allegations thrown at them by mainstream media, but so far no one has seriously proposed that they inculcate child abusers. The finger is occasionally pointed at the Internet at large, but not MMOs. Why is this so?

Well, it's because MMOs are populated entirely by inarticulate, spotty, teenage boys who never wash or change clothes.

Most of the time, false stereotypes work against us. However, on rare occasions they do work *for* us.

Preserving for Art

You can look at the Mona Lisa as a document of Sixteenth Century Tuscan life. You can look on it as an enigmatic image of a beautiful woman.

You can also look on it as an expression of artistic intent.

In this view, the artist is attempting to convey a message through his (in the case of Leonardo da Vinci) work. By experiencing the work, an expert can divine the artist's meaning.

A game expert playing old games gains insight into the minds of the creators of those games. They see how ideas develop and change over time. They can tell a Molyneux game from a Meier game as easily as they can tell a Mozart piece from a Beatles piece. In gaining this understanding, they are better able to create their own games.

If the designers and critics of the future are to understand how things got to be how they get to be, then games must be preserved. Only by understanding the rules can you willfully break them; only by understanding what has been said can you disagree; only by reading can you learn to write.

As for what to preserve, well for a good designer, the rules and the interface could be enough—they may well be able to extrapolate from there. They'd need to know about the context, but being designers they probably have an above-average understanding of that anyway.

For everyone else, though?

Prime Minister Suspect

In January 2008, Gordon Brown, at the time Prime Minister of the UK, announced his intention to stop developers from creating computer games that featured knives as weapons. This was in response to public concern over rising knife-crime figures.

Goodness knows what he would have said if he'd found out we had fireballs.

Human Rights and MMOs #14

To wrap up this long and full-of-unanswered-questions look at human rights and MMOs, here are some guiding principles for if you ever need to argue about the place of MMOs in society with people who don't play them (or with people who do play them but who are argumentative):

- Always remember that it's *players*, not characters, who have the rights.

- There is an implicit covenant between designers and players that affects rights.

- The relationship of player to developer is that of mortal to god, not of citizen to state.

- Frames and the magic circle are crucial.

- It's possible that the assertion of a right could be self-defeating (for example, being allowed to preach real-world religions in a strongly role-playing Fantasy world would kill it).

- Lots of this applies to simulations and to social worlds. Don't assume that game worlds are entirely unique.

Players who temporarily consent to giving up a right in order to gain what they see as a benefit will not like the interference of do-gooders. Always ask *why* a human right exists before mindlessly applying it.

Tomorrow's Lost History

Buying virtual goods for real money (whether allowed or disallowed by the MMO's operator) could become so endemic and so established that it's impossible to play an MMO that doesn't include it.

If it does become culturally expected, rather than merely grudgingly accepted, we could reach a stage where people don't even realize they ever had a *choice* about engaging in it, and never know that there used to be MMOs in which you could succeed through your strength of spirit and character rather than your willingness to part with your real-world wealth.

Local maxima are not always global maxima.

Preserving MMOs

All this about preserving computer games is fine and dandy, but MMOs aren't games: they're places. As with any place, the people who live there are part of the place.

What MMOs *are* is bound up with who inhabits them. You can't separate the two without missing half the picture. An MMO's players are an intrinsic part of the historical context, of the artifact created and of the medium through which any authorial message is delivered.

Preserving only the software of an MMO is like preserving only the buildings of a city. It's better than nothing, but its study basically amounts to archaeology. If we're preserving for a purpose, we need to help people *use* what we preserve; for MMOs, that means preserving the *players* in addition to the world.

Now I've looked into this, and apparently the cryogenic suspension of random players comes with some tiresome legal and moral implications. So, if we can't preserve the players themselves, the next-best solution would be to preserve studies of them.

Aha! There is actually a discipline for studying communities: Anthropology. Unfortunately, you can only undertake an anthropological study while your MMO is alive and well. That means we need to have anthropologists out there in the field playing MMOs *now* if we want to hope to preserve the essence of such worlds for future generations to study.

This isn't as simple as it sounds: the MMOs themselves change (the *WoW* of today is not the *WoW* of a decade ago); the players change over time; there can be cultural differences between servers. Despite all this, we could still help the people for whom we're preserving MMOs by doing things such as videoing people playing at various stages in their player career, collating the design documents, interviewing the designers and developers, ... The key is to archive what we think the people 200 years from now will need to know if they're to make sense of what we're preserving.

Today's MMOs will profoundly influence tomorrow's society. It's *essential* that we preserve them.

We're not going to, though, are we?

General Ignorance

British satirical magazine *Private Eye* tries its best, bless, but it really doesn't understand technology.

> *"He used to make up imaginary friends. Now the web does it for him"*

The web, virtual worlds, yes...

Pieces of Kangaroo

It's always entertaining when mainstream museums put on exhibitions about computer games (which they invariably call *videogames*). Their earnest attempts to increase visitor numbers by being relevant to the modern world despite being clueless never fail to amuse.

It's like those reality TV shows where some "celebrity" reluctantly eats a kangaroo's testicle in order to win food for the rest of the team. They don't like the idea, they don't like the taste, they question whether what they're consuming is even fit for consumption, but they do it for the common good.

The only difference is that in the celebrity example the smiles come from bathos, whereas in the museum example they come from pathos.

Changing Society

Why should I care if playing MMOs causes players to forgo the social structures of the real world? They'll have new social structures that are every bit as valid as the ones replaced. That works fine for me.

The only difference between real-world and game-world social structures is that we get to experiment, change, and adapt our virtual worlds, so that *their* social structures *evolve*. We don't get to do that in the real world, because we can't change its physics to support such changes. The virtual world structures we create will therefore, eventually, be superior to the real-world structures that constrain us at present.

Why would anyone want that not to happen?

Human Rights and MMOs: Coda

One of the worlds developed using the *MUD1* engine was *MIST*. *MIST* was run by a tyrannical administrator (hi, Lorry!) who would regularly delete or imprison characters, dock points from them, destroy property, ban players, insult them—all arbitrarily and on a whim. Newbies could equally well find themselves showered in points of killed by a finger of death from out of nowhere.

The players loved it! It was all *part of the game*. Should MMOs like *MIST* be allowed?

Yes, yes, yes, they should be allowed!

We've Already Won

I'm talking to you, you self-righteous politicians and newspaper columnists, you relics who beat on computer games: you've already lost. Enjoy your carping while you can, because tomorrow you're gone.

The BBC microcomputer was released in 1981. It was ubiquitous in schools, introducing a generation to computers and to computer games. According to the UK Statistics Authority, the median age of the UK population is 39. This means that over half the UK population has grown up playing computer games. They aren't addicted, they aren't psychopathic killers, and they resent those boneheads—that's *you*—who imply that they *are* addicted and *are* psychopathic killers.

Dwell on this, you smug, out-of-touch, proud-to-be-innumerate fossils: over half the UK population thinks games are fun and cool, and you don't.

Next year, another generation of game-savvy individuals will get the vote. The year after, another will. Scared yet? You should be: we have the numbers on our side. Do your worst—you can't touch us. We've already won.

Soon, the prime minister of the day will have grown up playing computer games, just as 30 years previously we'd had the first prime minister to have grown up watching television, and 30 years before that to have grown up listening to radio. Times change: accept it; embrace it! Don't make yourself look even more Twentieth Century than you do already. You've lost!

Understand? *Your time has passed.*

This anxiety you sense, this fear of what you don't comprehend: hey, it's OK. Parents who didn't play computer games *do* feel alienated, *do* feel isolated from their children; they do feel frightened, and naturally so, because they can't keep their children safe if they don't understand what they're keeping them safe from.

It's transient, though. Upcoming parents played games themselves, or if they didn't, their siblings did, or their friends did. They're no more concerned about "moral decay" or "aggressive tendencies" or any of the other euphemisms for "Ohmygod I don't understand this!" than you are about daytime TV. *They're* the present, not you: you're the ever-more-distant past.

Gamers vote. Gamers buy newspapers. They won't vote for you, or buy your newspapers, if you trash their entertainment with your ignorant ravings. Call them social inadequates if you like, but when they have more friends in *World of Warcraft* than you have in your entire sad little booze-oriented culture of a real life, the most you'll get from them is pity.

So we've won: accept it. Huff and puff if you must, but your audience grows smaller by the day. Your views are mortally wounded, and soon they will be dead.

Games are mainstream. Drown, or learn to swim.

Tarred with the Same Brush

Why should we care if people call online social networks "virtual worlds"? Why should we care if they call *Farmville* an MMO?

Well, we should care because it lumps MMOs together with things that they're not. When this happens, people draw false conclusions. This can give us a bad name that we don't deserve. People used to be wary of the Internet because of all those "My husband is addicted to the Internet" stories (whereas actually he was addicted to chat rooms, or porn, or *Poker,* or whatever). If people think that Facebook is anodyne, and Facebook is a "virtual world," then they'll think *Guild Wars 2* and *Black Desert Online* are anodyne because they're also "virtual worlds."

Look up terms such as "MMO" and "virtual world" on Wikipedia if you want to know what people you've never heard of have been quietly defining them to be.

Do Not Defer

If there were large numbers of gamers in their thirties and forties warning the youth of today about the terrible consequences of playing computer games, and stopping their own children from playing them, there might be something to the assertion that computer games are A Bad Thing. This is what happens with drug abuse, for example; the old fogeys who warn about the consequences of messing with brain chemistry are replaced by new fogeys who, having decided to ignore the old fogeys, find themselves agreeing with them in the light of their experience.

With games, though, we don't see people who grew up playing them begging their own children "Just say no." What we see is them telling their children that they can't go on the PlayStation until they've finished their homework, much the same as their own parents wouldn't let them watch TV until they'd finished their homework.

I've had it with anti-games people and their selective use of bad research to justify their prejudices. I don't see why we should defer to *any* of them any more, knocking down their arguments patiently, one at a time, waiting for them to repeat their damaging assertions regardless. All we have to do is tell them they've lost. It doesn't matter what charts they wheel out, what distressed mothers who lost their children to *World of Warcraft* they parade, what opinions they state as fact: they've been overtaken by events. They may as well be Zeus-worshippers for all the relevance they have.

The Byron Report

In March 2008, the Byron Report, *Safer Children in a Digital World*, came out.[4]

How pleased the British government must have been with itself! By appointing a parenting expert, Dr. Tanya Byron, to lead it, they were practically guaranteeing they'd get 266 pages of ammunition to use against computer games. Just thinking about the popularity boost from cracking down on this evil would have had them salivating with glee!

Except that Dr. Byron was born in 1967. When the Sinclair ZX Spectrum came out in 1982, she was only 15. She knew what the government didn't: computer games are here to stay. So long as parents understand the dangers, they can make informed decisions. She didn't recommend lining game designers up against the wall and shooting dead every last one of them. Her report was balanced and fair. She suggested *education* as a solution—education of the *parents*.

That's a level of reason rarely seen in the context of UK government.

---

[4]Tanya Byron: Safer *Children in a Digital World: the Report of the Byron Review*. Department for Children, Schools and Families, March 27, 2008. http://dl.uksites.futureus.com/cvg/static/7578-ByronReview- Bookmarked.pdf

Queen's Counsel

The Times, December 4, 2008. Cartoon: *Queen's Counsel.*

Panel 1:

> Lawyer A: I can't believe a woman would sue for divorce just because her husband had an affair in *"Second Life"*.

Panel 2:

> Lawyer A: What is society coming to when people litigate because of a fantasy website?

Panel 3:

> Lawyer A: Next thing you know … people will be…

Panel 4:

> Lawyer B: Opening a divorce law practice on *Second Life?*
>
> Lawyer A: Exactly! Why didn't I think of it before?

Real-world law firms had had a presence in *Second Life* for some time before this cartoon appeared (a fact which had even been reported in *The Times* itself), so it wasn't entirely a new idea. Still, it was nice to see virtual worlds appearing in the mainstream press as things you can joke *about*, rather than as jokes themselves.

Breaking Up

Over the years, I've seen real-life weddings as a result of MMO romances, and I've seen real-life divorces, too. The weddings have been outnumbered by the divorces by a ratio somewhere between five and ten to one, but times are changing as games in general and MMOs in particular become more mainstream.

The reasons for the divorces don't change a great deal, though, and can typically be characterized in of one of the following ways:

- **Distance.** One partner plays the MMO, in so doing consuming a great deal of their free time. The other partner feels neglected. If the nonplayer can hold on for 18 months without either leaving home or having an affair, then the player will come out of it and things will return to normal. The cause of the problem here is basically that the nonplayer neither understands what the player is doing nor why. If it was something "normal," as going down to the pub every night is in some places, there wouldn't be an issue—lots of people who are happily married still like to have some time to themselves. It's the fact that the nonplayer doesn't understand (or, worse, they misunderstand) what's going on that's at the heart of the break-up. I expect that a generation down the line, time spent playing games will be better understood as a social activity and people won't be any more worried by it than they would if their partner were to drop in at the gym after work or whatever.

- **Temptation.** One partner plays the MMO and the magnifying of emotions they experience plus the degree of anonymity they enjoy leads to their having an affair with another player. I've watched these unfold, and although they can be very intense for about a month they will then often start to slide. The parties will frequently look for other online lovers to try to recapture the feeling, so it's not entirely a case of "wait a couple of months and you'll get your wife back," but it can be close to that. Nevertheless, there's a trust issue here. Sure, your spouse hasn't had a physical affair with someone else, but a nonphysical affair is still an affair. What the aggrieved partner does as a result depends on the extent to which they understand this, with the current tendency being to err on the side of forgiveness. Nevertheless, I expect that as more people come to understand what MMOs are, the more this kind of activity is likely to lead to marriage break-ups (although it can also strengthen marriages if the philanderer comes to believe that the affair was a mistake).

- **Touchstone.** The marriage is in trouble anyway, and the MMO is merely a catalyst that brings on what was always inevitable. If it didn't happen online, then it would happen at work, at social events, outside school or wherever. It always has, and it always will. You can get a happy ending out of this, as when two people meet each other virtually and leave existing unfulfilling relationships to start anew, but even so it's not without side-effects (because those unfulfilling relationships still have to be left).

Well wasn't that was a jolly monologue?

Glitterball

GCHQ is the UK's Government Communications Headquarters. Its primary purpose is intelligence-gathering, especially the intercepting and decryption of communication signals.

In July 2014, it was revealed that among the tools that GCHQ has in its armory is Glitterball, the description of which reads "Online Gaming Capabilities for Sensitive Operations. Currently Second Life."[5]

Second Life today, whatever MMO you're playing tomorrow?

Don't assume that what you say in a virtual world stays in that virtual world.

The *Mass Effect* Effect

It's July 22, 2013, the day the eldest son of the eldest son of the eldest son of the Queen is born, and the hottest day in seven years. I am in the feebly air-conditioned underground offices of the Department for Business, Innovation and Skills in London for a roundtable discussion regarding the draft Consumer Rights Bill, which affects digital goods and services such as MMOs.

I do this so you don't have to.

At one point, among a group of 30 or 40 people interested in every piece of digital content except games (TV, music, anti-virus software, mobile phone apps), I ask for reassurances (which were given) that if a game has an unsatisfactory ending, that doesn't mean it can be regarded as an unsatisfactory product for which players can ask for their money back. I mention the ending of *Mass Effect 3* as an example.

There is laughter in the audience. These people may be there to represent nongame digital content delivery systems, but they know about *Mass Effect 3*. Some of them are in their twenties, but most are in their thirties and forties. They're game-aware.

To those who still think that playing games is deviant behavior: your days are numbered. Time is on our side. We're coming for you.

---

[5]GCWiki: *JTRIG tools and techniques*. GCHQ. 2012. https://s3.amazonaws.com/s3.documentcloud.org/documents/1217406/jtrigall.pdf

Showing Respect

In December, 2011, *The Economist* had a special on computer games. Here's the opening line of the article:

> IN NOVEMBER 2010 *"Call of Duty: Black Ops"* was released.

It's great to see a major international publication according games the same kind of respect they accord other works of art (such as movies or books) by putting the names of games in quotation marks (or italics). I've been moaning about the mainstream printed media's not doing this for years.

If only a few more people who work in the game industry itself italicized game names, they might realize what artistic power we *have* here.

Industry Support

Here's some advice for governments out there that are looking at ways to support their MMO industry. Note to the UK government: you don't have to read this, I've already told you it.

- Don't disparage games. The UK lost its film industry because mere entertainment was considered vulgar whereas documentaries were worthy. Most of the movies we watch today hail from Hollywood, which had no such issues of cultural snobbery. With MMOs, we're seeing research money being ploughed into making "serious games," but none going to making "fun games." There isn't even a research council that covers the concept in its brief. Stop treating MMOs as if they were the stuff of children; they're not. They're here because of how they entertain, not for their business or education potential.

- Move on from the old stereotypes. Half the population of the UK was born in the 1970s or later. They grew up playing games. MMOs are here to stay. All this "they're addictive" or "they incite violence" or "they turn people into pedophiles" nonsense is just that: nonsense. Move on. Take games seriously as creative endeavors.

- Give the industry some respect. How are we going to get investors to put money into MMO development if people think the industry is geek heaven? Bring it into the cultural establishment. Hand out a few medals or honors: it's not expensive.

- Be careful to whom you listen. There are high-profile academics and non-MMO developers willing to pontificate about MMOs without actually having any deep understanding of them. There are others who are world-class. Solicit many views.

- Make the legal status of MMOs clear. Issue guidelines saying what is and isn't OK, what's optional and what's mandatory, what you will do as a government and what you won't. Lack of clarity is a big obstacle to investment, and if you can provide that clarity through a formal set of government guidelines, that could be a big help.

Oh, there's also tax breaks, but everyone asks for tax breaks so there's no surprise there...

Ask Dr. Psycho

From this week's *Practical Serial Killer:*

Dear Dr. Psycho

My son hopes to grow up to perpetrate mass shootings, because he's really into blood. In the past, you've recommended the TV news as a reliable source of gore, but I don't want to depress him with the stories of political chaos and economic gloom which all too often mar these otherwise excellent programs.

Can you perhaps suggest a computer game he could play that will satisfy his blood lust—but without the grim figures about rising inflation and falling house prices?

—Bella

Dear Bella

Your son should feel really proud that he has such a caring and protective mother; I, for one, hadn't considered the effects of discussing economic downturns on the young, impressionable mind. Kudos to you!

Unfortunately, I am unable to suggest a computer game that will help your son realize his dream of mowing down his school friends in a hail of bullets, because, to be honest, games are simply not realistic enough. The blood looks like red gloop; it doesn't wet clothes, it doesn't mat hair, and it doesn't pool properly.

However, there is an alternative! Many soap operas routinely show beatings in their storylines, and their make-up artists are experts in making the results look realistic. As a bonus, soaps will usually feature at least one role model for would-be killers such as your son—a positive attitude for which they rarely get the credit they deserve.

All this—and not a Chancellor of the Exchequer in sight!

—Dr. Psycho

Clash of Cultures

How to turn something fun into something boring:

I guess we can be thankful it wasn't *Monopoly* turned into an MMO.

(And for all you *WoW* fans who want to know what the most expensive property is: it's Darnassus).

X-Men Movie Addict

The front-page headline of the *Daily Mirror* for Monday, May 25, 2015 reads:

WOLVERINE FAN IS HUNTED OVER MURDERS

X-Men movie addict's mum, sister and stepdad are knifed to death

This was, as you might expect, a tragic story; the murderer was found the next day having committed suicide in a wood. Still, if you have newspapers to sell, you want a sensationalist headline so you go for—

Wait, what? He's an "X-Men movie addict," not a "video games addict"? Why is that?

Perhaps the result of the poll of *Daily Mirror* readers on page 40 of the same edition of the newspaper might be making itself felt:

Do you think video games are bad for you?

YES 30%

NO 70%

Face it, anti-games people: you've lost.

Be Proud, America!

Back in 2003, I attended the first *State of Play* conference, held at New York Law School. After it was finished, there was a limited-invite roundtable at which the director of the US government's eRulemaking initiative[6] and the Assistant General Counsel at the Department of Transport listened to suggestions as to how games could be used to educate US citizens regarding the process of commenting on public policy.

I didn't say much, because it wasn't really my place to lecture on ways to improve the democracy of a country I was visiting as a guest.

I would like to note, however, that I was hugely impressed that two high-ranking US government officials were willing to sit down with a bunch of game designers (and researchers interested in game design) to ask our opinions. I can't conceive of anything similar happening in the UK. The closest we'd get, the "game designers" would actually be heads of game development companies, heads of organizations of game development companies, the head of whatever division British Telecom has at the moment working on what they think are games, and perhaps some economics professor specializing in "game theory." No way would they talk to the people who actually *design* games.

Be proud, America. At least you get a discussion for your technology media to mischaracterize.

Don't Quote Me

I love looking through the business cards I get at MMO conferences. People have their character name in quotes right there in the middle of their real name.

The main culprits are journalists (showing they're gamers like the rest of us) or community managers (showing they're in touch with their customers). You could see something like it from pretty well anyone, though, even academics and developers. I think it's kinda nice.

Sadly, it's not something I could get away with doing myself. Richard "Richard" Bartle doesn't really have the same impact.

---

[6]http://www.regulations.gov/

Industry Hobbling

Here's some advice for governments that are looking at ways to hobble their MMO industry. Note to the UK government: you don't have to read this, I've already told you it.

- Badly thought-out legislation. If a government decides it wants to ban MMOs, fair enough, that's its right. However, a constant worry of developer legal teams is that a well-meaning but ill-informed government could enact legislation intended to help players or developers that actually has the opposite effect. For example, bringing out laws that enforced RMT in the belief that this would "promote trade" would be a death blow.

- Unfortunate application of existing legislation. If virtual goods have real-world value, then their sale should be subject to real-world tax regulations. This might just about make sense in an MMO that allowed RMT, but for ones that don't it would be a disaster.

- Caught-in-the-crossfire laws. Laws brought out to curb, say, gambling, are worded in such a way as to cover MMOs, too. Likewise, following a character around trying to steal their stuff might be OK under a game's rules, but if the player can call on anti-stalking laws, then that puts an end to that piece of gameplay.

- Mad patent laws. Patents are supposed to reward innovation, but they rarely do. Instead, they reward stating the obvious. Things which are so blindingly self-evident that most people who work with them don't consider them as patentable nevertheless get patents awarded such that it takes the blood of 12 freshly-slain virgins to revoke them. Software patents, which are thankfully not allowed in the EU, are particularly insidious in this regard.

Oh, there's also promising us tax breaks but not giving them, so investors hold off indefinitely in the hope that sometime soon you'll be as good as your word.

Ludium II

In 2007, the Synthetic Worlds Institute ran a game (*Ludium II*), the aim of which was to come up with a list of proposals to guide real-world policy regarding virtual worlds. Here's the result:

Whereas virtual worlds are places with untapped potential, providing new and positive experiences and effects, we resolve that:

1. A self-governance group of virtual world stakeholders should be formed.

2. A players' bill of rights should be drafted and should include the right of free speech and the rights to assemble and organize.

3. A universal age verification system should be created to support the individual rights of all users.

4. Virtual world designers should have freedom of expression.

5. Virtual worlds should include plain-language End-User License Agreements (EULA) to enable all individuals to understand their rights [in addition to the legalese EULA].

6. There are different types of virtual worlds with different policy implications.

7. Access is critical to virtual worlds, so net neutrality must be maintained.

8. Game developers shall not be liable for the actions taken by players.

9. Fair use may apply in virtual worlds that enable amateur creation of original works.

10. The government should provide a comprehensive package of funding for educational games research, development, and literacy.

As a *Ludium II* player, I signed my agreement to this, although when the final text appeared I found that it didn't entirely match what I believed it was going to say. In particular, I see a conflict between points 2 and 4; I thought point 4 had priority, but apparently they simply conflict. Of the others, point 3 is impractical, point 5 assumes that all virtual worlds have EULAs (some don't need them), and point 10 is wishful thinking. All the rest are reasonable, though.

The reason this is an inconsistent hodgepodge of ideas at multiple levels of abstraction is that it was distilled during the playing of the game from dozens of competing ideas. Here's how they were derived:

1. Members of a group of three people propose ideas to get a platform of ten ideas in total. Ideas lacking the approval of at least two of the three members therefore wouldn't get through unless the group was short of ideas.

2. Three groups of three debated which ten ideas to put forward as the group of nine's platform. If subgroups had come up with similar ideas, those were merged together into one. The practice by which statements made it to the final ten was much as in the earlier round: discussion, votes if necessary, general consensus.

3. There were three groups of nine. A preliminary round of horse-trading took place between these three groups to combine their statements into single ones acceptable to all. There was a lot of this, and ideas were often watered down in the process.

4. The elected leader of each group of nine got to add a new statement of their own. One group's leader did this; the other two leaders basically sponsored existing statements.

5. A final round of voting took place to determine the final ten statements.

Given this approach, it's amazing that anything sane made it through at all. However, it did.

I'm not sure that any of the top-flight American politicians to whom a copy of the declaration was sent actually read it, though.

Jeez, I *hope* they didn't; the embarrassment…

Zeitgeist

Here's the character Spoilt Bastard, from the British adult comic, *Viz*:

It doesn't matter that *Viz* is a profanity-filled send-up of children's comics that's read mainly by students. What matters is that it can drop a casual reference to *Runescape* without having to explain what the blue cheese it is.

This strip appeared in 2007. Few of those students are students any more.

The Bleak Mundane

The steps being taken to make MMOs ubiquitous will strip most of them of their soul, and the people who are brought up playing them will regard those few that didn't sell out as oddities frequented by latter-day geeks.

Just saying...

Ask Dr. Psycho

From this week's *Practical Serial Killer:*

> *Dear Dr. Psycho*
>
> *When I was a teenager I had no trouble working myself up into a frenzy of blood lust, but as I got older I noticed that it was becoming harder and harder to get into the right frame of mind to wish to maim random strangers.*
>
> *I was therefore delighted to hear last year about MMOs—a kind of "brain training" computer game that would put the zip back in my mutilation mojo and be fun and entertaining at the same time! I bought a subscription to Age of Conan: Hyborean Adventures and played it religiously for 4 hours every evening to let it work its magic.*
>
> *Nothing happened! Worse, I now read in the newspapers that social networking sites are where all the slasher-inducement action is. Have I wasted my time playing superficial games when, if I really wanted to hurt people, I should have been insinuating myself into their lives on Facebook?*
>
> —Eric

> *Dear Eric*
>
> *Yes.*
>
> —Dr. Psycho

Be Proud, Germany!

On May 27, 2008, I was shown around the Reichstag by a member of the German parliament. The next day, I sat on a panel next to a different member of the German parliament and answered a question directed at me by a third member of the German parliament who was in the audience.

I can't conceive of anything remotely similar to this happening in the UK, yet the Germans seem to think that *they're* the ones whose legislature is behind the times.

I did try to tell them how impressed I was, but I don't think they believed me…

Real-World Extensible

Some facilities that are available in MMOs aren't available in the real world, but they should be. Take the Looking For Group channel, for example.

Suppose I'm an academic and I want to find some people to hook up with so I can trick funding agencies into giving me money. How do I do it? Right now, I can only ask people I know (my friends list) or send out a blanket request on some general channel (yell).

I *want* to be able to post to a special channel without fear that I'm going to annoy anyone with unwanted solicitations; a channel read by people who are looking to join a group (LFG) or who are looking for more members of an existing group (LFM). Anyone not LFG or LFM wouldn't have signed up to the channel and so wouldn't be bugged by constant requests of no interest to them.

How many accountants read the latest papers about game design? How many game designers read the latest papers on accountancy? OK, I'll tell you the answer: it's close to zero in both cases. If you want to do a game about accountancy (for example, to make accountancy fun or games boring), where do you look for a partner?

If there were an academic network for people LFG, then it's conceivable that I could find some group of, say, geographers from the University of Central Nowhere struggling to design a game that I could really help them with; I in turn would benefit in my own research from their knowledge of how to organize spaces. I don't know they exist, they don't know I exist: without a LFG channel, how are our paths ever going to cross?

MMO concepts that can be used in the real world are called *real-world extensible*.

You remember from when I mentioned this regarding FOD and LOL, right?

Real Life API: Consumption

CMedia::Consumption

void Consumption(CPlayer *cPlayer*, **real** *rCons***)**

- *cPlayer* Specifies which player's consumption changes.
- *rCons* Specifies the percentage rise in consumption.

Remarks

Changes by *rCons* the medium's consumption by *cPlayer*. Suggested values for *rCons* by medium are:

- Television: Large and negative
- Print media: Small and negative
- Film (including DVD/Blu-ray): Close to zero
- Online media (excluding virtual worlds): Small and positive
- Music: Small and positive
- Virtual worlds: Large and positive

Social Interaction

Sometimes, people who think all computer games are the same will criticize them for ruining human interaction. Games are not all the same, however, and MMOs in particular actually foment interaction, rather than repress it.

Human beings are very adaptable. If a game allows freeform communication, its players will communicate. They will be able to express every emotion between love and hate through the medium of that channel, even if it's only in words; after all, books have been doing that for millennia. Anyone who is worried about the effects of virtual worlds on social interaction should direct their concern at television long, long before they look at MMOs.

However, when all is said and done, *Reality* is far more detailed than virtuality can ever be. There are some forms of social interaction that you can't get any other way. *Reality* always wins in the end. A kiss in a virtual world or a kiss over the phone is never going to be the same as a kiss in real life.

It could be a prelude to one, though.

Talent-Spotting

Players are what make MMOs what they are.

Sadly for me, there's a preconception among many MMO commentators that I am somehow aloof from the general player population—and even the general designer population. I don't know how that came about, but it's definitely there. It means that anything MMO-related I say that makes it to the public domain is viewed first and foremost with this in mind. I'm deliberately massaging my own ego, or seeking legitimacy, or trying to recapture past glories, or lording it over people I regard as serfs. I know that all this and more will be rolled out in MMO-related forums when people hear about this book. Now this is fair enough if those who post have read its text (hi!) and formed their opinion as a result, but a good many won't have (although they may have read one or two of the articles, taken out of context).

I don't want to be in this position, where what I say is reported (or misreported) merely because it was me who said it. I don't want to be relevant. Other people should be way ahead now, so that when I read their articles I think, "Wow, why didn't I think of that?"

Here's the thing, though: they probably *are* there already, but we don't hear about them. I only have to post on a blog read by fewer than 100 people and I'm torn to shreds in forum posts I don't even see until months later. Other people are probably writing great stuff elsewhere, but they're not noticed because there's no "Kill the boss and win a nice blue" kudos in attacking them.

I urge you, if you see something you like, that takes MMOs in a new direction, that says something that makes you *think* (you don't have to *agree* with it—so long as it makes you think), please give it publicity. Tweet about it, blog about it, link to it on your favorite social media site.

Do this, and eventually, we'll have MMO commentators who genuinely deserve attention, not people who are merely where they are through an accident of history (which is the case for me).

Genius

When you look at the creativity of past generations, the major scientific discoveries and works of art were generally made by people from a very small social stratum. The same applies to the philosophical writings of the ancient world: there were only a relatively few people in a social class that allowed for the kind of free time necessary to think about such things.

I don't believe that people in one social class are brighter or more imaginative than those in another. I don't believe that people from one culture are brighter or more imaginative than those from another, either. There are geniuses scattered everywhere.

So where are they?

Is it simply that society is missing them, or is it that they're somehow being prevented from harnessing their genius by social conditions aimed squarely at the mediocre and by gatekeepers denying access to opportunity? If Newton and Einstein and Darwin and Aristotle and Alhazen and Pasteur and Faraday had been born the children of farmhands, what would have happened to their genius then? If they'd been born female, what would have happened to it?

You're smart. For all I know—for all *you* know—you're a genius. Be inspired! If anything in this book has given you ideas, run with them! Let loose your imagination. Soar!

Genius isn't rare, it's just rarely discovered.

Game Graffiti

I was driving along the M23, heading in the direction of Gatwick Airport, when I overtook a Star Alliance airline truck. It was filthy on the back, and so of course some wag had written in the dirt.

They'd crossed out the word "Alliance" and underneath had put "Horde."

Anatomy

I've said a lot about MMOs in this book and its companion, *MMOs from the Inside Out*. If I were to write them again ten years from now, I'd still say a lot; however, it would be a different lot.

The field of MMO design is more unknown than known; so much so, in fact, that not only is it waiting to be discovered, it's waiting to be *shaped*. The worlds we create today will determine the direction taken by the worlds we create tomorrow.

All would-be physicians begin their studies with anatomy. Anatomy has been well understood for hundreds, if not thousands of years; nevertheless, everyone entering the medical profession has to understand it, because if they don't, they'll have a hard time understanding anything else.

For MMOs, these books book are like anatomy. That doesn't mean they're "an anatomy of MMOs"; it means the books describe the basics of what you need to know if you're to design MMOs. They point at some interesting features worth investigating, and even go into some of them in a little depth. However, they can't tell you everything there is to know about making MMOs because most of this is still to *be* known. All they can tell you is a portion of the basics.

MMOs can and will be so much more than they are at present. To future generations of players, *World of Warcraft* will be like *MUD1* is to today's players and *Metropolis* is to today's film audiences: revolutionary for its day, recognizably a part of the same art form, but left behind as the medium has moved on.

As for who's going to move the medium on: you are. All it will take is for you to break free. Stop looking at MMOs in terms of what they are today, and instead think in terms of what you *would* want them to be like if you'd never, ever played one.

You have an idea for a world that's different from anything you've ever seen? That's fresh and different? That *says* something?

Good. Now *design* it.

Real Life API—Exceptions

CException: public CObject

Remarks

CException is the base class for all exceptions in the Real Life foundation class library. Because **CException** is an abstract class, you must create objects of derived classes. Derived classes and their descriptions are listed below.

Class	Description
CSocialException	Undefined societal change.
CTechnicalException	Undefined technology change.
CEnvironmentException	Undefined environmental change.
CPhilosophyException	Undefined moral or philosophical change.
CTransitionException	Undefined transitional change.
CLifeException	Undefined quality of life change.

A Time and Place

Imagine you are standing on a badly-paved road with a cemetery to the north and the home of a grave-digger to the south. An inscription on the cemetery gates reads, "RESTING PLACE OF LOST SOULS".

In late 1978, that's where I was.

Thirty years later, I stood on the rim of the Sholazar Basin and gazed down onto its green, steamy mangrove swamp.

Where will I be in another thirty years?

Who knows? All I can say is that it hasn't been created yet and I desperately want to be there.

Index

Get the eBook for only $5!

Why limit yourself?

Now you can take the weightless companion with you wherever you go and access your content on your PC, phone, tablet, or reader.

Since you've purchased this print book, we're happy to offer you the eBook in all 3 formats for just $5.

Convenient and fully searchable, the PDF version enables you to easily find and copy code—or perform examples by quickly toggling between instructions and applications. The MOBI format is ideal for your Kindle, while the ePUB can be utilized on a variety of mobile devices.

To learn more, go to www.apress.com/companion or contact support@apress.com.

Printed in the United States
By Bookmasters